Library of
Davidson College

Economic Policy in an Interdependent World

Economic Policy in an Interdependent World

Essays in World Economics

Richard N. Cooper

The MIT Press
Cambridge, Massachusetts
London, England

© 1986 by The Massachusetts Institute of Technology.

All rights reserved. No part of this book may be reproduced in any form by any electronic or mechanical means (including photocopying, recording, or information storage and retrieval) without permission in writing from the publisher.

This book was set in Palatino by Asco Trade Typesetting Ltd., Hong Kong, and printed and bound by Halliday Lithograph in the United States of America.

Library of Congress Cataloging-in-Publication Data

Cooper, Richard N.
  Economic policy in an interdependent world.

  Bibliography: p.
  Includes index.
  1. Economic policy.   2. International economic relations.   I. Title.
HC59.C697 1986   338.9   85-7923
ISBN 0-262-03113-2

Contents

Preface   vii

1   **Economic Interdependence and Foreign Policy in the Seventies**   1
    [*World Politics* 24, no. 2 (1972): 159–181]

2   **Managing Risks to the International Economic System**   23
    [*Managing International Risks*, ed. R. J. Herring (Cambridge University Press, 1983)]

3   **Global Economic Policy in a World of Energy Shortage**   53
    [*Economics in the Public Service*, ed. J. A. Pechman and N. J. Simler (New York: Norton, 1982)]

4   **Economic Mobility and National Economic Policy**   71
    [Wicksell Lectures 1973 (Uppsala, Sweden: Almqvist & Wiksell, 1974)]

5   **Worldwide Regional Integration: Is There an Optimal Size of the Integrated Area?**   123
    [*Economic Integration: Worldwide, Regional, Sectional*, ed. F. Machlup (New York: St. Martin's, 1976)]

6   **Towards an International Capital Market?**   137
    [*North American and Western European Economic Policies*, ed. C. P. Kindleberger and A. Shonfield (New York: Macmillan, 1971)]

7   **Macroeconomic Policy Adjustment in Interdependent Economies**   155
    [*Quarterly Journal of Economics* 83 (February 1969): 1–24]

8 Monetary Theory and Policy in an Open Economy 179
[*Scandinavian Journal of Economics* 78, no. 2 (1976): 146–163]

9 An Analysis of Currency Devaluation in Developing Countries 199
[*International Trade and Money*, ed. M. B. Connolly and A. K. Swoboda (London: Allen & Unwin, 1973)]

10 Borrowing Abroad: The Debtor's Perspective 229
Richard N. Cooper and Jeffrey D. Sachs
[*International Debt and the Developing Countries*, ed. G. W. Smith and J. T. Cuddington (Washington, D.C.: World Bank, 1985)]

11 Economic Interdependence and Coordination of Economic Policies 289
[*Handbook in International Economics*, vol. 2, ed. R. W. Jones and P. B. Kenen (Amsterdam: Elsevier, 1985)]

Acknowledgments of Sources 333
Index 335

Preface

The articles brought together here, written over a period of fifteen years, continue and develop the central theme of my 1968 book *The Economics of Interdependence*: "how to keep the manifold benefits of extensive international economic intercourse free of crippling restrictions while at the same time preserving a maximum degree of freedom for each nation to pursue its legitimate economic objectives." This present volume focuses on the opportunities for and the constraints on national economic policy that are created by the fact that nations pursue their objectives in an environment in which goods, services, capital, and even labor are increasingly mobile internationally. The international economic environment thus strongly conditions the effectiveness of national economic policy. Earlier contentions notwithstanding, this is true in a regime of floating exchange rates as well as in a regime of fixed exchange rates, although there are important technical differences between the two environments.

The focus here is on the individual nation, possibly in interaction with others. A second volume, also to be published by The MIT Press, will address the nature and the consequences of alternative monetary systems—that is, the international rules and conventions that govern financial transactions among countries.

The articles will be much too theoretical or abstract for the tastes of some readers, yet far too loose and nonrigorous for others. The reliance on abstraction reflects my view that economic analysis of real events cannot proceed successfully without sharpening distinctions and differentiating among different circumstances. That in turn requires abstract reasoning—looking at limiting cases or possibilities as thought experiments. On the other hand, preoccupation with pure theory does not by itself illuminate the economic forces that actually operate in the world, which is the appropriate object of useful economic analysis. Thus, abstract theory must be adapted—

"loosened"—to allow for greater real-world complexity than that found in thought experiments concerned with limiting cases.

I find the judgmental use of abstract reasoning to help understand and illuminate actual circumstances or choices very satisfying. I hope readers will share this enthusiasm, which in my own case has been heightened by my occasional participation as a policymaker in the U.S. government (although not on a scale so grand as that covered by many of the articles collected here).

The articles are not arranged in the order in which they were written, but are grouped partly by difficulty of treatment—the first several are less formal and represent a somewhat easier introduction to the subject than some of the later ones—and partly by logical connection among the subjects examined. Except for corrections of typographical errors and other minor alterations, the articles have not been revised. Together, they reveal some evolution in my reflections, but the same underlying themes have absorbed me for nearly two decades.

Article 1 was written in 1970 for a Council on Foreign Relations study group. It attempts to lay out for foreign-policy specialists how growing interdependence will affect international relations, at first by engendering national frustration at the lessening ability to influence national events—a theme that is taken up somewhat more formally in articles 4, 7, and 11. It was written when fixed exchange rates still prevailed among major currencies, although President Nixon's bombshell that eventually led to floating occurred in August 1971, as the article was going to press.

Article 2 leaps forward a decade. It was written, for the centenary celebration of the Wharton School of the University of Pennsylvania, in 1981—after external debt had become a source of concern, but well before the debt crises of August 1982. It takes the view that the world economic system in the early 1980s, while not without its risks, was fundamentally sounder and less subject to devastating decline than the world economy in the 1930s, although there were a number of striking parallels. Since 1981 the world economy has been put under enormous strain by a divergence of macroeconomic policies in the major countries. Monetary contraction combined with fiscal expansion in the United States, in the presence of fiscal contraction in the other major countries, has resulted in high unemployment in Europe and unprecedentedly large American trade deficits, and this has raised alarmingly the likelihood of an erosion of the liberal trading system that is predicted in the article.

Article 3 was written in 1980 for a Festschrift for Walter W. Heller, under whose tutelage I began my professional career at the Council of Economic

Advisers in 1961. That was an extraordinary and exhilarating experience. The Council included James Tobin and Kermit Gordon, while the staff included Kenneth Arrow, Richard Nelson, Arthur Okun, Robert Solow, and many other stimulating colleagues, working for an adminstration that was open to new ideas even if not always willing or able to implement them. At the Council I learned a tremendous amount about how government works, about the value and the limits of an academic economic training in helping to formulate and execute national policy, and above all about the importance of the acceptance of a set of consistent and interrelated guiding principles by the president and his chief aides if "policy" is to be something other than a collection of pragmatic *ad hoc* decisions.

Article 3 briefly characterizes the impact of the oil shocks of 1974 and 1979–80 on the world economy and the dilemmas they created for macroeconomic management. It describes the world economic situation as it appeared in late 1976 and the response of the new Carter administration (which I, as Undersecretary of State for Economic Affairs, had some role in formulating). In particular, it explains the underlying rationale for the so-called locomotive theory of world economic policy, under which the United States, Japan, and Germany (the three largest non-Communist national economies) would coordinate an expansionist policy to pull the world out of its slump and to relieve the dangerous debt burden on many developing and smaller industrialized countries while avoiding such a disturbance of trade relations among major economies as might occur with uncoordinated policies in a period of floating exchange rates. The article describes both the failures and the successes of this effort, also discusses the "public goods" dimension of the world demand for oil, and ends by noting the need to prepare for another major oil disruption before the end of the century.

Article 4 takes a much longer historical perspective on the formulation of national economic policy, linking it to the evolution of regional, national, and international markets for goods, investments, and even labor. I was invited to give the Wicksell Lectures in Stockholm in 1973, and I chose as my theme the influence of the economic environment—in particular, the extent of markets—on the effects and hence the character of various instruments of economic policy. This article adopts the perspective of nations as economic agents whose capabilities and choices are limited by the wider economic environment in which they operate. I believe this perspective was then novel at the international level, although it could be found in the literature on local governments within a nation. The article points out the limits on governmental action in an international system in which labor and capital are mobile.

Article 5 focuses on one issue implicitly raised in the previous article and is really an essay on the theory of government. It asks, from the perspective of an economist, what is the optimal jurisdictional area. It suggests that the entire world would be optimal except for the presence of public goods and diverse preferences among individuals for those public goods. Thus, "states" are formed to cater to these diverse preferences by offering different quantities and qualities of the public goods, and each family locates in the state catering most closely to its preferences. This way of looking at states is highly abstract and unrealistic as a historical characterization, but it indicates one rational source of resistance to the many pressures to shift authority to levels of government with ever greater geographical jurisdictions in response to geographical widening of markets.

Article 6, written in 1970, asks what it means to suggest that national capital markets are "integrated" with one another, offers some empirical evidence for the increasing integration of capital markets under the regime of fixed exchange rates prevailing during the 1960s, and suggests the limits that this increasing integration would put on national pursuit of economic policy (especially monetary policy). Not long after the writing, these restraints became all too evident, and countries attempted to relax them by shifting to flexible exchange rates in March 1973.

Article 7, published in 1969, addressed in a formal (nonempirical) simulation model the impact of increased openness in trade and financial transactions on the effectiveness of monetary and fiscal policies pursued by two interdependent countries with a fixed exchange rate between their currencies. In general, it finds that increased openness reduces the effectiveness of national economic policy, in that countries on average are farther from their targets than in an environment with less interdependence. Another finding is that the need for foreign-exchange reserves increases with increased openness. The article demonstrates that by coordinating their policies countries can on average remain closer to their desired positions, the gains being greater the greater is the interdependence.

By 1975 the major countries had moved to flexible exchange rates, and this provoked an outpouring of academic analysis on the impact of macroeconomic policy under flexible exchange rates. (It should be noted that before the switch many economists were advocating a move to flexible rates.) Article 8 attempts to review the then-prevailing analysis of a comparison of fiscal and monetary policy under fixed and flexible rates. Much more sophisticated work has been done since the article was first published, and the gist of that work is that some form of managed flexibility is generally optimal but that the exact rules for management depend crucially (and hence unusefully) on the detailed objectives and economic structure of the country in question and on the disturbances it has to cope with. Article 8, however, finds that the claim that flexible exchange rates "insulate" economies from foreign disturbances was seriously misleading.

Article 9 shifts the perspective to economic policy in a small capital-importing country. The work was stimulated by my study of the economy of South Vietnam in the 1960s and by my conclusions that devaluation of the piaster could improve the country's foreign-exchange earnings modestly and that currency devaluation could be used as an instrument of economic contraction in the expansionary environment. This result was at sharp variance with the conventional analyses of currency devaluation that existed at that time, which held that successful devaluation must be expansionary and therefore required monetary and/or fiscal contraction to sustain its success. I began a more systematic study of currency devaluation, empirical as well as theoretical, and some of my conclusions were given in the Frank K. Graham Lecture at Princeton in 1971. The article published here is a somewhat extended version of that lecture. I believe it is still relevant, despite many changes that have taken place since then, because many developing countries continue to be (or aspire to resume being) net importers of capital on government account, and in practice most of them continue to fix their exchange rates, engaging from time to time in substantial discrete currency devaluations of the type analyzed here.

Article 10, written with Jeffrey Sachs in 1984, reverts again to the capital-importing country, this time focusing on the appropriate size and composition of its external debt. The article's novelty (due to Sachs) is that it addresses the incentives to default somewhat more systematically than had been done hitherto. It also draws attention to the crucial importance of the need to service foreign debt in external currency and to the implied need to invest foreign capital in ways that will save or generate foreign exchange. It finds that, with productively invested foreign borrowings, countries could sustain external debts considerable larger than the large external debts that were such a source of concern after the Mexican debt crisis of 1982. In short, debt problems in the early 1980s arose not so much because of the scale of debt *per se* as because of misuse of some of the debt, which, combined with a liquidity crisis which raised questions about the ability of countries to service their debts in the short run, resulted in a self-fulfilling prophecy as banks hesitated to lend new money.

The final article returns to the macroeconomic management of interdependent economies and the influence of economic structure (and especially the degree of openness) on the effectiveness of monetary and fiscal policy. It draws heavily in its underlying theme on several of the earlier articles, but it formalizes that work somewhat and draws on contributions by others made in the intervening years.

The switch of major currencies to flexible exchange rates alters the nature of interdependence, but it has not altered the fact that growing interdependence creates new challenges to the formulation of economic policy and generally increases the gain from coordinating one's economic policy with one's major trading partners. This is a challenge that has not yet been met successfully, despite accumulating experience with the consequences of misaligned policies among the major industrial countries. The subject of this volume, then, is likely to grow rather than diminish in importance.

1

Economic Interdependence
and Foreign Policy in the
Seventies

A casual reading of contemporary news reports suggests that during the past decade economic issues have taken on growing importance in the relations of non-Communist developed countries. The disputes between the United States and Japan over textiles, between the United States and the European Community over agricultural trade, and between France and Germany over currency alignments come readily to mind. It is perhaps symbolic of the enormous success of early postwar foreign policy that issues no graver than these play such a prominent part in relations among countries that, earlier in the century, were sporadically at each other's throats. But I contend that economic issues are becoming, and will continue to become, more problematic in relations among advanced non-Communist countries, and that their relative prominence today is not merely due to the fact that other, more fundamental issues have been resolved. Indeed, the trend toward greater economic interdependence among countries will require substantial changes in their approach to foreign policy in the next decade or so.

To clarify this proposition, we first need some delineation of the terms "trends," "economic interdependence," and "foreign policy." By "trends," I mean developments that can be confidently projected into the future on the basis of information now available, but not, of course, projected with certainty, since future developments are also influenced by future policies. Indeed, a principal reason for ascertaining trends is to suggest what policies will be required in order to change those that are disagreeable. Moreover, trends represent a projection of observable forces, not a description of present reality.

"Economic interdependence" normally refers to the dollar value of economic transactions among regions or countries, either in absolute terms or relative to their total transactions. I shall use it in a more restricted sense: to refer to the *sensitivity* of economic transactions between two or more nations to economic developments within those nations. This approach means that two countries with much mutual trade would still experience a low degree of interdependence if the value of that trade were not sensitive to price and income developments in the two countries; on the other hand, two countries would be highly interdependence if their transactions were greatly sensitive to economic developments, even if their mutual trade were initially at a low level.[1] *Inter*dependence implies two-way sensitivity; one-way sensitivity leads to a dependent economy. The reason for this focus on sensitivity rather than on level will become clearer as the argument proceeds; for the moment I will simply observe that the economy of the United States is becoming highly interdependent with that of Europe and Japan, even though total U.S. exports to those areas account for only about 3 percent of total output and (so far as we can tell) international financial transactions are a similarly small proportion of the total financial transactions in the United States.

"Foreign policy" is the most difficult term to define. It may be interpreted to mean all points of contact between the residents of one country and those of another, but surely that—although important—would be too broad. The term "policy" would seem, at a minimum, to reduce the term to mean all points of contact between national governments. But even this is broader than is usually understood in the press and in casual discussion; it probably refers to points of contact between governments concerning the territorial integrity of the nation-state and the security of its citizens (and possibly their well-being, but that broadens the meaning considerably)—in short, what has come to be called national security, broadly defined. A third notion of foreign policy is a grand conception of world economic and political order that provides a consistent framework for, and guidance to, the month-to-month decisions that nations must take in their relations with other nations.

There is, of course, a continuous gradation between grand conceptions and day-to-day operating decisions, with many proximate objectives advanced for guidance in specific instances, on the (sometimes incorrect) assumption that those proximate objectives will serve to advance the grander and inevitably more general conceptions of what is desirable. Despite this continuous gradation, I believe it is useful to distinguish between the grand conceptions of desirable relations among the peoples of the world and the usually all-absorbing concerns for day-to-day decisions that typically govern foreign ministries.

Growing economic interdependence has important implications for the first and third of these concepts of foreign policy—for the number and the character of contacts between governments and, more importantly, for the conception of a world economic and political order that is both desirable and attainable. In particular, it bears on the viability of the nation-state as the principal unit of decision-making. The implications for the second concept of foreign policy—national security—are less immediately compelling and are largely derived from the other two.

In the observations that follow I take up, in turn, the fact of growing economic interdependence, the challenge this poses for domestic economic policies and balance-of-payments adjustment, the actual and potential national responses to this challenge, and the implications of the resulting tensions and pressures for foreign policy in the 1970s.

Growing Economic Interdependence

The extraordinary and unprecedented growth in international trade has frequently been mentioned. The increase in international travel has been even faster, and is equally unprecedented. It is not clear whether international trade has grown in relation to total economic output (GNP); the relative growth of "services" would argue against this. But, in any case, that is less important than the sensitivity of international transactions to domestic economic developments such as taxation, inflation, and interest rates. There is no question that this sensitivity has increased in certain dimensions. Although merchandise imports account for only 4 percent of total U.S. expenditure, for example, imports account for a much larger share of the increment during periods of rapidly rising expenditure (17 percent in 1968, in real terms). When demand runs ahead of output, the rest of the world fills the gap. This process has long been more operative in other countries than in the United States, but even there the response has become more rapid and more complete.

It is less clear whether the *price* sensitivity of international demand has increased. Improved transportation and communications, wider acceptability of foreign styling, and narrowed cost and quality differences among nations suggest that it has; but growing product differentiation, with each major firm trying to establish its secure niche in the market, cuts the other way. So does the growing importance of the multinational firm wherever market-sharing conventions prevail among its various components. But these firms have also contributed to the convergence of cost and design and to the wider acceptability of "foreign" products. On balance, price sensitivity for international trade has probably increased as well.

This increased sensitivity has extended even to labor, an area in which the integrative forces of policy and technology are undoubtedly weaker than in any other. In 1967, when Germany slumped into its first postwar recession, one-third of the unemployed workers who lost jobs were foreigners on short-term contracts. On returning to their homelands they raised unemployment there and reduced it in Germany, literally representing an exportation of unempolyment. The reverse occurred once Germany expanded again. When reductions in federal funding, the stock market slump, and rising prices combined to bring about a sharp reduction in new hiring of university teachers in the United States, graduate students in Britain—whose higher educational establishment continues to grow at a rapid pace—nonetheless also felt the pinch: Britons and Commonwealth students studying in the United States started to look for jobs in Britain to replace those they could not find in the United States.

The greatest growth in interdependence has undoubtedly been in investment, both real and financial. The great growth in direct foreign business investment in the 1960s testifies to the new search for earning opportunities everywhere, not merely in the national market. Barriers of language and law have gradually been broken down or surmounted by large and even not-so-large American firms, who have flocked to Europe to exploit new or newly perceived market opportunities and tax advantages. Financial capital has also become much more sensitive to yield differentials among major financial markets, and an increasing number of both borrowers and lenders scan a world horizon for sources of funds and investment opportunities; in doing so, they tie national markets more closely together. German firms can borrow from Arabian sheiks and Iowa farmers in London's Eurodollar market. Even national stock markets, although they are subject to diverse influences, have shown increasing parallelism of movement during the past decade.[2] As in other areas of economics, it is the marginal transaction that counts in linking markets together.

This growing interdependence may be confidently projected into the future, in the absence of strong government action to retard the process, because it is based on the technological advances in transportation and communication which increase both the speed and the reliability of moving goods, funds, persons, information, and ideas across national boundaries—in short, the same forces that are producing the much-touted shrinking world, in terms of both economic and psychological distance.

Although this process is worldwide, it is much further advanced among the industrial countries of the non-Communist world—Western Europe, North America, and, increasingly, Japan—countries that, in the last few decades, have converged remarkably in their objectives of social and economic policy and in their political processes for reconciling differences and for executing policies. Although these countries will continue to be concerned about the Second and the Third World, their concerns will derive largely from considerations other than growing economic interdependence. (Economic interdependence must, in this context, be distinguished from the growing psychological interdependence brought about by increasing direct exposure through television and other media.) The remarks that follow will largely concern relations among the Western industrial countries.

A second kind of growing economic interdependence, institutional rather than structural, can be discerned among industrial nations. This institutional interdependence occurs when these countries must, by prior agreement, confer, and even reach joint decisions, on matters of economic policy. The two outstanding examples of this, neither of them present a decade ago, are the periodic decisions leading to the creation of Special Drawing Rights (paper gold) at the International Monetary Fund, and the decisions concerning the formation of commercial and agricultural policies within the European Economic Community. Both involve truly supranational decision-making, although of course only after prior negotiations among nations. Less dramatic instances are the attempts by donors to coordinate foreign aid to particular countries in "consortia" under the general direction of the World Bank, and the attempts, so far largely unsuccessful, to coordinate trade policies of the developed countries with respect to the products of the less-developed countries. This kind of institutional interdependence is in some measure a response to the growing structural interdependence, but it often also has a quite different, more strictly political origin, and thus is a separately identifiable factor in the economic area.[3] It will therefore be ignored in my argument, as will British accession to the EEC.

The Challenge of Growing Interdependence to National Economic Policies

Domestic Policies

Most national economic policies rely for their effectiveness on the separation of markets. This is true of monetary policy, of income taxation, of regulatory policies, and of redistributive policies (whether the last be through differential taxation or through direct transfers). Increased economic interdependence, by joining national markets, erodes the effectiveness of these policies and hence threatens national autonomy in the determination and pursuit of economic objectives. The term "threaten" is used nonpejoratively; there are also economic advantages to the joining of markets, and in some—but not all—cases these outweigh the resultant loss of economic autonomy; indeed, that is what creates the predicament. It is aggravated by the fact that during the past few decades the peoples of all industrial countries have substantially raised their expectations of governmental activity in managing the economy with respect to employment, inflation, growth, income distribution, and a host of other objectives, leading to the emergence of what is sometimes called the welfare state.

The loss of autonomy has been most prominently discussed in the area of monetary policy.[4] As national money and capital markets are joined by international flows of funds, interest rates in various markets are drawn together. Subsequently, if an individual country wishes to pursue a contractionary monetary policy in order to discourage a domestic boom, it will find, in the course of trying to tighten monetary conditions, that it is merely drawing funds from abroad; the more its central bank tightens, the more its would-be domestic borrowers will satisfy their needs by borrowing abroad rather than at home. Under these circumstances, monetary policy becomes an effective tool for influencing the short-term balance-of-payments position of a country, since it can attract or repel short-term funds; but it has become an ineffective tool for its customary objective of influencing the course of domestic economic activity.

The international mobility of firms and funds also erodes the tax policies of nations. It is no secret that the nascent international bond market has thrived on funds that engage in tax evasion. Host countries such as Luxembourg have a disincentive to police carefully the taxation of interest earnings on foreign funds: they thereby attract financial business. Without the full cooperation of countries where the earnings take place, the difficulty of enforcing tax laws on residents holding funds abroad will enable the wealthy and astute residents of all nations maintain a tax-free source of interest income; as more people become aware of the possibilities open to them, this will, in turn, increasingly erode both the revenue and the redistributive objectives of many countries.

For operating business firms it is more difficult to avoid an accurate declaration of earnings. But by adjusting the prices at which transactions take place among branches in different countries, they may sharply reduce their total tax liabilities and thereby thwart the fiscal objectives of countries with high tax rates.

In both of these cases—tax evasion and transfer pricing for tax avoidance—national authorities are not without countervailing courses of action. But, as will be made clear, in some respects these courses of action either infringe on the sovereignty of other nations or place their own international firms in a difficult competitive position. So a dilemma remains.

The same is true of regulatory policies of business, such as antitrust regulations, capitalization requirements, disclosure requirements, trading regulations, and the like. In each case the international mobility of funds and firms erodes the national capacity to impose and enforce limitations on business behavior. A Swiss corporation, faced with local requirements to give initial rights to new equity to existing stockholders, found it convenient to establish a subsidiary in Curaçao instead, and to raise its new equity from that base, drawing on international (including Swiss) sources of funds. If it were not for laws extending the jurisdiction of the United States to its citizens everywhere—a powerful irritant to some countries—American firms could escape U.S. proscriptions on trade with Cuba simply by locating in countries more sympathetic to such trade.

Although labor is still far less mobile than capital, the mobility of certain groups of people is sufficiently high to limit policies designed toward redistribution, whether through taxation or, as in the case of the British Health Service, through imposed conditions of work. This force can be seen most clearly within the United States, where states and municipalities with generous welfare programs have been swamped by immigrants from elsewhere in the country; in the end this requires a fiscal bailout by the federal government.

Mobility unites previously fragmented markets, and in so doing threatens policies that, for their feasibility, depended on the fragmentation of markets. As nations become increasingly interdependent, as capital and skilled labor become less exclusively national in their orientations, countries desiring to pursue tax or regulatory policies that deviate widely from those policies in other countries will find themselves stimulating large inflows or outflows of funds, firms, or persons; these induced movements will in turn weaken the intended effects of the policies, or make them more costly. Economic policies that have hitherto been regarded as exclusively domestic will come under increasing influence from the international environment.

Balance-of-Payments Policy

In addition to affecting domestic economic policies, increased interdependence will also, and more importantly in the immediate future, affect our methods for dealing with imbalances in international paymemts. Under the present rules of the game, laid down in the Bretton Woods Agreement in 1944, countries are required to fix their exchange rates and to finance out of reserves, or by borrowing at the International Monetary Fund, any temporary imbalances in payments. "Fundamental" imbalances are to be corrected by moving a country's fixed exchange rate parity to a new level. This system requires a governmental judgment concerning when a given imbalance is fundamental rather than merely temporary; while this judgment is being made, the public at large can speculate on whether or not the value of the currency is going to be changed. In the event of a change, this speculation results in both a redistribution (from government to successful domestic speculators) and a loss (from government to successful foreign speculators) of national wealth.

This system presupposes fragmentation of the markets for financial assets. Such fragmentation was implicit in the Bretton Woods Agreement, to be achieved, if necessary, by the imposition of controls on movements of capital. [Article VIII, Sec. 2(b) requires all members of the IMF to help police the capital controls of any member.] For various reasons, restrictions on capital movements have seemed both less desirable and less feasible than they appeared 25 years ago; therefore, as the barriers of ignorance and cost in undertaking international transactions have fallen, the potential speculative movement of funds has increased enormously. Just as the reduction in barriers has increased the sensitivity of funds to transnational interest-rate differentials, and thereby eroded the effectiveness of national policy, it has increased the sensitivity of funds to prospects for speculative gain, and thereby rendered more difficult (because more costly) the use of changes in the exchange rate to correct imbalances in payments. A crude quantitative indicator of these developments is provided by contrasting the maximum daily speculation of under $100 million against the pound sterling, in the "massive run" of August 1947, with the maximum daily speculation of over $1.5 billion in favor of the German mark in May 1969, and the movement of over $1 billion into Germany in less than an hour in May 1971. Moreover, as the barriers of ignorance fall further, there is no reason why $1.5 billion should not rise to $15 billion, or even to $50 billion, in a day. A 10 percent gain over the weekend is a tidy rate of return; if the speculator guesses wrong, he has lost, under the Bretton Woods arrangements, only the relatively modest transactions costs. Such huge speculative movements impose proportionate losses on countries that do change their exchange parities.

Reluctance to make an adjustment in the exchange rate will induce a search for alternative devices for correcting payments positions, and these, in turn, will impinge—as, indeed, they already have—on both domestic politics and foreign policy. One can make a plausible case in conjectural history that the governments of France, Germany, and Britain were turned out in 1969–70, as was that of Canada in 1963, on grounds that fundamentally reflect this growing economic interdependence among nations and the resulting influence on the ability of countries to cope satisfactorily with balance-of-payments difficulties. The exchange rate figured explicity in the German election. De Gaulle was ostensibly rejected on the basis of his proposals for regional government in France, but one may argue that the more fundamental reason for his rejection can be found in the economic factors that led to the disruptions of May–June 1968, namely France's restrictive economic policy after 1965. This policy represented an attempt to halt the deterioration in France's balance-of-payments position, and, *inter alia*, it involved sharp cuts in the planned educational budget and produced the highest level of unemployment in France since the 1930s. Harold Wilson's promise that the devaluation of the pound in 1967 would not devalue the pound in the pocket of the average Briton, which was followed by the most rapid price increases in two decades—linked in turn to the devaluation and to Britain's dependence on the world market, where prices were also rising—despite growing unemployment, played a key role in his electoral defeat in 1970.

Responses to the Challenge to National Autonomy in Economic Policy

Domestic Policies

The intrusions of growing interdependence into domestic economic policy, which are already visible but are likely to become much more intense in the next decade, have elicited five quite different but not mutually exclusive types of response by national governments: passive, exploitative, defensive, aggressive, and constructive. These designations are meant to be descriptive, not normative.

A *passive* response involves acceptance of the loss of domestic economic autonomy and virtual abandonment of any attempt to pursue courses independent of those determined by the countries to which the passive country is closely linked with ties of trade and finance. It is largely a resort of small countries who have become aware of their dependence on others and for whom the costs of independent action (i.e., of forgoing the benefits of linked markets) are likely to be high.

Some of these countries also pursue an *exploitative* course, which attempts to take advantage of the growing interdependence in ways which are successful if pursued by only a few countries, but which cannot be generalized for the world economy. Thus, we observe countries offering flags of convenience on ocean shipping, light registration and disclosure requirements for securities, nominal taxation on certain forms of business activity (tax havens), and generous subsidies to foreign investment.[5] So long as only a few countries create especially favorable conditions for certain forms of economic activity, they will succeed in attracting that kind of activity from elsewhere; if many countries begin to compete for the same activities in similar ways, international location will be little influenced, and net benefits will accrue to the favored activities at the general expense of governments, consumers, or labor. This kind of policy competition is already noticeable in the tax concessions, and even direct subsidies, given by many less-developed countries to foreign investors; as the practice spreads, revenue bases will be eroded while the effect in attracting investment will diminish. Competition can also be observed in the export credit terms given by the industrialized countries, in subsidies to hotel building and other aspects of tourism in Europe, and in the use by municipalities *within* the United States of tax-free industrial development bonds to attract industry. (This development has recently been restrained by congressional action.) Success in exploiting the new mobility is therefore limited to those countries that *begin* the process, and continues only so long as other countries do not follow or retaliate.

A *defensive* response involves attempts to reduce economic interdependence by preserving or restoring the fragmentation of markets in order to retain some economic autonomy. An early example was the imposition of restrictions on immigration into the United States. This was done, among other reasons, in order to protect the distribution of income then prevailing and to reduce the flow of new immigrants to a level which might reasonably be assimilated. More recently, Britain, Denmark, and Switzerland have all imposed limits on the number of foreign workers. The reasons are both political (on the assumption that certain minimum requirements of homogeneity in the population must be met in a functioning democracy) and economic (concerning in particular the distribution of income between relatively unskilled labor and other factors of production). The United States has long maintained an escape clause on its commitments to lower tariffs that can be invoked if foreign competition creates insuperable adjustment problems for domestic firms and labor. Some countries have for years imposed impediments to the movement of financial capital across their boundaries. Others have started to do so more recently. The United States has its interest-equalization tax on purchases of foreign stocks and bonds, and its mandatory restrictions on foreign lending by U.S. firms and banks. Britain and France have even more stringent controls. These restrictions are often imposed under the heading of balance-of-payments measures, but they are more correctly viewed, I think, as devices to insulate national capital and money markets from one another in order to preserve some degree of national monetary control. This view is supported by the fact that countries such as Germany and Switzerland, with strong or neutral payments positions, have also resorted to such measures.

Some countries have engaged in *aggressive* as well as defensive actions to preserve national autonomy. Rather than reduce mobility, these actions attempt to extend national control to the mobile factors wherever they be. Thus, the United States (which because of its size and relative importance is in the best position to engage in extraterritorial extension of its laws and regulations) has from time to time extended its antitrust laws to the foreign subsidiaries of U.S. firms and even to the foreign parents of foreign subsidiaries operating in the United States. For example, it has demanded the disclosure of financial information by foreign firms whose securities are traded informally in the United States, prevented foreign subsidiaries of U.S. corporations from selling to certain Communist countries, imposed minimum limits on repatriation of earnings by American firms operating abroad, and attempted (unsuccessfully) to compel submission of certain business information by foreign sea and air carriers. These various actions invariably provoke cries of outrage from other countries,[6] for they attempt to extend U.S. regulatory jurisdiction to economic agents that are the legal entities of other countries and hence under their jurisdiction, despite their American ownership. On the other hand, failure to subject these foreign entities to U.S. regulations or their equivalent invites circumvention of the regulatory intent through movement abroad. If the records of American-owned firms outside the United States are not subject to subpoena, for example, firms which are prevented by law from conspiring to fix prices or share markets within the United States may do so abroad, with impunity. Or, if American firms operating from foreign bases are not affected by the U.S. proscription on exports to Cuba, the restrictive policy can be vitiated simply by locating abroad. (This observation is not meant to imply approval of this proscription—only that a national policy can be undercut by international mobility of its firms.) In other words, while the response of the United States in these cases has been aggressive, it has not been capricious; it is addressed to a real problem in which the decisionmaking domain of businesses covers a wider geographic area than the jurisdiction of government.[7]

A fifth type of response involves the *constructive* attempt by governments to frame their policies jointly, so that mobility among the cooperating countries ceases to offer an escape from governmental jurisdiction. Examples of true coordination of policies are rare, although in the area of monetary management there have been several faint signs of coordinated action, notably in the general lowering of interest rates in 1967. There have also been attempts, partially successful, to limit export-credit concessions by government-sponsored export-credit institutions. Bilateral tax treaties have, of course, been used for years to reconcile the conflicting claims of tax jurisdiction over business income. But this approach through coordination could go much further, and encompass a wide range of policies concerning taxation, the regulation of business structure and activity, the framing of monetary policy, and other "domestic" policies. It is an approach that requires considerable patience, however, for joint regulation can proceed only as rapidly as the most laggard participant; since some potential participants have successfully exploited the new mobility, they will be reluctant to give up their gains.

Balance of Payments Policies

The same five types of response can occur in the area of balance-of-payments adjustment. The passive response, which represents a return to the feature of the nineteenth-century gold standard that required domestic economies to be keyed to balance-of-payments conditions, has proved acceptable to few countries. There is a wider danger, already observable, that, in their attempt to avoid exchange-rate adjustment, some countries will engage in exploitative responses. By altering the domestic tax system to take advantage of a feature of the international trading rules (embodied in the General Agreement on Tariffs and Trade) that permits certain types of border tax adjustments but not others, these countries will attempt to improve their trade positions; by subsidizing the tourist industry, they will try to increase foreign exchange receipts.

A defensive response involves imposing restrictions on various payments to foreigners in order to improve the balance of payments—restrictions that could in the past be observed with respect to virtually all international transactions: trade, tourist expenditures, foreign aid, private capital movements. Canada in 1970, and Germany and the Netherlands in 1971, adopted quite a different defensive response in allowing their exchange rates to float freely, to be determined by market forces. This expedient, long urged by many academic economists but prohibited by the Bretton Woods agreement, insulates those economies from inflows of interest-sensitive and speculative funds.

The United States is in the unique position of being able to adopt an aggressive response in this area. It has been suggested by some that the United States should cease to pay gold for dollars offered by other central banks, in order to force the world onto a dollar standard or to induce other countries to allow their currencies to float against the dollar—in the expectation that most countries would reject the latter option and prove willing to accept and hold large (unlimited?) numbers of dollars, thereby relieving the United States of concern over its balance-of-payments condition.[8] Others have claimed that for all practical purposes we have already reached this state. But in terms of foreign policy, there is a vast difference between an explicit arrangement that most governments would find deeply offensive and an implicit arrangement with many of the same features in practice. The former would create considerable public as well as official resentment, which might lead to actions on grounds of national pride that are neither in the economic interests of the countries undertaking them nor in the interests of the world economy; the latter would have enough ambiguity to permit both the United States and other like-minded governments to maintain with semi-truth that nothing has changed and that each country retains its freedom of action while still enjoying the benefits of international intercourse.

Finally, it is possible to imagine truly cooperative forms of payments adjustment, in which rules or conventions are established to determine which countries should make what adjustments, with derogations subject to international consultation. The rules of Bretton Woods made an attempt in this direction, but the possibilities for private speculative gain surrounding discrete alterations in exchange rates that are the system's keystone have in practice rendered the IMF consultative procedure a dead letter. Nevertheless, in recent years tense and sometimes acrimonious consultation on exchange-rate changes has taken place outside the IMF among the major countries.

Economic Interdependence: Implications for Foreign Policy

The foregoing excursion into the challenge that increased interdependence constitutes to domestic economic policies and the possible national responses sets the stage for an examination of the implications for foreign policy.

Obviously, the impact on domestic politics is one route whereby economic interdependence can influence a nation's foreign policy; hence the problems facing the foreign policy of the United States. The shift from De Gaulle to Pompidou and from Labour to Tory may not basically alter the shape of world affairs, but it can affect them in important details. For example, France's willingness to consider Britain's entry into the European Economic Community blunted Britain's general foreign-policy role as long as negotiations were in process and will divert British and European official attention and energy from other matters for some time. Another example is the restoration of Britain's military commitment east of Suez before the withdrawal had proceeded so far as to become irreversible. The important influence of domestic politics on foreign policy is also demonstrated by election of a communist as president of Chile. It has been alleged that the very rapid growth of foreign ownership in Chilean manufacturing in the late 1960s, much of it in the form of takeovers, played a significant role in the public appeal of Sr. Allende, who during his campaign raised the specter of foreign domination of Chile's infant manufacturing sector.

The impact on political leadership may possibly lead to the most important effect of interdependence on foreign policy, but it is too subtle and too uncertain in direction to be analyzed with any confidence. More direct and clearly identifiable effects arise from the challenges to national autonomy in the realms of economic policy. These challenges take foreign policy right into the thicket of domestic politics. On the whole, foreign policy, in the narrower sense of national security and military-strategic considerations, has in all countries been elitist—the interest and province of a relatively small group of persons. Strategic considerations do become political issues, but generally in a rather abstract fashion, as broad issues and postures. Even the foreign-policy budget—largely military—has until recently been relatively immune from domestic political considerations. (This is equally true of foreign aid, where one small group is pitted against another, and the public remains passive and uninterested.)

With the advent of increased economic interdependence, however, foreign developments will intrude on a whole range of policies that are traditionally domestic, and these bread-and-butter domestic political issues will in turn influence and greatly complicate the management of foreign policy.[9] It follows that foreign policy in the sense of all official relations between countries will become more intricate both in the range of issues and in the frequency with which they arise. National reaction in the 1970s will undoubtedly blend all five types of response. Many of these responses will create frictions between countries, and diplomats will be kept busy at their traditional task of smoothing ruffled feathers. If foreign policy is to be regarded as successful, it will have the additional task of channeling and controlling the reactions to greater interdependence in order to prevent the dominance of those exploitative, defensive, and aggressive responses that, if generalized, are detrimental to international order and hence to all participants. This means, in particular, confining the exploitative responses to *de minimus* cases and introducing some kind of order into the defensive and aggressive responses so that they will not provoke retaliation that is damaging to all parties.

To say this, however, is to say little more than that in times of tension and conflicting objectives it is in the interest of all to avoid outcomes that are detrimental to all. It is far more difficult to define the maximal task for foreign policy (even in an area limited to economics), for that depends, among other things, on our basic objectives and in particular on the value we attach to the preservation of *national* autonomy as such. We must sooner or later face in a global context the issue of centralization or decentralization that is so prominent within the United States. In thinking about these issues, I find it helpful to consider three extreme cases—Weberian "ideal types." None of them will be realized during the next 10 years, but each may serve as a model, or general guideline, toward which we might move; all of them accept as given the fact of extensive government influence on the operation of market forces.

The first is a regime of nation-states, each successfully pursuing its own objectives that have been determined in its own way, democratically or otherwise. As noted above, successful pursuit of economic objectives at the national level requires markets that are fragmented at least to the national level, and this in turn implies that each nation is sufficiently insulated from other nations to pursue its independent course (although groupings of likeminded nations need not be excluded). This does not rule out trade and capital movements, but it does presuppose some instrument of policy (tariffs, quotas, taxes on international transactions, flexible exchange rates, or other defensive measures) that will permit a country to prevent emaciation of its domestic policies by international transactions that are highly sensitive to them. It is the sensitivity of international transactions that must be reduced, and that objective does not require autarky.

The second regime involves a supranational state that will take over many of the functions that are now performed by the nation—an extreme form of "constructive" response. In the area of economic policy this would mean economic stabilization, taxation of mobile factors, regulatory policies concerning businesses and unions, and even, up to a point, redistributional policies. In other words, the span of government control would be brought into correspondence with the decisionmaking domain of mobile businesses and individuals. Such a superstate need not be global in scope. Businesses, funds, and labor are not free to move globally, and they will not be for some time. The Communist countries and many less-developed countries are effectively insulated from the main economic centers of the industrial world, either by policy or by the uncertainty inherent in the absence of policy under politically unsettled circumstances.

There is a natural historical analogy here. It is the gradual passage of responsibility for increasing areas of economic management from the American states to the federal government. As American business became truly national rather than regional or local in character, the states found it increasingly difficult, in a country within which free trade prevailed and contracts made in one state had to be honored in others, to regulate business activity effectively. Businesses simply left the states that imposed onerous restrictions on their activities, or at least the head offices migrated. Consequently, the federal government gradually took over regulatory responsibilities.

The third regime involves American hegemony, an extreme form of "aggressive" response. Rather than turn responsibility over to a superstate, the United States would gradually extend its regulations to cover U.S. citizens abroad and foreigners residing in, or dealing with, the United States. By a combination of persuasion and (nonmilitary) threat, it would either bring other countries into line or drive them into the first regime, thereby insulating them from such contact with the United States as they find offensive to their sovereignty. The world would be on a dollar standard, and many nations would adopt systems of regulation and taxation similar to those of the United States in order to avert punitive reactions from it and to avoid internal embarrassments arising from differential treatment favoring American over domestic enterprises. This state of affairs could not be brought about, of course, without the overcoming of a certain amount of domestic American opposition, concerning, for instance, the taxation of income from foreign sources even when it is not repatriated.

None of these regimes is immediately foreseeable, for none is politically feasible. But the model regime which we implicitly use at present—autonomous and purposeful nation-states in harmonious and unrestricted economic intercourse, through the competitive marketplace, at fixed exchange rates, governed by occasional treaties and conventions to ensure good conduct and to iron out modest problems of overlapping jurisdiction, leaving virtually all economic decisions to national governments—is simply not viable in the long run, for the reasons already given. Unless we develop some new conception of world economic order, the search for specific solutions to specific problems will run a substantial risk of slipping into practices that are detrimental to all. We will enjoy neither the full benefits of economic integration on a "global" scale nor the full benefits of national autonomy in the establishment and pursuit of economic and social objectives. In short, it is the third notion of foreign policy, the grand conception of a world economic order, which will be profoundly affected by the impact of increased economic interdependence, for greater interdependence will inevitably compel a basic reexamination of the kind of world we ultimately want.

Various viable compromises among these three regimes are of course possible, and we should no doubt work toward one of them in the near future rather than toward the ideal types. Three come to mind. The first leans toward preservation of national autonomy by reducing the degree of interdependence through action by individual governments; such actions would be governed by international conventions to ensure that they were mutually consistent and that they went no further than necessary to achieve their purposes. Thus, agreement might be reached, and controls instituted, to limit movements of financial capital between countries. The blockage would not have to be complete to preserve some degree of national autonomy in monetary policy, but it would have to cover the major sources of flows. Similarly, taxes could be imposed on the outflow of business capital to prevent modest national differences in taxation and regulation of business from influencing the location of industry. Tariff quotas might be used to inhibit any rapid growth of imports that would greatly disturb domestic industries; the quotas could be allowed to grow automatically so that loss of competitiveness would be reflected in a relative but controlled decline in the domestic industry.

A second, preferable approach accomplishes much the same objective by introducing somewhat greater flexibility in exchange rates, with international rules governing the changes in rates and surveillance of adherence to the rules.[10] This approach would, I believe, help enormously with respect to balance-of-payments adjustment, and considerably with respect to the movement of yield-sensitive funds and price-sensitive goods from country to country, but it would still leave the whole area of business regulation untouched. It might therefore be combined with a third approach, involving intensive efforts to discover areas of potentially overlapping jurisdiction with a view to reaching common tax and regulatory policies among countries—preferably while the process of extensive foreign investment is still at a relatively early stage, so that a reasonably firm framework of expectations regarding corporate practices is available. (Recent inconclusive discussions between the United States and Swiss authorities regarding the prosecution of tax evaders indicate just how difficult agreement will be in some areas, and with some countries.)

The new requirements of the international scene will undoubtedly revive the debate between those with a *dirigiste* philosophy of economic policy and those who lean toward laissez faire. The former have largely carried the day domestically,[11] with governments committed to stabilize the economy, ensure growth, and establish an equitable distribution of income. The latter will therefore welcome a chance to reopen the issue in a new context; they will resist attempts to restrict international transactions and to regulate international firms and financial transactions through intergovernmental cooperation. International mobility offers a welcome escape from domestic regulation. The new circumstances will also result in some major realignments on broad issues at home. American labor has generally been internationalist in outlook and position, but it correctly sees the mobility of American firms as a threat to its welfare. Its opposition to "tariff factories" has begun to spread to all foreign investment and even to liberal trade policy, just as, in a somewhat different context, British Socialists regarded a restriction-free international economy as a threat to their plans for domestic social reform in the late 1940s. Laissez faire might logically be regarded as a fourth extreme regime, reflecting a universal passive response, but its manifest conflict with accepted domestic objectives warrants its exclusion.

In summary, increased economic interdependence will result in more varied and more frequent official and semi-official contact between nations—far more than foreign ministries can handle in volume, scope, or technical detail. As a result, the relative importance of foreign ministries in relations among the Western industrial countries will decline. Increased economic interdependence will also compel a reassessment of the prevailing model of world economic order.

The impact on foreign policy in the sense of national security is not likely, in the medium run, to be any greater than it was in the 1950s or the 1960s.[12] Such influence as there is will come through two channels: the tone of public attitudes toward foreign nations and the process of adjustment to imbalances in international payments. Public feelings of benevolence or malevolence toward particular foreign nations are easy to underrate because of their intangible quality; although they rarely prove decisive, they can influence the flexibility with which the executive can pursue foreign policy. In the absence of an adequate adjustment mechanism, balance-of-payments pressures can of course have very tangible effects on a nation's flexibility, as Britain and France have both learned during the past 15 years. These limits have been brought home to the United States in a variety of ways that range from the perceived need to tie foreign aid to procurement in the United States (the most important irritant in our relations with some countries) to the persistent pleas for reduction of force levels in Europe and elsewhere on balance-of-payments grounds. Such pressures erode the confidence of other nations in our ability to carry out our stated commitments and objectives. What is clearly needed is the introduction of some instrument of control that would achieve a balance-of-payments adjustment among major countries but would also further the cause of international cooperation.

It is important to recall that most of the tensions between international transactions and the autonomous pursuit of domestic economic policy arise from the sensitivity of movements of goods, services, funds, firms, and persons to economic developments at home and abroad, and not from the absolute magnitude of the flows. The value of trade to a country, in terms of its contribution to national welfare, may depend neither on the sensitivity nor on the magnitude of the flows, although it is more likely to be related to the magnitude than to the sensitivity. Indeed, value and sensitivity are inversely related in one important respect: High sensitivity results precisely from the capacity of a country to substitute domestic for foreign production or investment, in response to relatively small margins of advantage; yet when such substitution is easily possible at relatively low cost, the value per dollar of trade or investment to the country is correspondingly diminished. (It is of course possible that the total gains from trade remain high even when the gains close to the margin are small, so that sensitivity is high up to a point but not beyond that point.) Where the total gains from trade are high, preservation of trade becomes a matter of high foreign policy, as it is sometimes called, or even of national security. Thus, a high value placed on trade may lead countries to war over it, as it led Japan in 1941 to attack the Philippines and the U.S. fleet at Pearl Harbor to remove threats to its oil trade with the East Indies. Increased interdependence in the sense used here will greatly reduce that risk, but it will also greatly increase the intrusion of international transactions into domestic affairs, thereby augmenting and aggravating a very different range of problems in foreign policy.

Growing economic interdependence thus negates the sharp distinction between internal and external policies that underlies the present political organization of the world—sometimes called the Westphalian System, after the treaty that marked an end to the universalism of the Middle Ages—into sovereign, territorially-based nation-states that are inviolable in their domestic actions and subject to voluntarily agreed rules and conventions in their foreign policies (including war).[13] The growing interdependence of the world economy creates pressures for common policies, and hence for procedures whereby countries discuss and coordinate actions that hitherto were regarded as being of domestic concern exclusively. These pressures arise because market forces increasingly circumscribe the ability of nation-states to achieve their desired aims, regardless of their formal retention of sovereignty. Where autonomy implies success in achieving objectives and not merely the freedom to make futile attempts to achieve objectives, some autonomy in policy can actually be restored by yielding sovereignty in certain areas.

The Westphalian System formally treats all nations as equals, and diplomatic forms preserve that fiction. But there are many important asymmetries in the world, so that "interdependence" is not always even-handed in its circumscribing impact. The asymmetries do not, however, always favor the larger countries. It is true that the United States, by virtue of its relative economic size and the international use of its currency (which in turn is partly related to size), retains much more autonomy in the use of monetary policy for domestic purposes than do other countries, for its own actions strongly influence world monetary conditions. Tight money in the United States means tight money in the world (as in 1969), with capital inflows eroding the tight-money position only modestly. Similarly, the importance of American investment abroad means that American corporate-tax practices (and in particular the provisions for crediting foreign taxes against U.S. corporate-tax liabilities) have a strong influence on corporate-tax treatment in other countries, thereby preserving some autonomy for the United States.

On the other hand, small countries are sometimes in a more favorable position to exploit the international rules and the increased mobility of firms and funds than large ones. Like an oligopolistic firm, a large country must be alert to the reactions of others to its own actions; it must concern itself with the viability and stability of the system as a whole. The small country, in contrast, can, within limits, consider the system as being beyond its influence and can therefore act freely in ways that, if generalized, would alter the system, often for the worse. It can act with impunity so long as the resulting movements of funds or firms remain relatively small—that is, so long as they do not threaten the system as a whole. Thus we see the emergence of "flags of convenience" and their analogs in matters of corporate structure, disclosure of information, and taxation.

Throughout this dicussion the less-developed countries have been largely excluded from consideration. This is not because their problems are unimportant, but because economic interdependence among the developed countries is moving so rapidly that it creates a common range of problems among countries with broadly similar objectives and institutional setups and therefore calls for common and often collectively agreed solutions. The European Economic Community as a center for economic decisionmaking is rapidly becoming obsolete in the face of growing economic interdependence; the United Nations, on the other hand, is much too large and reflects much too diverse a range of economic concerns among its members to be a useful instrument for international collective action in this area. An unhappy by-product of relying on a small group of largely industrial nations, a rich man's club, is the accentuation of the perceived differences between the rich and the poor. As time goes on, problems facing the initial group will undoubtedly spread; therefore the club should have a flexible approach to membership, as required by the problems at hand. A much broader group will be appropriate for some issues, for example in defining the relationship between foreign-controlled firms, host governments, and home governments. But even here the concerns and anxieties of less-developed countries, still groping for national identity, may have quite a different character from those of more mature and more self-confident countries, and this in turn will require different solutions.

Notes

1. This definition of interdependence contrasts with that implicitly used by Kenneth Waltz, who emphasizes the importance of foreign trade to the welfare and security of the countries under consideration. See his "The Myth of Interdependence" in C. P. Kindleberger, ed., *The International Corporation* (Cambridge, Mass., 1970). As will be made clear below, trade may become less valuable to countries at the same time that it is becoming more sensitive to price, income, and other economic variables, and indeed for the same reasons.

2. For a more systematic review of the evidence of increased interdependence, see Cooper, *The Economics of Interdependence* (New York, 1968), chaps. 3–5; Cooper, "Towards an International Capital Market?" in C. P. Kindleberger and A. Shonfield, eds., *North American and Western European Economic Policies* (New York, 1971).

3. This second form of integration corresponds to what Karl Kaiser has called "intergovernmental regional subsystems," to be distinguished from "transnational society subsystems," of which economic integration through joined markets would represent one possible example. But joined markets also create pressures for intergovernmental action. See his "The Interaction of Regional Subsystems," *World Politics* 21 (October 1968): 84–107.

4. The term "autonomy" is preferred here to the more usual "economic sovereignty." In fact, nations retain actual as well as legal control over their instruments of policy (sovereignty); the problem arises because these instruments of policy lose their effectiveness, so that countries find themselves able to pursue their objectives but unable to achieve them.

5. For a general discussion of these issues as they affect foreign investment, see Charles P. Kindleberger, *American Business Abroad* (New Haven, Conn., 1969).

6. Or worse. In 1963 Britain threatened to seize Pan American and TWA planes if the CAB did not back down from its insistence on regulating transatlantic fares.

7. The actions by Britain, Denmark, and the Netherlands to halt "pirate" radio stations operating off their coasts in international waters also represent extraterritorial claims to jurisdiction, as does the unilateral extension by Ecuador, Peru, Chile, and Iceland of territorial claims far into international waters in order to control rich fishing grounds.

8. C. Fred Bergsten ["Taking the Monetary Initiative," *Foreign Affairs* 46 (July 1968): 713–732] discussed the proposal but rejected it. It was, however, put into force by President Nixon while this essay was going to press.

9. This has long been true of trade policy, of course, and this fact has set trade policy apart from other aspects of foreign policy—a much wider range of political interests and persons had to be brought into the picture. Indeed, in the early 1930s, tariffs were considered exclusively a matter of domestic concern. Such success as trade policy has had as foreign policy has hinged on the brilliant idea of reciprocity, which in effect pits one set of domestic economic interests against another and thereby restores to the executive some of the freedom of action that he has in other areas of foreign policy. On the general relationship between domestic politics and foreign policy in Britain and the United States, see Kenneth N. Waltz, *Foreign Policy and Democratic Politics* (Boston, 1967). Curiously, Waltz does not discuss trade policy at all; if he had, he might have qualified his judgment that the American executive has more scope for pursuing foreign policy than does the British prime minister.

10. A proposal along these lines can be found in Cooper, "Sliding Parities: A Proposal for Presumptive Rules," in George N. Halm, ed., *Approaches to Greater Flexibility of Exchange Rates* (Princeton, N.J., 1970). This volume contains extensive discussion of a number of similar proposals.

11. Some years ago Gunnar Myrdal identified and lamented the tension between the national pursuit of domestic objectives that are desirable in themselves and the preservation of an integrated international economy. He argued that the growth of the welfare state had led to disintegration of the world economy. I believe that this judgment unduly idealizes the "integration" of the world economy before the rise of the welfare state and that, in any case, it is premature; however, the tension between national pursuit of national economic aims and the attainment of harmonious and unrestricted international transactions is certainly present, and indeed will become more acute. See Myrdal, *Beyond the Welfare State* (London, 1960), especially chap. 10.

12. This statement did not anticipate the extraordinarily aggressive response of the United States in President Nixon's New Economic Policy of August 1971. The imposition of the 10 percent surcharge on imports and the declaration that the dollar would no longer be convertible into gold, without any prior consultation even with our closest allies, are bound to induce others to reexamine their dependence on and their trust in the United States in matters of national security, and may even accelerate the proliferation of nuclear weapons.

13. See Richard A. Falk, "The Interplay of Westphalia and Charter Conceptions of International Legal Order," in Richard A. Falk and Cyril E. Black, eds., *The Future of the International Legal Order*, vol. 1, *Trends and Patterns* (Princeton, N.J., 1969).

2   Managing Risks to the International Economic System

We live in a period of high uncertainty. John Kenneth Galbraith has called it the Age of Uncertainty. The purpose of this article is to assess the risks or threats to the international economic system that arise from this uncertainty, and the suitability of present institutional arrangements to deal with those risks.

By "risk" I mean the possibility of an unforeseen development that influences our welfare. "Risk" as used here bears little relationship to the "risk" involved in games of chance, where the outcome is uncertain before the dice are rolled but the nature of the outcomes is understood and their relative likelihood or probability is known. One might say that there is statistical certainty in games of chance. In sharp contrast, the principal efforts to deal with risk in social systems, as with hang gliding, is to try to influence the probabilities.

If a development is foreseen, it can be allowed for and it is not a risk. For the most part, we will be dealing with unforeseen adverse developments. Favorable developments are generally of less concern, although in some cases if they are mishandled they may influence the future adversely, as when a firm finds itself with demand for its products that it cannot satisfy and thereby loses customers, or when the discovery of oil creates public expectations that a country cannot satisfy.

A period of change almost always creates uncertainty, for the field of possible outcomes is wider than during a period of relative stability. The current international economy is in a period of rapid changes. Some of those changes are driven by technology, such as improvements in transportation and communication that integrate the world market and thereby reduce the natural protection of regional or national markets, partly by simply removing barriers of ignorance so that the "foreignness" is removed from foreign trade and investment. These developments create new opportunities for business firms, but they also stiffen the competitive environment in which firms must operate. Governments too are affected; the globalization of markets undermines some of their traditional modes of intervention into economic activity, but it also creates new opportunities to exploit the mobility of business firms.[1]

Rapid change has also emanated from the political arena, mainly from decolonization and its continuing aftermath, which keep the political framework in which economic transactions take place in a constant state of flux. Breaking political ties with former colonial powers removed an element of stability and relative certainty; however, it also reduced the privileged position of the colonial power, creating new opportunities (with their attendant uncertainties) for outsiders.

During the past decade, developing countries have not merely altered the basis for doing business at home; they have also become important actors on the world scene, partly as rapidly growing exporters of manufactured goods and partly as political actors calling for fundamental changes in the international economic system and thus creating uncertainties about the durability of the existing "rules of the game."

Finally, the thawing of the Cold War and the emergence of detente removed a comprehensible (if not always sensible) framework for East-West relations. Again new opportunities for trade have been created, but they remain uncertain because of continuing ambivalence of American officials and the American public toward trade with Communist countries.

It will prove useful to distinguish among different degrees of adverse development, ranging from a *disturbance* (an adverse development which is unfortunate but which we can take in stride) to a *crisis* (a disturbance that threatens more serious consequences and the possibility of a *breakdown*, or *collapse*, which causes us to change fundamentally the way we do things) to a *catastrophe* (a breakdown from which recovery is difficult, prolonged, and very painful, if indeed the process can be spoken of as "recovery" at all).

This article will be concerned with the international economic system as a whole, by which I mean the framework in which firms and nations undertake international transactions. The framework comprises the formal rules, the informal conventions, and the accepted practices that govern international economic transactions, along with the institutional arrangements for policing the rules, resolving disputes, and changing the rules in the face of altered circumstances.

Obviously some participants in the international economic system can be in crisis or even experience a breakdown (as when a firm declares bankruptcy) while leaving other participants, and the system as a whole, free of crisis and far from collapse. Indeed, the system can be said to be resilient precisely to the extent that it is able to absorb disturbances and even crises and breakdowns among its participants without generating a systemwide crisis, much less a breakdown. A system is supportive to the extent that it helps its participants to keep a disturbance from becoming a crisis leading to a breakdown for the participants.

The time dimension must also be mentioned. A series of crises may seem to have been absorbed satisfactorily but may lead over time to undramatic but cumulatively substantial changes. Do we call this a breakdown of the old system if the cumulative changes are sufficiently large? In historical perspective, the answer will almost surely be yes. But contemporary participants may have no sense of such a breakdown, only a sense of adaptation to altered circumstances and/or new information. Thus, both "crisis" and "collapse" have a time dimension; to warrant the label, events must occur rapidly. (How rapidly they must occur will itself vary with the time perspective of the observer.)

This article, then, will be concerned with disturbances that are sufficiently large and concentrated in time that they lead to crises for firms (and perhaps governments) of such a magnitude that they threaten to cause a breakdown of the international economic system or some substantial part of it. We must then ask the following: What types of disturbances are most likely to do this? What mechanisms do we have in place to prevent a crisis for the system? What mechanisms do we have in place to mitigate the effects of a crisis and prevent a breakdown? What improvements are possible to prevent system-wide crises and to mitigate the effects of those that occur? Implicit in these questions is the judgment that breakdowns are undesirable and should be avoided. Some breakdowns, however, will be welcome to some observers, and they may even be preferable (if the damage is limited) to the continuation of a crisis-prone regime. For instance, the shift to flexible exchange rates that followed the partial breakdown of the Bretton Woods system in the early 1970s may fall into this category.

The Great Depression: A Catastrophe

The catastrophe of the Great Depression offers examples of complete breakdowns in several parts of the economic system, and a brief examination of those aspects provides background for the institutional innovations that arose from the Great Depression and that still provide the core of the existing international economic system.

The basic causes of the Great Depression are still a source of controversy and dispute. For our purposes, it involved three separate but mutually reinforcing kinds of crisis: a tariff war, a banking crisis, and a balance-of-payments crisis. They all contributed to, but were also aggravated by, sharp declines in industrial production and prices, which in turn were worsened by restrictive fiscal policies and efforts to deflate in the mistaken notion that, if only factor costs (especially wages) could be reduced enough, national economies would right themselves.

Consider first the tariff war. Tariffs had already been raised after World War I, to protect industries that had expanded during the war and now experienced new postwar competition. After 1925, world agricultural prices began to slump under the pressure of large supplies. Farm income dropped and pleas for support of agricultural prices spread. Herbert Hoover campaigned in 1928 on a platform that promised tariff protection to American farmers, and Congress started hearings in January 1929 with terms of reference not confined to agriculture. The Smoot-Hawley bill wound its way through Congress, passing the House in May 1929, to the growing anxiety and formal protest of foreign governments. In June 1930 (against the advice of 1,028 petitioning American economists) President Hoover signed into law the highest tariff in American history. Spain, Canada, Italy, Cuba, Mexico, France, Australia, and New Zealand retaliated with higher tariffs on American (and other) goods within a few months, and other countries followed suit. Switzerland even promoted a boycott of American goods.[2]

Under the combined onslaught of falling real income, falling prices, and higher tariffs, international trade fell by two-thirds between 1929 and early 1933. Tariffs no doubt were the least important of the three causes, but they made a contribution to the decline and, more important, they both reflected and reinforced inward-looking national perspectives that hindered international cooperation of any kind to mitigate the forces that were pushing the world into ever-deeper depression. Kindleberger attributes the breakdown to a lack of world leadership; Britain (which supported a tariff freeze and maintained its economy open until 1932) was unable to provide it, and the United States was unwilling.

A second crisis was that in banking. Under the pressure of declining agricultural prices and incomes, a number of banks failed in 1929 and 1930 in the rural areas of the United States. Temin argues, however, that these failures were no greater than those that were typical in depressions of a magnitude that had been frequent in the United States in the previous century and thus cannot explain the depth of the Great Depression and the subsequent rash of bank failures.[3] More serious was the failure of the Bank of the United States in December 1930. This bank had 57 branches in New York and $25 million in capital, so its failure was a major event. This failure was due to fraudulent and illegal activities by its owner, Bernard Marcus, and cannot be attributed directly to the depression. However, it surely lessened public confidence in banks.[4]

Two French banks failed at about the same time, and one of these failures also involved fraud and the complicity of several officials.[5] But the major banking crisis came the following spring. Foreign lenders began to withdraw their funds from German banks—which had borrowed heavily abroad at short term—after the German election of September 1930, in which both the Communists and the Nazis greatly increased their representation in the Reichstag. This weakened the German banks. A second wave of withdrawals started in May 1931—a few before and many after the announcement of the collapse of the Austrian bank, the Credit-Anstalt. This bank had made some bad acquisitions in the preceding two years, and its weak financial position gradually came to light. The wave of distrust spread to banks in Hungary, Czechoslovakia, and Romania (parts of the former Austro-Hungarian Empire) as well as to Poland and Germany. The spread suggested that American lenders lumped all these countries together, unaware of their separate identities. In June 1931, Nordwolle (a German firm that had speculated unsuccessfully on a rise in the price of wool) went into bankruptcy; in July the great extent of its losses and the exposure of its creditors (especially the large Danatbank) became known and the withdrawals accelerated. Banks had to be closed temporarily. Emergency loans were raised and support was extended, but the damage to confidence in banks had been done. The continued withdrawal of foreign deposits and loans led to a balance-of-payments crisis.

In this period the major countries adhered to the gold standard, which meant that gold provided the legal backing for the issue of currency and that central banks would pay out gold on demand at a fixed price in exchange for their currency. In the 1920s it had become a widespread practice for some central banks to hold as reserves the currencies of other countries, most notably sterling, on the understanding that those currencies could readily be converted into gold. Hence, the regime has been called the gold exchange standard. France chafed under this arrangement (which had been advocated to conserve monetary gold), and after the franc was stablized in 1926 (at an undervalued rate) France began to convert some of its holdings of sterling into gold on a more or less regular basis. These conversions accelerated in the second half of 1928, and in 1929 the extent of U.S. lending abroad slackened to the point that the United States, too, began to pull in gold from the rest of the world. Between early 1929 and the summer of 1931, France and the United States together acquired $1.7 billion in gold, about 10 percent of world gold reserves. This occurred at a time when London was still the acknowledged financial capital of the world and the Bank of England the principal regulator. Britain burdened itself with an overvalued currency when it returned to the gold standard at prewar parity in 1925, and Germany was burdened with reparations payments as stipulated in the Dawes Plan of 1924. Both countries borrowed abroad to cover their payments, and both were financially vulnerable to the withdrawal of foreign funds that came in 1931.

Hoover proposed a moratorium on all payments of reparations and intergovernmental war loans, but it was too late. Funds streamed out of Germany until a standstill on the withdrawal of all foreign funds was agreed upon in July. The pressure then shifted to London, where the Reports of the Macmillan Committee and the May Committee had just been released, respectively indicating the extent of Britain's foreign liabilities and the extent of the upcoming budget deficit, along with sharp disagreement among its members on how to reduce it, but urging new loans from abroad. Two emergency loans were raised from France and the United States, but they were not enough to stem the wave of distrust and pessimism among private holders of sterling and among the smaller central banks. After erroneous press reports of a mutiny in the British navy, withdrawals accelerated, and Britain went off the gold standard on September 21, 1931.[6] Two dozen countries followed, and the international monetary system, as it had been known until then, collapsed. The United States held onto gold until 1933, France and the Continental "gold bloc" until 1936. Germany declined to allow the mark to depreciate with sterling, as some recommended, out of continuing fear of inflation engendered by the hyperinflation of 1923; instead, it introduced controls over international payments, a practice that was to be emulated widely during the subsequent three decades and that continues in some countries even today.

Once countries ceased to peg their currencies to gold, the possibility arose for exchange-rate manipulation, active or passive. Under financial pressure, sterling depreciated by one-third by December. This was far more than was necessary to correct Britain's trading imbalance, and the drop stimulated Britain's sluggish economy. Japan, too, enjoyed the stimulus of an undervalued currency, and in 1933 the United States abandoned gold with the deliberate aim of "raising prices" within the United States. The dollar was re-pegged to gold at $35 an ounce the following year, which also resulted in an undervaluation of the dollar relative to Continental currencies.

International cooperation was not wholly lacking during this turbulent period; it was merely hopelessly inadequate. Few national governments had the courage or the domestic political support for any international cooperation that seemed to involved sacrifice. Hoover did, it is true, successfully propose a moratorium on intergovernmental debts; but it came only in July 1931, and even then France had to be threatened with isolation before agreeing to go along. A series of special loans were arranged, usually with the Bank of England in the lead, to help countries in distress—Austria, Germany, then Britain itself. Central banks were the principal parties, and when the question of a massive new loan for Germany was raised in the summer of 1931, Hoover declined on the grounds that the U.S. budget deficit was already too large. On several occasions France stipulated political conditions on new loans, especially in an attempt to head off economic cooperation between Germany and Austria.

Once banks were seen to be in serious trouble, the distrust spread to other, unrelated banks. Withdrawals, both domestic and foreign, occurred apace. Finally, the decline of commodity prices and export earnings led a number of primary producing countries to default on international bonds they had issued during the more buoyant 1920s (although other countries went through extraordinary deflation at home in order to continue payments on their bonds); these defaults in turn led to the drying up of the international capital market.[7]

Rebuilding the International Economic System

The experience of the Great Depression governed the institutional arrangements that were established during and immediately after World War II, which in crucial respects prevail at the present time. Much, of course, was done in domestic legislation. The Glass-Steagall Act, the Banking Act, the Securities and Exchange Act, and the creation of the Federal Deposit Insurance Corporation were all designed to strengthen the financial system in order to prevent a repetition of stock-market excesses and the rash of U.S. bank failures that had taken place between 1928 and 1933. Above all, the Full Employment Act of 1946, and its counterparts in other countries, committed governments to act as the balance wheel of national economies, to prevent the deflation of prices and incomes, the loss of production, and the rise of unemployment that had taken place during the Depression.

On the international front, the main institutional arrangements were set out in the Bretton Woods agreements and in the General Agreement on Tariffs and Trade. These agreements establish both general norms of international behavior enjoining cooperation and a concern for the system as a whole and particular rules designed to avoid what were perceived as the worst behaviors of the Depression. They also established institutions to perform a facilitating role and to police the new norms and rules.

Briefly, the Bretton Woods agreements required that each country establish a "par value" for its currency, which it would alter only to correct a fundamental disequilibrium in its international payments, and then only on notification and with approval of other countries. These provisions were designed to prevent the evil of competitive depreciation of currencies. Moreover, each country was to make its currency freely available both to residents and to nonresidents for payments for goods and services, a reaction to the exchange controls of the 1930s (but note the significant omission of a requirement for currency convertibility for capital movements). Each country was also obliged to convert its currency on demand from other *monetary* authorities (but not the public) into gold or some currency itself convertible into gold. Finally, two new institutions were to be established. The International Monetary Fund (IMF) would police the above rules, and would lend to countries at medium term in order to tide them over temporary balance-of-payments difficulties, thus providing a source of balance-of-payments support that was absent in the 1930s. In addition, the International Bank for Reconstruction and Development (now known as the World Bank) was created to provide long-term loans to countries, to be raised in private capital markets. It did so by providing guarantees to the buyers of World Bank bonds backed by all the members of the World Bank. This arrangement permitted the resumption of long-term international lending.

On the side of trade, the General Agreement on Tariffs and Trade (GATT) established the principle of nondiscrimination in international trade (aimed to avoid bilateral trade agreements of the type set up by Germany and other countries during the 1930s, and, unsuccessfully, to reduce the Imperial Preference System established in 1932 among Britain and its dominions and colonies). It prohibited quantitative restrictions on international trade (except for balance-of-payments reasons, with the approval of the IMF) and subsidies to exports. It involved a commitment to reduce tariffs over time through a process of multilateral negotiation, and a commitment not to raise tariffs previously in place. Finally, it established procedures for resolving disputes between contracting parties and for controlled retaliation in the event that disputes could not be resolved satisfactorily. The last feature was a novel one, designed to limit sharply any "trade wars" that might develop and to keep them on their own track so they would not sour other cooperative relations among countries.

These various agreements made allowance for exceptions, and they have been administered flexibly over time (some observers would say too flexibly in the case of the GATT[8]); nonetheless, they established a framework of norms which, along with the domestic legislation mentioned above, laid the basis for a remarkable world economic prosperity over a quarter of a century—probably the most prosperous period of that length that the world has ever experienced.

The "Breakdown" of the Bretton Woods System

The present threats to the international economic system are similar in kind to those that contributed to its breakdown in the 1930s: banking crises, balance-of-payments crises, and trade wars. In addition, we can now contemplate—because we have experienced a taste of it—an oil crisis. We will return below to these four possible sources of disturbance in a contemporary setting. But first it will be useful to digress briefly on the alleged breakdown of the Bretton Woods system that occurred in the early 1970s.

The breakdown arose, as had the collapse of the gold exchange standard 40 years earlier, from a balance-of-payments crisis in the world's leading economy and leading financial center, now the United States. For a variety of reasons that need not concern us here, the dollar had become overvalued by the early 1970s. The U.S. payments position deteriorated both on current and on long-term capital account (especially direct investment), and when the protection provided by high interest rates in 1969 melted during the recession of 1970 and the recovery of 1971, capital began to flow out of the United States on a massive scale. Alarmed by the inflow of dollars (which under the rules of the Bretton Woods regime they were obliged to purchase at the going exchange rate), many central banks began to convert their dollar acquisitions into gold on a considerable scale. U.S. gold reserves were inadequate to cover the large outstanding dollar liabilities (a point that had been under discussion for some time), and in August 1971 the United States ceased to convert dollars into gold for foreign monetary authorities. It also imposed a 10 percent surcharge on all dutiable imports in order to improve the competitive position of American firms, at least in the home market.

In December the surcharge was removed, after a negotiated depreciation of the dollar and an appreciation of other leading currencies amounting to a net (weighted) depreciation of the dollar by about 7 percent—an amount that American officials considered inadequate. The par value system was salvaged, but with the important difference that the United States did not undertake to convert dollars into gold. When in early 1973 a large outflow of dollars resumed, therefore, other countries faced a choice of accumulating dollars without limit or allowing their currencies to "float" against the dollar. In March they chose the latter course, and the world entered an era of floating exchange rates, at least among the major currencies.[9] This system was formally sanctified in 1978.

It is an error to believe, however, that this development represented the demise of the Bretton Woods system. Rather, it represented the loss—some would say a welcome loss—of one feature of the Bretton Woods system, namely the commitment to fixed exchange rates. The other features of the Bretton Woods system—the convertibility of one currency into another and the role of the IMF as a guiding hand and a lender to countries in difficulty—continued, in addition to the IMF's newly acquired role as an issuer of Special Drawing Rights, a new form of international reserves.

While pressures on the dollar were the precipitating event for the move away from fixed exchange rates, tensions in the old system had been evident for some time—around sterling in the mid 1960s and around the German mark in 1969. These tensions were relieved with revaluations of those currencies (downward in the case of sterling, upward in the case of the mark), but only after much turbulence in foreign exchange markets and with monetary policy.

Indeed, the fixed-exchange-rate feature of the Bretton Woods system contained a fatal flaw: National autonomy in monetary policy, fixed exchange rates, and free movement of capital are incompatible. One of the three had to give way. The Bretton Woods system did not require the freedom of capital movements, but as a practical matter it was impossible to separate capital from current transactions, and in any case several countries (including the United States) were committed to a high degree of freedom of capital movements. This remained true in spite of the restraint that the United States imposed on outward movement of some forms of capital after 1963. Nations were not yet ready to give up their autonomy in monetary policy and, in effect, return to the domestic version of the "gold standard" without the actual use of gold. That left the fixed exchange rates to give way, and they did.[10]

The collapse of the system of fixed exchange rates had long been foreseen by a number of specialists in international finance (and had been urged by some of them), but it nonetheless came as a surprise and a shock to the wider public, and to this day it is still usually considered as a "breakdown" (with the unfavorable connotations of that word) rather than as an improvement in the international economic system which, to be sure, was brought about in a disorderly fashion under the pressure of events.

Current Threats to the International Economic System

Let us return to the 1980s. Four possible sources of crisis are frequently mentioned, and we will take up in turn the nature of each threat and the institutional arrangements in place to prevent or to contain it. These four are a foreign-exchange crisis, a banking crisis, an oil crisis, and trade wars. As will become clear in the course of the following discussion, I believe that these possible threats are real, but that governments are well aware of them and that, with the possible exception of an oil crisis, they are manageable. The most serious threat to the existing system does not come from a crisis at all—although there will certainly be crises from time to time—but from a gradual, piecemeal erosion of the international rules and conventions under the pressure of various national economic crises, such that after a period of, say, a decade the fabric of international transactions and international economic cooperation that has been successfully built up over the past 30 years may have disintegrated. But let us first turn to the possible sources of crisis.

Foreign-Exchange Crisis

A foreign-exchange crisis arises when there is a rush—for whatever reason—from one currency to another, or, when the option is available, from a currency into monetary gold at a central bank. Foreign-exchange crises brought down the gold standard in 1931 and part of the Bretton Woods system in 1971. These days, a foreign-exchange crisis could be precipitated by an attempt by any large holder of liquid funds to convert them into some other currency, such as Iran threatened to do with its dollar holdings in November 1979. Or it could be precipitated by market perception that monetary policy in one country is way out of line with that in other major countries. Whatever the reason, once the movement starts it is subject to bandwagon effects; that is, foreign-exchange dealers initially buy or sell in sympathy with the initial impetus rather than counter to it.[11]

Then what happens? I will leave for discussion below the possibility that some banks might run into difficulty because of large-scale conversions from one currency to another. With floating exchange rates among major currencies, large-scale conversions will lead to a depreciation of the currency being sold initially (it is of course also purchased—the rate moves enough to induce a purchase). Psychological bandwagon effects for or against a currency may lead to a sharp movement in its exchange rate. But sooner or later buyers will appear for a depreciating currency (sellers for an appreciating one).

The exchange rate will move until they do. Flexible exchange rates thus provide a safety valve—not always a comfortable one—in balance-of-payments crises; a country cannot be "driven off gold" now as in 1931 or 1971. The dilemmas for policy are more subtle, involving management of the domestic economy (a depreciating currency aggravates inflation) and export cometitiveness. (Export competitiveness is reduced by a currency that appreciates more rapidly than differential inflation rates would require.) Countries with rapidly appreciating currencies will find imports more competitive and exports less competitive, and their governments may be called upon to protect imports, even though import restrictions would perversely accelerate the appreciation of the currency and worsen further the position of exports. Countries with depreciating currencies will be tempted to restrict outflows of capital (as Germany did informally in 1980–81) or to tighten monetary conditions (as the United States did in October 1978).

Central banks can break the movement in exchange rates, and sometimes even reverse it, by intervening directly in exchange markets. They act as counterspeculators. For an appreciating currency, there is no limit to the possible intervention, since the central bank is selling its own currency of issue; but large sales entail expansionist monetary policy, which cannot always be easily or fully offset by open-market sales of securities.

For a depreciation currency, the extent of intervention is limited by the country's foreign-exchange reserves and its capacity to borrow abroad, including credit lines with other central banks. The major central banks now have extensive access to funds. Once again, exchange-market intervention influences monetary conditions, in this instance in a contractionary direction.

Some countries still peg their currencies to the dollar or to a weighted average of other currencies. A number of European currencies are confined within a series of bilateral exchange-rate limits by the European Monetary System. In these cases a country can of course be forced off its previous rate by sufficiently large movements of funds across the foreign-exchange market. But that is not likely to represent a threat to the monetary system as a whole, no matter how traumatic it may be for the particular country. We have now had many cases of exchange-rate adjustment. The International Monetary Fund often oversees—indeed recommends—such a change, and accompanies it by a loan to facilitate the post-devaluation adjustment. Recently the IMF has greatly augmented the funds it will make available during these stabilization programs, and it has also adapted the conditions it lays down for a loan to fit the diverse circumstances that may lead a country into balance-of-payments difficulty.

One inhibition to currency devaluation these days may be the large amount of external indebtedness denominated in foreign currency. Currency devaluation increases the local-currency cost of servicing these debts, and unless that possibility has been allowed for (e.g., through reserve funds) the debtor may be forced into bankruptcy. The problem of external indebtedness will be discussed futher below.

To sum up, flexible exchange rates provide a considerable shock absorber for the international economy. Balance-of-payments crises are not likely to threaten the system as a whole, except insofar as they give rise to banking crises or lead to trade restrictions.

Banking Crisis

A bank insolvency can ricochet through the banking community, leaving a field of illiquidity and even further insolvency. This is because of the great extent to which interbank transactions dominate bank lending, especially international banking. The so-called Euro-currency market had grown to an astounding $1.3 trillion by the end of 1980, of which over half was made up of interbank deposits. Thus, if one bank becomes insolvent, it freezes and perhaps reduces the assets of other banks. Moreover, the insolvency can influence other banks by reducing confidence in them and thus leading depositors to withdraw their funds.

The precipitating event may be a withdrawal of funds by a major depositor; a default by a major debtor; or losses in operations of the bank due to its management's bad judgment, bad luck, or malfeasance.

Despite the attention it has received in recent years in connection with the massing of large surplus funds by oil-exporting countries, the first cause—a major withdrawal of funds—is not likely to cause a banking crisis these days. If we are dealing with a single currency, any withdrawal of funds must be redeposited, directly or indirectly, elsewhere in the banking system. Unlike in the 1930s, withdrawals cannot take place in specie, and large depositors are unlikely to withdraw bank notes. Thus, banking funds will be moved about but cannot be reduced except through contractive central-bank action. A run from small deposits into bank notes is conceivable, but in the United States this is inhibited by deposit insurance, an institutional bulwark that many other countries have not yet adopted.

Large withdrawals create a problem for the particular bank that is subject to the withdrawals; however, as long as that bank is perceived to be sound, it can borrow funds in the interbank market to cover the withdrawals to the extent that it cannot liquidate some of its assets. Thus, large-scale withdrawals become a serious problem only if the bank is in trouble for other

Table 1
Long-term external debt, 1973 and 1981 (billions of dollars).

	1973	1981
East European countries (bank claims only)	9.0	55.1[b]
OPEC members (bank claims only)	3.0	59.8[b]
Non-oil-producing developing countries	97.3	436.9
Official creditors	49.1	175.6
Private creditors	48.3	261.4
financial institutions	34.5	223.6
Oil exporters	15.6	90.6
Others	81.7	346.3
Debt-service payments	16.1	92.3
Ratio of debt service to exports[a] (percent)	14.0	21.0

a. Exports of goods and services.
b. 1979.
Sources: IMF, *World Economic Outlook*, June 1981, tables 27, 29, 30; IMF, *International Capital Markets*, Occasional Paper no. 1, September 1980, tables 2, 3.

reasons and has effectively lost access to the interbank market. Even then it will generally have access to the discount window of its central bank. Understandings on this point with respect to foreign banking will be taken up below.

More serious is default by a major debtor. During the past decade, and especially since the oil-price increases of 1974, there has been an enormous increase in international debt. While the increase has been virtually universal, the increase to developing countries (other than members of OPEC) has been the source of the most articulated concern. Official institutions have greatly increased their lending, but bank lending has increased even more—by a factor of 6 between 1973 and 1981 (see table 1). The largest single debtor countries were Brazil and Mexico, whose external debts were huge, both absolutely and relative to the capital of some lending banks. Thus, lending to all developing countries (other than members of OPEC) by the nine largest U.S. banks amounted to 204 percent of their capital by the end of 1980, up from 156 percent in 1977. Moreover, there were 80 instances in which loans by U.S. banks to a single developing country exceeded 30 percent of its capital (up from 36 instances in mid 1979).[12] These figures are somewhat misleading, since a consequential amount of bank lending involves guarantees by third parties (typically governments of the major exporting countries), and this is even more true of non-U.S. banks than of U.S. banks. Still, there is no question that banks these days are highly leveraged. The ratio of equity capital to total assets of the nine U.S. banks most heavily engaged in international business was only around 4 percent.[13]

Given the huge magnitude of external debt, and the varied economic and political disturbances to which countries around the world are subject, default is a major source of concern. At the end of 1980, a total of 26 countries (most of them in Africa and Central America) had payments arrears amounting to over $6 billion—the equivalent of 42 percent of their 1980 export earnings. This represented an increase in arrears from just under $1 billion in 1975, involving 13 countries.[14]

The situation is intrinsically more precarious than it was in the 1930s, when most lending to developing countries was in the form of bonds, many of which were held by nonbank holders. Under those circumstances, the likelihood of a domino effect through the banking system was less. If the banks in question are sound and well diversified, even several defaults can be absorbed. But the possibility of multiple defaults and resulting interruption of the continuing flow of funds through international markets leads banks and debtors alike to go to considerable lengths to avoid formal defaults. The practice of rescheduling debts that are in threat of imminent default has been developed precisely to avoid the possible consequences of default, both for creditors and for debtors. Under these arrangements, a debtor country threatened by the possibility of default asks for a meeting of major creditor nations, usually under the chairmanship of the French ministry of finance. The debts in question are official and officially guaranteed claims with maturity over one year, including official export credits or guarantees. An assessment of the economic prospects of the debtor is made, and the creditors agree to reschedule the principal payments of the outstanding debt due in the coming year, often with a grace period of several years during which no payment of principal is required. An agreement with the IMF on a stabilization program has been required as a condition for rescheduling (except in the recent case of Poland, which is not a member of the IMF). Moreover, the debtor undertakes to reschedule its debts to private creditors, mainly banks, on terms no more favorable to the creditors than was the case for the official debts. Thus, a framework is established for working out a rescheduling with the leading bank creditors.

This system, which falls short of the "standstills" that were introduced in several instances in the 1930s in that interest and some nonrescheduled principal continue to be paid, has the advantages of avoiding formal default, keeping the debtor country formally credit-worthy, and maintaining the loans on the balance sheets of the lending banks at full value. Thus, the

Table 2
Multilateral debt rescheduling (official and officially guaranteed debt).

	Number of debtor countries	Total amount rescheduled
1972	5	$ 650,000,000
1973	2	290,000,000
1974	4	1,594,000,000
1975	2	397,000,000
1976	2	330,000,000
1977	2	200,000,000
1978	2	1,780,000,000
1979	4	2,750,000,000
1980	3	3,036,000,000
1981[a]	5	4,020,000,000

a. January–July.

possibility of insolvency is avoided, albeit at the expense of increased maturities on the loans and reduced liquidity for the lending banks.

Over thirty debt reschedulings have taken place during the past decade, involving amounts in excess of $1 billion for Turkey (1978 and 1980), Zaire (1979), Poland (1981), and Indonesia (1970). (See table 2.)

The banks are rather well diversified in their international lending, with their loans spread among developed countries, Eastern European countries, oil-exporting developing countries, and oil-importing developing countries. They have tended to avoid lending to the poorest countries, leaving them to official institutions such as the World Bank. So default would become a major problem only if several substantial defaults occurred at the same time, due most likely to a common cause such as another large increase in oil prices or a major world recession, or both.

Withdrawals of deposits or default by a major borrower can, however, become a serious problem if a particular bank is already in trouble for other reasons, such as having incurred large losses on foreign-exchange dealings or on real-estate loans. In that case the bank in question may not have access to adequate liquidity through the interbank market. It may even become insolvent in the traditional way, through bad commercial loans or operating losses. Two examples of bank failures, Bankhaus I.D. Herstatt and the Franklin National Bank, did greatly disturb the international banking system during 1974, a year of rapid change in banking because of the recent fourfold increase in oil prices and the consequent OPEC surpluses and general economic uncertainty.

Herstatt had suffered large losses on foreign-exchange transactions, which it had concealed through false bookkeeping. When this was discovered, the German banking authorities declared Herstatt bankrupt in June 1974. It was a medium-size bank, with $800 million in assets, but it had $200 million in outstanding spot foreign-exchange contracts. The difficulty arose because the bank was closed immediately after the close of business, European time, after it had been credited for its purchases, but several hours before the close of business, New York time, before it had been debited. Thus, numerous banks found themselves without expected receipts on a spot transaction, and as a consequence the foreign-exchange market virtually came to a halt for several days. It was resumed (on a scale reportedly only about one-third of what it had been) through the expedient by the New York Clearing House of allowing payments to be recalled up to a day after they had been made. Moreover, smaller and less-well-known banks had great difficulty dealing both in foreign exchange and in the Eurocurrency market, and had to pay a premium on transactions when they were readmitted to the markets.

The Franklin National Bank had also lost substantial sums in its foreign-exchange dealing, and had attempted to conceal the loss through manipulation of its books. Rumors about the difficulties of Franklin had been circulating for some months after December 1973, but the difficulties did not become public until May 1974, whereupon there was a rapid withdrawal of funds, both domestic and foreign, from Franklin and its London and Nassau branches. The scale of Franklin (the 94th largest American bank, with assets totaling $4.8 billion), and in particular its foreign-exchange commitments of $2 billion, caused concern in the Federal Reserve about the impact of a precipitous collapse by this bank on the international financial system. To avoid this, the Federal Reserve lent to Franklin through its discount window on an unprecedented scale ($1.8 billion by the time Franklin actually closed its doors). The loan was also unprecedented in its duration and in its availability to cover deposit withdrawals from Franklin's foreign branches as well as from the home office. Once it became impossible for Franklin to carry out foreign-exchange transactions, the Federal Reserve purchased and sold foreign exchange on its behalf, and in the end it took over Franklin's remaining foreign-exchange book of some $800 million for settlement, subject to indemnification for losses or nonperformance by the other parties.[15] Without this assistance from the Federal Reserve, the ramifications of Franklin's failure would no doubt have been very wide indeed.

Both Herstatt and Franklin were banks operating within their home jurisdictions, although foreign-exchange transactions played a crucial role in the demise of each and Franklin was heavily in debt in the Euro-currency market as well. Both thus had important ramifications going beyond national boundaries. But what about the possible failure of banks operating outside their home jurisdiction? How would the difficulties of, say, an Italian bank operating in London in U.S. dollars have been handled?

The possible problems created by the growth of international banking were brought home to central bankers during the banking crises of 1974, but they were unable in several meetings at the Bank for International Settlements to resolve their differences fully. They issued a communiqué after their September 1974 meetings saying that they "recognized that it would not be practical to lay down in advance detailed rules and procedures for the provision of temporary liquidity" but were "satisfied that means are available for that purpose and will be used if and when necessary."[16] This vague statement was not entirely comforting to the banking community and others concerned with the stability of international banking. As host to the largest international banking center, the Bank of England tried a more precise definition of responsibilities, one that would limit its own exposure. It stated that branch banks were clearly the responsibility of their parents and, through their parents, of the regulatory authorities of the home country of the parents—something the Federal Reserve implicitly acknowledged in its handling of the Franklin case. It went on to suggest that in the case of subsidiaries and consortium banks the parent-owners had a moral responsibility for their support, defined as "responsibility to support those investments beyond the narrow limits laid down by laws of limited liability and, above all, ... responsibility to protect depositors with those banks."[17] The Bank of England sent letters to owners of consortium banks and parents of subsidiaries operating in London asking them to accept such moral responsibility, and they did so.

It is unclear that the central banks in the home countries take a similar view of their responsibility. Extensive cooperation among national bank supervisors arose out of the banking crises of 1974, and they divided responsibility between home and host countries (home countries are to worry about the solvency of their banks on a worldwide consolidated basis, host countries are to worry about the liquidity of the banks operating under their jurisdiction). In summarizing this cooperation, however, Peter Cooke has stated that the agreed division of responsibility "is not, and was never intended to be, an agreement about responsibilities for the provision of lender of last resort facilities to the international banking system, and there should not necessarily be considered to be any automatic link between acceptance of responsibility for ongoing supervision and the assumption of a lender of last resort role."[18]

Thus, despite the important strides that have been made in international cooperation, most notably in data collection and consolidation and in exchange of information among bank supervisory authorities, important ambiguities remain. These are perhaps necessarily present because of the potential inability of any central bank to be a lender of last resort in a currency other than its own, and because of the understandable reluctance by the Federal Reserve (and other central banks whose currencies are used internationally) to take on that responsibility for banks around the world that fall wholly outside of its regulatory reach and involve no American ownership.

Despite the remaining ambiguities, the fabric of cooperation among central banks and their sense of common purpose in preventing a collapse of international banking are both sufficiently strong that the banking crises that will surely arise from time to time are not likely to lead to a collapse of international banking. Given the extensive swap network between the Federal Reserve and other central banks (now amounting to over $20 billion) and the unlimited short-term credit that is afforded between central banks that are members of the European Monetary System, even the lender-of-last-resort function in another currency can be carried quite far.

An Oil Crisis

Modern economies are extremely dependent on petroleum, and by 1977 53 percent of the petroleum for the non-Communist world originated in the Persian Gulf, Libya, and Algeria. A cutoff of all or even a substantial fraction of this oil would have devastating effects on the economies and even the political systems of the western world. Even the fear of a cutoff, or a price increase based on those fears, is a major disturbance to Western economies.

An oil crisis is no longer hypothetical. The world experienced two during the 1970s. The first was in 1974 when, after a brief embargo by the Arab oil producers of the United States and the Netherlands for their support of Israel in connection with the Yom Kippur War, the Organization of Petroleum Exporting Countries (OPEC), led by Iran (which had not participated in the embargo), raised the posted price of Persian Gulf crude oil by a factor of 4. The second was in 1979, when the revolution in Iran deposed the Shah and led to a reduction in Iranian production by about 2 million barrels a day—the immediate reduction was considerably larger—and a worldwide scramble for oil.

It is worth recalling that the world has been subjected to four other interruptions of oil from the Middle East, although none of them caused the widespread damage of the 1974 and 1979 price increases. Iran nationalized its oil production in 1951, whereupon Iranian oil was boycotted by Western firms for nearly 3 years. The Suez Canal, through which most Persian Gulf oil flowed to Europe, was closed in 1956–57 and again in 1967 (for 8 years). And Iraq invaded Iran in September 1980, with the result that Iraqi and Iranian oil exports together declined for a time by about 3.5 million barrels a day. While these interruptions, particularly the one in 1956, created some turbulence, they did not create the devastation of the 1974 and 1979 disturbances because in each case there was new or excess productive capacity that was brought into production, because (in the case of 1967) Europe was already reducing its dependence on the Suez Canal with large tankers going around the Cape of Good Hope, and because (in the case of 1980) there were exceptionally large stocks (built up in panic buying during 1979) combined with a downturn in demand for oil brought about by the 1979 price increases and the attendant economic recession.

Because of the importance of oil, major increases in oil prices greatly complicate the management of modern economies. An immediate effect is to raise the general price indices, such as the consumer price index. That, in turn, may stimulate demands for higher wages and for higher prices of items not directly related to oil. At the same time, higher oil prices involve a tremendous transfer of wealth from oil-importing to oil-exporting countries—over $90 billion in 1974 and about twice that in 1980. This transfer reduces the real standard of living in oil-importing countries (which wage earners and others may fruitlessly attempt to recover through higher wages and prices) and creates large imbalances in international payments until the oil-exporting countries are able to adapt their expenditures to their new levels of income—a process that may take several years. Moreover, until this adjustment takes place, the world is likely to experience contractionary tendencies, since oil consumers (because of the inelasticity of their demand for oil) will reduce their purchases of other goods and services faster than oil producers will increase their demand. Thus, the economic decisionmakers in industrial countries are faced with a sharp dilemma. To maintain demand and avoid an unnecessary rise in unemployment, they should for a time pursue an expansionist economic policy. To do so, however, will provide an environment in which heightened wage demands are more likely to be satisfied, thus building the oil-price increase into a wage-price spiral. The extent of this latter danger depends on the state of the economy at the time of the oil-price disturbance and on the extent to which wage settlements are responsive to slack in the labor market.

Additional disturbances in the oil sector cannot be ruled out; on the contrary, they are likely to occur, although it is difficult to predict just how they will occur (as late as mid 1978, few were predicting a revolution in Iran). No preparation can be fully adequate to deal with a stoppage once it occurs, but without any preparation an oil stoppage would threaten the smooth functioning of modern economies and even the basic political institutions in many countries. The loss of real income and the secondary impact on economies would provide fertile ground for radical political movements offering paneceas and making scapegoats of established political figures for the inflation and unemployment. (The rise of Hitler through democratic processes in depression-ridden Germany comes to mind.) Or there could be military coups as parliamentary governments demonstrated their inability to cope with the economic distress, as in Turkey in 1980.

Most governments are aware of these dangers, but it remains the case that both national policies and international cooperation are not fully adequate to deal with the risks. The failure to act arises from the high costs of the various possible courses of action to reduce dependence on Middle Eastern oil, from the distributional consequences of some of those actions, and from sharp disagreements over which actions would be most efficacious. One school of thought, dominant in Germany and now in the U.S. government, holds that allowing the market free reign offers the best approach to allocating scarce resources, even in an emergency. There are, however, several proper concerns of governments that market participants will not take into account without some kind of government interference. Market participants will of course take actions to prevent damage to their own direct interests from any likely interruption. But they will not, in their individual decisions regarding consumption of oil or its substitutes, allow for the dangers to national and international institutional structures arising from excessive dependence on imports from an unstable part of the world. Second, market participants do not allow for the undesirable macroeconomic effects of excessive dependence on imported oil. Finally, market participants do not allow for the collective impact that they can have on the price of oil (their monopsony power, taken together). It is the role of government to look after these external effects, particularly those (such as macroeconomics and national security, broadly defined) that fall directly under their charge.

In 1980 (a year of recession) the United States accounted for 37 percent of the non-Communist world's oil consumption and about 20 percent of the world's oil imports. Thus, active U.S. participation is necessary in any scheme to reduce the Western world's dependence on Middle East oil; but moderate action by the United States alone would not be sufficient. To deal with the possible risks adequately, some kind of collective action is necessary. The objectives of such action should be to avoid disturbances to the oil market insofar as that is possible; to reduce dependence on potentially uncertain sources of oil, so as to reduce the impact of a disturbance in the oil market; and to take emergency measures in the event of a crisis to mitigate both its immediate impact and its longer-range impact through the ratcheting of prices.

The first of these objectives is the task of general foreign policy. We have learned in recent years that some disturbances are beyond the control or even the influence of Western governments; in any case, foreign policy has its own conflicts and dilemmas such that it cannot typically be directed at a single, exclusive objective, however important that objective may be. But avoiding turbulence in world oil markets should be a major objective of American (and European) foreign policy in the 1980s.

The second and third objectives have become lively sources of discussion and action in the International Energy Agency, a Paris-based organization of 20 industrial countries created in the wake of the 1974 energy crisis; within the European Economic Community; and at the seven-nation economic summit meetings in 1979 and 1980. With respect to the second objective, the IEA established medium-range (1985 and 1990) collective objectives for oil imports, along with a reporting and monitoring framework for national actions designed to achieve these collective objectives. It established year-by-year national "yardsticks" in order to measure national performance against the collective objectives. The heart of this program is the national actions that are taken to reduce dependence on imported oil, but the IEA mechanism provided an international framework for assessing the adequacy of those national actions and for encouraging all IEA member countries to take action to avoid the tendency of small countries to adopt the "free rider" position of allowing the larger countries to take the difficult actions alone and solve the problem for all.

This medium-range program now seems to be in abeyance, since the present U.S. administration takes a negative view of medium-range targets for oil consumption and of national actions to reduce oil consumption, other than allowing the price to rise (which as far as it goes was an appropriate and indeed desirable action to take). If other governments adopt a similar position, the United States will be open to the same risks of large disturbances that have already been experienced, unless one takes the view (which was also taken by some observers after the 1974 price increase) that at today's oil prices conservation and switching to substitutes are sufficiently attractive that an adequate reduction in import dependence will take place even in the absence of additional actions.

The third objective, coping during an oil interruption, has been addressed by the IEA in two ways. First, the IEA has established minimum oil inventory targets for all member countries—90 days of imports—so that there will be some cushion against an interruption in supply. Consideration is being given to raising these stock targets to 120 days of imports. Second, the IEA has established an emergency sharing scheme to be brought into play if a shortfall in supply exceeds 7 percent of IEA consumption. Under this scheme, each member country would undertake to reduce home consumption by the amount of the shortfall; this would be accompanied by a prorated sharing of the available oil among all participating countries, if possible on a voluntary basis (through the leading oil firms) and if necessary on a mandatory basis. This emergency sharing scheme is designed not only to ensure the availability of oil to friendly nations but also to offer enough security to them so that they will not engage in a competitive scramble for limited oil supplies in a fashion that sharply drives up not only the spot-market price but also the posted OPEC (term contract) prices, as happened in 1979.

The emergency sharing scheme was not invoked in 1979 because the global shortfall did not in fact reach 7 percent, as other oil producers (most notably Saudi Arabia) increased their production to make up for the loss of Iranian production. But the uncertainties generated by the loss of Iranian production (combined with the low level of stocks, which had been depleted during the "oil glut" of 1978) induced firms and countries to build stocks during a period of prospective shortage. The heightened demand in turn bid up prices on the thin spot market for crude oil, which in turn induced the members of OPEC to raise their posted prices several times during the course of the year.

The U.S. government remains formally committed to the IEA sharing scheme, but with great ambivalence because of its working assumption that the market can allocate scarce resources in a superior way even during an emergency. Apart from its professed willingness to draw down the Strategic Petroleum Reserve in an emergency shortfall, therefore, it leaves the international system exposed to the considerable risks that have already materialized twice in the oil domain.[19]

The assumption that a major disturbance in the Persian Gulf would be so threatening to the Western world as to call for military action overlooks the nature of the problem. Military force is necessary in sufficient strength to deter the Soviet Union from engaging in military action or even plausible (and perhaps implicit) military threats to the area, and an effective U.S. military presence in the area might well deter takeovers by radical political minorities; however, military presence cannot ensure the continued functioning of the oil facilities, wherein Western interest lies. Military preparedness is therefore not a substitute for energy preparedness.

Trade Wars

Countries are tempted to protect their economies from import competition for a variety of reasons: to encourage "infant industries" with the prospect of development, to improve their international payments position, to protect employment in particular sectors that are experiencing import competition, to grant favors to particular firms or individuals who have supported the government in power, to retaliate against similar actions by trading partners, and so on. Some of these reasons are relatively unchanging over time, but calls for import protection are likely to be more strident and more favorably received—or more difficult to resist politically—during times in which growth is sluggish, unemployment is high, and international payments are in deficit. Unhappily, these are the consequences, as we have just seen, of an oil crisis. Thus, the prospect of trade wars are enhanced by an oil crisis. But they could also arise simply from the efforts of countries to run tight monetary and fiscal policies in order to combat inflation.

Fortunately, there are several countervailing tendencies. First, governments are much better apprised these days of the strong positive links between trade and economic growth that have benefited the world economy during the past three decades. They are also aware that major actions to restrict imports are likely to be emulated elsewhere, so exports would suffer. This factor is reinforced by the presence of flexible exchange rates, whereby import restrictions would lead to a currency appreciation and thus would discourage exports. (Erratic movements in exchange rates that affect a country's competitiveness adversely have, however, led to some pleas for protection against seemingly arbitrary movements of currency value.) And governments are aware that, both in reality and in perception, import protection is inconsistent with fighting inflation. Finally, since the 1940s we have had institutional mechanisms (mainly the GATT, but the IMF and the OECD have also played important roles) which have served as forums for reminding governments of the consequences of protectionist actions, for strengthening their collective resolve not to engage in them, for settling trade disputes that arise, and for maintaining some momentum toward continuing trade liberalization, even in difficult times.

On the whole, governments behaved well during the extreme provocations of the two oil crises and the economic recessions they aggravated. The industrialized countries, through the OECD, pledged in June 1974 not to introduce trade-restricting measures to help them out of their current difficulties, recognizing that a round of such restrictions would in fact hurt rather than help. This pledge was repeated annually and was broadened and made permanent in 1980. The now annual economic summit meetings among the heads of government of the seven largest industrial countries have also recognized the importance of avoiding restrictions. And the Multilateral Trade Negotiations, launched in 1973, were successfully completed during 1979. They also extended the trade rules into some new areas (such as government procurement), clarified and tightened them in some old areas (such as the role of subsidies to industry and their impact on trade), and introduced new dispute-settlement mechanisms associated with the seven codes that were negotiated as part of the MTN.

In light of this recent experience, the prospect of trade wars does not seem to be high. Rather, the risk is that there will be creeping protectionism—gradual erosion of the relatively liberal trading environment that has been established since World War II. This erosion could take place through government takeovers of commercial enterprises and subsequent manipulation of their purchases and sales abroad, which would lead to results different from those that would have been achieved under a private, competitive regime; through "voluntary" restraint agreements under which a successful exporting country would restrain its exports under the threat of more onerous restrictions by importing countries; and through the misuse for the restriction of imports of the growing number of health, safety, and environmental regulations that national governments may quite legitimately impose on both imported and domestically produced goods.[20]

Gradual Erosion of the System of Cooperation

On the whole, the institutional bulwarks are reasonably strong against breakdowns arising from crises in the four areas that have been discussed: balance-of-payments difficulties, banking difficulties, oil, and trade (with the possible exception of oil, where cooperation in the process of development now seems to have been set aside). Where the bulwarks are less strong is against a gradual erosion of the international economic system. From the perspective of, say, the year 2020, observers may look back on the 1970s and the 1980s as a period of major transformation of the international economic system, and they may well speak of a "breakdown" of the postwar system of international economic cooperation.

Those of us who are living through it may not recognize any such breakdown, however. Crises, yes, because people are always impressed with their own difficult moments and tend to underrate the difficulties of past periods provided they turned out reasonably well. But not breakdowns. For those who live through this period, it will appear as an evolution of the international economic system, sometimes in an orderly way, sometimes as *ad hoc* responses to urgent and pressing developments.

The most important question, of course, will be the nature of the response to an oil disruption. Whether, when, and how large an oil disruption may occur will be a major source of uncertainty through the 1980s and perhaps beyond. For many, an equally large source of uncertainty will be whether the governments of oil-consuming nations will respond to an oil disruption by economic contraction or by introducing price and allocation controls, and even whether they will survive such a disruption politically.

A second major source of uncertainty will be the changing role of developing countries. Despite all the rhetoric that suggests they are being victimized by the industrialized nations, some of them have done extraordinarily well, and others have been positioning themselves to grow faster through changes in their own economic policies and can be expected to do well during the 1980s barring major disruptions to the world economy. Others, in contrast, continue to blame the international economic system and the industrialized nations for their economic backwardness.

There is bound to be much economic transformation during the next decade whatever happens, and, as noted at the outset, change creates uncertainty. How will developing countries actually develop? As they develop, will they see it in their interest to integrate more fully into the existing and evolving international economic system, or will they call for radical changes in that system? Or will they simply take advantage of the opportunities the system permits without actually supporting it by taking on its obligations, and thereby induce an erosion in the system as it becomes more difficult for developed nations to ignore deviations from its rules?[21]

How the industrialized countries will respond is another source of uncertainty, both with respect to maintaining open markets for the products of developing countries and with respect to admitting those countries to the circle of decisionmaking on changes in the international rules as they become able and willing to take on the obligations of full membership.

The large and growing disparity of circumstances and of views among developing countries is a further source of uncertainty. They have learned the advantages of bloc voting in the international political arena, and the Group of 77, as it is called, has shown remarkable cohesiveness. But will the "moderates" or the "radicals" come to dominate the G-77? Or will it be a standoff, resulting in an incompatible and contradictory mixture of proposals for moderate and radical change, combined with immobilizing indecisiveness in the international community? And how much difference will that actually make? The international economy has its own dynamic of change, clearly influenced but not fully determined by the actions of national governments and certainly not fully determined by international agreements or their absence. The evolution of the international monetary system took quite a different course in the mid 1970s, for instance, from the direction in which the Committee of Twenty, set up to reform the system, was pointing. On the other hand, continuing international disagreements over the nature of a seabed regime—disagreements between those countries in the G-77 who want maximum governmental involvement in management and even mining of the seabed and those (mainly developed) countries who want maximum reliance on private enterprise—have almost certainly postponed by 5 or more years the inauguration of manganese-nodule mining from the deep seabed. Moreover, radical rhetoric concerning "national sovereignty over natural resources," even when not embodied in damaging fashion in international agreements, fosters a climate of uncertainty about the security of investment in mineral industries in developing countries by helping to legitimize the future abrogation of contracts that seem (after successful development of a mine or a well) to be inconsistent with one or another interpretation of this imprecise phrase.

Finally, continuing and sharp disagreements among developing countries may influence future decisions of OPEC, particularly insofar as some of the moderate members of OPEC feel politically insecure and must from time to time balance their generally moderate stance with more agressive actions.

It is the function of diplomacy to manage these sometimes imponderable processes as skillfully as possible, trying to secure a moderate, evolutionary course that is more conducive to economic prosperity. But whether diplomacy will succeed is itself uncertain.

Notes

1. This theme is developed at greater length in my *Economic Mobility and National Economic Policy* (Stockholm: Almqvist & Wiksell, 1974).

2. See Charles P. Kindleberger, *The World in Depression, 1929–1939* (Berkeley: University of California Press, 1973), p. 132.

3. Peter Temin, *Did Monetary Forces Cause the Great Depression?* (New York: Norton, 1976). Temin's answer to his title's question is unambiguously negative, but he leaves the Depression basically unexplained.

4. Curiously, in their massive *Monetary History of the United States* (pp. 309–311) Milton Friedman and Anna Schwartz argue that the Bank of the United States was fundamentally sound—despite the fact that it was insolvent—and fail to mention that its top officers were convicted of illegal activities, although it was a cause célèbre at the time. Perhaps such malfeasant private activity did not fit into their thesis that all the major mistakes were made by government, and especially by the Federal Reserve Board.

5. Kindleberger, *World in Depression*, p. 146.

6. Ibid., pp. 158–160.

7. For a brief discussion of the experience with defaults see R. N. Cooper and E. M. Truman, "International Capital Markets as a Source of Funds for Developing Countries," *Weltwirtschaftliches Archiv* 106 (1971), Heft 2; also Carlos F. Díaz-Alejandro, "Stories of the 1930s for the 1980s," in P. A. Armella et al., eds., *Financial Policies and the World Capital Market: The Problem of Latin American Countries* (University of Chicago Press, 1983).

8. See Gerard Curzon and Victoria Curzon Price, "The Undermining of the World Trade Order," *Ordo* 30 (1979).

9. For an illuminating history of this breakdown see Robert Solomon, *The International Monetary System, 1945–1976: An Insider's View*, (New York: Harper & Row, 1977), chapters 9–11.

10. Given this flaw, the interesting question is not why the Bretton Woods system broke down but why it took so long to break down. One possible explanation, based on the fact that it took nearly 15 years to implement the Bretton Woods system fully, is given in my *The Economics of Interdependence* (New York: McGraw-Hill, 1968), chapter 2 and pp. 234–242.

11. See the comment by Dennis Weatherstone (an important participant in the foreign-exchange market) on John Rutledge's "An Economist's View of the Foreign Exchange Market," in J. S. Dreyer et al., eds., *Exchange Rate Flexibility* (Washington, D.C.: American Enterprise Institute, 1978).

12. See Federal Reserve Governor Henry C. Wallich, LDC Debt—To Worry or Not to Worry, remarks to the Bankers' Association for Foreign Trade, Boca Raton La., June 2, 1981 (mimeo).

13. This compares with equity/asset ratios of around 13 percent in 1929.

14. See IMF, *Annual Report on Exchange Arrangements and Exchange Restrictions 1981*, p. 22.

15. For an excellent and detailed account of the collapse of Franklin National, how it got into its difficulties, and the interagency and international cooperation that was involved in isolating and resolving the problems, see Joan Edelman Spero, *The Failure of the Franklin National Bank* (New York: Columbia University Press, 1980).

16. Quoted in ibid., p. 155.

17. Bank of England, *Quarterly Bulletin*, June 1975, pp. 188–194.

18. "Developments in Co-operation Among Banking Supervisory Authorities," in Bank of England *Quarterly Bulletin*, June 1981, p. 240.

19. For an official statement reflecting U.S. ambivalence see Department of Energy, Domestic and International Energy Preparedness, July 1981 (mimeo).

20. For a discussion of some of these developments see Curzon and Price (note 8). For a brief description of the results of the MTN and their bearing on these developments see Thomas R. Graham, "Revolution in Trade Politics," *Foreign Policy*, fall 1979, no. 36: 49–63.

21. A problem similar in principle, but on a much smaller scale, arises from the gradual integration of communist countries into the international economic system. Trade and capital movements between market and nonmarket economies have grown sharply in the past decade. One Communist country after another has applied for membership in the GATT and the IMF, with Rumania entering the IMF in 1972, China in 1980, and Poland and Hungary probably in 1982. These developments, if they are not reversed, pose problems of adaptation for the guardian institutions, but they will not be insurmountable, nor will they alter radically the operation of those institutions.

3   Global Economic Policy in a World of Energy Shortage

My subject is international coordination of economic policy, a topic in which Walter Heller took an early and active interest as chairman of President Kennedy's Council of Economic Advisers. My main focus will be on the overall management of world economic activity in the period since 1974, although trade, energy, and balance-of-payments policies will play a part. I chose 1974 as a starting point because of the sharp increase in oil prices that took place in January of that year. It was a dramatic event, probably the largest shock per unit time the world economy has ever seen. In a mere 3 months, over 12 percent of the value of world exports were sharply redirected.

World economic troubles did not, of course, start with that sharp increase in oil prices. There was great turmoil in foreign-exchange markets in the period 1969–1973: a world shortage of grain leading to sharp price increases in 1972–73, a world economic boom in 1972–73 that pushed up dramatically the prices of minerals and agricultural raw materials, and the Yom Kippur War of October 1973 which led to an oil embargo by Saudi Arabia aimed at the United States and The Netherlands.[1]

It is also worth recalling that the world demand for OPEC oil grew steadily and sharply before the price increase in 1974, from 18.8 million barrels a day in 1968 to 23.5 million barrels a day in 1970 to 31 million barrels a day in 1973, the last figure being exceeded since then—slightly—only in 1977.

The Economics of an Oil-Price Increase

On January 1, 1974, oil prices were raised from $3.60 a barrel on Saudi marker crude to $9.60 a barrel (it had been as low as $1.35 a barrel as recently as 1970). Exports of OPEC oil amounted to nearly 30 million barrels a day, so this price increase represented a sudden rise in annual payments to the oil-exporting countries of about $66 billion. This sharp increase in prices represented at the same time a consequential worsening of the terms of trade for all oil-importing countries, leading to a loss of real income; a sharp increase in an important price in domestic markets; and a drastic worsening of the balance-of-payments position of oil-importing nations.

In addition to these relatively well-understood effects, there was a "fiscal" effect of the increase in oil prices in view of the fact that OPEC countries could not increase their spending nearly as rapidly as their income had been increased. If there was a fiscal effect, where did the revenue go? Certainly the U.S. government deficit increased sharply in late 1974 and again in 1975. It was said that the increase in this deficit was inflationary. Yet OPEC had, in effect, levied an excise tax on the world's consumers of oil, and the revenues from that tax, instead of being returned directly to the income stream, were devoted largely to the purchase of U.S. Treasury bills and other short-term assets. From an analytical point of view, we should have consolidated the budgets of Saudi Arabia (and some other OPEC countries) and the United States, since Saudi surpluses were devoted partly to the purchase of U.S. government securities. Such a consolidation would show a fiscal surplus in mid 1974, not a growing deficit as was perceived in the United States at that time. Moreover, it is difficult to understand how a U.S. deficit could be inflationary under these circumstances. On the contrary, the overall fiscal impact was strongly contractionary, i.e., it reduced the total demand for domestically produced goods and services. This contractionary impulse gave rise to a fall in output and a decline in employment.

The fall in output was not due exclusively to the fiscal effect. This Keynesian-type contraction was accompanied by—indeed, caused by—a large rise in the relative price of oil, a raw material critical to industry and agriculture. Thus, there was also what might be called a "supply-shortage" effect. Starting from a position of competitive equilibrium, a sharp increase in the price of a major imported raw material will shift the production frontier downward, reducing output. Moreover, if wages are inflexible downward, it will also lead (on plausible assumptions about factor substitutability) to a decline in employment. Real wages must decline to restore full employment of labor.

Thus, the contractionary impetus of the oil-price increase represented the combined impact of this supply-shortage effect and the contractionary fiscal effect. The result was to deepen greatly a recession that had probably already started as a result of anti-inflationary policies adopted in 1974 in the major countries, and it led to the deepest and longest world recession since the 1930s.

One can also look at this event from a monetary perspective. Each oil-importing country (and the world) experienced a rise in the money value of its total transactions at the initial volume of transactions, the increase being returned (via OPEC members) to financial markets. The rise in value of transactions should increase the demand for money, and this increase in demand would be reinforced by the decline in short-term interest rates which should follow, other things being equal, from the increase in supply of funds coming into financial markets. The increase in demand for money would aggravate the decline in demand for goods and services (other than oil). A once-and-for-all increase in the supply of money was therefore necessary in order to avoid the Keynesian contractionary effects.[2]

The wage-settlement process in modern economies further complicates macroeconomic management under the circumstances reigning in 1974. Wage earners demand, either through formal cost-of-living adjustments or through negotiated increases in wages, to recoup real income lost through inflation. Wage earners understandably do not distinguish among the possible sources of price increase. A deterioration in the terms of trade means that real income has been lost to the rest of the world, not merely to profit earners or government, and it requires a decline in the average real income of all residents relative to what it otherwise would be. A deterioration in the terms of trade on the scale implied by the 1974 oil-price increase (11 percent) was outside the experience of modern industrial economies during the postwar era.

The failure by wage earners to distinguish between sources of a price increase poses an acute dilemma for policymakers. If they fail to take expansionist measures, there will, as noted above, be higher-than-necessary unemployment—a self-imposed additional penalty to the loss in real income arising from higher oil prices. But if they take expansionary measures, they might unwittingly encourage the attempt of wage earners to recapture lost income through higher money wages. The once-and-for-all increase in money supply called for was at the *initial* level of money wages. But an increase in the money supply might be misinterpreted as supporting or ratifying increases in money wages, thus feeding a wage-price inflationary spiral. The direct sensitivity of the wage-settlement process, through expectations, to actions by the monetary authorities of course varies from country to country and may not be high; but the possible connection is troublesome.

One way out of the dilemma would be to have a tax cut concentrated on personal income. This could at least partially restore real (after-tax) wages without raising wage costs, and would stimulate demand at the same time. The suitability of this possibility of course also varies from country to country, since its effectiveness in this context depends on the willingness of wage earners to restrain their demand for higher (pre-tax) money wages.[3]

National Responses to the Oil-Price Increase

As can be seen from this all-too-brief sketch, the economic impact of such a sharp oil-price increase was very complex. Different national economies responded in different ways. Britain, Italy, and Japan, for example, experienced a wage explosion following the sharp increase in the prices of oil and other primary products (such as sugar), as did several smaller European countries. The United States, in sharp contrast, had only a moderate acceleration of money-wage growth, and as a consequence (alone among major industrial countries) experienced a decline in real wages in 1974 and again in 1975. West Germany fell between these extremes.

The economic authorities also responded differently. The United States, West Germany, Japan, and some developing countries (such as Korea) maintained or introduced tight monetary and fiscal policies to contain what was left of the 1972–73 boom and to inhibit inflation. Japan was able to limit its wage explosion to a year, whereas in Britain and Italy it became more endemic.

Several smaller European countries continued to pursue more expansionist measures, and as a consequence aggravated their oil-induced balance-of-payments difficulties. This was also the course followed by most developing countries. By and large, these countries did not experience wage explosions, but they did adjust their fiscal actions so as to "stay on plan" and continue their growth in output and employment, financing the increased fiscal requirements from abroad. Still other developing countries actually increased their rate of expansion, in some instances (e.g., Jamaica, Peru) based on the erroneous assumption that high prevailing export prices for raw materials would remain high. Many countries took a calculated risk that the world recession would be shallow and short. In the event they guessed wrong, but their actions had the salutary effect from a global point of view of sustaining exports from the major industrial countries and thereby cushioning the world recession.

International Cooperation in 1974–1976

The need for international cooperation was recognized at once. It ultimately took place under five headings: energy, trade, finance, macroeconomic coordination, and a new category called North-South economic relations. I will offer a brief summary of the other headings before returning to macroeconomic coordination.

Oil was the immediate problem. The partial embargo, followed by a dramatic increase in price, impressed this on everyone. The prevailing view within the U.S. government and among some economists was that the OPEC cartel would soon collapse and prices would return to something like their 1973 levels. The collapse could be hastened by solidarity among consumer nations. With this in mind, Secretary of State Henry Kissinger convoked the Washington Energy Conference in February 1974. The conference addressed a range of issues in the energy field, and ultimately led to the creation of the International Energy Agency (IEA), with its emergency oil-sharing plan in case of major disruptions (defined as shortfalls in excess of 7 percent) to world oil supplies.

Over time, the IEA took on other responsibilities in the energy field, including forecasting future world energy balances and establishing a broad common framework among member countries[4] for reducing their demand for imported oil. This framework involves the establishment of national "yardsticks" for oil consumption and close IEA monitoring of national actions taken to keep actual oil imports at or below the yardsticks. The value of this kind of international coordination lies in the fact that all but the very largest countries perceive the world energy environment to be beyond their influence. Each country's actions are therefore guided by actual and expected prices, and it discounts the impact its actions alone may have on the world price of oil. Yet, in a period of oil shortage, this kind of collective myopia could be devastating for all. By acting together, countries can turn a series of *de minimus* impacts into something substantial. Since the actions themselves are costly and politically controversial, the sense of equity involved in sharing responsibility among countries helps overcome the political resistance to national action.

Emergency action on energy was the first step. The second, which was more urgent and matured faster, was to ensure that countries did not act too quickly to correct their new and large payments deficits. The risk was that countries would take collectively damaging actions in an effort to eliminate their new or enlarged deficits. Yet the underlying global fact was a huge OPEC surplus, and so long as that was present the simple arithmetic of a closed world economy required corresponding deficits. Two steps were taken to avoid myopic balance-of-payments measures. First, the 24 members of the Organization for Economic Cooperation and Development (OECD) declared in June 1974 their "determination ... to avoid having recourse to unilateral measures ... to restrict imports" for a period of one year in the circumstances then prevailing. This pledge was renewed annually until 1980, when it was expanded into a more permanent trade declaration.

In addition, it was necessary to ensure adequate balance-of-payments financing so that countries would not be forced into mutually damaging actions by their inability to finance their payments deficits. This came to be called the "recycling problem." The OPEC surplus ensured that financing equivalent to the deficits was globally available (provided—and it is an important proviso—that the central banks of the world, and most notably the Federal Reserve System, did not take restrictive monetary actions to prevent the decline in short-term interest rates that the sudden emergence of the large OPEC surplus implied[5]). There was much debate at the time over whether the world banking system could handle adequately the large OPEC surpluses (they turned out to be $68 billion in 1974). There were numerous prognostications of inevitable financial collapse. We know now that the banks did handle most of this surplus, that we did not have financial collapse, and that the surplus itself declined much more rapidly than was forecast in 1974, practically disappearing by 1978.[6]

But even with the major part of the recycling problem covered by the private banking system, institutional improvement was necessary for those countries with little or no access to the private market. The International Monetary Fund (IMF) therefore created in 1974 an "oil facility," which borrowed directly from OPEC and other countries in balance-of-payments surplus and re-lent to oil-importing developing countries. The magnitudes were not large on a global scale—about $3 billion in the IMF fiscal year 1974–75 and around $4.5 billion in 1975–76. But these sums were crucial to some countries. In addition, the IMF began in 1974 to auction a portion of its gold. The capital gains, amounting to $4.6 billion over the five-year period of sales, were largely allocated to a newly created IMF trust fund for special low-interest loans to the most needy developing countries.

The balance-of-payments financing problem was seen to be a continuing one, however, so another product of the 1974 energy conference was the negotiation among OECD countries of a financial support fund that would recycle funds from financially strong OECD nations to financially weaker ones in amounts up to around $13 billion. Several key senators were hostile to this notion because it imposed financial obligations on the United States as a result of the oil-price increase without imposing any financial obligations on OPEC countries. Because of this antipathy, and because by 1977 most of the OECD countries were on the way to mastering their financial difficulties, efforts were switched to negotiating and implementing a supplementary financial facility to augment IMF resources by about $10 billion, which would be available for lending to developing countries as well as to OECD countries.

The fourth area of cooperation was "producer-consumer" dialogue. A dialogue on energy was urged by France as a less confrontational counterpoise to the American notion of close cooperation among consuming countries, and it led to the Conference on International Economic Cooperation (CIEC), under which 27 governmental entities came together in Paris over the period 1975–1977 to attempt to negotiate improvements in the international economic system. The OPEC-led developing countries would not accept an international dialogue, much less a negotiation, on energy alone. The agenda was therefore broadened to include financial assests, foreign aid, commodity policy, and a host of other issues. The developing countries hoped to use the "oil weapon" to extract concessions from developing countries on these other issues. The flaw in this strategy was that OPEC countries were basically not prepared to offer assurances on either the price or the supply of oil, and the industrialized countries were therefore not inclined to offer additional concessions in the other areas. The CIEC, therefore, produced only modest results beyond the educational value to those who participated in it.

Macroeconomic Coordination

It was recognized, belatedly, that the oil-price increase, reinforcing antiinflation policies, had driven the world into a deep recession and that common action was required to extricate the world economy from that recession. In November 1975 the first of what have become annual economic summit meetings among the world's largest industrial democracies took place in Rambouillet, outside Paris. The communique from the Rambouillet summit reported that "the most urgent task is to assure the recovery of our economies and to reduce the waste of human resources involved in unemployment." Unemployment in all of the major industrialized countries had reached postwar highs in 1975, and in many countries unemployment continued to rise.

In June 1976 the OECD produced its "medium term economic strategy," designed to achieve a steady recovery in the industrial economies without pushing them so hard that anti-inflationary objectives would be seriously threatened. The OECD had been involved in attempting the coordination of macroeconomic policy for nearly 15 years, since 1961. Its predecessor agency had played a similar role within Europe for even longer. As chairman of the Council of Economic Advisers, Walter Heller played a major role in overcoming instinctive bureaucratic resistance within the U.S. government to coordinating anything with foreigners at that time. He recognized early the importance of close collaboration—even if full coordination was not possible—with other industrial countries on the management of macroeconomic policy. With strong U.S. encouragement, Japan was admitted to the OECD a few years later. Through its Economic Policy Committee, the OECD has served as a forum for exchange of information and views on the macroeconomic outlook and on prospective actions in member countries. It was not suitable for close coordination of policies, even if member countries were willing (which they were not). Countries rarely discuss, in Walter Heller's words, "economic policy in the making." But the OECD has occasionally served as a very useful body for establishing a general climate of opinion on the appropriate course for macroeconomic policies.[7]

This work has been given much more public visibility and greater political commitment by the economic summit meetings, attended by heads of government. A second economic summit was held in Puerto Rico in June 1976. The resultant communiqué was largely self-congratulatory in tone, in part because economic recovery had gotten underway in the United States and several other countries.[8]

The World Economic Situation at the End of 1976

The world economic situation in early 1977, three years after the oil shock and at the beginning of the Carter administration, was still parlous. Economic recovery from the 1975 lows, though rapid, had proceeded less rapidly than the recovery from previous recessions when allowance was made for the depth of the 1975 recession. By the fall of 1976, the world recovery was faltering. Industrial production in Europe and Japan had leveled out or was clearly in the process of leveling out. Britain, Italy, and several small OECD countries were experiencing extremely severe balance-of-payments problems. These, in turn, put severe downward pressure on the exchange rates of their currencies and led to much popular theorizing about vicious and virtuous circles, running from inflation to exchange rates and back again. Raw-material prices had fallen sharply from their exceptional highs in 1973–74. Many countries had accumulated three years of exceptional external debt, with heavy debt service immediately in prospect as grace periods on official loans were expiring. Imports into oil-importing developing countries grew only 4.5 percent during 1976, reflecting foreign-exchange constraints that had begun to take a toll on their growth.

By the historical standards of each country, unemployment was high and still rising in most European countries and in Japan. Inflation, though down from the high rates of 1974, was still unacceptably high in most countries. Germany and Japan were the notable exceptions. By 1976 these two countries had reduced their inflation rates to levels close to their historical norms. The United States, Japan, Britain, and Germany had led the world into recession, and their combined current account surplus increased by over $18 billion between 1974 and 1975, thereby worsening the payments deficits of other countries. Part of this swing, however, reduced the surplus of the OPEC countries.

There were serious dangers inherent in this situation. Many countries might renounce their external debts and introduce tight exchange controls. The Group of 77 (a coalition of most of the developing countries of the world) called for a formal moratorium on all debt payments. Default or moratorium would have sent reverberations throughout the international banking system, which was still adjusting uncomfortably to the failure of the Herstatt Bank in Germany and the Franklin National Bank in the United States. Although in many respects the international banking system was much stronger than it had been 45 years earlier, the ghost of 1931 was clearly present. Discussions among central bankers in the Bank for International Settlements had gone only part of the way toward sorting out "lender-of-last-resort" responsibilities in the highly complex international financial system. Loans by the major banks had grown very rapidly during the preceding three years and were raising questions about the adequacy of their capital and the quality of some of their loans. In the United States, the Comptroller of the Currency was suggesting that several major countries should be considered dubious risks.

The dangers were not only economic. Governments attempting to be "responsible" in economic management in the face of serious external constraints risked having the batons of power taken away from them by political opportunists promoting economic nostrums to conceal their questionable political objectives. Because of growing economic hardship, democratically inclined leaders might be forced to choose between being ousted and resorting to authoritarian methods of control. In the face of these kinds of dangers, special support programs were put together for such countries as Egypt (by several Arab OPEC countries), Portugal (by the major industrial countries), and, later, Turkey. But the problem was potentially widespread.

The Locomotive Theory

It was in this context that the "locomotive theory" was advanced: Those countries that did not face serious external constraints and still had ample unutilized capacity should take actions to stimulate the faltering world recovery and thereby relieve the enormous financial pressures bearing on other industrial countries and developing countries alike.[9] Fortunately, the three countries that did not face serious external financial restraints—the United States, Japan, and West Germany—were also the three largest economies of the free world, together accounting for 37 percent of gross world production. Recovery led by these three countries would relieve the financial pressure on other countries and permit—indeed, induce—some modest expansion there. Unemployment could be reduced in Europe. This was especially important in Italy, where Communist strength at the polls was high and growing. Export earnings of developing countries could be bolstered sufficiently to sustain their economic growth and to avoid default on their external debts and the probable international financial turmoil that would follow any major default.

While a number of countries allowed their domestic economic policy to get out of control in the period 1974–1976, most countries pursued a course of action that was rational in light of the information that was then available to them. Moreover, it turned out to be globally helpful even if it posed subsequent difficulties for the countries in question. They gambled that the world recession would be short and shallow, like previous postwar recessions. In addition, eminent authorities were asserting that OPEC price unity would be short-lived and that the cartel would soon fall apart. The gamble turned out to be wrong on both counts, but the fact that many countries continued to pursue economic growth—borrowing abroad to do it—meant that the world recession was much less deep and prolonged than it might have been. The importance of developing countries as markets is sometimes overlooked. Non-OPEC developing countries now take a quarter of all U.S. exports, and a fifth of the exports of all OECD countries if intra–European Community trade is excluded.

The new U.S. administration in 1977 pursued the locomotive theory. President Carter introduced additional economic stimulus at home and tried to persuade Japan and Germany to do the same. Immediately after his inauguration, Vice-President Mondale traveled to Europe and Japan with this message, and more formal discussions took place at the London economic summit in May 1977 and at the June ministerial meeting of the OECD. The idea had the support of a number of other countries, but Japan and Germany balked at introducing any expansionary measures despite the fact that by mid 1977 industrial production had leveled off in both countries.

The United States went ahead anyway. The net result was some desired expansion of the world economy, including prices of raw materials, but also a sharp reallocation of payments imbalances. The United States developed very large payments deficits in late 1977 and 1978, whereas Japan and Germany developed very large surpluses. Corresponding pressure was reflected in the exchange markets, with the dollar depreciating sharply against the yen and the mark (and those other European currencies closely aligned to the mark). One of the noteworthy advantages of flexible exchange rates is that each country feels directly, through the exchange markets, the consequences of its own domestic economic policies. German and Japanese businessmen were extremely alarmed about the appreciation of the yen and the mark, respectively, and urged their governments to do something to stop it. The currency appreciation made clear that those two large countries could no longer substitute export-led growth for domestic demand. The American public and financial community, by the same token, were concerned about the depreciation of the dollar, but the depreciation also created important new export opportunities for the American business community.[10]

By the winter of 1977–78, the payments imbalances and exchange-rate movements had become sufficiently alarming to many people that by the Bonn economic summit in July 1978 it was possible to strike a package deal under which the United States would ease up on its expansionary policies (there were domestic reasons for doing this as well), but Germany and Japan—joined by Britain and France, whose external position had improved substantially by then—would take actions to stimulate their economies. Measures were introduced in Germany and Japan shortly thereafter.

The Bonn summit represents the first successful attempt to coordinate fiscal policies among major countries on a quantitative basis. The Bonn summit called specifically on France to increase its fiscal deficit by 0.5 percent of GNP, on Japan to take fiscal action to increase its real growth by 1.5 percentage points in excess of the previous year, and on Germany to provide fiscal stimulus equivalent to 1 percent of GNP. The summit also endorsed fiscal expansion in Britain and urged more general expansionary measures on Canada and Italy. This attempt was still primitive and halting, but it was effective.[11]

The Bonn summit came too late to avoid some of the avoidable overshooting in payments imbalances and in exchange-rate movements. If coordinated stimulus had begun 15 months earlier, in the spring of 1977, the huge growth in the payments imbalances of the United States, Japan, and Germany could have been mitigated, and the turbulence in exchange markets which so may people around the world found alarming could have been averted or muted. Earlier Japanese expansion also would have avoided some, but not all, of the bilateral trade frictions that bedeviled relations between the United States and Japan during this period.

There has been some criticism of the Bonn summit's results, especially in Germany, on the grounds that it contributed to subsequent inflation. In fact, the rise in the GNP deflator in Germany remained unchanged from 1978 to 1979 and actually fell in Japan from 4.0 percent in 1978 to 2.0 percent in 1979. In contrast, it rose in the United States despite the sharp decline in U.S. economic growth. The bearing of fiscal stimulus on the rate of inflation in periods of high unemployment and low capacity utilization has been and will continue to be debated extensively. Suffice it to say that I believe the inflationary pressures in Europe and Japan in 1979 have their origins elsewhere—especially in oil-market developments, driven mainly by the revolution in Iran. Appreciation of the mark and the yen helped to reduce inflationary pressure in Germany and Japan during late 1977 and 1978; that source of price stability was lost in 1979.

Economists teach that we should think in terms of choices among feasible alternatives. If the dangers sketched above as being manifest at the end of 1976 were real, and if they were largely averted, the actions taken during 1977–78 may, at least in part, be credited. That success must be set against that part of the subsequent acceleration of inflation that is attributable to expansionist actions by the United States in 1977 and actions of other major countries in 1978. The devils we see are always more formidable than the devils we cannot see. But the latter are out there, and the path the world economy actually took, while certainly not ideal, may still have been the best one available.

Is International Coordination of Economic Policy Necessary?

It is difficult enough to manage economic policy satisfactorily within each country. It becomes even more difficult if each country must coordinate with others in framing and executing its policies. The world would be simpler if this were not necessary. It is, therefore, worth asking under what circumstances genuine improvements will flow from a coordination of international economic policies. Unless such improvements are demonstrable, there is much to be said for allowing each country a high degree of autonomy in matters of economic policy. I see three broad respects in which coordination of policy results in gains for the international community as a whole and presumptively for each of its members.

The first involves the coordination of targets of economic policy. If targets are incompatible, policy actions by countries are bound to be unsuccessful, yet costs may be associated with their pursuit. Examples of potentially incompatible targets involve different views on what an exchange rate between two currencies should be, or the desire of all countries to run trade surpluses, or, more subtly, targets involving trade deficits and surpluses that do not balance out. A less obvious example involves sharply divergent desired growth rates under a liberal trading regime when the underlying structure of demand cannot sustain such divergences, resulting in ever greater imbalances in payments.

Second, coordination of economic policy may avoid unnecessary costs that arise from cycling around feasible policy targets. A path of target variables that involves overshooting the target will leave a country, on average, further away from its objectives than would a direct approach, and a direct approach is more easily attainable with some coordination of policy. Moreover, economic adjustment—the movement of real resources from one sector to another—is not, in fact, costlessly reversible, as it is typically portrayed in blackboard renditions of national economies. If major economic variables overshoot their desired values and have to be brought back to them, resources may be moved unnecessarily and avoidable costs are incurred. These costs do not always accrue to the private decisionmakers, as when workers are laid off and then rehired.

Sometimes overshooting can be avoided or greatly reduced simply by an exchange of appropriate information among countries on their prospective policies, followed by an adjustment by each country of its actions to take the prospective actions of other countries into account. Monetary and fiscal measures are framed on the basis of forecasts of the near future, and in open economies these forecasts should depend on the macroeconomic policies (as well as other developments) of other countries.

Sometimes the avoidance of overshooting requires more active coordination of policy actions, that is, aligning them to some extent. If the national economies are in synchrony, then anticyclical actions must also be synchronized if large imbalances in payments and/or movements in exchange rates are to be avoided. By the same token, however, these actions must be coordinated so that their combined impact does not overshoot the objective. Moreover, some divergence of cyclical movement in national economies is stabilizing for the world economy as a whole, and thus is helpful if the resulting payments imbalances do not provoke harmful reactions.

The third respect in which international coordination of economic policy can result in general gains is when it improves the cost-benefit calculation that each country faces in determining its own actions. Fiscal policy, for example, may seem to the authorities in a small, open economy to be hardly worthwhile since the import leakages are so high that the residual impact of a given fiscal action on the domestic economy is quite small. The authorities in each one of a group of closely connected national economies may reason in precisely the same way, so that no fiscal action is taken, even though, for the countries as a group, it would make sense. Through coordination, such a group of countries may "internalize" the leakages and restore fiscal policy to the (collective) position it deserves.[12]

Countries may actually fear the consequences of acting alone, not merely the low advantage of doing so. For a small country in recession with a floating exchange rate, economic stimulus will generally depreciate the currency, which will raise the domestic-currency prices of all goods closely related to the foreign-trade sector. The country thus confronts an adverse short-run inflation-unemployment tradeoff. This fact will inhibit expansionary action. Its trading partners may find themselves similarly inhibited. Through action in concert, the short-run Phillips curve can be improved for all.

As already noted, energy policy offers an example whereby collective action can improve the future terms of trade. A small country reasons that it cannot influence the world environment in which it trades. It therefore bases its actions on present and expected future energy prices, which are taken to be independent of its own (generally costly) actions. By acting in concert, a group of small countries is able to influence its future terms of trade, so the actions become worthwhile.[13]

Energy and Macroeconomic Policy

As we look ahead into the 1980s, macroeconomic policymakers in the industrialized nations are confronted with a serious dilemma. On past relationships, policies for moderate economic expansion will sooner or later run into a shortage of oil at existing prices. OPEC production cannot be expected to increase above 1979 levels (nearly 31 million barrels a day) for a number of years. The competing demand for those supplies originating elsewhere, including domestic demand in OPEC countries, will continue to grow. The more rapid is economic growth in the OECD, the sooner an oil crunch will arise. We have had bottlenecks in economic expansion before, but none with such great and pervasive influence over the entire economy. Sharply rising oil prices in response to an oil shortage, as we have already seen twice, can bring economic growth to a halt, partly as a result of direct contractionary impact and partly as a result of government monetary and fiscal response to restrain the inflation generated by the oil-price increases.

High oil prices are necessary signals to consumers and producers, so they represent part of the solution to an emerging oil shortage. But sharp increases in oil prices are part of the economic problem as well. They must be avoided if we are to have steady economic growth during the decade and if we are to have any prospect of reducing inflation. I conclude from this brief discussion that during the 1980s an active energy policy is a necessary component of a successful macroeconomic policy. Without government actions to reduce the demand for oil that go beyond simply allowing the market to work, macroeconomic management will be continually plagued by the energy problem. Without an active energy policy we will have higher-than-necessary rates of inflation and lower-than-desirable rates of growth.[14] Thus, an energy policy is necessary to protect rational anti-inflationary and growth policies, not to mention rational foreign policy. In this regard the 1980s pose a very different set of problems from those posed in the 1960s, when I began my tutelage in public policy under Walter Heller.

Notes

1. Even mentioning some of these factors as important macroeconomic events identifies me as a "Keynesian," although a rather neoclassical one, because I do not consider monetary magnitudes—however they are defined—as either the first or the last word of macroeconomic problems or policy. They are themselves part of the interwoven economic and political process.

2. For a formal analysis of the impact of supply shortages on the overall market for money and goods and services, see E. S. Phelps, "Commodity-Supply Shocks and Full Employment Monetary Policy," *Journal of Money, Credit and Banking*, May 1978.

3. I suggested such a tax cut for the United States at President Ford's Conference on Inflation in 1974. Walter Heller made a similar suggestion, but he would have offset the revenue loss by higher taxes elsewhere or by lower expenditures.

4. This was ultimately to include all the industrialized countries except France, which had objected to the formation of a consumer bloc on political grounds. France, however, cooperates with IEA programs through the European community.

5. The investment preferences of OPEC countries in 1974–75 focused heavily on short-term, highly liquid dollar-denominated claims, including U.S. Treasury bills and Eurodollar deposits. This preference, *ceteris paribus*, would lower short-term interest rates. To the extent that the Federal Reserve targeted interest rates in framing monetary policy, there was a risk that the Federal Reserve would restrict monetary growth in order to prevent a fall in interest rates. The funds to be recycled would thus be withdrawn from the monetary sytem. In fact, U.S. Treasury bill rates

rose to a peak in August 1974 and then fell sharply until May 1975. And, far from pursuing steady monetary growth, the Federal Reserve allowed considerably less monetary growth in 1974 than had taken place in 1973, on all the usual monetary magnitudes.

6. The cumulative OPEC surplus from 1974 through 1978 was $180 billion. This was about half the prospective cumulative surplus that was frequently mentioned in 1974. To be sure, a part of this smaller cumulative surplus resulted from a recession that was much deeper and longer than most analysts had imagined it would be.

7. If length of ministerial communiqués can be taken as a reliable guide, coordination of policy within the OECD grew markedly during the 1970s. The annual communiqué increased from 2 pages in 1972 to 11 pages in 1979. Or was this a sign of growing desperation about global economic management, as if throwing words at the problems might help to solve them? If so, there is some encouragement in the slight decline in the length of 1980's communiqué.

8. But perhaps also in part because the more complacent Secretary of Treasury Simon had dominated the preparatory work, whereas George Shultz had been engaged from outside government to prepare for the Rambouillet summit.

9. The origin of the term "locomotive theory" is unclear. The term seems to have originated in Japan. A plausible hypothesis is this: I gave an interview to the Nihon Keizai Shimbun in the fall of 1975, in which I argued that the United States, Japan, and Germany should become the "engines of growth" of the world economy. "Engines" may well have gone into Japanese and come out into English again as "locomotives."

10. One line of thought asks why the locomotive theory need involve several countries. The United States, acting alone, would have less impact, but perhaps enough to make the difference. Moreover, since deficits represent transfers of real resources from the rest of the world, would it not be to U.S. advantage even to have a deficit sufficient to offset the entire OPEC surplus alone? The answer has two parts, not wholly consistent with one another. First, large trade deficits alarm the public and generate public support for protectionist measures, which those who seek import protection are quick to exploit. Second, large deficits lead to a depreciation of the currency, and that (while stimulating exports and making imports less competitive) alarms the public, aggravates inflationary pressures, and (wrongly) conveys the impression both at home and abroad of an absence of economic leadership. Lay opinion has not yet grasped the full implications of floating exchange rates.

11. A year later, the Tokyo summit created an analogous quantitative framework for coordinated action to reduce the demand for imported oil, with followup to be pursued in the IEA.

12. This phenomenon is discussed more extensively in my Wicksell lectures, *Economic Mobility and National Economic Policy* (Stockholm: Almqvist and Wicksell, 1974) (article 4 in the present volume).

13. There may be a more complex factor at work here. Clearly, expected prices may be higher in the absence of collective action, and that prospect should produce a

strong self-interest in oil-conserving measures. However, public opinion tends toward myopia in such matters, weighing present prices heavily and discounting doomsday projections. Hope springs eternal that developments will turn out not all that badly and costly actions can thereby avoided. A large part of such hope is the expectation that the United States will somehow solve the problem not only for the United States but for others as well. This free-rider attitude does not take into account the fact that American public and congressional opinion is increasingly sensitive to what other countries are doing, so Americans are less likely to agree to difficult and costly measures if others are not also seen to be taking comparable actions. A collective framework for action helps to overcome these attitudes.

14. William Nordhaus offers rough quantification of the gains from an active energy policy in terms of growth and (anti-) inflation in "Economic Performance in Industrial Countries," *Brookings Papers on Economic Activity*, no. 2 (1980). See especially tables 8 and 9.

4   Economic Mobility and National Economic Policy

It is a great honor to have been asked to deliver some lectures commemorating Knut Wicksell, who surely had one of the most original minds in economics of all time. My topic in these lectures does not rise directly out of Wicksellian thought, but I believe that he would approve of it. Furthermore, as will become clear as I proceed, it is closely linked to and draws on other strains in Swedish economic thought—on colleagues and followers of Wicksell such as Heckscher, Lindahl, Myrdal, and Ohlin.

I begin with the observation that economic policy in all modern industrial non-Communist countries relies very strongly on the existence of markets. This is true of fiscal policy, of monetary policy, of regional policies, of investment policy, of competitive scholarship awards, and of a host of other government actions to influence the course of economic events. Given the historical background of these economies, there is little remarkable in this fact. It is the natural thing to do, since effective markets make up these modern economies. But the relationship is more subtle, less obvious than meets the eye. In particular, I hope to show that policy as it has evolved depends intimately on the existence of national markets, that the evolution of policy has followed (but also contributed to) the development of national markets, and that as markets grow beyond national boundaries national economic policy as we know it will be undermined, and must be replaced either by actions to retard the growth of markets beyond nations or by actions to take advantage of the new internationalization of markets.

By a "market" we can take August Cournot's definition, cited with approval by Alfred Marshall, as "the whole of any region in which buyers and sellers are in such free intercourse with one another that the prices of the same goods tend to equality easily and quickly"—after allowing for transport costs. We will be concerned not only with markets for goods, but also with markets for services, funds, factors of production, and even ideas.

The argument to be developed here is that a substantial range of economic policy presupposes a national market in Marshall's sense of the term, and that internationalization of markets will tend to undercut some important components of national economic policy while at the same time strengthening new instruments of policy.

Dichotomies such as that between "national" and "local" or "international" markets generally have no place in economics. Reality is more continuous than that; "nature takes no leaps," to cite Marshall again. But it often helps, in identifying important forces at work, to examine extreme cases and to explore what happens when a set of limiting assumptions obtains. That indeed is strongly in the tradition of Wicksell, many of whose contributions to economics involved precisely the rigorous exploration of limiting cases. We can then introduce whatever frictions are necessary to take us back to reality, after having usefully identified important underlying forces that are constantly tugging at the economic variables in which we are interested.

The extensive contemporary reliance on markets stands in sharp contrast to the character of economic policy in medieval Europe, or in China today. Medieval Europe was replete with direct controls on economic activity—on geographic mobility, occupational choice, prices, wages, and profits. There was relatively little free trading, and that was frowned upon as a despicable (even if necessary) social activity, to be carried on largely by persons who were outside the mainstream of society. Very much the same condition applies in China today. Trade is officially a "nonproductive" activity, socially inferior to manufacture. Individuals are told where they should live and what activities they should engage in, in the interests of the new society. Prices and wages and fixed by decree and rarely altered. Change takes place by directive rather than by incentive.

Medieval Europe (and contemporary China) involved a very different conception of society, and of the role of the individual within it, from that underlying modern "Western" society. It was assumed that the interests of the social organism could be defined independent of the personal interests of its members, that each member had a well-defined place and function essential to the smooth working of this social organism, and that each member would accept his place and identify his welfare with that of society. A gradual rise in incomes, due in part to plague and in part to technological change, increased the scope for individual maneuverability in the slowly evolving medieval society. The reintroduction of classical thought during the Renaissance, with its strong emphasis on the individual, resulted in a further loosening of the bonds of each member to an organic social system. The move toward free markets was an exceedingly gradual one, from the feudal period through a long "mercantile" period to the laissez faire of the nineteenth century and the managed economies of today. In parallel to this development, the objectives and the instruments of economic policy also evolved to correspond to and take advantage of the growth of markets—though not without delays and tensions in the process of adjustment to new circumstances and new opportunities.

In what follows I first illustrate the dependence of national policy on the existence of well-functioning national markets. I then suggest how the effectiveness of some major instruments of national economic policy will be eroded as markets grow beyond national boundaries and become increasingly global, and how at the same time other instruments of policy will become more effective. The treatment is quite general and touches on all four major economic functions of government: stabilization, allocation, distribution, and regulation (i.e., the choice and enforcement of a legal regime). A third section offers a brief historical sketch of the gradual evolution of markets and of the attempts of economic policy to keep up with markets, from medieval to modern Europe, within the United States, and today among nations. A concluding section speculates on the implications of observable market developments for national economic policy in the future.

The Dependence of National Economic Policy on National Markets

Fiscal Policy

Perhaps the most straightforward illustration of the dependence of national economic policy on national markets concerns the use of fiscal policy for economic stabilization. The condition to be corrected here is an excess or a deficiency of aggregate demand in some nation, leading to price inflation or to unemployment of resources. Suppose for concreteness that demand is deficient. The Keynesian solution, now widely used by modern governments, is to stimulate aggregate demand through an expansionary fiscal policy, either an increase in government expenditure or an increase in private expenditure induced by a reduction in taxes. Although there has been considerable debate on which types of action will have the greatest effect on aggregate demand, and especially on whether a cut in corporate taxes will have as much effect as a reduction in income taxes on low-income families or an increase in government expenditure, very little attention has been paid to the implications of where the expenditure or tax reduction occurs geographically. It is implicitly assumed that no matter where the additional expenditure is made, it will diffuse rapidly throughout the nation, generating employment wherever necessary or drawing the unemployed to the new jobs. In other words, market forces will spread the secondary spending effects more or less uniformly throughout the land, so the location of the initial impetus to demand is of no importance.

It is worth noting that the application of input-output analysis to modern economies has shown that the commodity pattern of a new expenditure has relatively little effect of the final pattern of incremental demands. The secondary commodity pattern of expenditure is pretty much the same over a wide range of primary expenditures. By analogy, is this also true of the geographic pattern of expenditures? Modern macroeconomic policy generally assumes that it is, although the recent attention paid to "regional" policies acknowledges that the spatial diffusion of demand does not adequately reach certain locations in the economy, making necessary some geographic specificity.

Indeed, the very concepts of Gross National Product and Gross National Expenditure assume a meaningful method of aggregation of thousands of individual demands over the national territory in question, and this in turn requires the presence of a common market, if not literally in the sense of commodity price equalization then at least in the sense of parallel movement in prices for similar commodities.[1] Although it is not always recognized, these notions lose some of their value in application to less-developed countries, where markets are often badly fragmented. The problem of aggregation over fragmented markets is also one strand in the debate between those economists who focus their attention for controlling the level of unemployment on concepts of aggregate demand and those "structuralists" who draw attention to the occupationally or geographically specific nature of unemployment and urge government measures aimed directly at the occupations or locations where unemployment is most heavily concentrated. The latter group assumes that markets will *not* operate so as to transmit any injection of demand quickly throughout the economy, creating employment (perhaps after a number of intermediate steps) where it is utimately needed.

Monetary Policy

The dependence of national economic policy on national markets is even clearer in the case of monetary policy. Rediscounting of bills or open market operations by the central bank affect credit through credit markets. Even without markets, rediscounting can of course assist the particular bank or broker or merchant whose bill is rediscounted. But as monetary policy, it works only if that action in turn provides some general easing of credit conditions, i.e., if the effect is diffused throughout credit markets. Similarly, open market operations as monetary policy (as opposed to an indirect way of financing the government) have their effect through market linkages. Typically such purchases or sales are made only in the principal financial center of each country, but the effects of these purchases or sales are assumed to be transmitted quickly throughout the land. Otherwise, monetary action would influence monetary conditions only in the financial center. It was Walter Bagehot's perception, just 100 years ago, that the Bank of England could affect credit conditions throughout the whole of England. This condition permitted a national monetary policy, and Bagehot argued that the Bank of England should take that responsibility upon itself—an illustration of how new possibilities create new responsibilities.[2] If geographical interest arbitrage or its functional equivalent in the availability of credit does not take place, action in a single financial center will not diffuse throughout the nation and it is not meaningful to speak of national monetary policy.

Allocational Incentives

Much of national economic policy is concerned with the allocation of resources. Indeed, this is a more traditional function of government than is economic stabilization, which in its current forms and scope dates only from the 1940s in most countries. Governmental concern with resource allocation in market economies arises both from the need for collective consumption and from the need to oversee the efficient functioning of private markets. Three sources of this concern can be especially identified, apart from a desire to redistribute income: (1) economies of scale, and their special case, indivisibilities in production; (2) externalities, and their extreme form, noncompetitiveness in consumption, combined with the difficulty of internalizing these external effects, that is, combined with high costs of exclusion; and (3) failure of markets in capital and in risk to function properly, due especially to the nonappropriability of human capital, to scale that inhibits proper risk-spreading, and to moral hazard involved in insurance against risk. This is not the place to discuss the various dimensions of collective consumption and their origins in the failure of markets or to provide efficient solutions, but a few illustrations can be offered of how governmental attempts to correct these deficiencies in markets often rely on the presence of markets. In other cases, of course, they do not.

Governments often introduce special subsidies or taxes to encourage or discourage economic activities. For example, due to the nonappropriability of "human capital" in the forms of skills and learning, and indeed of most general knowledge, including especially useful scientific knowledge, there will tend to be underinvestment in these activities because capital markets will not function adequately to permit borrowing now against future returns. What lender will undertake investment in a scientific investigation which is risky at the outset and the results of which will immediately be available to all? Society has developed a number of devices to overcome this problem, including the awarding of patents on certain forms of knowledge and substantial prizes (such as the Nobel awards) and other forms of reward to successful scientists. But these may not be enough. As a partial remedy, some governments finance scientific research through research grants, inviting applications from a wide class of investigators and making awards to those whose projects pass some form of critical review. This process presupposes a "market" in scientific talent, willing to respond to the prospect of research grants.

Similarly, capital and risk markets function badly when it comes to education, especially education that is not best acquired through an apprenticeship system (where the master craftsman makes the "investment" but is assured of repayment through lower-than-market wages to the apprentice during the period of apprenticeship). In the absence of government assistance, students cannot easily borrow against their future earnings and hence often cannot undertake investment in education even when that is both in the individual's and in the social interest. Governments have therefore stepped in with tax-financed subsidies to educational institutions (to permit a charge to students that is below costs) and scholarships to individuals, ultimately to be repaid through taxes on the increases in income permitted by the additional education. Scholarship awards, like research grants, are typically given on a national basis, to permit students to select the best institution for their needs and capabilities. Again, a national market is assumed to exist. Education can be and often is financed locally, but the disadvantage of this in a mobile society is that educated individuals may leave the community that provided the financing, and this prospect reduces the incentive of local government to provide educational support. So as persons become nationally mobile, the financing of their education must also be done, at least in part, at the national level.

Governments use taxes and subsidies for a host of other activities as well—to encourage investment in exceptionally risky ventures, such as oil exploration, or in exceptionally durable ventures, such as housing and sewage treatment facilities and forests. Often investment in general is subsidized, e.g. through an allowance for accelerated depreciation for tax purposes, on the grounds that capital markets are imperfect even for tangible investments or that private aversion to risky investment exceeds the appropriate degree of social aversion to risk. Once again, this form of incentive assumes that markets exist to the extent necessary to respond to the incentives.

To be sure, these activities would not have to operate through markets, and indeed in some cases do not. If additional investment is desired in China, the government simply increases taxes on output and undertakes the necessary investment. Some direct government investment also takes place in the Western world. Moreover, education is made compulsory up to a certain age, a less expensive alternative to providing financial incentive to individuals to go to school, on grounds that the external effects of a better-educated populace redound to everyone and that rational choices cannot be made in today's world without at least some formal education. Universal compulsory medical insurance is imposed in some Western countries to avoid the risk-splitting that would otherwise occur. And some governments engage directly in the production of desired goods or services, e.g. housing (which is often motivated by redistributive considerations, taken up below) and scientific research. Finally, public debate is still intense on whether anti-pollution action should be undertaken primarily with financial disincentives or with direct regulation of effluent quality.

Despite the emphasis that modern industrial countries place on markets, their governments at the same time rely as well on direct regulation of certain activities. One of the important functions of government is to establish the legal regime in which economic transactions take place—the rules of contract, liability, disclosure, and fraud, and the procedure for resolving disputes. While it is conceivable that these vital features of any modern economy could be established through the market (that is, by a system of taxes and subsidies keyed to the attainment of socially desirable behavior), it is customary and indeed more effective in most cases to stipulate minimum conditions of compliance expected of all traders and producers. To the extent that the sanctions against noncompliance are merely fines, it could be said that we do use a system of economic incentives to encourage compliance, and a business firm or individual finding a particular regulation especially onerous can simply violate it and pay the fine. But a certain moral and social opprobrium is associated with such violation, and this form of sanction is often far more important in inducing compliance than a fine. We really define the members of a social community by specifying certain minimal standards of good behavior, and a sharp dichotomy between good and bad behavior is very different both in intent and in effect from a system of financial incentives that leaves each firm and individual to balance out the gains against the losses associated with alternative forms of behavior.

But the effectiveness of a system of regulations is also sensitive to the presence of markets, and in particular to the mobility of individuals and firms relative to the boundaries of the community laying down the regulations. This is a theme to which we will return below.

Erosion and Transformation of National Economic Policy with the Internationalization of Markets

The foregoing discussion has suggested that economic policy today relies to a great extent on the existence of markets, and often on markets that are national in scope. We now want to consider the consequences of having efficient markets that exceed the nation in scope. Obviously the consequences for any particular policy instrument depend on the particular markets that are most germane to it, and the scope of other markets is of less consequence. In many cases it will prove to be factor markets that are of greatest relevance, although in some cases commodity markets alone are of considerable importance for this issue and in still other instances there is some degree of substitutability between commodity markets and factor markets.

Stabilization Policy: Fiscal Action

As the first example of the consequences of larger-than-national markets, let us return to a detailed analysis of the impact of fiscal policy on national aggregate demand. For concreteness, let us suppose that a government desires to increase aggregate demand, and that to accomplish this it engages in an additional public-works expenditure at a particular location. Unemployment is assumed to be uniformly spread throughout the nation. How effective is a public expenditure at a specific location in reducing widespread unemployment? The answer depends in part on the mobility of labor within the nation—will unemployed workers be drawn readily to the site of the expenditure, or will other workers be drawn there, leaving jobs available elsewhere for the unemployed?—and it depends in part on the marginal propensity to "import" from the rest of the nation by the community at the site of the additional expenditure.[3] For the moment let us concentrate on the second of these two effects. If the tendency to "import" goods and services from the rest of the nation is high, then of course the transmission of additional demand throughout the nation will be rapid and the locus of the

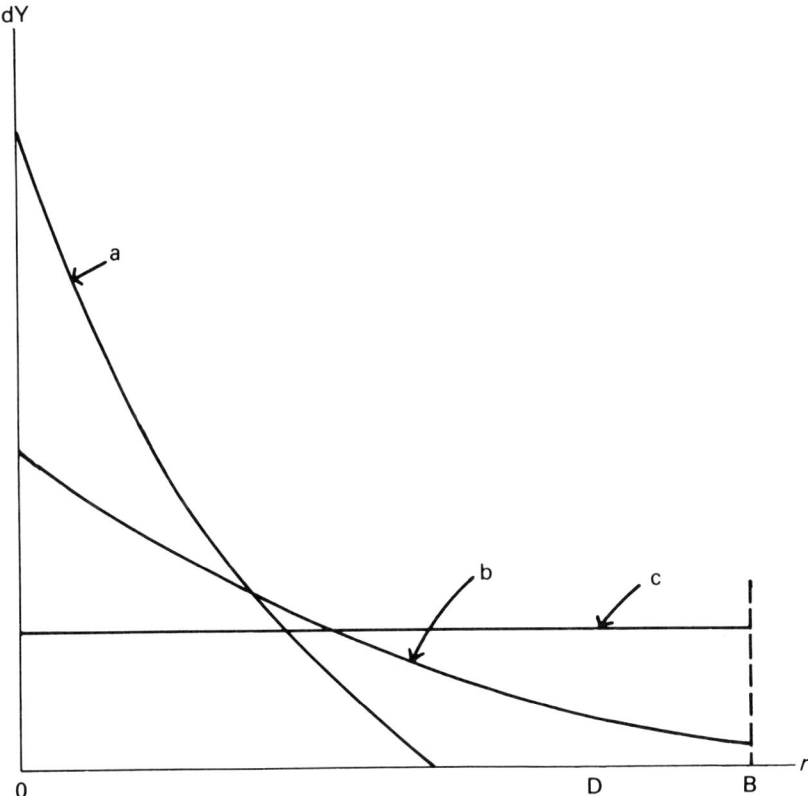

Figure 1

initial expenditure will be of little consequence—although of course the stimulus to demand may still be somewhat greater there than elsewhere, so that locus is not totally a matter of indifference. If, in contrast, the tendency to import goods and services from the rest of the nation is low, if in other words most of the incremental expenditure is spent locally, and the proceeds of the increases in local income so generated are also spent locally, and so on, then of course the stimulus to the rest of the economy will be slow in coming and it will be substantially less, relative to the initial injection of demand, than the stimulus to income in the community where the expenditure first takes place.

These points are illustrated in figure 1, which depicts on its vertical axis the increase in total income induced by a given increase in government expenditure. The change in income is the "equilibrium" change, after a period of adjustment.[4] Economic distance, i.e. distance measured in terms of economic impact, is measured along the horizontal axis. The expenditure is assumed to take place at the origin; the farthest boundary of the country, assumed in figure 1 to be closed, is at B. Three different schedules are shown in figure 1, reflecting three quite different degrees of market integration of the country. Schedule a assumes a country whose markets are quite fragmented, so that an increase in expenditure at the origin affects income very strongly in the neighborhood of the expenditure, but its diffusion throughout the rest of the country is highly attenuated and it has no impact on incomes in the farthest reaches of the country. That is, there is no income-induced trade between the extremities of the country. Schedule c, in contrast, reveals a highly integrated country, so that an injection of expenditure at the origin will have, after a period of adjustment, the same impact on incomes everywhere else in the country as it does at the point of injection. Schedule b represents a case in between the other two, with some income-induced trade linkages among all parts of the country but with enough frictions so that there remains a substantial difference between the impact on income at the point of expenditure and the effect on income far from the point of expenditure. Market linkages are present, but they are very imperfect; the marginal propensity to "import" from the rest of the country is positive but low.

It should be noted that the total effect on income of the enlarged government expenditure is the same in the three cases, for the initial expenditure is assumed to be the same in all three cases, and the marginal propensity not to spend is assumed to be identical throughout the country. As a consequence, the areas under the three schedules are the same.[5] But they are distributed very differently across space.

Figure 1 thus illustrates the point made earlier that national fiscal policy can be framed independent of locational considerations only if the country as a whole represents a highly integrated market, so that expenditure injections, no matter where they take place, are rapidly transmitted to other parts of the country. An unemployed worker located at D may view an expenditure at the origin with relative equanimity if schedule c is operative, but will rightly be aggrieved in the other two cases.

Two further points can be made about this closed economy. First, spatial diffusion of new expenditure does not take place instantaneously. The schedules in figure 1 can be reinterpreted in terms of the impact on income at different times during the period of transition, with schedule a representing the period soon after the new expenditure was made, schedule c representing the "equilibrium" impact on income after full transmission in a fully integrated economy, and schedule b representing an intermediate point of time. This contrasts with the earlier interpretation put on all three schedules as the equilibrium impact on income. To the extent that adjustment is not instantaneous, then of course sectional interests have a strong interest in where the fiscal policy impact first falls, for that location will get a temporary boost to income above the equilibrium value and will receive the impact earlier. The second point is that we have been concerned here with the transmittal of an expenditure injection through the markets for goods and services through commodity trade with the rest of the country. To the extent that labor is highly mobile, even the market relationship depicted by schedule *a* may alleviate unemployment throughout the country, for unemployed workers (or their equivalent) will migrate to the origin of the expenditure. Total income will have been increased there relative to other parts of the country, but if labor mobility is perfect the employment generated at the point of expenditure will have reduced unemployment uniformly throughout the country because of the migration of workers. Thus, the proposition advanced earlier about the necessity of national markets for the effectiveness of fiscal policy should be qualified to mean the necessity of national markets either for goods and services or for persons, but not necessarily for both.

Consider now the consequences of opening this country to trade with the rest of the world. Under these circumstances, some portion of any additional expenditure will be spent on imports from the rest of the world. As a result, incomes will be stimulated there as well as in the country in which the government expenditure is made. But, by the same token, some of the desired effect on national income will be lost to the country taking the action. As in the closed economy, the extent of this dissipation (we called it diffusion in the earlier case) will depend on the marginal propensity to import from abroad. The impact of a given fiscal stimulus on the country undertaking it will depend on how closely that economy is integrated with the rest of the world. The greater the degree of integration, the lower the national impact (that is, the less effective fiscal policy will be as an instrument of national stabilization policy).

This point is shown in figure 2, which is drawn on the same principles as figure 1 but is extended to include the whole world or some large part of it. As before, the vertical axis measures the "equilibrium" increase in income following a given increase in expenditure at the origin, and the horizontal axis measures economic distance from the origin, with *B* representing the borders of our country and *W* representing the ends of the earth. (Of course, some areas outside the country might well be economically closer to the point of expenditure than are some areas within the country; but we abstract from that possible complication here.)[6] Three of many possible relationships

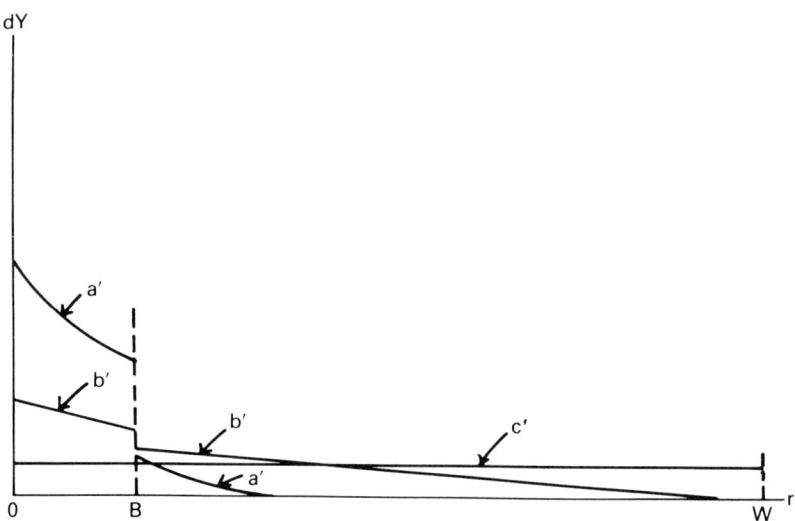

Figure 2

are depicted by schedules a', b', and c'. Schedule a' reveals (among those shown) the lowest degree of interdependence between our country and the rest of the world. As far as income-induced imports are concerned, the country is virtually a closed one: an expenditure at the origin diffuses throughout the country, but very little of it is transmitted beyond the nation's borders. Furthermore, a discontinuity is shown at the border. This may arise because of a national preference for domestic goods per se, because of tariffs or other barriers to imports that create an artificial preference for domestic goods, or because of movements in exchange rates that inhibit sharp changes in expenditures on imports. In any case, most of the impact on income of the new expenditure takes place within the country, with very little leakage or spillout into the rest of the world.

Schedule c' depicts a strongly contrasting case, in which there is no differentiation between "foreign" and "domestic" as far as expenditures are concerned, so the impact of an incremental expenditure at the origin affects income throughout the world in equal degree. Schedule b' depicts a case of moderate but not high interdependence. Since the total income effect throughout the world is the same in the three cases (implying equality of the area under the three schedules), the impact on national income in the initiating country is very much greater in case a' than it is in case c', with b' lying between them. In case c', the leakage to the rest of the world is very high—a fact that may be either welcome or unwelcome, depending upon economic conditions there. Indeed, in the limiting case of a small country in a world of high interdependence, the national impact of fiscal action may be totally dissipated through leakages to the rest of the world. (Under case c', the share of total increase in income taking place within the country is OB/OW in figure 2, which for a small country will be negligible.) Even for moderate-size countries, the final stimulus to national income may be less than the initiating incremental expenditure. In either instance, fiscal policy becomes quite an inefficient instrument for influencing the level of national income, and this may explain the relatively little emphasis that small, open economies (or fiscally autonomous regions within countries, such as states within the United States) place on fiscal policy as an instrument of economic stabilization. For large countries, fiscal policy retains some influence even in case c' merely by virtue of the size of the country relative to the world economy, but in that instance fiscal action by that country creates a large "externality" with respect to the rest of the world—a spillover effect that will be welcome there if economic conditions and objectives are similar to those in the country that initiates the expenditure but unwelcome if economic conditions in the rest of the world differ substantially or if preferences as regards the pressure of aggregate demand differ sharply. In these instances, stabilizing fiscal action by one country becomes an external disturbance to the rest of the world.

In interpreting the relationship between national fiscal action and stimulus to national income in the alternative cases shown in figure 2, it is necessary to keep in mind that fiscal action is assumed here to be used to stabilize aggregate demand in the face of shifts in private or foreign-government demand. When the world economy is not highly integrated, disturbances in one part of it will not be strongly transmitted to other parts, so that fiscal action will not be needed elsewhere. In contrast, when the world is highly integrated, shifts in expenditure in one part of the world will be rapidly and strongly transmitted to other parts, thereby mitigating the unwanted impact on income at the source of the shift but creating a disturbance in other parts of the world. Thus, economic integration has the effect of spreading disturbances more widely and thinly. To the extent that exogenous shifts in expenditure in different regions occur independently, an integrated economy acts as a kind of insurance pool, or a diversified portfolio, spreading deviations widely and thus, through averaging, damping down the magnitude of variation in incomes or prices *without* stabilization measures. This "pooling of disturbances" represents one argument for encouraging greater economic interdependence, so long as the disturbances in different parts of the economy are not perfectly correlated.[7]

But greater economic interdependence does not always represent an unmitigated gain in this respect. In the first place, the same forces that increase the interdependence between two regions in the sense of rapid and strong transmission of disturbances also probably increase the positive correlation between those disturbances, so that the benefits of diversification are diluted. Thus, waves of pessimism or optimism among consumers or among investors are likely to occur in different nations at the same time if the economies are closely linked in many ways. In the second place, individual regions may find themselves experiencing a *greater* degree of economic disturbance in an interdependent economy, even though overall variance has been reduced, because the absolute size of disturbances coming from outside the region overwhelms the disturbances arising within the region. Some form of compensation, e.g. through countercyclical compensatory transfers, may therefore be warranted from the regions whose gain in stability is substantial.

In the third place, preferences may differ from one country to another on the degree of demand pressure that should be maintained on the economy, so that a greater interdependence that spreads disturbances more widely and thinly will also reduce the scope for accommodating these differences in national preferences. Both international ill will and national economic distress will be created when one country "imports" the disturbance of another and has to take corrective action—corrective action that will be weakened by the openness of its economy—when the other country is slow in taking corrective action itself. The most striking examples of this in recent history are the French economic expansion associated with the Algerian war in the mid 1950s and the U.S. expansion associated with the Vietnam war in the mid 1960s. Both led to payments deficits and exported inflation, and in both cases the initiating countries were slow to take the required restrictive economic measures, thereby imposing a burden of unwanted "imported inflation" on other countries.

In summary, then, to be effective at the national level fiscal policy requires a national market, in the sense that the marginal propensity to "import" from the rest of the country into the locality in which the expenditure is made is high. On the other hand, a large propensity to import from the rest of the world weakens fiscal policy as an instrument of stabilization policy, for much of its demand-creating or demand-dampening effect is dissipated abroad. It is perhaps not an accident that Keynesian fiscal policy was born in the protectionist 1930s, after national markets had formed, but during a period in which barriers to international trade bottled up the expansionary actions within each country. By the same token, it is perhaps not surprising, in light of these observations, that local governments have rarely in recent years pursued Keynesian fiscal policy. The effects are quickly dissipated beyond the local jurisdiction, so this instrument is not an effective one. As we will see below, however, other actions are open to a local government to stimulate local economic activity when its jurisdiction is located in a larger national economy with high mobility of economic factors.

The above discussion has presupposed a regime of fixed exchange rates, or at least of exchange rates that are inhibited in their movement by official intervention or private speculation. If exchange rates are freely flexible, then standard analysis shows that fiscal policy will have the same effect on aggregate demand in the absence of international capital mobility as would occur in a closed economy, for movements in the exchange rate will automatically ensure no "leakage" of demand to the rest of the world.[8] With international capital mobility, however, some of this insulation is lost, e.g. by the inward movement of funds in response to fiscal expansion, which inhibits depreciation of the currency.

Moreover, standard analysis does not allow adequately for the influence of movements in the exchange rate on the demand for money and other financial assets denominated in local currency. In a small open economy, a sharp depreciation of the exchange rate, by reducing the real value of money balances and other financial assets within the economy, may cause a reduction in private spending that offsets the fiscal stimulus, and since this effect is roughly proportional to the relative importance of the foreign trade sector in the local economy, the free flexibility of exchange rates does not provide the desired insulation after all. Thus, the degree of openness, or economic interdependence, is a more important factor in determining the effectiveness of fiscal policy than is the exchange-rate regime—unless, of course, the mere existence of floating exchange rates reduces the degree of interdependence, e.g. marginal propensities to import, by discouraging trade and capital movements.

Stabilization Policy: Monetary Action

Monetary measures suffer much the same disability as fiscal measures when a national economy is in close financial intercourse with other parts of the world. For a small country whose financial markets are linked to the great financial centers, the rest of the world becomes for practical purposes both an infinite source of funds and an infinitely large repository of funds. Any attempt to deviate sharply (and, in the limiting case, at all) from world monetary conditions will merely provoke a movement of funds into or out of the country sufficient to bring national monetary conditions back into line with those prevailing elsewhere. Monetary actions lose all of their grip on domestic aggregate demand.

A large country, of course, does not fare quite so badly simply by virtue of its size; its monetary actions influence world monetary conditions, so that monetary easing by a large country in a world of integrated financial markets will still exert some influence on its own domestic demand, just as fiscal stimulus does, but it will be muted because much of the stimulus is transmitted abroad. (It has been suggested that the United States today determines monetary policy for the world, and thereby experiences an attenuated but still noticeable impact on demand at home.)

The situation becomes more complicated in a world with flexible exchange rates, not least because the mere presence of flexible rates may preclude a high degree of interdependence among financial markets. If the risk associated with a regime of flexible exchange rates is perceived to be high, then money-market investors will be reluctant to place their funds in foreign money markets except on a fully hedged basis, and that behavior will provide some considerable insulation between national money markets. In that case, monetary action by a single country will have some effect on domestic aggregate demand, largely through inducing movements in the exchange rate which in turn will lead to shifts in expenditure between home and foreign goods and services. Thus, if a country engages in open-market sales of securities or other actions to restrict credit, the dampening of demand for goods will lead to an incipient decline in imports and thus to an appreciation of the currency. This appreciation, in turn, will stimulate imports and discourage exports, thus reducing inflationary pressures on the economy. Or, to put the same point in terms of monetary analysis, the reduction in the money supply will lead to a curtailment of expenditure and to an attempt by residents to borrow abroad, both of which will result in some appreciation of the spot exchange rate.

For a small open economy, however, there is the possibility that residents will choose to hold their money balances in foreign currency rather than undergo what might be substantial fluctuations in the value of their money balances in terms of the foreign goods and services they purchase. Holding foreign currency would then insure against such fluctuation.[9] But if this development has proceeded very far, active use of monetary policy by the country in question, by increasing the variability of the exchange rate, may merely induce a further shift in the public's holding of money to foreign currency, thereby reducing the effectiveness of domestic monetary action. Thus, the sought-after insulation would be lost after all.

Even if this development does not occur, monetary action under a regime of flexible rates achieves its influence on aggregate demand by altering the exchange rate, that is, by "exporting" the excessive or deficient demand. This exportation of the disturbance may be even more unwelcome abroad than the spreading of disturbances (and corrective action) under a regime of fixed exchange rates.

To sum up, we reach the same general conclusion that we reached in the case of fiscal policy: As an instrument for stabilizing the national economy, monetary policy requires a national credit market to work efficiently; but if effective markets transcend national boundaries, then monetary policy loses its grip on domestic aggregate demand for all but the largest countries, and even there its influence is weakened. To be effective, in other words, monetary policy requires impermeable, or at least imperfectly permeable, national boundaries. A regime of flexible exchange rates serves to introduce some insulation between markets whose assets are denominated in different currencies, but the insulation is only an imperfect one if trading relationships are extensive relative to total income.

Taking the observations on monetary and fiscal policy together, we discover that open economies have a hard time maintaining aggregate demand on an even keel using these now traditional instruments. With high mobility of factors of production, however, they will be tempted to turn to other, more competitive instruments of policy to achieve their objectives toward economic growth and stabilization. We will return to this question below.

Allocation and Distribution

High factor mobility across jurisdictional boundaries in some respects reduces the inefficiencies associated with the provision of public goods, but it makes redistribution of income within jurisdictions virtually impossible. Though some redistribution of income within modern societies takes place through direct transfer from the taxable public to the beneficiaries, such as the transfers that take place through welfare payments or through nonactuarial pension systems, much of the redistribution is accomplished through the medium of public expenditure. Some public expenditure, such as low-cost housing, is specifically for the benefit of certain income groups. But most public expenditure benefits much of the population, or in any case benefits particular segments of the population selected on grounds other than income. This expenditure is generally financed by taxes on the whole population, taxes that are typically based on income, consumption, or property. The tax systems of modern economies generally aim to tax more heavily those residents who are relatively well off. The benefits of public expenditure are not distributed in the same way, so some redistribution takes place through the tax/expenditure system.

The problem of how best to finance public expenditure has attracted the attention of economists for many years. Knut Wicksell suggested a solution for a just system of property that was designed to achieve exactly the right amount of public expenditure and to finance it in exactly the right way, i.e. by taxing those who benefit from the expenditure. He suggested that each proposal for public expenditure should be associated with a particular mode of financing it, and that the joint tax/expenditure proposal should be put into effect only with unanimous approval by the affected citizenry. With this procedure, a series of hypothetical iterations on both the level and character of the expenditure and the nature and distribution of the tax burden would ensure that the right amount and distribution were achieved. Unfortunately, the proposal does not make due allowance for the presence of bargaining tactics and the closely related temptation to conceal one's true preferences in the hopes of becoming a "free rider" by enjoying the benefits of a particular expenditure without having to pay for it. Each voter might threaten to hold up the whole package unless he achieved a more favorable distribution, even though he were willing to accept the initial proposal. The procedure therefore carries the risk that through zero-sum bargaining tactics the benefits of a particular proposal might be lost altogether. Wicksell's follower in public finance, Erik Lindahl, attempted to make Wicksell's underlying principle more operational by proposing that all public goods whose consumers could be identified should be financed on the benefit principle; that is, the direct beneficiary should pay the cost, much as he does for a private good. To finance "generalized" public goods such as national defense, where discovering the level of "consumption" by each individual is a hopeless task in view of the incentive of each to conceal his true preferences, Lindahl proposed that the ability-to-pay principle be used.[10]

A strict benefit principle is not usually applied to public goods, even when the direct beneficiary can be identified. This is partly for administrative reasons (e.g. the burden of applying user taxes to those who drive on city streets), partly because some public goods are thought to derive their "publicness" from externalities that are not readily measured (e.g. the provision of education at public expense), and not least because of the desire to achieve some redistribution of income through the tax/expenditure system. In practice, therefore, the provision of public goods and the accompanying taxes is accomplished through majority voting, with the consequences that neither the level nor the composition of public goods is optimal,[11] and that many individuals are paying more for the public benefits they receive than they would on the basis of individual preference while many others, in contrast, would be willing to pay more for additional public benefits and even for the public benefits they receive.

This divergence between private preference and public provision, however, reflects a low degree of inter-jurisdictional mobility. If individuals are mobile, they can group themselves according to their preferences for public goods, and in the limiting case all but highly idiosyncratic individuals or those tied to particular localities will live and work in communities that cater exactly to their preferences for public goods according to their willingness to pay for them. In other words, the selection of one community among many possible communities becomes, for the mobile individual, much like the purchase of a private good: he can choose the tax/expenditure combination that most suits him, and the results will be optimal so long as "prices" (including now tax-prices) reflect true social cost, that is, so long as public goods are produced under constant or increasing costs and so long as there are no externalities either between jurisdictions or arising from the addition of an individual to or the subtraction of an individual from each community.[12] Thus, high mobility, by permitting individuals to sort themselves according to preferences for public goods, contributes toward the efficient allocation of resources. By the same token, however, it prevents any community from using the tax system to redistribute income if that does not accord exactly with the preferences of the taxed individuals—in which case it is similar to voluntary charity managed through the public sector. Any overtaxed individual will leave the community in question, while undertaxed individuals will flock to the community offering the subsidy. In practice, of course, the presence of relocation costs allows some room for variation from exact preferences.

It is worth pausing for a moment to see exactly how the sorting takes place, and to show that, at least to a rough approximation, even the presence of indivisibilities in the production of public goods does not disturb the optimality of the provision of public goods where mobile persons can choose among a large number of communities.

Consider the case in which the sole tax in all communities is the real property tax (a close approximation to reality for local authorities in many industrial countries), in which there are no external effects beyond the jurisdiction of each community (an assumption that is obviously weak when new knowledge is being produced or disseminated) and in which the addition of a new resident does not impose nonpecuniary costs, e.g. through congestion, on the residents of the community. Suppose further that the usable land in each community is fixed in amount and that the benefits of all public goods are proportional to the amount of property owned or rented. (The last assumption will be close to the truth for such public goods as street lighting, streets, and police and fire protection, but it is obviously strained in the case of primary education or public parades.) Under these circumstances the new resident will exactly pay for the public services that he expects to receive, and therefore he will choose the community that most suits his tastes in terms of level and quality of public goods. The resident will exactly pay the price either in the rent he pays, which in competitive equilibrium will include the property taxes, or in the taxes he pays in combination with the price of the land that he has purchased. If public goods entertain a difference between marginal and average cost due to some indivisible expenditure made at some time in the past, then the price of the property the resident buys will be increased by the discounted future excess value of the public services over the taxes he will expect to pay. In effect, the new resident is asked to pay an admission fee, through the price of land, to cover his share of the fixed costs—much as is required by many clubs.[13] Rent will similarly reflect the average service flow from public goods. Thus, those residents who originally "invested" in the initial expenditures for public goods (e.g. the physical facilities of a school system or a water and sewage system) can recoup their investment through rental or resale.

If public goods are produced under constant returns to scale, and the area of the community is enlargeable through development, the addition of a newcomer to the community will require a proportionately higher level of service, which is just covered by taxes.

When (as is generally the case in reality) public services are not proportional to real property owned or rented, or when property taxes do not distinguish between land and improvements, newcomers will exhibit some tendency to underinvest in land or improvements, respectively, for the taxes will exceed the associated benefits. In the latter case, however, since tax revenues on improvements will lower any fixed debt service to the resident population, there will be some tendency to relieve the excessive tax burden on newcomers. We will return to this phenomenon below.

Of course, our assumptions about externalities in this example have not been wholly realistic. Additional residents often do cause congestion, and hence impose nonpecuniary costs on the rest of the population, because public goods cannot always be readily increased to accommodate newcomers. Moreover, it would be unusual in a world of the perfect mobility that we have assumed if there were not some effects that were external to the jurisdiction. Indeed, the movement of educated persons and the transmission of scientific and technical knowledge via mobile persons both represent external effects in that the benefits accrue in part to communities that have not paid for the education or the generation of knowledge. Such externalities create pressures to enlarge the jurisdiction of government, to "internalize" them.

Moreover, the same underlying forces of technology and communication that increase mobility also tend to increase the efficient scale of at least some public goods. Defense expenditures and weather forecasting and control are two illustrations. These forces also create pressures for enlarged communities, to capture the advantages of scale.

We return to a point with which this section started, the redistribution of income. Fiscal systems in the modern world are frequently devoted to redistributing income from the rich to the poor, and in the medieval world they were often designed to redistribute from the poor to the powerful. Sometimes the redistribution is direct, as when taxes are used to finance welfare programs under a tax/transfer system. But more often it arises as a by-product of an expenditure program that accomplishes other objectives as well, such as farm-income stabilization programs, or the use of a progressive income tax to finance public expenditure of all types, or (in medieval times) the imposition of a corvée or the invoking of obligations of fealty to build an army which among other functions may plunder one's neighbors.

Except under special circumstances, redistribution through a tax/expenditure system requires that those who are heavily taxed (i.e. those whose tax burdens exceed their benefits from public goods) be immobile. This was true under the feudal system of levies, which gradually broke down as the peasant population became more mobile. It is also true today, when thanks to cheap and convenient transportation a person can often escape a local tax jurisdiction without even changing his job. In a closed economy with a single jurisdiction, redistributional taxation on income will affect factor supply only through the route of discouraging saving, effort, or risk-taking. If savings, risk-taking, and work habits are totally unresponsive to reward, redistributive taxation can be accomplished at no economic cost. But in an open economy, alternative jurisdictions can attract or repel factors from the jurisdiction engaging in redistributive taxation. With full information and low transfer costs, factor supplies to the jurisdiction in question will be much more responsive to relative rewards than would be true if the jurisdiction were closed. An attempt to impose a tax burden (net of public services) on capital or on a particular group of persons will simply induce the capital or the persons to move elsewhere, where the burden can be avoided. An attempt to favor a particular group of persons, by the same token, will attract the favored group from elsewhere, thereby increasing the tax burden on those factors from which income is being redistributed or else diluting the benefits for those original residents for whom favored tax treatment was intended.

If all factors of production except land are mobile, then any redistributive taxation can fall only on land, and in particular on the owners of land at the time the redistributive taxation is applied. (Subsequent purchasers of land will only be willing to pay an appropriately lower price for it; that is, the tax will be capitalized in the market value of the land.) If only some factors of production are mobile, redistributive taxes can be effectively levied on the immobile factors, since their immobility implies that part of their reward is economically equivalent to rent(assuming the factors are in perfectly inelastic supply). If, more realistically, most factors are immobile in the short run but mobile in the long run (where by mobile we mean willing to move, not merely capable of moving), then redistributive taxation can be applied effectively in the short run but the effects will gradually be eroded through inward or outward movement from the jurisdiction in question. Geographic inertia arises from the costs of movement to new locations; from locational preferences arising from loyalty to employer, preference for unique or rare natural or man-made characteristics of the area, ties to family, sentimental associations with the area, etc.; and from preference for the particular tax/expenditure mix in that jurisdiction compared with other jurisdictions. For all these reasons, redistributive taxes can be imposed on existing residents up to a point without provoking movement, even in the long run. For the prospective newcomer, these considerations carry less weight, particularly if the jurisdiction is small, for he can often indulge any locational preference by locating just outside the jurisdiction in question (e.g. in the suburbs of a preferred urban center).

The bearing of all this on our main topic is that if the domain of mobility has increased, for example through lower transport costs and reduced ignorance of other locations, the jurisdiction of the taxing authority must increase to keep up with the growing domain of mobility if redistributive taxation of factors other than rents is to have any role. Otherwise the mobile will escape the taxman, leaving the immobile to bear the tax burden.

Regulation

Governmental or private regulation represents a special form of "public goods," with the characteristic that a large number of persons can enjoy the advantages (or the disadvantages) of regulation at zero marginal cost and often cannot be readily excluded form enjoying the advantages. The need for regulation most frequently stems from one or another imperfection in markets. The need may arise from monopoly in ownership of some key material, or from strong economies of scale or a large indivisibility in the production or distribution process. It may arise from inadequate information for effective consumer choice. This is especially important in the area of food and drugs, in some professional services, and in financial markets, where it is difficult to insure against possible damage because of inadequate markets for risks.[14] It may arise from redistributive considerations, such as those designed to increase the incomes of farmers or doctors by restricting supply. (Historically, an important "redistributive" motivation for regulation was to raise revenue for the government, or, more accurately, for the ruling power, e.g. through the sale of monopolies.) And it may arise from considerations of national defense or public safety, as when the government attempts to control the market in drugs or in dangerous weapons.

Regulation involves direct prescription or proscription and represents an exception to the generalization made above that we have come to rely heavily on markets in framing economic policy. Indeed, the gradual move to market measures frequently displaced an earlier emphasis on direct regulation. But the consequence for regulation of enlarged mobility is similar to its consequence for market-oriented policies: the possibility of relocation outside the regulating jurisdiction may erode the effectiveness of regulation. Each jurisdiction can in principle apply regulations to activities within the jurisdiction, whether the objects of regulation be goods, persons, firms, or funds. Hence it can regulate the goods that residents consume at home, and it can regulate the production processes (including the provision of services, such as legal or medical services) located within the jurisdiction. But it cannot regulate goods or services consumed abroad or productive processes abroad (except when imported goods are distinguishable by the process). Nor can it regulate the financial structure and the degree of disclosure by nonresident issuers of securities and other financial claims, although it can do so for securities formally traded within the jurisdiction. Thus, as mobility increases, an increasing portion of economic activity by the residents of any given jurisdiction may escape regulation by that jurisdiction. Persons can travel abroad for abortions or for surgery, firms can locate abroad to escape safety regulations or anti-pollution requirements, and mutual funds can operate abroad to escape disclosure requirements or taxation. High mobility limits the scope of many types of regulation.

Policy Response to High Mobility

Thus far, I have emphasized the tendency of international mobility to erode national economic policies.[15] But that is not the only consequence. High mobility also increases the effectiveness of certain instruments of policy, thereby creating an incentive to rely more on those instruments; or it may alter the effectiveness of certain instruments of policy. Thus, whereas with high international capital mobility monetary policy loses its grip on domestic aggregate demand under a system of nonfloating exchange rates, it becomes more effective as a short-run instrument for governing the balance of payments. Tightening up on monetary policy cannot, with high mobility of capital, damp down domestic demand, but it can readily attract short-term funds from abroad.

Similarly, while high mobility of goods weakens fiscal policy as an instrument of stabilization, high mobility of funds strengthens it by providing the necessary monetary expansion or contraction to support expansionary or contractionary fiscal policy. When the marginal propensity to import has become so high that even fiscal action supported by international movement of funds becomes relatively ineffective in influencing aggregate demand, the mobility of other factors may also have increased to the point at which alternative forms of fiscal action may succeed in influencing aggregate demand. Thus, an area with deficient demand may correct that condition (but not always quickly) by attracting real investment from outside the region through the offer of subsidies. The subsidies may take the form of free or low-cost land, cheap credit, or tax holidays for a period of years, during which time the firm is enjoying the public services financed by other taxpayers. The construction of new plant with outside funds raises local demand for goods and services, except in the limiting case in which all the investment, including the labor, is done from outside the country (which comes close to the case for certain investments in less-developed countries today); and the new productive capacity permits the region to sell more to the rest of the world on a continuing basis, thus generating demand for local goods and services. In effect, the tax-financed subsidy lowers the after-tax factor rewards to the resident factors of production, thereby making the region's goods more competitive in markets outside the region. This is the principle that underlies regional policies, which have recently come strongly into fashion, although in those cases the subsidy itself may be provided from outside the region, thereby (through the inward movement of investment) increasing demand for local labor without lowering local after-tax income.[16]

But of course this route, like currency depreciation, generalizes only clumsily. It may work well for a single region or even for a few regions, but it does not work well if demand is deficient throughout the world or over large regions of the world. Competition among regions for the location of mobile firms will not much affect the actual location of firms, but it will serve to redistribute income away from the immobile factors of production to the mobile firms. To the extent that the neoclassical hypothesis that unemployment is caused by downwardly rigid money wages is valid, a tax/transfer system that lowers real wages (and the costs of production) while leaving nominal wages unchanged has merit. Taxes levied on immobile labor lower the after-tax wage, and subsidies (e.g. in the form of public services) to mobile capital raise the after-tax return to capital, thus tilting relative factor prices toward the greater employment of labor. Competition in subsidization among regions will reduce the real wages of employed labor, and that reduction may serve to increase total employment.[17]

Redistribution of income is not ruled out altogether in the presence of high mobility. Some factors will always be immobile, especially land, and they can be taxed for the sake of redistribution to others. With inward mobility, any given jurisdiction may be swamped with immigrants of those qualified for the net benefits, however, and the redistributive gains to members of that class of persons will be attenuated. In those instances beneficiary residents will desire limits on immigration, such as most modern welfare states have employed, or limits on the eligibility for net benefits to those resident in the region before a certain date or for a certain period of time. Professional licensure requirements often serve the purpose of protecting or raising the incomes of those who got there first.

Finally, we must not assume that erosion of policy instruments through high mobility is always a bad thing. Recall the Tiebout hypothesis, alluded to earlier: mobile persons can form communities on the basis of relatively homogeneous tastes for public goods, and under many circumstances that formation will be economically superior (that is, will represent a superior use of limited resources to satisfy individual wants) to the necessarily imperfect satisfaction of divergent preferences through some form of voting system. The satisfaction of individual preference for two or more public goods is bound to be frustrated if the preferences of residents in a region are bimodal, or even if they show wide dispersion around a single mode. Many of the celebrated migrations of history have occurred for the purpose of accommodating preferences that differ substantially from the prevailing norm: the Jews out of Egypt, the Pilgrims to America, the Mormons to Utah, and so on. To be sure, in those instances the total social and cultural environment was at issue, not merely the satisfaction of demand for public goods in the narrow economic sense. However, the less dramatic but more massive movement of middle-class Americans from urban to suburban residences can be traced in large part to different preferences for public goods from that prevailing in central cities.

The extreme Tiebout hypothesis rests on rather restrictive conditions: perfect mobility of all individuals, absence of economies of scale beyond the scale of each jurisdiction, and absence of external effects beyond each jurisdiction. These conditions do not fully obtain in practice, as has been suggested on several occasions above. Individuals do have locational preferences; costs of movement are often substantial even when knowledge about alternative locations is complete, which it is not; external effects do often extend beyond a jurisdiction; and for some public goods economies of scale surmount local jurisdictions and occasionally even national jurisdictions. But even with these qualifications the point that high mobility often improves allocation of resources carries some force. One currently relevant area of application involves the regulation of productive processes. With appropriate collective decisionmaking, some communities may vote for very stiff labor laws, safety requirements, or anti-pollution regulations, while other communities, with equally good collective decisionmaking, may impose less stringent controls in these areas, either because of different circumstances or because of different preferences. There is little lost and much gained by such divergence of view, so long as full employment is maintained (so that relaxation of regulations is not conditioned by the desire to attract industry to increase employment) and so long as the external effects (e.g. from air or water pollution) do not extend beyond each jurisdiction to other communities. Nor should it be a cause for regret when a pollution-producing industry moves from A to B, provided the residents of B attract the industry in full knowledge of the implications. The movement may raise wages in B and improve the air (while lowering wages) in A, in accordance with the preferences of each community.

Economic Policy and the Historical Growth of Markets

I have suggested above that governments of modern industrial countries of the "West" rely on markets to a high degree for the execution of their economic policies, that in many cases the successful execution of economic policy requires a market that is national in scope, and that when markets evolve to the point of becoming international in scope the effectiveness of tradition instruments of economic policy is often greatly reduced or even nullified. In this section I will try to give these hypotheses a semblance of verisimilitude by drawing (selectively) on the history of economic policy in Europe and North America over the past few centuries.

From Detailed Regulation to Laissez Faire[18]

In the late Middle Ages economic transactions were subject to regulation in minute detail. Each manor and town set wages and prices, the latter especially for food. Occupational choice was governed largely by heredity, and crafts were closely regulated as to entry, training, and quality and price of work. These detailed local regulations greatly impeded the resettlement of persons from manor to town or from town to town as that became increasingly possible and desirable with the gradual extension of effective royal authority over England and over parts of France in the sixteenth century, an extension that greatly improved the conditions of travel through the reduction of brigandage and the extension of law and order.[19] In 1563 Queen Elizabeth of England promulgated the Statute of Artificers, which provided a procedure for setting maximum wages and established rules of apprenticeship throughout England. It was viewed as a liberating move, supplanting the local regulations that impeded movement. But it still provided for detailed regulation. Some of the medieval regulations—such as the prohibitions on forestalling, engrossing, and regrating (buying goods before they reach market, buying in large quantities, and selling to persons other than consumers)—survived into the nineteenth century. There were many prescriptions as well as proscriptions: the English woollen industry was protected by banning the export of wool and prohibiting the import of wool cloth, but also by requiring every Englishman to be buried in wool and (for a time) requiring all Englishmen to wear woollen caps on Sunday.[20]

Today we associate detailed regulation of production and trade with the policy of mercantilism, dating roughly from the seventeenth century and running into the nineteenth (or, some would say, the twentieth). But the originators of mercantilist policy thought of it as a liberalizing (and nationalizing) move, compared with its antecedents. Axel Oxenstierna, chancellor of Sweden and a leading mercantilist thinker, argued as early as 1636 that prohibitions on production or trade should give way to deterrents and stimulants, that the state's ends should be accomplished through persuasion, with friendliness and good will, not with force. The great architect of French mercantilism, J. B. Colbert, was of a similar opinion, as were Robinson and Coke in late-seventeenth-century England. And Mandeville argued in the early eighteenth century that "private vices by the dextrous management of a skillful politician may be turned into public benefits"—that is, tax and other incentives might be used by the state to steer economic activity.[21] Heckscher suggests that neither Colbert nor Axel Oxenstierna was "able even approximately to attain the ideal of a completely restriction-free state of affairs" but that "such was their ideal."[22]

Medieval regulation survived through the period of mercantilism. But an interpretation of the period must allow for possible discrepencies between law and practice. Administration was weak, and many violations went unchallenged.[23] There was much smuggling and evasion. Some violators paid fines, and others paid off corrupt officials or threatening informers—actions that could be interpreted as "market" transactions. Indeed, a cynical view of mercantilist policy is that it was really aimed at redistribution from producers and traders to officials and informers. But this tempting hypothesis is not consistent with the fervor with which the regulations were sometimes enforced. It has been estimated that upwards of 16,000 people died in seventeenth-century France over the question of printed calicoes, many through executions for dealing in this prohibited good, others in armed frays between proponents and opponents.[24]

Over the course of time, prohibitions and detailed regulations gradually gave way to taxes and tariffs and a degree of latitude. Adam Smith attacked even these relatively mild market incentives, and his arguments paved the way for total repeal, leading to free trade in nineteenth-century Britain and a high degree of laissez faire in many other countries. The residue of medieval and mercantile regulations were largely removed during the mid nineteenth century.

The English prohibition on forestalling, engrossing, and regrating offers a useful illustration of the interplay between markets and economic policy. These prohibitions were aimed primarily at foodstuffs, although they were applied to other unmanufactured products as well. In the medieval days of limited transportation, with each town and its surrounding countryside relatively isolated, getting grain and other foods to the town market was a life-and-death matter for the town's residents. The prohibitions were designed to keep prices in the towns down by ensuring supply from the surrounding countryside and to protect both farmers and consumers from "middlemen" who might corner the market on a particular product and charge monopolistic prices. As transportation improved, however, the degree of potential competition increased. This was especially so with the great English turnpike and canal boom of the late eighteenth century, which was followed somewhat later by similar developments on the Continent. (The overland travel time between London and Edinburgh dropped from 14 days to 48 hours between 1750 and 1850, one rough measure of the improvements in transportation.) Under these circumstances, as Edmund Burke pointed out, the provisions against "forestalling and regrating" actually increased the price of food in the towns rather than holding it down as intended. With the widening of markets, regrating—that is, wholesaling—became a necessary economic function to move food and other materials from areas of surplus to distant towns. Burke successfully led a move to repeal the relevant statutes in 1772, but the prohibitions continued to be enforced occasionally at common law for another quarter-century.[25]

The sweatshop abuses of a laissez faire system led in the late nineteenth century to new regulations concerning industrial safety, hours of work, and minimum (rather than maximum) wages. But by and large the Western economies are still relatively free of regulations compared with the situation before the nineteenth century.

Money Markets and Monetary Policy

It was argued earlier that national monetary policy requires a national money market. Such money markets were slow to develop, and they evolved with the art and sophistication of banking. By 1810 there were already substantial flows of short-term credit between different regions of England, but marked interest-rate differentials continued to exist for several decades; the flows of credit were not of sufficient magnitude to weld the various regional markets into one national market. In 1826 the Bank of England set up a number of branches throughout the country to compete with local banks for deposits, and in the 1850s commercial-bill brokers and the London discount houses established agencies in different parts of the country.[26] These extensions were facilitated by the improvements in transportation and by the rapid spread of the railroad and the telegraph throughout the country, which made communication far more rapid and reliable than before. Already by 1873 Walter Bagehot could write (with some exaggeration) that savings from the agricultural districts "are first lodged in the local banks, are by them sent to London, and are deposited with London bankers, or with the bill brokers. In either case the result is the same. The money thus sent up from the accumulating districts is employed in discounting the bills of the industrial districts.... Lombard Street is thus a perpetual agent between the two great divisions of England—between the rapidly-growing districts, where almost any amount of money can be well and easily employed, and the stationary and the declining districts, where there is more money than can be used.... Thus English capital runs as surely and instantly where it is most wanted, and where there is most to be made of it, as water runs to find its level."[27] Bagehot observed that England in his day had achieved a single money market, and he at once drew the conclusion that the Bank of England, as by then the sole bank of issue in England, could and should influence national monetary conditions through its discount policies in London. Up until that time the Bank of England had played the role of central bank with respect to government financing, and it had responded on occasion to support particular banks that were in financial difficulty by rediscounting their short-term assets. But the 1870s marked the period in which the Bank began to take responsibility for the general monetary condition of the country.[28] Even then the new task was taken up only gradually and with caution. It was not until World War I, when treasury bills were first issued in great volume (they had been introduced in 1877, on Bagehot's suggestion, as a possible instrument of monetary policy), that the Bank of England engaged in open-market operations on any scale. By then an extensive system of branch banking had spread throughout the country, ensuring the unity of the national money market.[29]

A similar pattern appears in other countries, but at later times. The market for short-term credit in the United States was still quite localized in 1870, although considerable interregional lending was taking place. By 1900, however, there was a strong convergence of interest rates in all major regions of the United States, suggesting the existence of a truly national market. As in England, commercial bills provided the key link between regions; bills issued in regions of high interest rates would quickly be purchased by banks in regions with ample funds. The emergence of a national money market not only pulled regional short-term interest rates together, but through greater competition it also reduced bank commission rates from as high as 0.5 percent in the 1870s to 0.125 percent by the late 1880s. The development of a national long-term capital market took place more slowly, but the same general forces could be observed. Here the principal instruments of integration were the insurance companies, especially after state regulatory restraints on their purchase of out-of-state corporate bonds and mortgages were removed around the turn of the century.[30]

The Federal Reserve System was created in 1913 in response to the felt need for a national monetary policy and to the new capacity to have a national monetary policy. The system contained twelve districts, and it was envisaged that these districts would exercise a certain amount of independence in their pursuit of monetary objectives—an expectation that reflected a view that regional money markets were reasonably cohesive but were less closely linked to one another. But by the 1920s (as in the case of England, World War I had led to a great expansion in the volume of treasury bills) it was clear that the regional markets were so closely linked to one another that the regional banks could not pursue independent rediscount policies for more than a short period of time. Open-market operations to affect general credit conditions began in the early 1920s, and they took place predominantly and later exclusively in New York, in confident expectation that the market impact would rapidly diffuse throughout the country.

In Europe, bank mergers toward the end of the nineteenth century played a central role in the creation of national markets for short-term funds. This was true in England, France, Germany, and, at the turn of the century, Italy.[31] National monetary policy on the Continent lagged behind that in Britain, largely because the development of national money markets was slower and, when it came, rested in the hands of relatively few banks, so that policy could be effected as easily through directives to those banks as by market transactions of the central bank. Both instruments were used, and in any case the transmission of monetary impulses throughout the economy depended, as in the United States and Britain, on the existence of a national market, even if that market was sometimes made by relatively few banking institutions.

The contrast between these countries and many less-developed countries today is noteworthy. Many less-developed countries do not have, and cannot have, monetary policy in the sense of instruments that influence national credit conditions through actions by the central bank, for they have no national financial markets. At best, they can try to influence monetary conditions by directives to commercial banks, and by providing some regional banking facilities of their own. Even then, monetary control is impeded by the very large currency holdings in most such countries relative to short-term credit. Currency holdings are subject to periodic waves of hoarding and dishoarding (that is, changes in velocity), making monetary control difficult.[32]

Regulation and Taxation within the United States

The consequences of increased mobility and enlargement of the market for the economic policies of jurisdictions smaller than the market can be observed in the attempts of the various states of the United States to regulate and tax business enterprise over the years. Under the American constitution, large powers are reserved to the individual states of the union. But they are also placed under the obligations not to impede interstate commerce and to honor contracts made in other states. With vast improvements in transportation permitted by the railroad, the steamship, and the telegraph, markets grew over the nineteenth century from local to statewide to national in scope. A parallel and closely related rise in the mobility of firms, which were increasingly able to serve a wide market from a variety of locations, gradually eroded the capacity of the states to regulate and to tax business.

State corporation laws were originally the most popular and effective way of regulating incorporated businesses.[33] In 1886, for example, Massachusetts passed new corporation statutes designed to prevent fraud or mismanagement by firms incorporated in the state. The directors and officers of Massachusetts corporations were made personally liable to creditors if the firms' debts exceeded their capital. The valuation of new stock had to be approved by the state commissioner of corporations. So long as similar laws prevailed in other industrial states, Massachusetts corporations had little to gain from incorporating elsewhere.

The system of corporate regulation through state law became unstable during the following two decades. First New Jersey, then Delaware began to exploit the provisions in the U.S. constitution prohibiting impediments to interstate commerce and requiring that contracts made in any state be honored in any other state. New Jersey liberalized its laws of incorporation in 1896 by allowing new stock valuation to be entirely at the discretion of the corporation directors; it had earlier permitted debts to exceed capitalization. Both provisions laid the basis for the Standard Oil Company and other giant firms incorporated in New Jersey. The state benefited from a modest tax on the value of corporate capital.

New Jersey's bid for corporations undermined the regulatory corporation laws of other states. Massachusetts corporations, for example, could circumvent regulation simply by incorporating in New Jersey, and a strict Massachusetts law would fail in its purpose. In 1902 a special Massachusetts commission reported "a general practice" of organizing corporations outside Massachusetts to do business within the state. The commission drafted a new, permissive corporation law, which was enacted virtually without change a year later. The restrictions of 1886 were largely eliminated.

In a series of laws starting in the first decade of the twentieth century, Delaware relaxed greatly its restrictions on incorporation, and in the end maintained virtually no requirements regarding the capital structure of a corporation registered in the state. Directors were not closely bound by their charters in issuing new stock. Illinois had tried to police the capital structure of corporations, but in 1933 it virtually adopted the latest Delaware revisions of 1927 and 1929, illustrating a kind of Gresham's Law in corporate regulation. In the same year, however, the federal government undertook much greater responsibility for regulating public stock issues under the Securities and Exchange Act.

State taxation provides a second, more recent illustration of the severe constraints imposed on the states by close competition with their neighbors.

Wide taxing powers are nominally reserved to the states. Yet, although authorities in state taxation complain bitterly about the large differences in tax structure and tax treatment of business income and commodities from state to state, these differences are very narrow compared with those between countries. Commodity taxation is predominantly at the retail level—the administratively simpler manufacturers' excise tax is virtually nonexistent—and the rates are very close to one another, particularly between contiguous states. State taxation of corporate income also tends to be much the same from state to state, and differences in rates, coverage, and definition of taxable income have narrowed over time.[34]

The reasons for increasing uniformity are obvious enough. The freedom of commodities, capital, and persons to move from state to state without legal impediment, and the ease with which they do so, reduces greatly the scope for wide differences in tax treatment, since both purchasers and sellers will leave the high-tax states. A striking example of the pressures toward uniformity is provided by North Carolina's adoption in 1957 of a new tax law which changed the basis for calculating state taxes on the net income of corporations engaged in interstate commerce. The new law had the effect of reducing the tax burden on out-of-state corporations making interstate sales from bases in North Carolina; moreover, it relieved in-state corporations from paying North Carolina income taxes on income derived from out-of-state sales.[35] The tax change was frankly designed "to encourage more industry to locate and expand in the State."[36] Within three years South Carolina and Virginia had adopted essentially the same formula—as the governor of South Carolina explained, "to keep competitive."[37] In the same vein, an Indiana state Tax Study Commission wrote in 1952 that "it is of the utmost importance to maintain Indiana's tax position [vis-à-vis business] as compared to competing industrial states, and any adjustments in rate or structure must give this position first consideration."[38]

Under this pressure of acute competition for industry, measures are taken which benefit industrial firms but which, since most states are following similar practices, may not much affect the actual location of industry. It is not surprising, therefore, that there are perennial cries for greater coordination of state taxation, and even for uniformity. In 1957 the National Conference of Commissioners on Uniform State Laws approved a model Uniform Division of Income for Tax Purposes Act which would eliminate the pointless competition among states in their tax laws. But no state acting alone has much incentive to adopt it. Hence, even state tax commissioners and others who might be supposed to be jealous of states' rights have called on the federal government to impose uniformity on state taxation of corporations engaged in interstate commerce (which means in effect virtually all direct taxes on business).[39]

Much of this competition among the states arises from the mobility of business. Taxation and regulatory activities are less effective if the range of feasible business locations exceeds the jurisdiction of the taxing or regulatory authorities. State regulatory laws began to lose effect around the turn of the century when American corporations increasingly became truly national in their operations.

Just as high locational mobility eroded the capacity of the states to tax and regulate business activity because of competition to retain industry, it also provided an incentive to subsidize new industries in various ways, in order to attract them for the sake of their employment, their local spending, and their incremental contribution to local revenues. Competition among the states for mobile industry has taken the form of tax concessions, low-interest loans, site preparation, and free land. The progress of one form of this competition is instructive. Under U.S. tax law the interest on bond issues by states and municipalities is exempt from federal income taxes. This practice results in substantially lower interest rates on state and local bonds than on corporate bonds. In the mid 1950s several municipalities began to issue "industrial development bonds" in their own name, entitling the interest to exemption from tax, for the purpose of re-lending to business firms that located in the issuing municipalities. In 1956 this practice existed in only three states, with total issues amounting to less than $2 million. By 1967, the practice had extended to 40 states and total industrial development bonds issues were $1.3 billion.[40] At that magnitude, these bonds pushed up the interest rates payable on all state and local bonds, and of course with so many states employing the same incentive the net effect on industrial location was greatly diminished. The practice had come to represent merely a transfer from the immobile taxpayers of each jurisdiction (and, in this case, from the federal treasury) to the business firms benefiting from the loans. In 1968 the U.S. Congress interceded by placing severe limits on the scope for such financing.

A final illustration is provided by the efforts of many cities to provide welfare payments to their poorest residents, i.e. to redistribute income from taxpayers to the poor. Welfare payments in the relatively wealthy cities, such as New York and Philadelphia, were attractive to many individuals from poorer parts of the country, who flocked to these cities in large numbers during the 1950s and the early 1960s. The tax burden on other residents became onerous, and they in turn moved out of the cities to the suburbs, which were separate local jurisdictions with their own taxes and expenditures, often lower but in any case more closely tailored to the preferences of the mobile, middle-class suburbanites. Once again, the federal government interceded to at least a modest degree by providing welfare payments (to those with dependent children) out of national tax revenues. An effort to "nationalize" the entire welfare system in the United States has been mounted.

In all these instances, mobility of firms or persons greatly altered the capacity of local or state jurisdictions to carry out their aims of economic policy, and a much larger jurisdiction—the federal government—ultimately took over at least part of the responsibility.[41] This is an evolution with lessons for the world economy.

Increased Mobility in the World Economy

Signs can be seen today that suggest the beginnings of a similar process of transformation of national policy through the growth of international markets. The example that has perhaps received the greatest attention is monetary policy, where it has been argued since the early 1960s that the United States exerts a strong influence on monetary conditions in other countries, through its own monetary policy in interplay with the structure of the international monetary system, and that it fails to take adequately into account their policy objectives in framing U.S. monetary policy. In particular, it was said in the early 1960s that U.S. monetary policy was too expansionary, and that the United States was thereby exporting inflation, even though U.S. unemployment was well above target during that period and prices in the United States were virtually stable. Then in 1969 the United States was accused of putting other economies through a monetary wringer because of its inappropriately tight monetary policy. The linkage in both cases was short-term capital movements, primarily between the U.S. banking system and other countries—in the latter period through U.S. bank borrowing in the Eurodollar market in London and other European financial centers. These linkages affected other economies directly because of the commitment, before 1973, by each country to maintain a fixed (though alterable) exchange rate between its currency and the U.S. dollar. Under those conditions, monetary easing in the United States led to capital outflows to other countries, which in turn led to monetary expansion in those countries as the central bank bought dollars in exchange for local currency. Monetary autonomy is lost, except for those few countries—the United States and possibly Germany—that are large enough to influence world monetary conditions and have adequate reserves or other means of finance to do so. In resisting this implication of world monetary integration through markets, countries first imposed various kinds of controls or other impediments on the movement of financial capital, then in 1973 allowed their currencies to "float" so that the link between U.S. monetary conditions and local monetary conditions would be broken or at least weakened.

The foreign trade flows of most countries are not so great as are interregional flows within the countries, a point that is germain to the effectiveness of fiscal policy as an instrument of economic stabilization. But already in the late 1950s economic ties were sufficiently close among the six members of the European Economic Community that member countries would have been ill advised to ignore either the "leakages" from their own actions into the economies of other member countries or the impact on their own economies of fiscal actions in other countries. On one estimate, for example, a 5 percent increase in government expenditure in Germany would in equilibrium have increased the German gross national product by 1.64 percent, but it would also have increased the French GNP by 1.53 percent. The leakages from Belgium and the Netherlands were sufficiently high that the income multiplier associated with additional government expenditure was barely above unity.[42] Fiscal leverage has surely declined further in the ensuing years.

Moreover, even among nations, as among the U.S. states, competition for industrial location has occasionally become fierce in recent years. Many nations now offer tax holidays, free or low-cost land, site preparation, cheap credit, and even cheap utilities in order to attract internationally mobile manufacturing establishments to their shores. Ireland, Britain, Belgium, France, and Italy all maintain aggressive "regional" policies designed to attract industry, and though the industry sometimes comes from elsewhere within each country, more often it involves new location by a foreign firm. And of course such firms will shortly be able to export throughout a virtually tariff-free European market.

Extensive competition among developing countries for foreign firms has developed in Southeast Asia and in the Caribbean area. In 1965 Taiwan promulgated its Statute for the Encouragement of Investment and gave it much publicity in foreign circles. This act in some respects only consolidated a number of favors that were already available to foreign investors, but it also augmented them. Within three years, similar acts were promulgated in the Philippines, Malaysia, Singapore, Thailand, and Indonesia, all trying to attract export-oriented manufacturing industries and all relying on tax holidays, rapid depreciation, import-duty exemption, and various assistance in getting them established.[43] Similarly, the smaller countries bordering the Caribbean all maintain relatively low corporate tax rates and provide tax holidays and other forms of encouragement to foreign investors. In this case there has been some loose coordination among countries within the Central American Common Market, but stiff competition remains among them. (Of course, countervailing forces of nationalism and xenophobia are also present in many less-developed countries, and these act as deterrents to foreign investments.)

In addition, various countries have established a reputation as "havens" for corporate headquarters or as sales or finance subsidiaries from onerous national regulations: Switzerland for taxes, Luxembourg for corporate regulation, the Bahamas and Curaçao for regulation on securities and banking. Indeed, the entire Eurocurrency market represents something of an escape from national banking regulations, for, while it is located in European countries with a long tradition of bank regulation, the fact that Eurocurrency deposits and loans are denominated in currencies other than that of the host country serves as a rationale for excusing these operations from many of the standard regulations. Competition among centers inhibits the imposition of regulation by any one, for the business may simply move elsewhere.[44] The rapid growth of the international bond market also reflects in substantial degree the evasion of national measures, in this case income taxes on interest earnings.[45]

International mobility has now reached the point, moreover, at which it plays an important role in the framing of domestic economic policies. Business argues successfully against certain domestic tax reforms on the grounds that it will place firms at a disadvantage vis-à-vis their foreign competitors. A leading Canadian company, Massey-Ferguson, successfully threatened to move its headquarters and other operations out of Canada if certain changes were made in Canadian regulations. And, as noted above, the prospect of losing the financial business has been an important factor inhibiting regulation of the Eurocurrency market.

The new mobility affects individuals as well as banks and firms. International tourism has become a booming business, providing opportunities for consumption of items that may be proscribed at home (such as liqueur-filled chocolates, Cuban cigars, or abortions). South Africa is doing a growing international business in surgery, which has become enormously expensive in the United States. Mexico and the state of Nevada do a thriving business in granting divorces to refugees from U.S. states with stricter requirements. In the late 1960s, summer excursion fares across the English Channel were low enough to permit French housewives to do their weekly grocery shopping in Britain, where prices for meat, butter, cheese, tea, and other products were about half what they were in France. (Britain's adoption of the

European common agricultural policy put a stop to that type of arbitrage.) Tens of thousands of American draft evaders found haven in Canada, Sweden, and other countries during the Vietnam War.

The "brain drain" reflects a high and growing locational mobility on the part of skilled individuals throughout the world, and this mobility imposes increasingly severe constraints on the ability of countries of origin to tax heavily or otherwise impose regulations on the activities of these individuals. Indeed, this mobility will create acute difficulties on the ability of poor countries to achieve a more equitable distribution of income, for they will have to pay something closer to the "world price" to keep these individuals from emigrating, but incomes will be greatly above average incomes in most developing countries.[46]

Some Speculations about the Future World Economy

These lectures can be concluded with some broad generalizations about the past and some bold speculations about the future. I have argued that the economic policies of western countries are market-oriented and are heavily dependent on markets for their effectiveness, that in some important realms of policy (especially economic stabilization) the markets must be national in scope, and that when markets exceed the jurisdiction of governmental action many economic policies are greatly weakened in their effects and at the same time governments are drawn toward new measures that take advantage of the wider mobility. To this must be added the observation that markets are being widened, and have been for many years, largely under the impetus of lower costs of transportation and communication, with the latter playing an especially important role in the widening of financial markets and in overseas investment.[47] Therefore, the problems sketched here will materialize in one form or another.

A broad view of the history of economic policy suggests that for many centuries its purposes were to augment the wealth of the ruler, and secondarily to provide public works, to stabilize prices (especially food and the closely related rate of interest for consumption loans), and to control the quality of goods and services. The person and the position of the ruler were gradually separated in Western countries, and the function of economic policy was correspondingly altered. Moreover, under the influence of libertarianism it diminished sharply in the nineteenth century. As late as the 1920s government responsibility for the economy in most Western countries was minimal, confined to eliminating the worst abuses of the sweatshop, maintaining the gold value of the national currency, and providing the bare rudiments of social security. The tragic experience of the 1930s shocked governments into action, and a revolution in economic thought, associated in the Anglo-Saxon world with Keynes and built on new national income concepts and measurements, gave them the tools. They set out not only to tame the business cycle but also to reduce other sources of insecurity by providing unemployment compensation, disability payments, old-age pensions, and, more recently, medical care. Since World War II we have placed ever greater responsibilities on government—that is to say, although it is not always so perceived by the public, we have accepted greater collective responsibility—by laying down more exacting standards for social security and for stabilization and employment and by adding economic growth, price stability, and control of the physical environment to the list of objectives.

Because of the social conflict involved, our distributional objectives have been more modest and less fully articulated. The desire for price stability can be interpreted as reflecting distributional concerns. So can the desire for economic growth, which bypasses questions of redistribution by enlarging the economic pie for all and even by permitting some redistribution out of the increment to national income. Much redistribution, of course, is incidental to reduction in the hazards of life, such as insurance, and some takes place through differential financing of public goods, such as education and housing. We no longer hear mention of Keynes's radical proposal for euthanasia of the rentier by driving the rate of interest to zero, which arose from a now-discarded theory of the chronic proclivity of capitalist systems to oversave. But contemporary currents in thought suggest that redistributive aims will be much more prominent in the next decade than in the recent past.

In sum, our desires and expectations have increased with and even beyond the capability of governments to manage the economy, and that capability itself has improved with technological improvements in transportation and communication and with the closely related growth in markets. The growth of markets increased the span of effective control of national governments; indeed the very formation of nations—England and France in the sixteenth century, the United States in the eighteenth century, and Germany and Italy in the nineteenth century—is linked in part to this growth of markets. The growth of markets continues, outrunning governmental jurisdictions as it has done in the past and calling for further adaptation of economic policies and further enlargement of jurisdictions.

If markets exceed the span of national control, then the economists' models of market behavior come into play, where the decisionmaking units are nations in competitive or oligopolistic relationship to one another.

Competitive relationships with perfect markets would lead to complete erosion of many national policies. To take the most obvious and topical example, national monetary policy would be completely frustrated (under fixed exchange rates) in any attempt to influence domestic demand or credit conditions by inflows or outflows of funds. Similar arbitrage would penalize nations that attempt to maintain business taxes or regulations more severe than those prevailing elsewhere, since firms would move away from the country with onerous conditions. Thus, there would be strong (and, in the limiting case, irresistible) pressure for each country to conform to the international norm. Government actions would be strongly conditioned by an environmental constraint. Just as we would lose much control in the physicists' ideal world without friction, governments would lose much control in a frictionless economic world of high mobility.

What would determine the international norm? This is difficult to say exactly, for it depends on precisely what nations are trying to accomplish and on the instruments they employ. But competition among nations might completely erode regulation and taxation of all those firms and individuals whose presence is strongly desired in several areas. Thus, we would observe two processes in this kind of world: arbitrage that pushes many national policies toward some common norm, and competition among nations that determines the norm. The mechanism is analogous to that in competitive markets, in which all firms find themselves to be price-takers and in which unrestricted entry drives marginal supranormal profit rates to zero.

It was the genius of Adam Smith, and the major contribution of economic analysis to the history of ideas, to point out conditions under which business enterprise in its attempt to maximize profits would paradoxically compete them away completely through entry-and-exit arbitrage and therefore allow private self-seeking to lead to a social optimum. This proposition laid the intellectual foundation for the extreme individualistic philosophy of the nineteenth century. But does Smith's normative analysis apply also to free competition among nations? This depends in part on one's attitudes toward government action. Those who think that government interference with free market forces already far exceeds prudence will welcome any erosion in the direction of laissez faire. Others will deplore it. But reference to a "free-for-all" in policies does not settle the matter analytically, for, as Smith showed, a "free-for-all" under competitive conditions will lead to one concept of a social optimum.

The application of Adam Smith's normative proposition depends in part also on the particular issue. In the case of control over products and over productive processes, there is much to be said for decentralization among nations, except when external effects beyond the national jurisdiction are large. Extensive use of the oceans or the atmosphere for disposal of long-lived noxious substances (such as DDT or radioactive material) or extensive weather modification represent actions that clearly transcend merely national concern. But external effects would not be large for most productive processes, and it would be a mistake to impose uniform standards of pollution or safety on all processes, wherever located. Rather, full information concerning the polluting effects or the dangers associated with each productive process should be made known to all. Countries will then compete for the location of mobile firms. That competition will, in general, be optimal for the world so long as it takes place with full information and so long as the international monetary system has an adequate adjustment mechanism so that the competition does not take place for balance-of-payments reasons. At the margin, a higher level of pollution or a lower level of safety may be acceptable to some countries for the sake of higher real incomes or for distributional reasons.

While allocational efficiency will fare well under a decentralized system of governments competing for mobile resources, many redistributional aims will be undercut. It will be difficult (in the limiting case, impossible) to tax mobile factors of production on any basis other than the benefit principle. Immobile factors may, of course, be taxed more heavily than would be warranted on the benefit principle for the sake of subsidizing mobile factors. To the extent that distributional considerations are given weight in many countries, therefore, it will be desirable to address the principles that should govern taxation of income and wealth in the world as a whole, or at least within the domain of high mobility, and to agree on a code of behavior among the relevant countries, much as the General Agreement on Tariffs and Trade represents a code of behavior governing tariffs and other restrictions to trade. In the absence of such codes, improvement in the mobility of capital and skilled individuals relative to unskilled individuals will worsen the distribution of income among the total world population.[48]

Economic stabilization is another area of economic policy that will not fare well under a decentralized system of government with efficient world markets. Actions by individual nations (except the largest, which by virtue of their size can hope to influence world economic conditions) will lose their effectiveness through "leakages" to or from other countries. To protect their control over national economic developments, nations will be tempted to impose barriers to transactions with foreigners. Indeed, many such barriers, especially to the movement of funds, have already been imposed to preserve some degree of national autonomy in matters of economic policy. The more constructive course of action would be to begin framing macroeconomic policy at a regional or global level. A start has been made in the European Community, but in these matters the community is perhaps already too small, for the domain of mobility of some factors of production already exceeds its span of control.

Such international public goods as anti-monopoly control, public health, and weather modification also have to be dealt with at a level well beyond national states.

To sum up, in a conclusion that is thoroughly Wicksellian both in its utopian quality and in its practical necessity, we need a system of functional federalism among nations, with different economic functions handled at different levels of government—some at the present national level, but others at the supranational level and still others at the subnational level. The growth of markets, efficient in itself, makes such a development increasingly imperative.

Mathematical Appendix

1. Consider first a two-country world characterized by the following relationships:

$Y = C + X - M + Z,$

$C = C(Y),$

$M = M(Y),$

$X = X(Y') = M'.$

Here Y is national income, C is consumption, X is exports of goods and services, all in constant prices. Z represents all other autonomous expenditure. Let a similar set of relationships apply for a second country, designated by primed variables.

Combining terms and differentiating completely yields the following system of simultaneous equations:

$$\begin{bmatrix} s+m & -m' \\ -m & s'+m' \end{bmatrix} \begin{bmatrix} dY \\ dY' \end{bmatrix} = \begin{bmatrix} dZ \\ dZ' \end{bmatrix}$$

where $s = 1 - \partial C/\partial Y$, $m = \partial M/\partial Y$, and similarly for the primed country. Solving:

$$\begin{pmatrix} dY \\ dY' \end{pmatrix} = \frac{1}{\Delta} \begin{bmatrix} s' + m' & m' \\ m & s + m \end{bmatrix} \begin{pmatrix} dZ \\ dZ' \end{pmatrix}$$

where $\Delta = (s + m)(s' + m') - mm' = ss' + sm' + s'm$. This gives the familiar Keynesian foreign-trade multipliers with allowance for foreign repercussions.

We want to know both the impact on world income and the impact on country income of an increased expenditure in, say, the unprimed country as the degree of interdependence—measured here by m and m'—varies. Suppose there is a proportionate increase k in both m and m'. Then it can readily be shown that

$$\frac{\partial}{\partial k}\left(\frac{dY}{dZ}\right) = \frac{1}{\Delta^2}(-s'^2 m) < 0,$$

$$\frac{\partial}{\partial k}\left(\frac{dY'}{dZ}\right) = \frac{1}{\Delta^2}(mss') > 0.$$

That is, as the degree of interdependence rises, the impact of a given increase in expenditure on income in the country of expenditure declines, and the impact on income in the other country rises. Moreover, in the special case where $s = s'$, $dY + dY' = (1/s)dZ$, that is, the change in world income is not influenced by the values of m and m', and any gain in impact in one country's income as a result of changes in m and m' is exactly offset by a reduced impact on the other country's income. (If $s \neq s'$, interdependence brings out compositional effects on the aggregate world saving rate, and hence on the total impact on world income.)

2. Generalization of these results to three countries is relatively straightforward, although some new complexities are introduced. The basic structure becomes

$$\begin{bmatrix} s + m_1 & -m_{12} & -m_{13} \\ -m_{21} & s + m_2 & -m_{23} \\ -m_{31} & -m_{32} & s + m_3 \end{bmatrix} \begin{bmatrix} dY_1 \\ dY_2 \\ dY_3 \end{bmatrix} = \begin{bmatrix} dZ_1 \\ dZ_2 \\ dZ_3 \end{bmatrix}$$

where (to avoid compositional effects on the world savings rate) s is assumed to be the same in all three regions, m_{ij} is the marginal propensity of region j to import from region i, and $m_i = \Sigma_j m_{ij}$.

It is necessary here to introduce some assumption concerning "economic distance." This can be done by assuming $m_{31} \leqslant m_{21}$, $m_{12} = m_{32}$, $m_{13} \leqslant m_{23}$. In words, the second region is assumed equally "distant" from the first and the third, and these two regions are assumed to be farther from each other than they are from the second. The additional assumption $m_1 \leqslant m_2 \leqslant m_3$ is then sufficient to establish

$$\frac{dY_1}{dZ_1} > \frac{dY_2}{dZ_1} \geqslant \frac{dY_3}{dZ_1},$$

as can be readily shown by solving the above system of equations for these magnitudes. Once again, $\Sigma\, dY_i = (1/s)dZ$, that is, the change in world income is independent of the values of m_{ij}, but a proportionate increase in those values will reduce dY_1/dZ_1 and increase the impact of dZ_1 on incomes in the other two regions.

A generalization of this result for continuous regions leads to

$$\int_0^w dY(r)dr = (1/s)dZ$$

and to the other results associated with figures 1 and 2. The results shown there as schedules c and c' can be achieved if $m_{ij} = m$ for all $i \neq j$ and in addition if the marginal propensity to spend in each region directly out of the initial expenditure, dZ, is equal for all regions. They can also be achieved even when the initial expenditure is made exclusively in the region of origin if the marginal propensity to import into that region is sufficiently higher than the marginal propensity to import into other regions. For the two-region case the requisite condition is $m = s' + m'$. An analogous but more complicated condition is required for three or more regions.

3. The formulations above assume that a country can sustain an imbalance in trade for some time. Incomes adjust to expenditures regardless of the effect on the trade balance. McKinnon and Oates have analyzed an alternative model of a single country with an expenditure (dZ) financed by selling bonds to foreigners—the case of a small country embedded in a perfect international bond market.[49] They also require that in equilibrium international payments must be in balance and that private holdings of assets are unchanging.

If the further assumption is made that the marginal propensity to import out of the initial expenditure is the same as it is out of additional income, then $dM = dZ$ (exports assumed exogenous and imports rise to equal capital inflow) and $dM = mdZ + md Y$, from which it follows that $dY/dZ = (1 - m)/m$, independent of s. Also,

$$\frac{\partial(dY/dZ)}{\partial m} = \frac{-1}{m^2} < 0,$$

so that a rising m reduces the impact of expenditure on income. Indeed, for

$m > \frac{1}{2}$, $dY/dZ < 1$. The effect of fiscal policy is weakened as the economy becomes more open in trade. This result is reached by supposing that any change in private asset holdings arising from a payments imbalance (a surplus in the case of a country financing its government expenditure by selling bonds abroad) will shift the level of expenditure and income by enough to eliminate the payments imbalance. Thus,

$$dY = cdY - mdY + (1-m)dZ + adA,$$

where dA is the change in net private assets, c is the marginal propensity to spend out of income, and a is the marginal propensity to spend out of changes in assets. This formulation does not incorporate secondary repercussions arising from induced changes in income in the rest of the world, as our previous model did.

4. Let us return to the two-country model of the first section of this article and interpret the autonomous expenditure terms dZ and dZ' as random disturbance terms with zero means and standard deviations σ and σ' respectively. Then, with no trade, the standard deviations of Y and Y' will be σ/s and σ'/s', respectively, in the absence of offsetting action. World income is $Y + Y'$, and its standard deviation in this world of closed economies is

$$\omega = [(\sigma/s)^2 + (\sigma'/s')^2 + 2(\sigma/s)(\sigma'/s')\varrho]^{1/2},$$

where ϱ is the correlation between disturbances dZ and dZ'.

If the two countries engage in trade, then

$$\begin{pmatrix} dY \\ dY' \end{pmatrix} = \frac{1}{\Delta} \begin{bmatrix} s' + m' & m' \\ m & s + m \end{bmatrix} \begin{pmatrix} dZ \\ dZ' \end{pmatrix}$$

in the absence of offsetting action. The standard deviation of income in the unprimed country, σ_y, is then given by

$$\sigma_y = \frac{1}{\Delta}[(s' + m')^2\sigma^2 + (m'\sigma')^2 + 2m'(s' + m')\sigma\sigma'r]^{1/2}$$

where r is the correlation between disturbances dZ and dZ' when the two countries are joined in trade. An analogous expression holds for $\sigma_{y'}$, the standard deviation of income in the primed country.

Then the standard deviation for world income is

$$\omega^* = [\sigma_y^2 + \sigma_{y'}^2 + 2\sigma_y\sigma_{y'}r]^{1/2}$$

$$= \frac{1}{\Delta}[(s' + m' + m)^2\sigma^2 + (s + m + m')^2\sigma'^2$$

$$+ 2(s' + m' + m)(s + m + m')\sigma\sigma'r]^{1/2}.$$

In the special case where $s = s'$, so that regional composition effects are not present,

$$\omega^* = \frac{1}{s}(\sigma^2 + \sigma'^2 + 2\sigma\sigma'r)^{1/2}.$$

Thus, $\omega^* \gtreqless \omega$ as $r \gtreqless \varrho$. Unless the opening of trade changes ϱ, the variation in world income is not affected. However, individual countries are more interested in the variation of national income. One measure of this national variation for the world as a whole is the sum of the variances in national income:

$$\Omega^* = \sigma_y^2 + \sigma_{y'}^2 = \frac{1}{\Delta^2}\{[(s' + m')^2 + m^2]\sigma^2 + [(s + m)^2 + m'^2]\sigma'^2$$

$$+ 2[m'(s' + m') + m(s + m)]\sigma\sigma'r\}.$$

How does this compare with $\Omega = (\sigma/s)^2 + (\sigma'/s')^2$, the sum of the national variances in the absence of trade? If savings rates differ between the two regions, cases can be found for which $\Omega^* > \Omega$ for $\varrho = r$. Also for $r > 0$ cases can be found for which $\Omega^* > \Omega$ when $s = s'$. However, for $s = s'$ and $r \leq 0$ it can easily be shown that $\Omega^* < \Omega$. Thus, in a world of trade with uncorrelated disturbances the sum of the national variances is reduced. If disturbances are strongly positively correlated, however, it is possible (depending on the exact values of the other parameters) that trade will raise the variation in income in both countries.

Moreover, even if the sum of the variances declines with trade, it is possible for the variance of income of either country alone to be larger with trade. This is most obviously so when the variance of disturbances is much higher in the trading partner than in the home country. In the very special case of two identical trading partners ($s = s'$, $m = m'$, $\sigma = \sigma'$), trade will reduce income variation in both countries so long as $r \leq \varrho < 1$.

Notes

1. If this condition were not met for at least some commodities, the notion of GNP would be nonsense. For example, if grain prices differed radically between two nontrading regions of a given country, a drop in grain production in the low-price region matched by a physically equivalent increase in production in the high-price region, with no change in prices, would show a rise in both measured nominal and measured real GNP. Yet total output, by assumption, has not changed. If prices were to respond to changes in quantities in each region along a rectangular hyperbolic demand curve, the shift would show no change in nominal GNP but an increase in

(base-weighted) real GNP. Under these circumstances, except on highly restrictive assumptions about interpersonal welfare comparisons between two regions, the notion of GNP loses any meaning either as a measure of real output or as a measure of welfare.

2. Walter Bagehot, *Lombard Street* (Homewood, Ill.: Irwin, 1962). Originally published in 1873.

3. This marginal propensity to import is more general than the usual simple Keynesian marginal propensity, for the latter assumes perfectly elastic supply of goods and services both within and outside the community in which the injection of new expenditure takes place. What is relevant here is an elastic supply of goods and services outside that community, but not necessarily inside it. In the limiting case of perfectly inelastic local supply, the relevant marginal propensity to import will be unity.

The blurring of the distinction between countries and regions is in the spirit of Bertil Ohlin's *Interregional and International Trade* (Cambridge, Mass.: Harvard University Press, 1933), for as he pointed out much of the analysis that we normally apply to countries is equally applicable to regions within a country.

4. The "equilibrium" here is a Keynesian one, making no allowance for the continuing flow of assets between one part of the country and another. It is best described as a quasi-equilibrium.

5. Formally, $dY/dG = \int_0^B dY(r)dr = k(s)$, where dG is the step increase in government expenditure, dY is the equilibrium increase in income, r is a variable that runs over regions of the country from the point of expenditure to its borders (B), s is the marginal propensity not to spend, and k is a constant parametric in s. This condition holds regardless of the shape of $dY(r)$, i.e. regardless of the values of the marginal propensity to import among various regions of the country. See the appendix for an algebraic analysis.

6. Where part of a national economy is much closer economically to external areas than it is to other parts of the nation, we may speak of an "enclave." Such enclaves were once frequent in certain export industries of many poor countries, but economic ties to national markets have increased substantially during the past two decades.

7. See the appendix for analysis.

8. The clearest brief exposition of this result is in J. Marcus Fleming, "Domestic Financial Policies under Fixed and under Floating Exchange Rates," IMF Staff Papers, 1962, reprinted in R. N. Cooper (ed.), *International Finance* (London: Penguin, 1969).

9. This possibility has been emphasized by Ronald I. McKinnon in his "Optimum Currency Areas," *American Economic Review*, 1963, reprinted in Cooper, *International Finance*.

10. For a discussion of the public-finance theories of Wicksell and Lindahl, see Carl G. Uhr, *Economic Doctrines of Knut Wicksell* (Berkeley: University of California Press, 1960), pp. 158–190.

11. The criterion for optimality for "pure" public goods, i.e. those with full jointness of consumption by all residents of the jurisdiction in question, is that the sum of the marginal rates of substitution for all individuals must equal the marginal cost of providing the public goods. See Paul A. Samuelson, "The Pure Theory of Public Goods," *Review of Economics and Statistics*, 36 (November 1954): 387–389. This condition will not generally be satisfied under schemes of majority voting, where the preferences of the median voter govern the level of public expenditure. For a rigorous discussion of voting for two or more public goods and the extreme difficulty in obtaining a consistent social ordering, see Gerald H. Kramer, "On a Class of Equilibrium Conditions for Majority Rule," *Econometrica* 41 (March 1973): 285–297.

12. This result was first expounded by Charles Tiebout. See his "A Pure Theory of Local Expenditures," *Journal of Political Economy* 64 (October 1956): 416–424.

13. See James Buchanan, "An Economic Theory of Clubs," *Economica* 32 (February 1965): 1–14.

14. See Kenneth J. Arrow, *Essays in the Theory of Risk-Bearing* (Chicago: Markham, 1971), especially chapters 5 and 9.

15. Some years ago, Gunnar Myrdal wrote perceptively of the deep tension between the national pursuit of national economic policies—what he calls the welfare state—and the integration of the world economy. He emphasizes the commodity disturbances that the world economy thrust on national economies, rather than the pull it may have on mobile factors of production, and the need perceived by governments, growing out of the 1920s and 1930s, to insulate their economies from these disturbances through protective measures. Myrdal perhaps exaggerates the extent of world economic integration before the advent of the welfare state, for high costs of transportation and communications provided a natural barrier of protection from foreign disturbances. See his *Beyond the Welfare State* (New Haven: Yale University Press, 1960), especially chapter 10.

16. Cases can be constructed in which local residents have an incentive to subsidize new investment from outside the region not only for the production of employment but even because it increases after-tax income in a fully employed region. This incentive will arise (1) when public goods have a heavy fixed cost, which can be shared in part with newcomers (i.e. the newcomer pays below average but above marginal cost for these public services), (2) when the newcomer's activity brings with it positive external effects, such as new knowledge not readily available to the community that raises productivity elsewhere in the community, and (3) when the new investment is sufficiently large to alter relative factor prices in favor of local labor at the expense of "foreign" investment already present in the region before the introduction of the subsidy, which is not made available to the old investment.

17. But it could worsen the picture. If the marginal propensity not to spend is higher for firms (and their owners) than it is for workers, a redistribution of income away from workers will reduce aggregate demand. And this technique of competition among regions, unlike competitive depreciation, does not provide any overall monetary stimulus to aggregate demand.

18. This section draws heavily on Eli Heckscher's celebrated treatise *Mercantilism* (trans. by M. Shapiro, rev. ed. by E. F. Söderlund) (New York: Macmillan, 1955). Also, William Letwin, *Law and Economic Policy in America*, (New York: Random House, 1965), chapter 2.

19. It is difficult to appreciate these days the importance of highwaymen and pirates as deterrents to travel. Extension of the rule of law can be just as important in reducing costs as technical improvements in the means of transportation.

20. Heckscher, *Mercantilism*, vol. I, p. 265.

21. Quoted in Heckscher, *Mercantilism*, vol. II, p. 293.

22. Ibid., p. 295.

23. For a discussion of weak enforcement of the apprenticeship rules under England's Statute of Artificers, see Margaret G. Davies, *The Enforcement of English Apprenticeship: A Study in Applied Mercantilism, 1563–1642*, (Cambridge, Mass.: Harvard University Press, 1956).

24. Heckscher, *Mercantilism*, vol. I, p. 173. In England, however, fines were almost exclusively used to penalize violators of the regulations, except in the case of food. Ibid., p. 267.

25. Letwin, *Law and Economic Policy*, pp. 37–38.

26. See W. T. C. King, *History of the London Discount Market* (London, 1932), pp. 272–274.

27. Bagehot, *Lombard Street*, p. 6.

28. Starting in 1839, however, the bank on several occasions rediscounted bills to relieve temporary credit panics. See M. H. de Kock, *Central Banking*, third edition (London: Staples, 1954), p. 147.

29. It was not until 1920, however, that Lloyds Bank established a single deposit rate in its branches throughout the country. See R. S. Sayers, *Lloyds Bank in the History of English Banking* (Oxford: Clarendon, 1957), p. 165.

30. An excellent discussion and analysis of the integration of American money and capital markets can be found in Lance E. Davis, "The Investment Market, 1870–1914: The Evolution of a National Market," *Journal of Economic History* 25 (September 1965): 355–399.

31. See Charles P. Kindleberger, *The Formation of Financial Centers: A Study in Comparative Economic History*, Princeton Study in International Finance no. 36, November 1974. Kindleberger discusses the forces that press toward a single financial center in each country.

32. Ronald I. McKinnon has emphasized the importance of fragmented money and capital markets as an impediment to economic development. See his *Money and Capital in Economic Development* (Washington: Brookings Institution, 1973).

33. This history is taken largely from Meredith Dodd, "Statutory Developments in Business Corporation Law, 1886–1936," *Harvard Law Review* 27 (1937): 32–35.

34. See Special Subcommittee on State Taxation of Interstate Commerce of the Committee on the Judiciary, State Taxation of Interstate Commerce, H. R. Rep. No. 1480, 88th Congress, 2nd Sess. pp. 95–136 (1964). See also J. Maxwell, *The Fiscal Impact of Federalism in the United States* (Cambridge, Mass.: Harvard University Press, 1946), especially chapter 13.

35. The first of these two features recalls some of the tax privileges of foreign corporations setting up sales offices in Switzerland. The second, amounting to a remission of direct taxes on export sales, would at the international level be a clear violation of GATT rules.

36. Advertisement in *New York Times*, Nov. 17, 1957.

37. Special Subcommittee on State Taxation of Interstate Commerce (note 34), pp. 123–126.

38. Quoted in John Due, "Studies on State-Local Tax Influences on Location of Industry," *National Tax Journal* 14 (June 1961): 172n.

39. The situation is actually somewhat more complicated than this implies. States, faced with rapidly increasing needs for revenue, widened their business taxes considerably during the 1950s to include a number of taxes touching significantly on interstate commerce. In 1959 the Supreme Court in *Northwestern States Portland Cement Co. v. Minnesota*, 358 U.S. 450 (1959), upheld the right of Minnesota to tax the net income of an out-of-state business arising from sales in the state. A series of decisions on related cases made clear the wide taxing powers of the states. The business community was alarmed, and in late 1959 Congress passed a law limiting the rights of states to tax interstate commerce. Many states resented the limitation on their taxing powers, but—caught between rising revenue needs and competition with other states—urged the Congress to legislate uniform standards for defining tax base, apportioning income, etc. See Hearings on State Income Taxation of Mercantile and Manufacturing Corporations before a Special Subcommittee of the House Committee on the Judiciary, 87th Congress, 1st Sess. 367 (1961).

40. Advisory Commission on Intergovernmental Relations, *Fiscal Balance in the American Federal System*, vol. I, Washington, 1967, p. 117.

41. Apparently the long-run tendency for the share of the national government in total government expenditures to rise is a general one. Wallace Oates summarizes the evidence for a number of countries. In the period 1950–1965, however, he finds a widespread reversal of this tendency, which he associates with greater reliance in the recent period on intergovernmental grants. Grants from the central government to local governments provide one method for maintaining some influence on the national distribution of income while still supporting public expenditure at the local level. See Wallace E. Oates, *Fiscal Federalism* (New York: Harcourt Brace Jovanovich, 1972), pp. 230–236. This book, which I discovered after these lectures were prepared, covers well a number of the issues raised here, especially those concerning stabilization and local expenditure on public goods.

42. See Stephen A. Resnick, "An Emperical Study of Economic Policy in the Common Market," in Albert Ando et al., *Studies in Economic Stabilization* (Washington: Brookings Institution, 1968), p. 191.

43. Andrew Allen's *Guide for Investment in Developing Countries* (London: Knight, 1973) gives a country-by-country description of the many concessions available.

44. Escape from domestic banking regulation is not new. Kindleberger (*Formation of Financial Centers*, pp. 31, 76) reports that foreign lending by English financiers was stimulated by the usury law of 1571, which set a maximum interest rate on domestic loans of 10 percent, reduced over time to 5 percent in 1713 until its repeal in 1854. And in the mid nineteenth century the Darmstädter Bank was found close to the financial market of Frankfurt but just outside Prussian jurisdiction to circumvent Prussian prohibitions on additional incorporated banks. The Eurodollar market received substantial encouragement first from U.S. limits (through Regulation Q of the Federal Reserve) on interest rates that could legally be paid on deposits, then from limits placed on American bank lending to foreigners from the United States.

45. For a discussion of this growth and some of its implications, see R. N. Cooper, "Towards an International Capital Market?" in C. P. Kindleberger and A. Shonfield (eds.), *North American and Western European Economic Policies* (London: Macmillan, 1971).

46. For a discussion of various facets of this problem, see the essays in Walter Adams (ed.), *The Brain Drain* (New York: Macmillan, 1968). The problem is especially acute with those individuals who have taken advanced study in Europe or North America. Some countries require return to the home country for a minimum period when the study abroad has been financed with public funds (and the United States requires that foreign students spend at least two years outside the United States after completing their studies there). Russia has recently acquired considerable infamy for its emigration tax on Jews, but many other countries are groping for analogous measures to provide a disincentive to emigration (without, however, having the same political overtones as the Russian tax). Jagdish Bhagwati has suggested that a special income tax be levied by rich countries on immigrants from poor countries for payment to the country of origin. This does not, of course, fully address the concerns of those alarmed by the brain drain, who claim that certain dynamic externalities are lost when skilled and educated individuals leave home. See Bhagwati, "The Brain Drain and Income Taxation," *World Development* 1 (1973): 94–98.

47. For some evidence on the internationalization of markets, see Richard N. Cooper, *The Economics of Interdependence* (New York: McGraw-Hill, 1968), especially chapters 3–5, and Assar Lindbeck, *The National State in an Internationalized World Economy* (Rio de Janeiro: Conjunto Universitario Candido Mendes, 1973). Lindbeck's work, which I saw after giving these lectures, covers some of the same issues that are treated here.

48. It may, however, improve world efficiency in the allocation of resources, for the marginal social product of some skilled individuals may be truly higher in countries that already enjoy high skills in quantity, because of better equipment and more stimulating colleagues there, i.e. because of economics of scale.

49. See Ronald I. McKinnon and Wallace E. Oates, *The Implications of International Economic Integration for Monetary, Fiscal, and Exchange-Rate Policy*, International Finance Section, Princeton University, 1966, pp. 16–17.

5

Worldwide Regional Integration: Is There an Optimal Size of the Integrated Area?

A skillful program committee chooses titles for conference papers that deceive in their simplicity, which on close inspection turn out not to be simple at all and which raise more questions than an author can hope to answer in the 5,000 words allotted. Thus the groundwork is laid for future research and future conferences. Certainly the title of this paper is deceptively simple, yet it cloaks a problem that goes to the heart of political theory: How should human beings organize their collective endeavors, especially those that require governmental action, so as best to achieve their diverse and often conflicting objectives? The discussion is necessarily normative and necessarily abstract.

The recent historical origins of the question posed in the title are clear enough. There has been a running debate since World War II (with antecedents in the 1930s) over whether the world economy would be better served by full multilateralism or by regional groupings that "discriminate" in favor of members and against nonmembers. This question arose especially with respect to customs unions and free-trade areas, where the principal instrument of discrimination was the import tariff. But it also arose with respect to balance-of-payments policy (with the Sterling Area and the European Payments Union representing the leading examples of regional groupings) and, more recently, with respect to the domain appropriate for fixed exchange rates among currencies or even for a common currency. As usually posed, these questions concern groupings among *nations*. However, similar questions, deriving from a different starting point, have been asked with increasing force about the optimal provision of public goods and services *within* nations—particularly those with a federal structure, which have shown increasing strain in recent years in trying to provide public goods both efficiently and with sufficient regard for local variations in preferences of the public.

Thus, from a theoretical point of view the issue posed in the title goes beyond possible regional relationships among nations. Put more generally, we can ask what is the optimal combination of communities or regions for an integrated area. In some cases the answer may involve grouping existing nations into a larger region; in others it might involve subdividing existing nations. Before proceeding further we should make a few distinctions about the meaning of "integrated area."

Some Important Distinctions Concerning "Integration"

Although alternative forms of integration will be covered in detail elsewhere, several distinctions are necessary before we proceed to a discussion of optimal integrated areas. First, "integration" can refer to the legal and institutional relationships within a region in which economic transactions take place, or it can refer to the market relationships among goods and factors within the region. This distinction becomes clear when we imagine a nineteenth-century laissez faire economy with no government barriers to interregional transactions but with markets not linked because of ignorance or high transportation costs. A region can be integrated in the first sense but not in the second. If there are institutional or legal barriers to trade and capital movements, on the other hand, markets of course cannot be fully integrated either, at least in the sense of equal product and factor prices. But even then prices may move in parallel with one another, indicating market integration at the margin, i.e., high sensitivity to developments elsewhere in the region.

Before we return to this distinction between institutional and market integration, it is useful to draw a second distinction: between integration as an end in itself or as a state of affairs and integration as a process. Much of the postwar debate on regionalism versus globalism was concerned with process rather than with state of affairs; the advocates of economic regionalism saw it as an effective route to some other objective—either economic globalism or regional political unification. The universalism of the Bretton Woods agreement and of the General Agreement on Tariffs and Trade, both laid down in the 1940s, stood in sharp contrast to the regionalism of the Sterling Area, the European Payments Union, the European Coal and Steel Community, and the European Economic Community. Each of the latter institutions was hotly resisted in its early stages as an undesirable retreat from the universalism which the architects of the postwar international economic system hoped to achieve. The regional institutions, for their part, were rarely justified as ends in themselves, although occasionally that strand of thought was present. Rather, they were regarded as superior means to more far-reaching ends.

Thus, Robert Triffin argued persistently that the European Payments Union, with its implied discrimination against the U.S. dollar, represented much the most effective way to achieve currency convertibility and to restore a truly multilateral system of international payments.[1]

Like-minded countries with similar problems would move more quickly together than they could either separately or when grouped with countries facing very different problems. To try everything at once would stymie progress, as the failure of the International Trade Organization seemed to suggest. On this formulation, the objective of both parties to the debate is the same, namely a multilateral world economy; judgments differed only on the best way to achieve it.

Unfortunately for clarity in the debate, another group, associated with Jean Monnet, had quite different objectives and sought to use the same instruments of economic regionalism to attain their objective of regional political unification. So a confusion was introduced; the probability that economic regionalism would eventually lead to economic universalism was reduced to the extent that it would lead to regional political integration.

Integration as a process on either basis involves establishing a situation that is not in long-run equilibrium; partial integration creates new problems, which in turn call for further integrative measures, and so on.[2] On the first version of integration as process, success among a limited group of countries breeds a willingness by others to join in, and eventually the regional approach becomes global. On the second version, one thing leads to another, and eventually political integration captures the minds of the people, creating durable political bonds within the region. In either of these frames of reference, the "optimal" region for integration is that which best achieves the desired objective rapidly and securely.

We return to economic integration as a state of affairs, rather than as a process. Markets are integrated if one price prevails for each product or factor, after allowance for transportation cost. On this market formulation, the optimum integrated area is the world as a whole, for any artificial interference with price equilibration (except those designed to eliminate market imperfections) will *ipso facto* represent a source of inefficiency in the allocation of resources. What then is the case for regionalism? It lies, I believe, not in the realm of private goods, but in the realm of public or collective goods, where these are defined broadly to include the nature of the economic regime itself, i.e., the system of property ownership, of contract, of risk-bearing, of resource allocation, and the like. Some individuals may not want an economic regime based on markets and may be willing to pay the economic price for that decision. Viewed from the perspective of public goods, "regions" really means governmental jurisdictions, and the enquiry must begin with the economic functions of government. The standard list calls on governments to provide public goods, to stabilize the level and growth of income, to redistribute income, and above all to provide a regulatory framework for economic and social transactions. Whether a region is "optimal" then depends on its optimal suitability for performing these various functions. "Optimal" means best able to serve the various social objectives, where "best" is in the Pareto sense of not permitting closer achievement of one objective without compromising the attainment of some other objective.

The perspective adopted here thus renders irrelevant Viner's classic distinction between trade-creating and trade-diverting customs unions, and their analog in the monetary area. As Cooper and Massel showed a decade ago, in terms of raising real national income a unilateral tariff reduction is superior to the formation of a discriminatory trading bloc, and the formation of customs unions must therefore be rationalized along different lines.[3] Harry Johnson has provided a more general framework for regarding protection in general and customs unions in particular as devices (perhaps inefficient ones) for the attainment of public goods, i.e. features from which the public at large derives some satisfaction, whether they be nationalism, redistribution of income, or a level of industrial production above what could be sustained by the operation of unimpeded market forces.[4] In this context the formation of regional groupings on a discriminatory basis might represent the most efficient method for attaining a given objective; but the results would have to be shown in each specific case, for the general optimality of discriminatory trade or payments arrangements cannot be assumed.

The Optimal Provision of Collective Goods

The optimal provision of public goods involves both technological considerations and the accommodation of public preferences. We will first consider the technological considerations, which generally (but not always) press for enlargement of governmental jurisdiction, while accommodation of public preferences generally (but not always) presses for relatively small governmental jurisdictions.

Three technical factors have a bearing on the provision of public goods: economies of scale, the presence of externalities (including the important special case in which some of the objects of regulation are mobile), and the possibilities for reducing economic disturbances through integrating markets. We will take up each of these considerations in turn, the last especially in the context of economic stabilization.

Economies of Scale

Scale economies offer a traditional argument for increasing the size of jurisdictions, at least up to a point. Certain public goods, especially those requiring for efficiency a high degree of specialization, experience strong economies of scale. Examples would be certain forms of scientific research, public health, police investigatory work, the penal system, some aspects of national defense, and flood control and irrigation. Where scale economies are substantial, the governmental jurisdiction (or its functional equivalent in facilities shared among jurisdictions) must be large enough to encompass the scale required, or else its residents will either enjoy lower-quality services or pay more than is technically necessary for those services.

The optimum scale for governmental jurisdiction will of course vary from public good to public good. Where jurisdictions can be effectively separated along functional lines, they can be tailored to the requirements of each different good. (Los Angeles and London both offer examples of urban areas with many overlapping jurisdictions, drawn in part along functional lines.) Where as a practical matter that is not possible, the choice of scale of a jurisdiction should (other things being equal) be governed by the minimum cost of the package of public goods that is to be offered. Because of organizational, managerial, and informational costs, the optimal jurisdiction will be well below the global level, in contrast to the optimal market area.

External Effects

External effects arise when activities within one jurisdiction affect directly the welfare of residents of another jurisdiction, other than through market prices. External effects can be either positive, as in the case of malarial control, or negative, as in the case of downstream water pollution. In one respect, external effects can be thought of as a more general case of economies (or diseconomies) of scale: Once a service (e.g. malarial control) is provided, the marginal cost of additional consumption (enjoyment) of that service is low or zero, and therefore the average cost to citizens is lower the larger the jurisdiction is in terms of taxable population. It is worthwhile to preserve the distinction between the two considerations, however, since economies of scale normally refer to technical input-output relationships in the production of a well-defined good or service, not to the consumption effects.

A special kind of externality arises from the mobility of the objects of policy action. Here the problem is that a "public good" by community preference may involve unwelcome restraints on certain elements of the community, e.g. its business firms, its radio stations, or its high-income members. Activation of these regulatory or redistributional policies will then drive the adversely affected parties out of a jurisdiction that is too small relative to their domain of mobility. They will escape the onerous action by leaving the jurisdiction in question.[5] To prevent this, the jurisdiction must either inhibit the mobility of its business activities or become large enough to encompass their entire domain of mobility. The latter course does not necessarily involve enlargement to the global level, because as a practical matter persons and firms are not globally mobile. Considerations of economics, geography, language, and culture all limit the actual domain of mobility.

The mobility of factors beyond a government jurisdiction limits the capacity of that jurisdiction to redistribute income. The heavily taxed will move out, and those who are subsidized will move in. Both movements undercut the fiscal viability of redistributional policies. Even trade in goods and services will affect the rewards to factors of production, as is underlined by the Heckscher-Ohlin-Samuelson theorem concerning factor-price equalization. But the imposition of tariffs can alter the free-trade distribution of income, and in any case the resulting factor rewards are *before* allowance for income taxes, which can serve redistributive objectives. It is factor mobility, not commodity movement, that really limits the possibilities for redistribution.

Similar considerations apply to attempts by jurisdictions to regulate business activity, e.g. capital structure, financial disclosure, safety, pollution, and so on. Once the regulations go beyond what is acceptable to the mobile firm, where "acceptability" will be influenced by the competitive environment in which the firm operates, it will depart for a jurisdiction with less onerous regulations.[6] Thus, mobility presses for the enlargement of jurisdictions to make policy effective.

Economic Stabilization

A third consideration for the optimal size of an integrated region concerns the objective of economic stabilization on the assumption that policy measures to stabilize the level of income or employment are uncertain in effect or costly to use. Under these circumstances, any arrangement that reduces the macroeconomic disturbances to the region in question will be beneficial. For a given region, macroeconomic disturbances (that is, disturbances that in the absence of countervailing action would alter perceptibly the level of aggregate income or employment) can arise either within the region or from outside it. Internal disturbances arise from shifts in private or governmental demand for goods and services, variations in weather, and other factors affecting domestic demand and supply; external disturbances arise from similar factors in other countries and are imported from abroad through international trade or capital movements. The region's economy will respond to these disturbances in some well-defined way which depends on (among other things) the openness of the region, and it can take steps to compensate for the disturbance with various regional instruments of policy, whose impact also depends on the structure of the regional economy.

How then should the boundaries of a region be drawn, from the viewpoint of maximizing the stability of the regional economy? By boundaries we mean here the limits of application of tariffs or direct controls on interregional transactions and/or a single currency or fixed exchange rates between currencies within the region.

First, consider the disturbances that create economic instability. If internal disturbances are low compared with those emanating from outside the region, the region should perhaps insulate itself from other regions, using the devices indicated above. This is analogous to risk-splitting in the writing of insurance: a low-risk group can gain by separating itself from the rest. In contrast, if internal disturbances are large relative to those emanating from outside the region, the region may gain by amalgamating with other regions and thus in effect exporting some of its disturbances to the larger area. Finally, if the relative importance of disturbances originating inside the region is about the same as those originating outside but the disturbances have different patterns (i.e. are less than perfectly correlated), then the interests of each of two regions will generally be well served by their joining, since the disturbances will partially offset one another and produce a lower net disturbance in both regions; that is, the regions will engage in risk-spreading rather than in risk-splitting by joining one another in a common region, analogous to enlarging an insurance pool.[7]

If we now take the net disturbance as given, reduced as it may have been through export or through import of partially offsetting disturbances, we can ask how much damage it will do to the region of our interest and how the region may take policy action to mitigate the remaining damage. Mundell has pointed out that, if factor mobility is high within a region, adjustment to some disturbances can take place quite smoothly, as shifts in demand among goods lead to prompt reemployment of any redundant factors. Kenen has made a related point in emphasizing the importance of diversity in an economy, both to reduce the net disturbance through mutual offsetting of uncorrelated disturbances and to spread the impact widely throughout an economy, thereby reducing the social cost.[8] In Mundell's formulation, stabilization requirements alone imply as small an area as possible (each with its own floating currency), for that leads as much as possible to a regime of complete price flexibility, and the market will always clear. Efficiency in the use of money leads Mundell's optimum currency area to stop far short of this atomism. Kenen's emphasis on disturbances suggests that, even in the realm of stabilization alone, the optimum area may be far larger than Mundell's argument implies.[9]

Moreover, extremely open (small) economies may find themselves bereft of useful instruments of policy to deal with disturbances. McKinnon has suggested that money illusion in an open economy may diminish to the point at which fluctuations in the exchange rate of the region's currency may cease to be effective in influencing patterns of demand, and indeed may simply induce residents to hold "foreign" currencies.[10] Also, a region may be so open that standard macroeconomic fiscal action ceases to be an effective instrument of demand management, because the great leakages abroad vitiate its domestic impact.[11] This vitiation of policy is a more complicated question than at first meets the eye, because of course the disturbances are also strongly attenuated in these very open economies, and we must therefore ask whether on balance the region is worse off in terms of macroeconomic management than it would be with more effective instruments of policy but also with larger net disturbances.[12] But the reduced effectiveness of policy instruments limits the region's capacity to compensate for disturbances arising outside the region, at least so long as some social cost is associated with their exercise at more intensive levels.[13]

Most of the considerations discussed above—economies of scale, external effects, escape from regulation and redistribution, effective economic stabilization—argue for increasing the size of jurisdictions. The entire globe would be the logical limit to this process. Only increasing difficulties of management (diseconomies of scale associated with management and bureaucracy) and (for those regions that can profit by it) risk-splitting cut in the other direction, toward smaller scale of the optimal jurisdiction. But we have not yet made allowance for the diversity of preferences for collective goods.

Diversity of Preferences

Individuals differ greatly in their preferences for collective goods, both of the systemic type (fundamental nature of regime, capitalist or socialist; strong preference for order; high respect for individualism) and of the specific public type (flood control; parks; scientific research). These strong differences are conditioned by differences in cultural background and in income level. The greater the diversity of preferences within a given jurisdiction, the more difficult it will be, obviously, to satisfy all the demands for public goods by the residents even approximately, since by their nature public goods are provided in roughly equal amount to all residents of the relevant area. There are, thus, large consumption losses in jurisdictions with a wide diversity of tastes, relative to what would be possible with different jurisdictions each catering more precisely to the preferences of its residents. This consideration pushes strongly toward relatively small communities that are homogeneous in their preferences for collective goods; it underlies much of the pressure for greater decentralization of government and more local control.

In the recent book *Size and Democracy*, two political scientists pose the tradeoff in a slightly different way. They point to the conflict between "system capacity" and "citizen effectiveness" (that is, the capacity of the governmental system to deliver public goods efficiently as against the ability of citizens to participate effectively in making governmental decisions affecting the level and composition public goods to be provided). They do at one point seem to suggest a positive value to diversity among the citizenship and to pluralism as such, however, particularly to provide an environment favorable to the dissenting citizen (which on one issue or another will be all of them), and this would suggest enlarging the jurisdiction despite the advantages cited above for having communities with homogeneous tastes. They do not, however, attempt to weigh this desire for pluralism against the necessary consumption loss on other public goods that arises from diversity in tastes.[14]

Considerations of liberty, however, press for smaller, more numerous jurisdictions, provided that individuals are free to move from one jurisdiction to another. Breton has put the point strongly: "The number of levels and sizes of units [of government] should be such that for any level of costs, the power of politicians—defined as their capacity to depart from the preferences of citizens—should be minimized."[15] Those fearful of the coercive powers of the state would set the scale of jurisdictions at a low level, even if that meant sacrificing some economic efficiency, for the sake of keeping politicians under check through competition with other jurisdictions.

Conclusion: What Is the Optimal Area?

How are these conflicting considerations to be weighed against one another? That itself is an issue involving the diversity of preferences, for different individuals will be willing to sacrifice differing amounts of income (as taxes) in the form of less efficient provision of conventional public goods in order to purchase some given amount of liberty or national prestige or sense of cultural identity. It is necessary, as Samuelson told us years ago, to have a social-welfare function that weights not only the provision of goods and services but also the individuals that make up the community. But to say we need a social-welfare function, while formally correct, merely passes the question to the agent who specifies that function.

Functional Federalism

Compromise among the various considerations is possible. Under a system of functional federalism, the tradeoff between scale economies and diversity of tastes is made for each public good separately, leading to many overlapping governmental jurisdictions, each dealing with its own set of highly specialized and closely related problems: police protection, weather forecasting and control, flood control, economic management. Each has its own autonomous decisionmaking structure and its own citizenry, which may differ from issue to issue. This in a way is the method of specialized international organizations, each established by separate treaties on civil aviation, tariffs, monetary arrangements, world public health, and so on, and it can also be seen in federal countries.[16] It is an attractive idea, and in practice it will be necessary, at least in some degree. The notion of sovereignty inevitably becomes ambiguous under a system of functional federalism, for there is no sovereign, only a series of partial sovereignties. But that ambiguity is necessary to achieve the objective of the optimal provision of public goods, unless of course the existence of an unambiguous sovereignty is itself regarded as the overriding public good.

However, a system of functional federalism with partial sovereignties has its disadvantages as well. In the first place, both technology and tastes are in flux. A particular organization that is optimal now will in general not be optimal 10 years from now. Yet an ongoing bureaucracy develops vested interests of its own and is very difficult to change. Every country is living with outdated but durable—not to say tenacious—governmental institutions. Flexibility would be lost through a proliferation of jurisdictions, none with overriding authority.

In the second place, a system of functional federalism would inhibit bargaining and political compromise across functional jurisdictional boundaries in the absence of a higher authority willing and able to sacrifice the vested interests in particular jurisdictions. For much of the time it is useful to have each issue operate on its own track, with its own set of conventions and sanctions to influence behavior. But from time to time the inability to bargain across issue areas would prevent communities from reaching an optimal configuration of public goods.

In the third place, decisionmaking groups drawn up along specialized lines seem often as a matter of experience to become dominated by the specialized producer interests, so broad consumer interests receive less attention than they should and than they would with more broadly based decisionmaking bodies.

Contemporary Relevance

I will close with some comments on the contemporary relevance of what are otherwise broad and largely inconclusive generalizations.

The pressures for enlargement of governmental jurisdictions are strong and growing in the modern world. Activities in each jurisdiction have impacts on other jurisdictions in an increasing number of areas. Economies of scale and externalities in some activities have been growing as well, so to the extent that those activities are desired as public goods the jurisdiction required to carry them with any efficiency has also increased in size. Not the least of the sources of "spillouts" in the modern world is the fact that governments have become active in pursuing a variety of social objectives, and these pursuits often vary from country to country, setting up strains, including those arising from the mobility of firms and persons, between different jurisdictions. Even when factor mobility is not present, one hears charges of "unfair" competition from a country that pursues practices somewhat different from one's own. Economic stabilization and income redistribution have become more difficult for countries to achieve acting alone. On all these grounds, therefore, an argument can be made for increasing the size of jurisdictions—for forming regional groupings out of nations.

The European Economic Community is one response to these pressures. The motivations behind the formation of the Community are many, and are mainly political, but at their root was a perception that European nations acting one by one would have a diminishing influence on the course of world events and hence even on their own welfare; thus, they joined together to pool their influence and to try to restore some autonomy to their evolution.

The EEC is relatively homogeneous by global standards, so the welfare loss associated with "harmonizing" various policies will be less than it would be for a larger and more diverse group of countries. Other successful attempts at economic integration—the Central American Common Market, and on a more limited basis the Andean group of countries—also reflect a high degree of homogeneity relative to the world at large (although we should keep in mind that homogeneity always looks greater from a distance than it really is). The United States has been relatively successful in part because, while very large, it is relatively homogeneous in taste and outlook, and it has a system of decentralized government capable of catering to variations in local preferences. Indeed, the greatest internal difficulties within the United States have arisen when local preferences, e.g. on racial discrimination, have offended a national norm.

Growing centralization and bureaucraticization in response to pressures for enlargement have created counterpressures for greater decentralization in governmental decisionmaking. These arise partly out of psychological revulsion at the growing distance between the average citizen and his government, partly out of the perception that centralization really reduces responsiveness to local preferences.

The Communist countries are committed to such a fundamentally different conception of the basic economic regime that is difficult to contemplate meaningful integration between those countries and other countries except along highly specialized and functional lines. Many less-developed countries are still groping for the appropriate underlying regime for themselves, trying to adapt a colonial legacy to new needs and to indigenous preferences, and until this process is completed it will be difficult to integrate such countries with others whose basic regime is settled and is generally regarded as satisfactory. Once again, integration along specialized functional lines is about all one should reasonably try at this stage, and even there such attempts as have been made are often plagued by difficulties because some countries question the fundamental propositions that others take for granted.

For these various reasons, therefore, regional integration regarding public goods seems to be a more promising route than global integration. (I emphasize that I am writing here about public goods—not private goods, for which the optimum region is the world.) Indeed, there should be no objection to groups of countries getting together to pursue their common interests, so long as neither their intent nor their effect is to gain at the expense of other countries. There are numerous opportunities for such "clubs" to form which are not at the expense of other countries, and indeed their activities may be beneficial to others.

I conclude, therefore, the same way Alec Cairmross did in his recent discussion of the optimal firm: There is no such thing.[17] Nor is there such a thing as an optimal region, at least at the high level of generality that has been considered here. Not the least of the difficulties is that close cooperation among nations or within regions *builds* close ties and more homogeneous preferences as well as reflecting them, a point well perceived by the advocates of the economic route to political unification of Europe. Rather, optimality calls for a much more complex array of jurisdictions, compromising between the desire for greater decentralization and the technical need for greater centralization in decisionmaking.

Notes

1. For a selection of Triffin's numerous articles and memoranda written in the early postwar era, see his *World Money Maze* (New Haven: Yale University Press, 1966), especially pp. 376–405.

2. On the theory underlying the neofunctionalist approach to political integration, see E. B. Haas, *The Uniting of Europe* (Stanford University Press, 1958) and J. S. Nye, *Peace in Parts* (Boston: Little, Brown, 1971), especially pp. 48–54.

3. C. A. Cooper and B. V. E. Massell, "A New Look at Customs Union Theory," *Economic Journal* 75 (December 1965): 742–747; "Toward a General Theory of Customs Unions," *Journal of Political Economy* 73 (October 1965): 461–476.

4. H. G. Johnson, "An Economic Theory of Protectionism, Tariff Bargaining, and the Formation of Customs Unions," *Journal of Political Economy* 73 (June 1965): 256–283.

5. A recent example of this process was the proposal by the Labour government in Britain in 1974 to tax the total income of foreign residents in Britain. The proposal was greeted with howls of protest, some foreign residents made their plans to leave, and the British government backed away from its initial position.

6. For a further discussion of these issues and of the influence of mobility on the formulation of government policy see R. N. Cooper, "Economic Mobility and National Economic Policy," article 4 in this volume.

7. For a more formal analysis of the impact of disturbances on the income levels of different regions, see the mathematical appendix to article 4.

8. R. A. Mundell, "A Theory of Optimum Currency Area," *American Economic Review* 51 (September 1961): 657–664; P. B. Kenen, "The Theory of Optimum Currency Area: An Eclectic View," in R. A. Mundell and A. K. Swoboda, eds., *Monetary Problems of the International Economy* (University of Chicago Press, 1969).

9. The contrary pulls on regional size of these two factors can be set down in informal mathematical terms as follows: $U - U^* = H(d, f)$, where U is the regional unemployment ratio, U^* is the unemployment ratio that is sustainable over time in the absence of disturbances, d represents the average level of net disturbances over a period of time, and f represents the factor-market frictions inhibiting immediate absorption of any unemployed labor. It seems reasonable to assume that

$$\frac{\partial H}{\partial d} > 0, \quad \frac{\partial H}{\partial f} > 0, \quad H(0,f) = H(d,0) = 0.$$

Suppose that we want to minimize H by a judicious choice of size for the region, within which trade is free and one currency prevails and beyond which trade is subject to tariffs and other currencies exist with flexible exchange rates between those currencies and that of our region.

$$\operatorname*{Min}_{s} H \to \frac{\partial H}{\partial d} \cdot \frac{\partial d}{\partial s} + \frac{\partial H}{\partial f} \cdot \frac{\partial f}{\partial s} = 0.$$

By the arguments in the text, $\partial d/\partial s < 0$ and $\partial f/\partial s > 0$, so a minimum may be assumed to exist. The resulting region would be "optimal" in this dimension only.

10. R. I. McKinnon, "Optimum Currency Areas," *American Economic Review* 53 (September 1963): 717–724.

11. Cooper, op. cit.; R. I. McKinnon and W. E. Oates, *The Implications of International Economic Integration for Monetary, Fiscal, and Exchange Rate Policy* (International Finance Section, Princeton University, 1966), pp. 16–17.

12. For a discussion of this issue, see R. N. Cooper, "The Relevance of International Liquidity to Developed Countries," *American Economic Review* 58 (May 1968): 636.

13. The last qualification is necessary because in its absence an instrument of policy could simply be worked at a sufficiently high level of intensity to deal with the problem, so long as it has any impact at all. But in fact there are limits to how hard we can push the use of each particular policy measure.

14. R. A. Dahl and E. R. Tufte, *Size and Democracy* (Stanford University Press, 1973), especially pp. 22–25 and 138.

15. A. Breton, "Theoretical Problems of Federalism," *Recherches Economiques de Louvain* 32 (September 1970): 114.

16. For a stimulating discussion of the division of labor among different levels of government, see M. Olson, Jr., "The Principle of 'Fiscal Equivalence': The Division of Responsibilities among Different Levels of Government," *American Economic Review* 59 (May 1969): 479–487.

17. A. K. Cairncross, "The Optimal Firm Reconsidered," *Economic Journal* 82 suppl. (March 1972): 312–320.

6 Towards an International Capital Market?

This article discusses the growth and development of the international capital market during the 1960s, considers whether it can be said that a genuine international capital market now exists, and discusses the advantages and disadvantages of one integrated capital market transcending national economies. "Capital markets" involve the mobilization of savings by those who want or are willing to accept financial claims, for investment (or consumption) by others who are willing to accept financial liabilities or share their equity. Capital markets are usually distinguished from "money markets" by the maturity of the claims that are traded there, the capital market referring to transactions in claims with maturities in excess (definitionally) of one year, and usually in excess of five years, although any clear distinction between the two must be arbitrary, for these markets may be, and typically are, closely related. Medium-term bank lending, for example, involves maturities in excess of one year but ordinarily does not give rise to marketable securities.

Several geographically distinct capital markets can be said to be integrated—that is, effectively one market—to the extent that a significant number of savers do not distinguish among claims on the basis of the geographical location of the borrower. In the international context, this means that a significant number of savers do not distinguish among borrowers on the basis of nationality. This failure to distinguish must include, of course, both the willingness to accept claims on foreigners and the ability to do so, the latter implying an absence of balance of payments and other restrictions against foreign investment.

The extent to which there can be said to be an Atlantic capital market, encompassing Canada, the United States, and many or most of the countries of Western Europe, can be approached empirically from two angles. We can ask about the absolute and relative volume of long-term financial transactions crossing national boundaries and about the nationality and other characteristics of the borrowers and lenders, or we can apply the economically more meaningful test of the extent to which bond yields and share prices have been brought into harmony. One market implies one price for identical goods or claims and similar prices for similar goods or claims. A genuine Atlantic capital market would therefore imply similar interest rates or yields for financial claims of similar risk and liquidity. The next two sections offer some sketchy evidence on both of these approaches. Following this evidence, I will draw some implications for economic policy of the tendency towards one market and offer an assessment of the advantages and disadvantages at the present time of a unified capital market spanning national boundaries.

Size and Growth of International Capital Movements

The rapid growth in foreign bond flotations during the decade of the 1960s has been a source of universal astonishment. From barely more than $200 million in 1958 (close to $400 million if the United Kingdom is included), foreign bond issues in Europe grew to over $4.7 billion in 1968, a compound growth rate of nearly 30 percent a year. The growth is far less dramatic, but still dramatic, if the U.S. market is included: Total foreign bond issues on both sides of the Atlantic rose from $1.5 billion in 1958 to $6.3 billion in 1968[1], a fourfold increase (table 1). A distinction may be drawn between foreign bonds issued in national markets, denominated in the national currency of the market in which it is floated, and "international" bond issues, which are denominated in a currency (usually U.S. dollars, but also German marks, two or more currencies, and units of account) different from that of the country or countries in which it is floated.[2] International issues grew from negligible amounts in the early 1960s to $3.5 billion in 1968.

The overwhelming bulk of the long-term foreign borrowing in the United States is by Canadians, although Japan, Israel, the World Bank, and (before the imposition of the interest-equalization tax in 1963) several European countries have also been important borrowers. American corporations and their subsidiaries have been the most important group of borrowers in European markets, accounting for nearly half of all new issues (many of them convertible bonds) in 1968. Non-American corporations accounted for nearly a quarter of the borrowing, and governmental bodies and international institutions for the remainder. Characterizing the lenders is more difficult, since it is not known who ultimately purchases these bonds. In the United States, insurance companies and pension funds provide a steady source of demand for new bond issues. In the European market, individuals

Table 1
Foreign bond issues,[a] 1958–1968 ($ million).

	Foreign issues on domestic markets		International issues[b]	Total
	U.S.	European[b]		
1958	1,138	302	82	1,522
1959	802	337	31	1,170
1960	636	393	29	1,058
1961	558	559	79	1,196
1962	1,185	430	—	1,615
1963	1,414	426	119	1,958
1964	1,191	263	838	2,293
1965	1,532	264[c]	1,192	2,989
1966	1,317	550[c]	1,155	3,021
1967	1,619[d]	404[c]	2,002	4,025
1968	1,576[d]	1,185[c]	3,517	6,278

a. Including private placements and convertible bonds.

b. Foreign bonds issued in Germany after imposition of 25 percent coupon tax on German bonds in March 1964 are treated as international issues, since they are exempt from the tax.

c. Including Canadian market.

d. Excluding portion purchased by foreigners.

Sources. 1958–1966: *Capital Markets Study*, vol. 3, Functioning of Capital Markets (Paris: OECD, 1968), p. 717. 1967–68: Department of Commerce, *Survey of Current Business*; Morgan Guaranty Trust Co., *World Financial Markets*.

and family trusts are more important (leading to correspondingly higher selling costs for the "retail" market). It has been estimated for the mid 1960s that about half the purchases of foreign bonds issued in Europe were by banks and trusts in Switzerland acting on behalf of customers from all over the world; another 20 percent of the funds came from other continental European countries.[3]

Over three-quarters of the international bond issues, narrowly defined, were denominated in U.S. dollars, and therefore over two-thirds of total foreign bond issues outside the United States were so denominated. Like a language, a currency is useful in proportion to the number of people who use it. By the use of a common currency, the market is widened and the potential liquidity of financial claims is increased—potential since this liquidity depends on the development of secondary markets where securities are bought and sold after issue and before maturity, and secondary markets in

Europe have developed more slowly than the new-issues market. During 1968 and 1969 use of the German mark became more prominent, as the German monetary authorities deliberately maintained low interest rates and took other steps to encourage the export of capital, making mark-denominated bonds less costly to borrowers than dollar-denominated ones.[4]

Foreign and international bond issues have grown rapidly relative to the total activity on the various national capital markets, as well as in absolute volume. Comparable measures are difficult to obtain, but on the basis of total net new bond issues on the eight major European capital markets plus the United States, as computed by the OECD, the share of foreign and international bond issues rose from 5 percent in 1960 to 11 percent in 1965 and to an estimated 14 percent in 1968.[5]

Equity shares are another part of the capital market. Here one must turn to the secondary market for relevant information, since it is far more important, relative to new issues, than is the case for bonds. Until 1967 and 1968, net movements of funds between countries on account of purchases of stocks (excluding direct investment, aimed at management control) was rather small. Americans added very little to their holdings of foreign stocks during the 1960s, while the British engaged in large-scale net liquidation of their foreign share holdings. Net foreign purchases of American stocks rose sharply after the mid 1960s, however: from $200 million in 1963 to nearly $2.3 billion in 1968, with purchases from Europe and Canada accounting for th bulk of them. Mutual funds spread rapidly in the late 1960s, especially in Germany and Italy, and many of these specialized in the purchase of foreign—mainly American—stocks.

From the viewpoint of the integration of capital markets, however, it is gross rather than net transactions that count. These have been substantial, even when net transactions were small. In 1968, for instance, foreigners bought $13.1 billion in American stocks, and sold $10.8 billion, over six times the levels of 1960; American purchases of foreign stocks (except for dealers, generally subject to the interest-equalization tax of 15 percent) amounted to $1.6 billion in 1968, while sales came to $1.2 billion, both over double the levels of 1960. These sums are of course small relative to the total gross value of stock sales ($125 billion on the New York Stock Exchange alone in 1968), but here, as elsewhere in economics, it is the marginal buyer that counts. The question, therefore, is whether international transactions in stocks and bonds were sufficiently large at the margin to influence or even to govern prices in the various national markets.

Before we turn to an examination of the evidence on that point, two other important dimensions of international capital movements should be mentioned. While they are not strictly part of "capital markets" as defined here, both short-term capital movements and direct investments provide potential indirect linkages between capital markets to the extent that there is some substitutability between short- and long-term financial claims, on the one hand, and between long-term financial claims and real assets on the other. Capital markets could be fully integrated in the economically meaningful sense of price equalization for claims of similar quality even with no movement of long-term portfolio capital between countries, for instance, provided that money and capital markets were tightly linked within each country and that national money markets were closely linked internationally.

National money markets are linked these days primarily through Eurodollars, a market in short-term dollar claims located in London and other European financial centres. Where national exchange regulations permit the outward movement of short-term funds, those with such funds to invest will compare their earning opportunities at home with those in Eurodollar deposits and will shift funds accordingly. Even where regulations limit the outward movement of funds, creditworthy borrowers will draw funds from the Eurodollar market when rates there are more attractive than in their home markets. In this way national money markets tend to be tied together.

The Eurodollar market has grown to substantial proportions. At an estimated $25 billion of total liabilities by the end of 1968, excluding interbank deposits, the Eurodollar market was roughly equivalent in size to the total money supply in Italy, Japan, or the United Kingdom, and was substantially exceeded only by the money supplies in France and the United States. It has shown surprising responsiveness, moreover, to new demands placed on it. Switches of borrowers or lenders between the Eurodollar market and domestic markets can therefore exert a powerful influence on domestic monetary conditions, and for many countries could in principle largely undercut monetary policy as an instrument of economic stabilization. This extreme has not yet been reached, in part because a switch between dollars and local currencies requires either that the switching party take on an exchange risk or that he insure against it, e.g. by selling forward the currency he has purchased. The presence of exchange risk serves to insulate national money markets from one another even when all the technical facilities for one integrated market are present.

Direct investment abroad can also provide a link between capital markets. Recent work on the motivation for direct investment has rightly emphasized the exploitation of quasi-monopoly powers arising from patents or other unique technological or managerial advantages. Many direct investors borrow in local markets, both to establish credit lines and to hedge against exchange risks, and this practice suggests that direct investment is not primarily in response to national differences in long-term bond yields. Nevertheless, direct investment does usually involve the transfer of funds from one country to another, and since the early 1960s such transfers have taken place on a substantial scale.

American takeovers of European firms bid up the price of existing assets and takeovers for cash shift funds from the American capital market to the capital or money markets of Europe. Investments in new plant and equipment are more ambiguous in their effects, since any flow of funds from the parent company is accompanied by an increased demand for funds that may more than offset it, depending on the extent of local borrowing and the size of multiplier effects. But many international corporations, with access to two or more national capital markets, are influenced in their source of funds by relative costs and hence tend to bring borrowing conditions in national markets into closer harmony. Direct investment also plays a role in bringing national money markets together, as corporations with temporarily idle funds place them where the yield-risk combination is most attractive or fill short-term cash needs by borrowing in the money market where costs are lowest. Indeed, international corporations have been among the major participants both in the Eurodollar market and in the Eurobond market.

In passing, it is of interest that both the Eurodollar market and the international bond market were encouraged by the imposition of national controls that inhibited the most advantageously situated national market from serving an international role. In 1957 the British commercial banks were circumscribed in their ability to lend sterling outside the United Kingdom but were left free to carry on in other currencies, so they began to accept deposits and lend in dollars. In 1963 the interest-equalization tax effectively closed the New York bond market to a large class of foreign borrowers and thereby generated a demand for issues in Europe—a demand that was greatly augmented two years later by the voluntary limitations placed on U.S. financing of direct investment abroad.

Interest Rates and Asset Prices

The flow of funds across national boundaries unquestionably increased sharply during the 1960s, both absolutely and relative to internal financial transactions. Identifiable international money and capital markets appeared. But were these developments sufficient to integrate the national financial markets in the sense of bringing together prices of similar financial assets? A

Table 2
International convergence of interest rates,[a] 1958–1968.

	Short-term[b]			Government bonds[c]		
	Mean	Standard deviation	Coefficient of variation[d]	Mean	Standard deviation	Coefficient of Variation[d]
1958	2.86	1.22	0.43	4.48	0.94	0.21
1960	3.37	1.21	0.36	4.66	0.93	0.20
1962	2.96	0.95	0.32	4.80	0.89	0.19
1964	3.66	0.74	0.20	5.36	0.93	0.17
1966	4.80	0.83	0.17	5.89	1.13	0.19
1968	4.74	1.75	0.37	5.97	0.81	0.14

a. Average rate for June of indicated year.

b. Unweighted mean and standard deviation of three-month Treasury bill or call-money rates for Belgium, Canada, France, Germany (West), Netherlands, Switzerland, United Kingdom, and United States.

c. With maturity in excess of 12 years, for countries listed in preceding footnote plus Italy and Sweden.

d. Standard deviation divided by mean.

Source. Underlying data from *International Financial Statistics.*

unified market requires a single price for the same commodity prevailing everywhere at each point in time. When this condition is not met, markets are to that extent fragmented.

It is difficult to test empirically the extent to which we have achieved integrated money and capital markets among the major industrial countries, since assets in different countries continue to be different in one important respect: They are denominated in different currencies. The possibility of changes in exchange rates among the currencies introduces an element of risk which, from the viewpoint of a resident of any particular country, is not present when all assets are denominated in a single currency. The assets also differ in other, less important respects. A comparison of interest rates on high-quality short-term assets and on long-term government bonds nonetheless reveals a marked tendency towards convergence following the move to currency convertibility by the major European countries in late 1958. Table 2 shows that the dispersion around the mean of short-term interest rates for eight countries declined substantially after 1958. The decline in dispersion was less marked for long-term bond rates, but except for 1966 the dispersion declined steadily relative to the mean bond yield, suggesting some convergence in the long-term capital market as well. The sharp increase in bond-rate dispersion in 1966 is attributable solely to a 2-percentage-point increase in German bond rates, to 8.4 percent, in a period in which the German state and local authorities were borrowing at an exceptionally heavy rate and the Bundesbank tightened credit to dampen total spending. The increase in absolute and relative dispersion of short-term rates in 1968 is attributable to a combination of high rates in Britain and France, reflecting doubts about the exchange rates of their respective currencies, combined with an exceptionally low rate in Germany designed both to stimulate capital outflow and to promote domestic capital spending in the aftermath of the recession generated by excessively tight monetary conditions in 1966.

In addition to coming closer together over time, interest rates showed a greater tendency to move together through time from 1962 to 1967 than before, indicating a greater influence of one market on another (fig. 1). This tendency was reversed in late 1967 and 1968, when a series of exchange crises disturbed interest-rate relationships and induced several countries to impose tight controls on capital movements.

Equity prices are more difficult to compare, for European firms publish too little financial information to compute price-earnings ratios and other measures of performance from the perspective of the shareholder. This fact not only makes analysis difficult but it also inhibits the effective integration of the markets for equities. Indices of share prices do show some sympathetic movement from country to country (fig. 2). The movement may reflect broadly sympathetic movements in national economic conditions rather than direct buying and selling links between equity markets, although the universal drop in equity prices in 1966, in the face of sharply divergent national economic developments, suggests more direct links. Expected or actual changes in exchange rates will also influence equity prices; currency overvaluation will weaken profit performance in manufacturing, while devaluation will improve it. Currency revaluation may have played a role in the fall in German and Dutch equity prices in 1961; on the other hand, Canadian equity prices closely paralleled those of the United States during 1961–1963 (indeed, throughout the 1960s), despite the Canadian devaluation of 1961–62.

The Challenge of and the Response to Financial Integration

All this evidence points to the conclusion that there has been some integration of money and capital markets during the past decade but that there is still a substantial way to go before we can speak of unified markets. Even

Towards an International Capital Market? 145

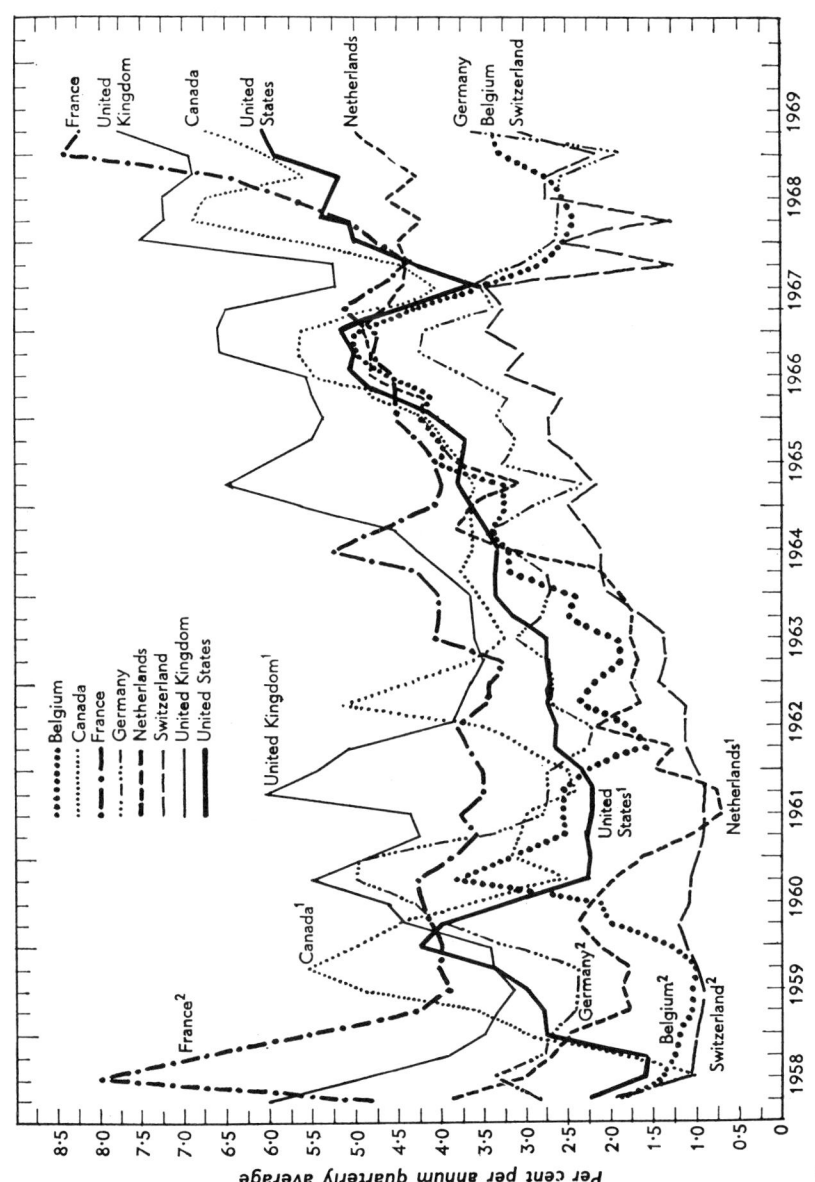

Figure 1
Short-term rates for United States, United Kingdom, Canada, France, Germany, Belgium, Netherlands, and Sweden, 1958–1969. (1) Average tender rate for 3-month Treasury bills; (2) average of daily or weekly call-money rates.
Source. IMF, *International Financial Statistics*.

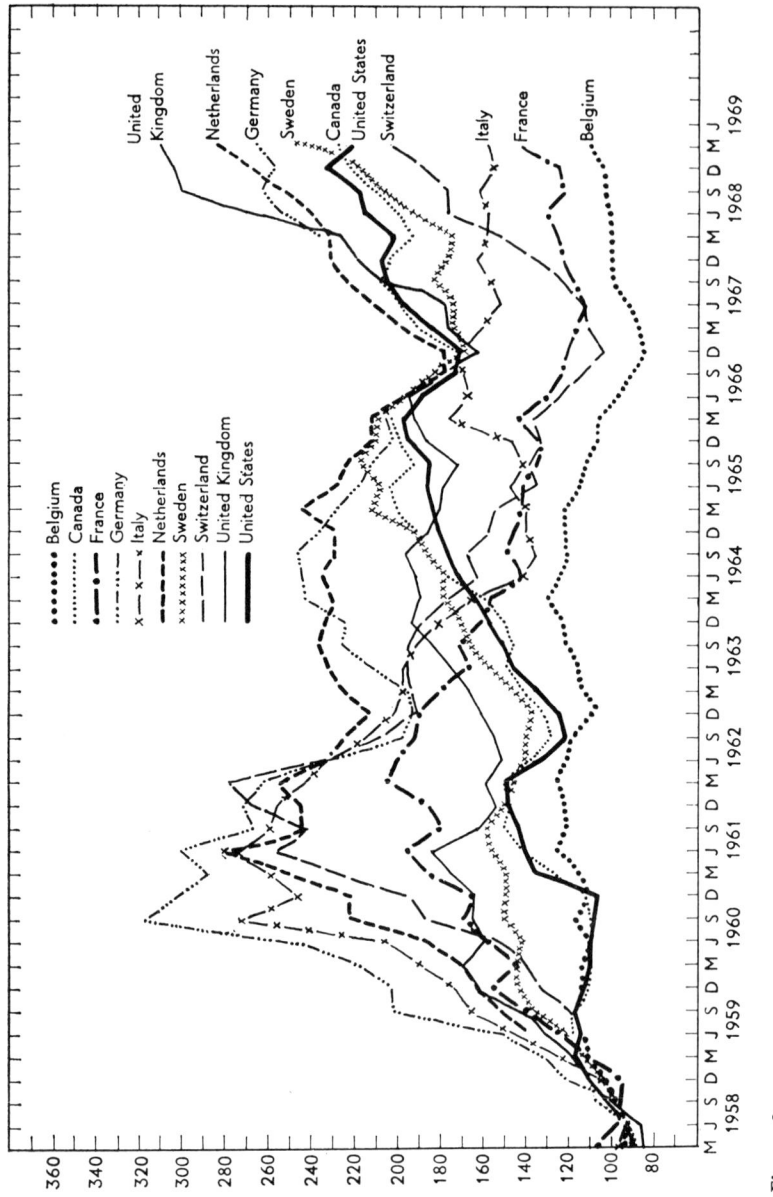

Figure 2
Index of industrial share prices, quarterly, March 1958 – March 1969.
(1958 = 100.)

the integration that has taken place so far, however, has important implications for the economies involved. The integration of financial markets limits the scope for the autonomous pursuit of national policy. This is most obviously the case for monetary policy, but it is also true for taxation and regulation of business and for exchange-rate policy.

Consider monetary policy first. In a world of high capital mobility under fixed exchange rates, a tightening of monetary conditions (e.g. through open-market sales by the central bank or through higher bank reserve requirements) will serve less to dampen domestic spending than to attract an inflow of funds from abroad. Similarly, an attempt to ease domestic monetary conditions to stimulate spending will instead simply stimulate an outflow of funds. Financial integration thus poses a profound threat to the traditional reliance on monetary policy for stabilization of the domestic economy. The effectiveness of monetary policy for this purpose is greatly reduced by high capital mobility across national boundaries, for the rest of the world in effect becomes a residual source of demand for excess domestic liquidity and a residual source of supply of funds.

By the same token, however, monetary policy becomes very effective as an instrument for influencing a country's short-run international-payments position. A slight tightening of domestic credit will attract funds from abroad and thus may be used to finance a payments deficit. Monetary policy used for this purpose will be more effective in the short run than in the long, partly because some of the initial inflow of funds in response to tighter monetary conditions will represent stock adjustment of a once-for-all character and partly because, in the absence of perfect capital mobility, higher interest charges on outstanding short-term indebtedness must be set against whatever continuing inflows there are.

An additional implication of increased capital mobility is that fiscal policy will become more effective at influencing domestic demend. The monetarist claim that the impact on aggregate demand of "pure" fiscal action (changes in the government budget position with no accommodating change in the money supply) will be largely if not wholly offset by interest-induced changes in investment demand ceases to apply in a world of high capital mobility. In the limiting case of perfect capital mobility, an increase in government spending can be financed by bond sales at unchanged interest rates by all but the largest countries without intervention by the monetary authorities, for funds from abroad will produce the required increase in the money supply. Thus, while the effectiveness of monetary policy in stabilizing the economy will decline with increased capital mobility, generating a need for alternative stabilization measures, the effectiveness of fiscal policy at influencing aggregate demand will increase.

The weakening of monetary policy for stabilization purposes nevertheless poses a serious problem for governments, since it is usually the most flexible instrument of policy at hand and for institutional reasons it is also more insulated from short-run political considerations. Not surprisingly, governments are loath to give up their reliance on monetary policy—indeed, it is not clear either that they should or that they can, politically—and they have therefore taken a number of steps to counteract the integrating tendencies evident in money and capital markets. These actions in turn make more difficult any analysis of the degree to which money and capital markets have become unified; the potential unification may be far greater than that actually observed, as summarized by the data in the preceding sections, because of deliberate countervailing steps to reduce the integrating pressures in the interests of preserving some degree of national autonomy in the exercise of monetary policy.

Government response to the greater interdependence between national capital markets has been widespread. These responses have often been taken under the guise of balance-of-payments policies, but that is merely the other side of the coin. Special measures to restrain capital outflows serve to protect the balance of payments in periods in which, for domestic reasons, the monetary authorities desire to maintain a greater degree of monetary ease than prevails abroad. That these measures are not governed principally by balance-of-payments considerations is indicated by the fact that countries in payments surplus have also taken steps to insulate their economies from high international capital mobility, even though balance-of-payments pressures were not so acute as for countries in deficit.

The devices used are well known. Virtually all countries restrict foreign access to their domestic capital markets, usually on the grounds that unlimited access by foreigners could create undue disruption of imperfectly developed national capital markets. Britain and the United States, however, restrict access on balance-of-payments grounds—in the case of the United States through an "interest-equalization tax" on U.S. purchases of European and certain other issues, which is to say that the authorities in those countries would not like to be obliged to maintain interest rates at the levels required to limit foreign borrowing. Both countries also limit purchases by their residents of outstanding foreign securities. The interest-equalization tax applies in the United States, and Britain in effect imposes a tax by requiring British residents wanting to invest abroad to buy foreign currency at a premium but to sell a portion of receipts from liquidation of foreign assets to the authorities at the official exchange rate. These and other countries also limit the amount of short-term investment that can be undertaken abroad.

High capital mobility can be as frustrating to countries wanting to tighten domestic monetary conditions as to those wanting to ease them. At various times France, Germany, the Netherlands, and Switzerland have all prohibited interest payments on deposits by foreigners, to inhibit an inflow of short-term funds. Special reserve requirements have been imposed on foreigners' deposits with the same aim. Since 1964 Germany has imposed special withholding taxes on interest paid to foreign holders of domestic bonds—a kind of negative interest-equalization tax. (Foreign bonds floated in Germany are exempt from this tax, so they command lower nominal yields and therefore draw funds largely from outside Germany.) Both Germany and Italy, and to a lesser extent the Netherlands and Switzerland, have encouraged their banks to channel short-term funds abroad through directives or attractive forward swap arrangements, thereby regaining some control over domestic monetary conditions. But this technique will work only so long as domestic nonbank borrowers do not have direct access to foreign sources of funds—a condition that has eroded over time.

International transactions in equities do not escape the national restraints. The taxes imposed by Britain and the United States apply to equities as well as to bonds. Several countries limit purchases of foreign equities by their residents to those quoted on the national stock exchange, which are restricted. In the late 1960s the growth of mutual funds in Europe provided a closer link between equity markets, especially in Germany and Italy, for they permitted residents to purchase balanced and diversified packages of foreign securities of which they had little direct knowledge. In 1969, however, the Italian government limited sharply the activities of these mutual funds, despite the fact that Italy was running a large payments surplus at the time, because they were drawing equity away from prospective domestic issuers at a time when the Italian authorities wanted to stimulate domestic investment.

In sum, national authorities do not yet seem ready to accept the limitations imposed on their own freedom to influence domestic financial conditions by an integrated capital market spanning national boundaries.

High international mobility of capital also imposes limits on national autonomy in matters of taxation and business regulation, although these limitations are both less obvious and far less evident than is true for monetary policy. There is little question, however, that one of the principal attractions of foreign bonds to investors is that income on them can be more easily concealed from the domestic tax authorities. Foreign bond issues registered on the London market, unlike domestic issues, are not subject to British withholding tax (where tax treaties eliminate British withholding on domestic issues, they also provide for exchange of information between taxing authorities), but they are not generally subject to withholding tax by the United States or by any other country either. High international capital mobility under these circumstances will erode the ability of national authorities to tax interest income except in those countries where the tradition of voluntary tax compliance is strong, for prospective bondholders can readily invest in international bonds to escape taxation.

High capital mobility also weakens national regulation of securities markets and corporate financial activity. In early 1969 a Swiss company subverted a Swiss requirement that existing stockholders be given preference on new stock issues by establishing a financial subsidiary in the Netherlands Antilles to raise desired funds through a convertible bond issue. This kind of escape from regulation through migration was a familiar phenomenon in the United States around the turn of the century; business regulation by the constitutent states was gradually eroded as the railroad and the telegraph transformed local markets into a national one. Those states most aggressive in the competition for business location set a tone for lax business regulation, and as a result regulatory responsibilities were gradually taken over by the federal government.

Pressures for supranational action in the field of business regulation and taxation have not yet reached an advanced stage, but the beginnings of such pressure can be seen both in the desire for increased intergovernmental consultation on such matters and in the attempts, largely so far by the United States, to tax "foreign" income and to extend national regulations beyond national boundaries. The Revenue Act of 1962 levied U.S. taxes on the income of U.S.-owned corporations operating from tax-haven countries, and the Kennedy administration had asked for a much broader extension of the U.S. tax than that finally passed by Congress. Similarly, in 1965 the Securities and Exchange Commission instructed a number of foreign (mostly Canadian) companies to submit information reports because their securities were being traded in the over-the-counter market in the United States. The foreign companies regarded this as an unwarranted intrusion into their business affairs, and they were supported by their governments, but the SEC was merely carrying out its congressional mandate to protect American investors from possible exploitation by unscrupulous corporate management. The problem of national jurisdiction arose because securities markets transcend national boundaries.

A third area in which high international mobility of capital has important implications is exchange-rate policy. A technically well-developed international money market, among other things, facilitates the movement of funds into or out of different currencies in anticipation of exchange-rate changes, so the volume of currency speculation is greatly enlarged during periods of uncertainty about exchange parities. The presence of exchange risk might be expected to inhibit the development of an international capital market.[6] When foreign loans are involved, the borrower and/or the lender runs an exchange risk. If the borrower's home currency is devalued, the burden of a foreign-currency debt will be increased in terms of his own currency. (Whether the real burden on the borrower is increased by devaluation depends on a host of other factors as well, such as whether devaluation raises the profitability of his local investment.) Nevertheless, financial integration may proceed rapidly when exchange risk is perceived to be low. The subsequent emergence of exchange-rate uncertainty will induce many lenders to insure against parity changes, either by borrowing or by selling forward. As the volume of outstanding international indebtedness increases, the volume of hedging activity in periods of uncertainty will also increase, resulting in corresponding pressure on national reserves. These large and sudden movements of funds may force reserve-short countries into unnecessary parity changes, or, on the contrary, may delay needed changes because of the reduction in national wealth (in the form of loss of reserves) implied by a change in the exchange rate when there is a large but temporary short (for devaluation) or long (for revaluation) foreign position in the currency.

The Advantages and Disadvantages of an International Capital Market

Turning now from the analytical and empirical to the normative side, we may ask whether such financial integration as has taken place is a good thing or a bad thing. To cast the question into policy terms, are the defensive reactions by governments desirable or undesirable? These questions cannot be answered sensibly without a point of comparison. What are the alternatives? On the standard competitive model, reducing artificial barriers to capital movements, whether by reducing ignorance or by removing policy restrictions, will lead to a more efficient use of the world's scarce resources and hence would generally be regarded as desirable. The economic theorist's presumption in favor of free markets is applicable to capital as well as to goods and services. Under competitive conditions, capital will seek higher rates of return, moving from regions of relative abundance to regions of relative scarcity. Total output will rise. In addition, free movement of funds permits individuals and institutions to diversify their risks, and this too is desirable to the extent that individuals deem high risks undesirable. Thus, there is a diversification argument as well as an efficiency argument for international capital mobility.

An assessment of the desirability of international capital mobility becomes more complicated when competitive conditions are not fulfilled, for example because of the presence of import tariffs or income taxes. International capital movements may either mitigate or aggravate the efficiency losses arising from the tariffs, depending on whether the tariffs raise the return to capital more in capital-poor countries than in capital-rich ones. Similarly, different national tax rates may either foster or inhibit the efficient allocation of capital among countries. Tax treaties strive for tax neutrality in the location of capital. However, lower tax rates combined with tax deferral or other tax-avoidance devices presumably contribute to better allocation when they draw American capital to Belgium than when they draw French or Italian capital to Switzerland, perhaps to be re-lent to the United States.

Arguments based on allocative efficiency assume that economies have adjusted fully to prevailing conditions. In particular, they assume that balance-of-payments equilibrium is ensured, so that real capital movements correspond to noncompensatory private and official movements of funds across boundaries, and they also assume that the various domestic economies respond quickly and properly to changes in the pattern and level of demand. Neither condition is met in practice. The failure of balance-of-payments adjustment to take place promptly and appropriately, in the short or even the medium run, may lead to no more than opposing movements of private and official capital. In this case the increased mobility of capital implies a need for additional international liquidity. But it may instead lead to the imposition of restrictions on other transactions, introducing resource misallocations or aggravating those already present; or it may lead to unwanted unemployment or inflation, the former entailing obvious resource costs and the latter involving costs of a more subtle sort. Although international capital movements are not ordinarily the source of unwanted deflation or inflation, they may inhibit the prompt correction of excessive deflationary or inflationary tendencies by constraining the use of monetary policy. Fiscal policy can in principle fill the breach left by monetary policy for stabilizing the domestic economy, though not without occasional help from changes in exchange rates if balance-of-payments equilibrium is also be to maintained. But if for political or other reasons fiscal policy is not in fact readily available for this role, the costs of international capital mobility are correspondingly higher. The United States during the period 1960–1964 offers perhaps the clearest and certainly the most costly case in which high capital mobility inhibited the use of monetary policy to stimulate a sluggish economy in a period in which fiscal policy could not be brought rapidly into play.

Finally, the increased international mobility of capital will affect the distribution of income. Real capital movements will raise the marginal product of labor in capital-importing countries and will lower the marginal product of labor (relative to what it would otherwise have been, except where the foreign investment has come entirely from increased savings) in capital-exporting countries. Under competitive conditions, labor will be made relatively better off in the former countries, capital better off in the latter. Even imperfect adjustment of real to financial capital flows will produce these effects, although to a lesser degree. In principle, of course, we can separate efficiency from equity, allow flows to take place on principles of efficiency, and correct for equity through the tax system. In practice, we have found great difficulty in incentive-free taxes, so a clear separation between the two considerations is not possible. Furthermore, redistributional taxation cannot be laid with impunity on internationally mobile factors, for they can escape taxation through migration or through evasion permitted by high mobility. Redistributive taxation relies on fragmented factor markets to be effective.

A second distributional effect of high capital mobility arises during the transition to a fully integrated capital market. Only the best-known (and generally the largest) firms and banks can borrow in the major international markets, and by shopping around such firms can lower the total cost of their borrowed funds—not least because of the lower international bond rates occasioned by tax evasion. Thus, the growing international capital market may foster the concentration of industry. (A countervailing tendency, at least during the transitional phase to full integration, is the invasion of national markets by new foreign competitors.)

How does one weigh these conflicting considerations in assessing the pros and cons of an evolution towards an Atlantic capital market? I conclude that such an evolution is desirable, provided we can coordinate monetary policies effectively among countries and obtain more active fiscal policies within countries and can ensure that real capital movements correspond closely to net financial flows. An international capital market is no substitute for changes in exchange-rate parities, and in fact its presence greatly aggravates the currency speculation that can take place in anticipation of changes in parities. It thus suggests the need for smaller and more continuous changes in exchange rates, which in turn may reduce somewhat the high mobility of capital. If balance-of-payments equilibrium is not ensured through coordinated monetary policies and if no provision is made for more frequent changes in exchange rates, however, high capital mobility will exert pressures for trade controls and/or unwanted domestic inflation or deflation. Under these circumstances, high international mobility of capital may well leave us with a third- or fourth-best world, and governments may be wise in the meantime to restrict international flows in the interests of attaining at least a second-best one.

Notes

1. Recent levels compare favorably in absolute magnitude to the average annual $2 billion in foreign bonds issued in Europe and the United States during 1924–1928, the alleged heyday of the international capital market.

2. Foreign bonds denominated in German marks are considered "international" bonds after March 1964, even when floated on the German market, since they were exempt from the coupon tax levied on interest payments to foreign holders of German bonds and hence had lower yields than German bonds floated on the domestic market.

3. David Williams, "Foreign Currency Issues in European Security Markets," *I.M.F. Staff Papers* (May 1967): 61.

4. Expectations of a future revaluation of the mark also helped lower coupon rates on mark-denominated bonds.

5. OECD, *Capital Markets Study* (Paris: OECD, 1968), statistical annex, pp. 122–123, and sources cited there.

6. Canadians floated fixed-interest bonds in New York (in U.S. dollars) on a large scale during the 1950s, when the Canadian dollar was on a floating rate. But expectations (and Canadian monetary policy) kept the Canadian dollar close to parity with the U.S. dollar. Moreover, Canadian borrowing in New York increased sharply in the 1960s, after Canada switched to a fixed exchange rate. How much of the dramatic increase in foreign borrowing was due to factors other than the change in exchange-rate regime is difficult to say.

7 Macroeconomic Policy Adjustment in Interdependent Economies

This article is concerned with the gains to be derived from coordination of economic policies, and with how those gains vary according to the degree of economic interdependence. It attempts to extend the discussion of economic policy formation in an open economy in two respects: by allowing for international capital movements and by exploring how well national policymakers, acting independently, can be expected to perform as the economic interdependence among countries increases.

Interest in these problems derives from two sources. The first is the great increase in international capital movements which took place after 1958, and the high sensitivity of some of these capital movements to interest rates. This change put new burdens and new restraints on national monetary policies. Analyses of the economic interactions among countries, such as Metzler's classic paper,[1] have generally been confined to trade flows, ignoring capital movements entirely. Those works which have incorporated the effects of international capital movements have been framed in terms of an "atomistic" country, one sufficiently small that the repercussions of its policies on the world economy, and hence back on itself, are negligible.[2] This assumption greatly simplifies the analysis, but it does so at the expense of relevance for a large economic area such as the United States, the European Economic Community, or the United Kingdom. The second source of interest is the evident increase in international consultation and cooperation which has accompanied growing economic interdependence among nations, a growing interdependence that appears in trade flows as well as capital movements.[3] Why has this interdependence apparently increased the pressure for international economic cooperation? The question is especially pertinent in view of the observation by Mundell[4] that when national economic authorities have several policy objectives and several policy instruments at their disposal, a division of labor can be found which will permit attainment of the objectives.[5] In a decentralized system of policymaking, each policy authority concentrates his attention on a single policy objective. Mundell's proposal concerns the division of labor between monetary and fiscal policies within a single country, but the "division of labor" principle would seem to be even more appropriate, and is certainly more evident, among countries; the same analysis should apply, and decentralization of policymaking should be successful. Close cooperation among policymakers should be unnecessary.

The analysis here attempts to show that as economic interdependence increases, the effectiveness of decentralized policymaking in the sense just described will decline, and the case for coordination of policymaking for directing all the policy instruments at all the targets will become more compelling. This conclusion is perhaps obvious and innocent enough as applied to policymakers within a single country, but it also has implications for the coordination of economic policies *among* nations, with a corresponding reduction in national sovereignty, which are only beginning to be appreciated.

The analytical framework used here is similar to that introduced by J. Tinbergen,[6] involving *targets* of economic policy (i.e., variables to which we attach some social importance, such as the level of unemployment or the rate of economic growth) and *instruments* of economic policy (i.e., those variables, such as government expenditures or open-market operations, which can be controlled by a nation's economic authorities, and which in turn influence the values taken by the target variables). "Effectiveness" of policy is measured both in terms of the speed with which policymakers restore the target variables to their target values after they have been disturbed by some exogenous and unforeseen forces and in terms of the size of international reserve movements required during the transitional adjustment period.

The approach taken here is to specify a simple two-country model of the world economy. Each country is assumed to have two policy instruments at its disposal. A process of adjustment to deviations from policy targets is specified, and the resulting dynamic adjustment model is simulated for different values of the parameters—marginal propensities to import and the interest sensitivity of international capital movements—which represent the degree of economic interdependence among countries.

The Model

The following macroeconomic relationships describe the economy of a major country:

$$Y = C + I + G + X - M, \tag{1}$$

$$C = C(Y), \tag{2}$$

$$I = I(Y, r), \tag{3}$$

$$M = M(Y), \tag{4}$$

$$L = L(Y, r), \tag{5}$$

$$V = H + R, \tag{6}$$

$$L = V, \tag{7}$$

$$B = X - M + K, \tag{8}$$

$$K = K_0 + K(r - r'), \tag{9}$$

where

Y = national income,
C = consumption,
I = domestic investment,
G = government expenditure,
X = exports of goods and services,
M = imports of goods and services,
L = demand for money,
V = supply of money,
R = central bank holdings of international reserves,
H = central bank holdings of domestic bonds,
B = balance of international payments,
K = net inflow (+) of foreign capital,
r = rate of interest on bonds.

All these variables (except r) are in money terms, but prices are assumed to be constant.[7] Relationships 1, 6, and 8 are identities, 2–5 and 9 are behavioral relationships, and 7 is a market-balance equation.

For simplicity it is assumed that all government expenditures are financed by the sale of bonds; there are no taxes. Thus, three assets are involved here: bonds, money, and real capital. But attention is focused on flows, and portfolio-balance considerations are ignored.

A similar set of relations (1′–9′) apply to the second region, which can be considered to be the rest of the world, whose variables are indicated by a prime. Exchange rates are assumed to be fixed throughout, and without loss of generality currencies are assumed to exchange one for one, so we have the following identities:

$$X = M', \tag{10}$$

$$M = X', \tag{10'}$$

$$K = -K'. \tag{11}$$

Together these imply

$$B = -B'. \tag{12}$$

Substituting equations 2–4 in 1 and 9 in 8, performing similar operations on the primed variables, differentiating totally the resulting equations, noting equation 12, defining $s = 1 - C_y - I_y$ for the first country and s' similarly for the second, and rearranging, we get five independent equations:

$$(s + m)dY - I_r dr \quad\quad - m'dY' \quad\quad\quad\quad = dG, \tag{13}$$

$$-L_y dY - L_r dr \quad\quad\quad\quad\quad\quad\quad + dR = -dH, \tag{14}$$

$$mdY - K_r dr \quad - m'dY' + K_r dr' + dB = 0, \tag{15}$$

$$-mdY \quad + (s' + m')dY' - I'_r dr' = dG', \tag{16}$$

$$\quad\quad\quad\quad - L'_y dY' - L'_r dr' - dR = -dH'. \tag{17}$$

Equations 13 and 16 concern the flow of goods and services in the two regions, equations 14 and 17 represent the monetary sectors of each region, and equation 15 is the balance of payments between the two regions. Thus, equation 14 indicates that changes in the demand for money must equal changes in the supply, which in turn are made up changes in international reserves plus open-market transactions in bonds.

Here subscripts indicate partial derivatives with respect to the indicated variable, and the differentials can be taken to indicate differences from target values, e.g., $dY = (Y - Y^*)$, where Y^* is the target value of Y. It is assumed that with all the variables on target initially, $B = B^* = 0$, so that $dB = B = dR/dt$. So long as $B \neq 0$, reserves will be changing and so will the money supply, unless offsetting action is taken. If we consider discrete (unit) periods of time and assume that the influence of *past* reserve changes on the money supply is neutralized by offsetting open-market operations (dS), leaving only B_t to affect the money supply in period t, we can replace dR in equations 14 and 17 by $dB = B$. In symbolic terms, while by the end of time period t, $dR = \sum_{i=1}^{t} dB_i$,

$$dV = dR - dS = dB, \quad \text{where } dS = \sum_{i=1}^{t-1} dB_i, \tag{18}$$

and similarly for the primed country. Therefore, dH and dH' must be interpreted as open-market operations deviating from dS and dS', respectively.[8]

Alternative formulations are to assume (a) that all reserve changes are immediately neutralized by open-market operations or (b) that incomes and interest rates always adjust fully and freely to ensure balance-of-payments equilibrium. With the first alternative dR would not appear in equations 14 and 17; with the second alternative dB would not appear in equation 15. The model used here is thus a peculiar hybrid of these alternative models, implying that the monetary authorities choose to neutralize the monetary effects of reserve changes, but that they do so only with a one-period lag. This formulation is adopted so that different degrees of capital mobility will have some effect on incomes and interest rates without ensuring complete elimination of payments imbalances.

Interest-rate differentials are assumed to influence the period-to-period *flow* of capital from one country to another. It would be more appropriate, but unduly complicating, to represent capital movements as a combination of stock adjustment and continuing flow in response to interest-rate differentials. The model assumes implicitly, therefore, that once an investor buys bonds he is "locked in" until maturity, so that only new saving plus the proceeds from (steadily) maturing bonds can be allocated between new domestic and foreign bonds in response to yield differentials.

It is assumed that s, m, L_y, and K_r are all positive and that I_r and L_r are negative (similarly for primed variables). The equations have been arranged so that all the target variables (Y, r, B, Y', r') are on the left-hand side and all the policy instruments $(G, H, G',$ and $H')$ are on the right. This permits the use of the economical matrix notation

$$Ay = x, \tag{19}$$

where

$$A = \begin{bmatrix} s+m & -I_r & 0 & -m' & 0 \\ -L_y & -L_r & 1 & 0 & 0 \\ m & -K_r & 1 & -m' & K_r \\ -m & 0 & 0 & s'+m' & -I'_r \\ 0 & 0 & -1 & -L'_y & -L'_r \end{bmatrix},$$

y is the column vector of target variables, and x is the column vector of policy instruments. As we will see below, the use of matrixes makes it possible to see clearly which interdependencies are being ignored in a policy adjustment process.

Note that interest rates on bonds are here regarded as *targets* of policy rather than as instruments, as they have been in some models.[9] Interest rates cannot be regarded as instruments of policy in an open economy with international capital movements, since no country can control its interest rate directly. It is open-market operations that are directly under the control of each country's monetary authorities. Interest rates can be regarded as a proxy for the target of economic growth or the distribution of income, just as the level of income proxies for the target of employment.[10] For example, full employment can be achieved with various combinations of consumption and investment. Lowering the bond rate can alter the "mix" in favor of investment and hence raise the growth in output. In this sense the rate of interest may be a proximate target of policy.

Comparative Statics of the Model

How small changes in each of the policy instruments[11] affect the "equilibrium" values of each of the target variables can be found by inverting the matrix A, since $y = A^{-1}x$ and dy/dx equals the transpose of A^{-1}. The elements of A^{-1}, even for this simple system involving only two countries, four instruments, and five targets, are formidably complicated.[12] For example, the normal foreign-trade multiplier for a change in government expenditure, allowing for feedbacks from the other country, for monetary effects in both countries, and for international capital movements, is

$$\frac{dY}{dG} = \frac{(L_r - K_r)[(s' + m')L'_r + I'_r L'_y] - L_r[(s' + m')K_r - m'I'_r]}{\Delta}, \tag{20}$$

where

$$\Delta = [(s + m)L_r + I_r L_y][(s' + m')L'_r + I'_r L'_y] - L_r m m' L'_r$$
$$+ m'I'_r(sL_r + L_y I_r) + mI_r(s'L'_r + L'_y I'_r)$$
$$- K_r[(s' + m')(sL_r + L_y I_r) + (s + m)(s'L'_r + L'_y I'_r)$$
$$+ m(s'L_r + L'_y I_r) + m'(sL'_r + L_y I'_r)].$$

Given the assumptions concerning signs made in the preceding section, both the numerator and the denominator of this expression will always be positive.[13]

It would be tedious to examine all the elements of A^{-1}. However, allowing for international capital movements between two regions does give rise to some possible outcomes which would not otherwise take place. We can consider three:

First, while an autonomous rise in domestic expenditure would normally be expected to hurt the balance of payments, if capital movements are sufficiently sensitive to interest-rate differentials a rise in domestic expenditure by raising interest rates may attract more than enough capital from abroad to finance the enlarged current-account deficit. The inflow of capital serves not only to purchase the bonds issued to finance the larger expenditure but also to help satisfy a larger transactions demand for cash.

Second, while a domestic boom in one country may normally be expected to "spill over" into the other country, raising incomes there as well as in the first country, it is possible that the flow of capital from the second to the first country, by raising interest rates in the second country, may induce a decline in investment more than enough to offset the stimulus from enlarged exports. A boom at home leads to recession abroad. This outcome will be more likely the higher is the interest sensitivity of international capital movements and of investment in the second country relative to the interest sensitivity of demand for money in both countries.

Third, tighter monetary policy (open-market sales of bonds) in one country may be expected to lower interest rates in the other country if international capital movements are small but to raise them if international capital movements are large. The first outcome results from the lower level of activity induced in the second country by a decline in exports to the first country. If capital is internationally mobile and interest sensitive, however, tighter monetary policy in the first country will pull funds out of the second country and raise interest rates there. This flow will mitigate the impact of a given open-market sale on the first country, but it will aggravate the decline in money income in the second country.

These examples should serve to indicate that allowance for international capital movements introduces a new range of possible outcomes into the traditional analysis of foreign-trade multipliers. It becomes especially important to specify the nature of the disturbance—whether it is an expenditure disturbance (e.g., a shift in the consumption function, an investment boom, or a change in government spending or taxation) or a monetary disturbance (e.g., a central-bank action or a shift in the public's portfolio between bonds and cash). Either type of disturbance may have quite different impacts on incomes and interest rates in the two countries, and on the balance of payments, depending on the relative sizes of the countries, on the relationship between the marginal propensities to import and the interest sensitivity of international capital flows, on the relationship between the marginal propensity to save and the transactions demand for cash, and on other factors.

The Policy-Adjustment Model

The preceding section was a digression on the comparative static properties of the model set out in the first section. Nothing was said there about the target values of the target variables. From the viewpoint of policy targets, the model of the first section is underdetermined. A well-known proposition of the theory of economic policy is that to achieve n targets (except by coincidence) there must be at least n instruments.[14] Here there are five policy targets and only four instruments,[15] so instruments are inadequate to secure any set of arbitrary values for the five targets. Here we are not interested in reaching arbitrary targets, however, but in how this model responds to small disturbances from policy targets which are assumed to be compatible. We can make the five targets (y^*) compatible by manipulating some parameter not a variable in this model, for example the exchange rate, so as to make them all compatible. Thus, the exchange rate is assumed to be correct for the desired levels of employment, rates of growth (as reflected in the interest rates), and balance-of-payments positions of the two countries. Initially $y = y^* = 0$ and $x = 0$, by choice of scale.

Now suppose this harmonious state is subjected to some disturbance. Disturbances can be specified in several ways and can enter the system in a number of places. For simplicity, however, we assume that the structure in equation 19 remains unchanged, that the parameters remain unchanged as a result of any disturbance, and that disturbances are confined to once-for-all shifts in expenditure patterns or in portfolio preferences in either of the two countries.[16] Thus, the disturbances (z) are step functions which enter the model linearly, like the policy instruments:

$$Ay = x + z, \qquad (21)$$

where z is a column vector. It is obvious from equation 21 that, for $y^* = 0$, $x^* = -z$, where x^* is the value of x required to ensure $y^* = 0$.

The policy authorities do not generally know the value of z. As a rule, they cannot observe disturbances directly, but only resulting deviations of target variables from their target values. They therefore must "grope" back toward policy equilibrium on the basis of signals from these deviations.

We assume that this groping process takes the form

$$\delta x = C(y^* - y), \qquad (22)$$

where δx is the time derivative of x and where C is a "coordination matrix."[17] C indicates the degree of coordination among policymakers in their pursuit of the targets, where coordination refers to the extent to which policymakers take into account the objectives and prospective actions of other policymakers in determining their own actions. Three cases can be distinguished.

(1) No coordination, or full decentralization, in economic policymaking. For example, the fiscal authorities are concerned only with the level of national income, not with the level of interest rates or the balance of payments. In this case C has only one element in each column. By rearrangement of the terms in equations 13–17 (i.e., by rearranging the columns of A), C can then be made diagonal. Each instrument x_i is assigned to a single target y_i, and adjustment takes the form

$$\delta x_i = C_{ii}(y_i^* - y_i), \quad i = 1, \ldots 4. \tag{23}$$

This is the case examined by Mundell[18] for two targets and two instruments.

(2) Internal coordination. In this case the policy instruments of each country are devoted to simultaneous achievement of the objectives of each country. The fiscal and monetary authorities of each country are concerned with the simultaneous determination of national income and interest rates, say, but they are not concerned with the values of these variables in the other country. C (after proper arrangement of A) is block diagonal.

(3) Full coordination. Here the policymakers take into account all the interdependencies of the economic system in using their policy instruments. C is a full matrix, identifying each instrument with all target variables on which it has an impact. It seems natural to relate the elements of C to the elements of A, and in particular when c_{ij} is not zero to set $c_{ij} = \alpha a_{ij}$, where α is a constant coefficient of adjustment and a_{ij} are elements of A. These values can be justified on the ground that within this general form of adjustment the most direct approach to equilibrium would be

$$\delta x = \alpha(x^* - x), \tag{24}$$

where each x is adjusted with a speed varying with the deviation from its (unknown) appropriate value. This seems to be an obvious standard for comparing speeds of adjustment under different degrees of coordination. But the system of full coordination reduces to this if $C = \alpha A$. Thus we have

$$C = \alpha \begin{bmatrix} a_{11} & 0 & 0 & 0 & 0 \\ 0 & a_{22} & 0 & 0 & 0 \\ 0 & 0 & 0 & 0 & 0 \\ 0 & 0 & 0 & a_{44} & 0 \\ 0 & 0 & 0 & 0 & a_{55} \end{bmatrix} \tag{25}$$

for no coordination,

$$C = \alpha \begin{bmatrix} a_{11} & a_{22} & 0 & 0 & 0 \\ a_{21} & a_{22} & 0 & 0 & 0 \\ 0 & 0 & 0 & 0 & 0 \\ 0 & 0 & 0 & a_{44} & a_{45} \\ 0 & 0 & 0 & a_{54} & a_{55} \end{bmatrix} \qquad (26)$$

for internal coordination, and

$$C = \alpha \begin{bmatrix} a_{11} & a_{12} & a_{13} & a_{14} & a_{15} \\ a_{21} & a_{22} & a_{23} & a_{24} & a_{25} \\ 0 & 0 & 0 & 0 & 0 \\ a_{41} & a_{42} & a_{43} & a_{44} & a_{45} \\ a_{51} & a_{52} & a_{53} & a_{54} & a_{55} \end{bmatrix} \qquad (27)$$

for full coordination. The zeros in the middle row merely remind us of the fact that there is no instrument to operate directly on the balance of payments, i.e., $x_3 = 0$.

Substituting equation 21 into 22 yields

$$\delta x = Cy^* - CA^{-1}(x + z), \qquad (28)$$

where the z are given. The solution to this system of simultaneous differential equations in x takes the form

$$x(t) = Ay^* - z + We^{-\lambda t}Z, \qquad (29)$$

and therefore

$$y(t) = y^* + A^{-1}We^{-\lambda t}Z,$$

where $y(t)$ is the value of the target variables at time t after the initial disturbance, W and Z are matrices determined both by the structure of the model and by the nature of the initial disturbance, and λ is a vector of the characteristic roots of CA^{-1}. If the target variables are to converge to their target values (y^*), the last term on the right must be transitory, which is ensured if all the roots are positive. The smaller these roots are, the longer the transition period will last and the longer the target variables will be away from their targets. Thus in general an adjustment system with large roots will be more efficient than a system with small roots. The length of the transition period, defined as the time required for $y(t) - y^*$ to reach some specified small value and stay below it in absolute value, will vary with the type of disturbance and the structure of the model, since these determine the weight to be associated with each root λ_i. But a system is more efficient with respect to many types of disturbance the larger is the smallest root, since this is the root whose term fades out least rapidly. Thus, in evaluating the different types of coordination we are concerned with the relative size of the characteristic roots of CA^{-1}, and in particular with the size of the smallest root.

Numerical Examples

Unfortunately, equation 28 cannot be solved analytically, even though it arises from a fairly simple model. It can be solved numerically, however, for particular values of the elements in A and C. Any set of values is somewhat arbitrary, but values have been selected here to correspond very crudely to the United States (unprimed region) and the rest of the world (primed region). All of the parameters have been fixed except for the two marginal propensities to import and the interest sensitivity of capital flows; these have been varied parametrically to allow for increasing degrees of economic interdependence between the two regions. Thus, the following numerical work is based on

$$A = \begin{bmatrix} 0.35 + m & 15.0 & 0 & -m' & 0 \\ -0.10 & 6.0 & 1 & 0 & 0 \\ m & -K_r & 1 & -m' & K_r \\ -m & 0 & 0 & 0.30 + m' & 15.0 \\ 0 & 0 & -1 & -0.24 & 12.0 \end{bmatrix} \quad (30)$$

The marginal propensities to import, m and m', were permitted to take on the following values in tandem, indicating a parallel rise in "openness" on current account in both regions:

$$\begin{aligned} m &= \quad 0.01 \quad 0.06 \quad 0.15 \quad 0.30 \\ m' &= \quad 0.007 \quad 0.04 \quad 0.10 \quad 0.20. \end{aligned} \quad (31)$$

The interest sensitivity of capital K_r, was given the following values:

$$K_r = \quad 0.0 \quad 2.0 \quad 10.0 \quad 20.0.$$

These numbers, like the values for I_r and I'_r in equation 30,[19] indicate the change in billions of dollars per unit of time (say, a year) resulting from a one-percentage-point change in the bond rate. Thus, $K_r = 2.0$ means that a one-percentage-point rise in r relative to r' would lead to an inflow of capital of $2.0 billion per period. The values for K_r range from no interest sensitivity of capital movements to very high (but not infinitely high) sensitivity.

Table 1
Smallest characteristic root[a] of CA^{-1}.

No coordination			Internal coordination		Full coordination	
K_r	0	20	0	20	0	20
m 0.01	$0.50 \pm 0.50i$	0.17	0.94	0.26	1.0	1.0
0.30	$0.52 \pm 0.40i$	0.18	0.41	0.18	1.0	1.0

a. All systems give rise to one root at zero, but this plays no role in the adjustment process so long as the disturbances do not affect the balance of payments directly, that is, so long as $z_3 = 0$.
Here $\alpha = 1$. For different α, characteristic roots will be the product of α and the roots shown.

Since there are five target variables and only four instruments, a choice must be made, for purposes of adjustment, among the target variables. It is assumed below that each of the two regions is primarily concerned with its level of employment and its rate of growth, and each directs its fiscal and monetary policies toward these ends. The balance of payments is thus left to follow the course dictated by the pursuit of these other objectives. Because of our assumption that all targets are compatible, the balance of payments will also adjust as the other target variables are brought to their targets.

An alternative assignment involves having one country, say the first, direct its monetary policy to keeping payments in balance, and allowing the rate of interest to adjust residually. Some remarks will be made below on this case, but attention will be focused on the first case.

Table 1 gives the smallest characteristic roots of CA^{-1}, where A is drawn from equations 30–32 and C is constructed as indicated in equations 25–27.

Several points stand out. First, when policies are not coordinated at all there is a considerable amount of "overshooting," as is indicated by the presence of complex roots (some not shown), which lead to oscillatory behavior in equation 29. When policies are coordinated internally, the oscillatory behavior disappears; the strong interdependencies, which when ignored lead to oscillation, were between monetary and fiscal policies in pursuit of the two domestic objectives in each region. Moreover, the smallest root is generally higher with internal coordination than it is with no coordination, indicating that convergence toward objectives will be faster when policies are coordinated internally. But the smallest roots are still below unity, indicating that convergence to targets after a disturbance may be slower with only internal coordination than it would be with full coordination of policies, which takes into account the interdependencies between nations as well as those within nations. However, with internal coordination there is also one root above unity (not shown), so for some types of disturbance convergence may actually be faster than it would be with full coordination.

The second point to note about the smallest roots for internal coordination is that they decline as the degree of economic interdependence between the two regions increases. This pattern suggests that the speed with which economic policymakers can return to their targets after disturbance, under a system of adjustment which ignores the interactions between national policies, will decline as the economic interdependencies grow. Lack of coordination becomes more costly and the case for better coordination is strengthened.

Simulated Policy Responses

The speed of response to any disturbance depends in part on the nature of the disturbance. Two types of disturbance of particular interest involve shifts in expenditure patterns (e.g., an "autonomous" investment boom or a change in government expenditure) and shifts in preferences among financial assets. The policy-adjustment model set out in section 3, modified to facilitate computer use, was simulated for the numerical values of the parameters given in section 4 and for these two types of disturbance. Some results of these simulations are set out in tables 2–4.

The policy model used for simulation was the system of difference equations 21' and 22' set out in note 17 rather than the differential equations 21 and 22. This change simplifies computation, but it also changes slightly the nature of the solution. The general solution to equations 21' and 22' is[20]

$$y_t = y^* + A^{-1}W(1 - \lambda)^{t-1}Z, \tag{29'}$$

where, as before, W and Z are matrices determined by the structure of the model and by the initial disturbances and λ is a vector of the characteristic roots of CA^{-1}. Here t takes on only integral values, representing discrete time periods. The second term on the right will be transitory so long as $(1 - \lambda)$ is less than unity in absolute value, i.e., so long as the real part of λ is between 0 and 2. Thus, in this case λ can be too large for stability as well as too small; indeed, if any of the roots is greater than unity, a cyclical response will be introduced. Uncoordinated policy responses will lead to overshooting the targets. Furthermore, roots which are near to 0 or to 2 will lead to longer transition periods than roots which are close to unity.

Thus, as before, the smaller the positive root, the slower the convergence

Table 2
Speed of adjustment to income targets (periods until $|dY| + |dY'| \leq 0.20$).

		K_r	Expenditure disturbance[a]		Monetary disturbance[b]	
			0	20	0	20
No coordination	m	0.01	17	17	22	38
		0.30	24	16	29	34
Internal coordination		0.01	10	26	11	36
		0.30	19	11	23	45
Full coordination		0.01	9	9	10	10
		0.30	9	9	10	10

a. $z_t = (20,0,0,0,0)$, $t \geq 0$.
b. $z_t = (0, -20,0,0,0)$, $t \geq 0$.

to policy targets; but here the additional possibility is introduced that too large roots can also lead to slow convergence, as well as to overshooting.

Table 2 indicates the time required for national income to be put back on target following an expenditure disturbance and a monetary disturbance under the three forms of policy coordination. The standard of performance was taken to be the number of time periods required to bring the sum of the deviations of national income (without regard to sign) in the two regions to within a specified distance from their target values, and to keep this sum below that figure. For concreteness, the initiating expenditure or monetary disturbance can be regarded as $20 billion per period, and the standard of performance is to bring the combined national incomes to within $200 million of their combined targets.

Table 3 gives similar results for the interest-rate targets, where the measure of performance is the number of periods required to bring the sum of the interest rates in the two countries to within 0.20 of a percentage point of the sum of the targeted rates of interest.[21]

Tables 2 and 3 confirm the two generalizations made earlier. First, the time period required for adjustment generally rises as capital mobility and import propensities increase, except when there is full coordination. In general, higher interdependence slows down policy adjustment. Even with internal coordination, the delay in achieving income targets following an expenditure disturbance is increased 10 percent in moving from the northwest to the southeast corner of the box in table 2, for instance, and the delay following a monetary disturbance is quadrupled. In addition, as we will see below, larger

Table 3
Speed of adjustment to interest-rate targets (periods until $|dr| + |dr'| \leq 0.02$).

	K_r	Expenditure disturbance[a]		Monetary disturbance[b]	
		0	20	0	20
No coordination	m 0.01	12	12	17	39
	0.30	26	24	30	39
Internal coordination	0.01	6	15	8	25
	0.30	13	7	17	34
Full coordination	0.01	6	6	8	8
	0.30	6	6	8	8

a. $z_t = (20,0,0,0,0)$, $t \geq 0$.
b. $z_t = (0, -20,0,0,0)$, $t \geq 0$.

reserves are required during the transition period when policy targets are being restored to their desired values.

Second, the delay in adjustment is reduced by increasing the degree of coordination, and the delay in adjustment from failure to coordinate policies rises with the degree of interdependence between regions. This conforms with common sense; if interactions are high, the losses from ignoring them will be larger than if interactions are low.

In addition, although it is not evident in table 2 and 3, the degree of overshooting targets is much greater in the case of no coordination than in the case of internal coordination, and overshooting is absent in the case of full coordination.[22]

These generalizations are not without exception. The tendency for high interdependence between countries to prolong the adjustment period is far less marked when there is no coordination than where there is internal coordination. This is because internal interdependencies—the influence of monetary policies on demand and that of fiscal policies on interest rates—are being ignored in the first case, and for the parameters tested here larger external interactions apparently do not add much; indeed, greater external interactions sometimes compensate in part for the ignored internal interactions.

Second, higher trade interdependence occasionally reduces the adjustment delay under the regimes of no coordination and internal coordination. High import propensities represent large leakages of demand, and if these are not quickly compensated by fiscal or monetary action abroad, they help to

Table 4
Reserve changes during adjustment (billions of simulated dollars, cumulative for ten periods following a disturbance).

	K_r	Expenditure disturbance[a]		Monetary disturbance[b]	
		0	20	0	20
No coordination	m 0.01	−1.2	+2.9	−0.1	−71.7
	0.30	−20.3	−6.8	−6.0	−74.3
Internal coordination	0.01	−0.7	+15.1	−1.6	−57.3
	0.30	−11.7	+5.7	−29.2	−74.4
Full coordination	0.01	−0.6	+5.3	−1.5	−20.8
	0.30	−5.7	−0.3	−14.3	−23.8

a. $z_t = (20,0,0,0,0)$, $t \geq 0$.
b. $z_t = (0, -20,0,0,0)$, $t \geq 0$.

stabilize the disturbed economy by transmitting some of the disturbance to the other country. But, of course, this failure in both countries to take into account high leakages contributes to the overshooting of targets.[23]

Table 4 indicates even more clearly the impact of high but ignored interdependence on the process of policy adjustment. It shows the change in foreign-exchange reserves (in billions of simulated dollars) during the first ten periods following an expenditure or a monetary disturbance amounting to $20 billion. The choice of ten periods is wholly arbitrary, designed merely to provide a common basis for comparison.[24]

The case of monetary disturbances can be considered first, since it shows a straightforward pattern. A shift in portfolio preference toward bonds and away from cash, or a series of open-market purchases of bonds by the central bank, will lower the interest rate, stimulate domestic investment expenditure, and induce a capital outflow. A persisting shift in demand for bonds will cause reserve losses which generally decline as the degree of policy coordination increases and, for each coordination regime, increase with interdependence both on trade and on capital account. Moreover, the difference between coordination regimes in the amount of reserve change increases with the degree of interdependence. Thus, as interdependence rises from $(m, K_r) = (0.06, 2)$, not shown, to $(0.30, 20)$, the conservation of reserves over ten periods arising from a move to full coordination of policies from internal coordination rises from $(16.8 - 10.9) = 5.9$ billion simulated dollars to $(74.4 - 23.8) = $50.6 billion for a monetary disturbance of $20 billion.

Reserve changes resulting from an expenditure disturbance also show a clear pattern, but a somewhat more complicated one than in the case of a monetary disturbance. An autonomous rise in expenditure will worsen the current account, tending to produce reserve losses. But it will also raise interest rates, leading to capital inflows and reserve gains. Whereas in the case of a monetary disturbance the effects on current and capital accounts reinforce one another, in the case of an expenditure disturbance they work in opposite directions. As we saw in the comparative static analysis of section 2, a rise in government expenditure (analytically equivalent to an expenditure disturbance) can either help or hurt the balance of payments, depending on whether the effect on capital account outweighs or is outweighed by the effect on current account. The range of possibilities in a dynamic context can be seen in table 4. For each coordination regime, reserve changes decline algebraically as the marginal propensities to import increase, and rise algebraically as the interest sensitivity of capital increases.

The fact that reserves rise with high capital sensitivity offers little consolation to an observer of the whole system, since a rise for one region implies a fall for the other; and an autonomous drop in expenditure in the first region will lead to a loss of reserves by that region. The pattern of reserve changes does suggest, however, that, as far as expenditure disturbances are concerned, for each degree of coordination and for each level of the marginal propensities to import there is an optimum interest sensitivity of capital which minimizes the need for reserves. As the marginal propensity to import rises, this optimum sensitivity also rises. Either higher or lower capital mobility would lead to larger reserve changes. Thus, it is not generally true, as is sometimes claimed, that a perfect capital market will reduce greatly or even eliminate payments imbalances by permitting "equilibrating" flows of capital. Very high interest sensitivity of capital movements may aggravate rather than mitigate balance-of-payments swings.[25] There is no guarantee, moreover, that the same degree of capital mobility will also minimize the impact on reserves arising from expenditure disturbances in the second region,[26] or that it will minimize the time required to restore income targets; and monetary disturbances will always result in larger reserve changes the higher the international mobility of capital in response to interest-rate differentials.

Figure 1 compares typical reserve changes in response to an expenditure disturbance under the three regimes of policy coordination. There is a clear tradeoff between reserve requirements and coordination of economic policies, with greater coordination generally reducing reserve requirements.

The results presented so far rest on a particular assumption about monetary policy (delayed neutralization of reserve changes), on a particular

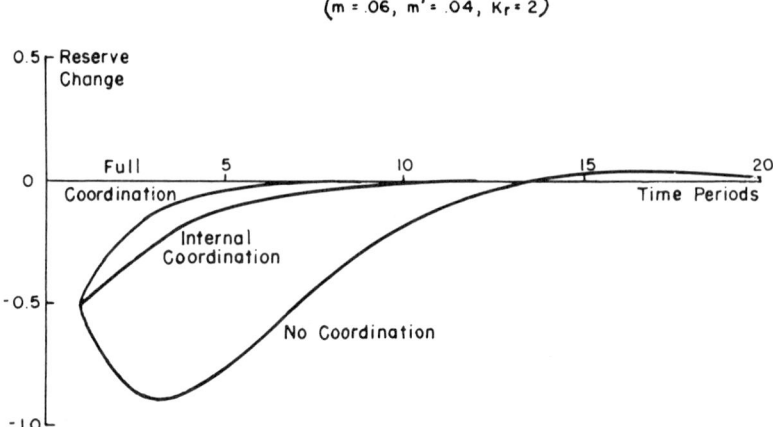

Figure 1

assignment of instruments to targets, and on a particular set of numerical values for the relevant parameters. It is of interest to know how sensitive the results are to these various assumptions.

With full and immediate sterilization of the impact of reserve changes on the money supply, the interest sensitivity of capital movements ceases to affect the time required after a disturbance to restore incomes and interest rates to their desired levels, since by assumption the effect of capital flows on domestic interest rates is neutralized. Nonetheless, the delays in reaching targets are lengthened by larger trade interdependencies, the delays decline with increasing coordination among policymakers, and the pattern of reserve changes is similar to that recorded in table 4, although the swings are larger because of the immediate neutralization of effects on domestic monetary conditions.[27] Thus, the conclusions above require little modification in this case.

The results presented so far for the case of no coordination (that is, each instrument associated with a single target) have been based on the assumption that monetary policy should be directed toward the objective of growth. Alternatively, monetary policy could be assigned the task of keeping international payments in balance.[28] In this case, broadly speaking, higher economic interdependence among regions speeds up the adjustment process rather than slowing it down. The result is not surprising, since the leverage of monetary policy on the balance of payments increases with higher interdependence. Restoration of income and growth targets at all levels of interdependence is much slower, however, than when monetary policy is directed toward the growth target.

Finally, separate simulations for substantially lower values of the marginal savings rates and the interest sensitivity of investment, and for higher values of the income and interest sensitivity of demand for money, suggest that the results reported in detail here continue to hold qualitatively and do not change radically in magnitude.

Conclusions from the Analysis

The model developed and simulated here has attempted to do several things at once. It has attempted to incorporate international capital movements in a systematic way, to allow for normal repercussion and feedbacks between two regions roughly equal in size, to explore the effects of coordination between policymakers on the path of adjustment to economic disturbances, and to suggest how the adjustment is affected by different degrees of economic interdependence between the two regions both on current and on capital account.[29] It is a medium-term Keynesian-type model, abstracting from longer-term adjustments in the stock of capital and the rates of return on capital, and it assumes that exchange rates are in long-run equilibrium throughout.

The numerical examples and simulations suggest that lack of coordination among policymakers

• delays achievement of national objectives such as full employment and a targeted rate of growth, and

• increases the requirements for international reserves when, under a regime of fixed but equilibrium exchange rates, the balance of payments is simply allowed to adjust passively to policy changes directed at other objectives.

They also suggest that these delays in reaching targets and their calls on foreign-exchange reserves increase with the degree of economic interdependence among nations.

These generalizations are not without exception, but they seem to be sufficiently well founded to suggest some implications for the "real" world of policy. Since the need to hold foreign-exchange reserves entails a national cost, and since prolonged deviations from national objectives of economic policy reduce national welfare, growing economic interdependence among nations calls for increased coordination between national policymakers. It also raises the requirements for foreign-exchange reserves, since given disturbances cause a larger drain on reserves when interdependencies are high even when policies are fully coordinated among countries.

There is little doubt that economic interdependence among nations—concretely, marginal propensities to import and the interest sensitivity of international capital movements—has increased sharply in the years since World War II, the period in which government responsibility for the speed and direction of national economies has become widely accepted. Hence, the analysis here suggests a need for greater coordination of national policies and for additional foreign-exchange reserves—or, alternatively, for steps to reduce the interdependencies—if welfare losses are to be avoided. Not surprisingly, both these forces can be recognized in official actions during the 1960s.[30]

The gains from coordination of policies here are "dynamic" gains, arising from better mutual timing. They should not be confused with the arguments for "harmonization" of economic policies on (static) efficiency grounds. Coordination of policies in the sense used here would be desirable under conditions of high interdependence even if one accepted the view that harmonization of economic policies beyond common agreement on maintenance of full employment is not necessary even in a free-trade area.

As a description of reality, the model developed here is deficient in a number of respects some of which can readily be corrected by further work. The model applies to only two regions rather than many. If coordination of policies takes place only within countries, many more interactions will be ignored when there are many regions. Second, the lag structure adopted here is far too simple. The only lags allowed are the lag in neutralization of reserve changes and those arising from the need for policymakers to grope toward their targets because they lack direct information about the disturbances. Everything else adjusts instantaneously. Adjustment lags should be allowed for, as well as different lags for different instruments of policy. Third, portfolio-balance considerations have been wholly neglected. In particular, international capital movements are assumed to respond to interest-rate differentials in a steady flow, with no allowance for a shift in stocks of private financial claims from one country to the other. Finally, for comparative purposes a uniform set of disturbances has been used throughout. But disturbances themselves may be influenced in size by the degree of interdependence among regions or by the degree of coordination among policymakers.[31] If so, it is not possible to say that higher economic interdependence among nations will call for more coordination without knowning also the impact of this higher interdependence on the disturbances.

Acknowledgments

I am grateful to Mrs. Melanie Weaver for programming assistance and to the Economic Growth Center of Yale University for financial assistance.

Notes

1. L. A. Metzler, "A Multiple-Region Theory of Income and Trade, " *Econometrica* 8 (October 1959): 329–354.

2. See, for example, M. Fleming, "Domestic Financial Policies under Fixed and under Floating Exchange Rates," International Monetary Fund *Staff Papers* 9 (November 1962): 369–380; H. G. Johnson, "Some Aspects of the Theory of Economic Policy in a World of Capital Mobility," in T. Bagiotti, ed., *Essays in Honor of Marco Fanno*, vol. 2 (Padova: Cedam, 1966); R. A. Mundell, "Capital Mobility and Stabilization Policy under Fixed and Flexible Exchange Rates," *Canadian Journal of Economic and Political Science* 29 (November 1963): 475–485; R. A. Mundell, "Flexible Exchange Rates and Employment Policy," *Canadian Journal of Economic and Political Science* 27 (November 1961): 509–517; R. A. Mundell, "The Appropriate Use of Monetary and Fiscal Policy for Internal and External Stability," IMF *Staff Papers* 9 (March 1962): 70–79; J. Tinbergen, *On the Theory of Economic Policy* (Amsterdam: North-Holland, 1952). Anne O. Krueger attempts in "The Impact of Alternative Government Policies under Varying Exchange Systems," *Quarterly Journal of Economics* 79 (May 1965): 195–208, to allow for such feedbacks for a regime of flexible exchange rates. See also R. A. Mundell, *International Economics* (New York: Macmillan, 1968), pp. 262–271, where a two-country model with perfect capital mobility is developed.

3. Tariffs, transportation costs, and other impediments to trade have declined, and in addition there has probably been a narrowing (at least among industrial countries) of differences in comparative costs. See R. N. Cooper, *The Economics of Interdependence: Economic Policy in the Atlantic Community* (New York: McGraw-Hill, 1968), especially chapter 3.

4. Mundell, "Appropriate Use."

5. Mundell has called this division of labor "the principle of market classification," and I have called it "the assignment problem." See R. N. Cooper, "The Assignment Problem: A Characterization," in R. A. Mundell and A. K. Swoboda, eds., *Monetary Problems of the International Economy* (University of Chicago Press, 1968). It is analogous to the identification of each commodity in a general market system with its "own" price.

6. Tinbergen, *On the Theory of Economic Policy*.

7. Prices could be allowed to vary in this model without affecting the basic results, so long as price changes were reversible with pressures of demand; however, to do so would complicate the model unnecessarily. Irreversible price changes would involve nontemporary disturbances of the balance-of-payments equilibrium, and these are outside the framework developed here.

8. I am grateful to Warren Smith and Jay Levin for drawing my attention to this implication of the analysis in an earlier draft.

9. See Mundell, "Flexible Exchange Rates and Employment Policy." Mundell modified this view of interest rates in "Capital Mobility and Stabilization Policy under Fixed and Flexible Exchange Rates."

10. It is, of course, the level of *real* income and not that of money income that determines the level of unemployment in the short run. In formulating the model in terms of money magnitudes I have assumed that money wages adjust to higher money national income far more slowly than the policy authorities.

11. Or, indeed, any other autonomous linear disturbance; see section 3 below.

12. There is a notational problem here. The elements of A^{-1} indicate how each of the target variables Y, r, and so on changes with a given small change in policy, allowing all the target variables to adjust but holding other *policy* variables unchanged, except for the delayed neutralization described above. Actually, dY/dG is not a true derivative, since it includes the effects on the money supply of reserve changes during a finite passage of time (one period). Moreover, "equilibrium" is of the medium-term Keynesian type and may represent a long-term disequilibrium.

13. With the Keynesian assumption regarding accomodating monetary policy, $dr = dr' = 0$ and equation 20 becomes the familiar foreign-trade multiplier with repercussions:

$$\frac{dY}{dG} = \frac{s' + m'}{(s + m)(s' + m') - mm'}.$$

14. Tinbergen, *On the Theory of Economic Policy*.

15. Actually, there are six potential targets, since each country may have a balance-of-payments target. However, such targets may be inconsistent. We assume here that the balance-of-payments targets are consistent, and therefore the number of targets reduces to five, since $B^* = -B'^*$.

16. To preserve the assumption that the initial equilibrium exchange rate can be retained throughout the analysis, it is necessary to rule out disturbances affecting the balance of payments directly, such as a shift in import functions or a change in portfolio preferences between cash and *foreign* bonds. Such disturbances would lead to an indefinite loss or gain in reserves and would require a change in the exchange rate or in other measures acting directly on the balance of payments. In the notation used here, we require that the third element (z_3) of the vector z be zero at all times.

17. This form of adjustment process follows naturally from a utility function quadratic in y; instruments are changed in proportion to the marginal utility of y if C represents the quadratic coefficients in the utility function. Here, however, C is determined on the basis of economic structure without regard to different welfare weights that may attach to the targeted variables.

The difference-equation analogue is used for simulation in the next section. The system then becomes

$$Ay_t = x_{t-1} + z_{t-1}, \tag{21'}$$

$$\Delta x = x_t - x_{t-1} = C(y^* - y_t). \tag{22'}$$

18. Mundell, "Appropriate Use."

19. A one-percentage-point rise in the government bond rate is assumed to lower domestic investment by $15 billion a year in both regions. This does not seem too

high when housing is included in investment. A one-point rise is assumed to lower the public's demand for (reserve bank) money, *ceteris paribus*, by $6 billion in the first region and $12 billion in the second. A range of values is given for the interest sensitivity of capital; of the values chosen, a flow of $2 billion perhaps comes closest to the situation prevailing in the mid 1960s.

20. Expression 29' is derived as follows: Substitute equation 21' in equation 22', which with reorganization becomes

$$x_t = C(y^* - A^{-1}z_{t-1}) + (I - CA^{-1})x_{t-1}.$$

Setting $y^* = 0$, $x_0 = 0$, $z_t = 0$ for $t < 0$, and $z_t = z$ for $t \geqslant 0$, we obtain

$$\begin{aligned}x_t &= [I + (I - CA^{-1}) + \cdots + (I - CA^{-1})^{t-1}](-CA^{-1})z \\ &= [I - (I - CA^{-1})^t](CA^{-1})^{-1}(-CA^{-1})z \\ &= -z + (I - CA^{-1})^t z \\ &= -z + W(1 - \lambda)^t W^{-1}z.\end{aligned}$$

Setting $W^{-1}z = Z$ and substituting in equation 21' gives equation 29'. Here λ are the characteristic roots of CA^{-1} and W is a matrix of characteristic vectors of $(I - CA^{-1})$.

This solution would have to be modified slightly for multiple roots different from unity, but the conditions for speed of convergence remain unchanged. For a discussion of simultaneous systems of difference equations, see P. A. Samuelson, *Foundations of Economic Analysis* (Cambridge, Mass.: Harvard University Press, 1947), pp. 418–429.

21. These standards of performance are, of course, arbitrary; "acceptable" deviations from target could be either larger or smaller than those chosen here; and they should be calculated for each of the regions separately, rather than taking the two regions together. But these measures seem reasonable (neither region alone can find itself farther from target than $200 million or 0.02 percentage point for national income and bond rates, respectively), and they serve to illustrate economically the relative speeds of adjustment under different coordination regimes and interdependence parameters.

Simulations were run for all of the parameter values in equations 31 and 32. Only four of the resulting sixteen cases for each of the three degrees of coordination are reported here.

22. The roots in table 1 suggest no overshooting in the case of internal coordination when the adjustment process follows equations 21 and 22. The use of discrete adjustment periods in equations 21' and 22' introduces a cyclical response pattern for $\alpha = 1$, since in that case $(1 - \lambda) < 0$ for some roots not shown. All the simulations reported here used $\alpha = \frac{1}{2}$, which eliminates this cyclicity for the parameters tested.

23. High values of m raise the largest characteristic root. As noted above, a root above unity introduces cyclicity in the solution to equations 21' and 22'. High values of m thus increase the likelihood of overshooting. Here $\alpha = \frac{1}{2}$ lowers the largest root below unity; but $\alpha = 0.8$ would lead to overshooting for $m = 0.3$, $m' = 0.2$.

24. With no coordination and high K_r, the arbitrary choice of ten periods for measuring reserve changes seriously understates reserve requirements, because reserves swing dramatically within the first ten periods and for a prolonged period thereafter.

25. For two regions that are similar in the sense that $mL_r = m'L'_r$, the formal condition for an expenditure disturbance to lead to no overall effect on the balance of payments (a worsened current account being exactly offset by an improved capital account) is that $-mL_r = K_r L_y$. If therefore $K_r > (-mL_r)/L_y$, a country experiencing a boom will increase its reserves at the expense of the other country. Under conditions of very high capital mobility, a boom could create large payments imbalances due to "disequilibrating" capital movements. Of course, monetary policy could be used to ensure external balance when K_r is high.

26. The condition that an expenditure disturbance in the second country has no effect on reserves is $-m'L'_r = K_r L'_y$, on the assumption $mL_r = m'L'_r$. This is obviously different from the condition in note 25 if $L'_y \neq L_y$.

27. The condition for $dB/dG = 0$ in this case is the same as that given in note 25, despite the different assumption regarding monetary policy.

28. This is an extension to two countries of the case considered by Mundell in "Appropriate Use."

29. F. M. Fisher, "On the Independent Use of Two or More Sets of Policy Variables," *Journal of Political Economy* 75 (February 1967): 77–85, has considered the question of ignored interdependence in a more general framework.

30. For empirical evidence on the growing interdependence and official response to it, see Cooper, *Economics of Interdependence*.

31. We are talking here about the "exogenous" disturbances, z, not the "disturbances" transmitted from one country to another through trade and capital movements. The latter are obviously influenced by the degrees of interdependence and coordination, and such influences are included in the simulations.

8
Monetary Theory and Policy in an Open Economy

Two developments in the world economy in recent years have created an immediate and practical interest in certain propositions which only a few years ago seemed to be merely of theoretical interest. The first development has been the great increase in the international movement of capital, with the presumption that this increased movement reflects increased mobility in response to given economic incentives. The second development is the movement for many currencies, since March 1973, from fixed to flexible exchange rates. Both developments raise important questions concerning the frequency and amplitude of disturbances to macroeconomic stability in national economies and the effectiveness of various instruments of stabilization policy (notably fiscal and monetary measures) at stabilizing national income and output under the new circumstances.

Relatively little systematic attention has been addressed to the first of these questions. The second was dealt with in theoretical terms by Mundell (1960–1964, collected in *International Economics*, 1968) and by Fleming (1962). This article will use the Fleming analysis as a starting point for a discussion of how their now widely taught results might have to be modified in the interests of better theory and greater realism. The article will not offer a systematic review of the rapidly growing professional literature on the subject of the title; rather, it will focus on several facets of what turns out to be an extraordinarily difficult set of related problems to deal with satisfactorily from a theoretical point of view while still retaining practical relevance. In a later section it will also address briefly the first question identified above: the impact of capital mobility and alternative exchange-rate regimes on the disturbances with which national monetary authorities may have to deal.

Monetary Policy in a Closed Economy

It is useful first to review briefly how monetary measures supposedly influence the aggregate demand for goods and services in a closed economy. It is now customary to identify three channels whereby monetary measures—specifically, an increase in the money supply—may be expected to influence aggregate monetary demand.

The first channel is through at least a temporary reduction in real interest rates—or, equivalently, an increase in the market value of physical assets relative to their reproduction costs or supply price. Expenditures on all forms of durable goods, especially housing and plant and equipment, will be stimulated by this discrepancy in prices, and in the process money income, output, and prices will also rise, the output-price division depending on the degree of utilization of the economy at the time of monetary expansion.

The second and third channels operate through changes in wealth and the influence such changes have on demand for goods and services. By reducing nominal interest rates, an increase in the supply of money will raise the market value of all assets whose yield is fixed in nominal terms and of close substitutes for such assets. As a result, wealth-holders will presumably find themselves with more wealth than they desire to hold and therefore increase their spending on goods and services.

The third channel also operates through its effect on wealth. This arises when the increase in money has come about in such a way as to increase total wealth held by the public even at unchanged interest rates, e.g. through a deficit in the government budget financed by money creation.

All these channels may also be expected to operate in an open economy, but with some important modifications. First, changes in the exchange rate, like changes in interest rates, will in general alter wealth held by the public, especially if they hold foreign securities. Moveover, changes in the exchange rate, like changes in interest rates, can create discrepancies between the current price of goods and services and their long-run supply prices, thereby stimulating or retarding demand. On both counts the influence of monetary actions on the exchange rate must therefore be taken into account. Third, the balance of payments offers another route whereby increases in the money supply will also increase wealth, a so-called outside source of new money.

Early Theory for an Open Economy: the Fleming Model and Its Results

Fleming deals with an open economy that is too small to influence world interest rates, world prices, or world incomes, so that the rest of the world can be treated parametrically. He excludes changes in the terms of trade from his analysis, but he allows for discrepancies between home-country interest rates and rest-of-the-world interest rates by permitting less than complete mobility of capital between the home country and the rest of the world. These "small-country" assumptions will be retained throughout this article.

The model is a simple Keynesian one, adapted to standard notation as follows:

$$Y = E(Y, i, r) + X(Y, r) + G, \tag{1}$$

$$L(Y, i) = M = H + R, \tag{2}$$

$$X(Y, r) + K(i) = B. \tag{3}$$

Here Y is national income (assumed equal to output), E is national expenditure, X is net exports, G is government expenditure on goods and services, L is the demand for high-powered money, M is the supply of high-powered money, H is central-bank holdings of domestic securities, R is central-bank holdings of international reserves, K is international capital movements, B is the balance of payments, i is the domestic rate of interest on government securities, and r is the exchange rate (domestic-currency price of a unit of foreign currency). All variables except i and r are measured in domestic currency, and prices of domestic output are assumed to be fixed. Parentheses indicate the variables that influence the variable they follow. Differentiating this system of equations and reorganizing items leads to

$$\begin{bmatrix} s+m & -E_i & -X_r \\ L_y & L_i & 0 \\ -m & +K_i & +X_r \end{bmatrix} \begin{bmatrix} dY \\ di \\ dr \end{bmatrix} = \begin{bmatrix} dG \\ dM \\ dB \end{bmatrix}, \tag{4}$$

where T_v indicates the partial derivative of T with respect to v, $s = 1 - E_y$, (the marginal propensity not to spend), and $m = -X_y$, (the marginal propensity to import). It is assumed that all of these structural parameters are non-negative except E_i and L_i, which are negative.

Within this framework, a system of fixed exchanges rates can be depicted by setting $dr = 0$, and a system of freely flexible exchange rates by $dB = 0$. Under a system of fixed exchange rates, the balance of payments, B, need not be zero, and as a result central-bank reserves will be changing. It is assumed that the central bank automatically sterilizes these reserve changes through offsetting domestic open-market operations (or in some other way), so that the balance-of-payments position does not directly affect the money supply. In other words, the monetary authorities are assumed to have full control over M, no matter what is happening to reserves. An act of pure monetary policy will therefore be a change in M, a stock variable, with G held unchanged. An act of pure fiscal policy, by the same token, is a change in G, a flow variable, with M held unchanged. We are interested in the impact of these two measures on Y under alternative exchange-rate regimes and as a function of K_i, the interest sensitivity of international capital movements.

The above system of equations can be solved for the policy multipliers $(dY/dG)_j$ and $(dY/dM)_j$, where j indicates the exchange-rate regime. The well-known conclusions from this analysis are

$(dY/dM)_{\text{flexible}} > (dY/dM)_{\text{fixed}}$,

$(dY/dG)_{\text{flexible}} \gtreqless (dY/dG)_{\text{fixed}}$ as $K_i \lesseqgtr -mL_i/L_y$,

and

$[(dY/dG)/(dY/dM)]_{\text{flexible}} < [(dY/dG)/(dY/dM)]_{\text{fixed}}$ for $K_i > 0$.

These results can be readily interpreted and have intuitive appeal. The first says that a given expansion in the money supply will be more effective at stimulating money income under a regime of flexible rates than under a regime of fixed exchange rates because under the latter some of the stimulus will leak away to other countries, whereas under the former the induced depreciation in the exchange rate will prevent this leakage on trade account. Moreover, a high mobility of capital will cause an even greater depreciation of the currency, thus stimulating domestic demand further.

The second result arises from the fact that under fixed exchange rates some of the fiscal stimulus will leak abroad, and this leakage is prevented with flexible rates by a depreciation of the currency. On the other hand, a fiscal stimulus without monetary support, as here, will tend to raise interest rates within the country. Under flexible rates, the resulting inflow of capital will tend to appreciate the currency, thus restricting demand. The inequality shows the conditions under which the second influence will outweigh the first. It is equivalent to fiscal stimulus leading a deterioration or an improvement to the balance of payments under fixed exchange rates. In the limiting case of infinitely large sensitivity of capital movements to interest-rate changes, the influence of fiscal policy on domestic demand disappears altogether under flexible exchange rates, for the induced currency appreciation fully offsets an initiating fiscal stimulus.

The third result clearly follows from the first two for sufficiently high mobility of capital. In the absence of capital mobility, equality holds between the two ratios; but any interest sensitivity of capital will give monetary policy a "comparative advantage" under a regime of flexible exchange rates

Table 1

	After one quarter	After six quarters
Impact on income of $100 in bond-financed government expenditure (dollars)		
Fixed exchange rate	101	171
Altered exchange rate	77	173
Impact on income of 1 percent increase in the rate of growth of the money supply ($ million)		
Fixed exchange rate	4.3	4.4
Altered exchange rate	63.8	19.0

Source. Caves and Reuber 1969, p. 69.

because of capital-induced movements in the exchange rate. By the same token, with any capital mobility monetary policy under a regime of fixed exchange rates has a comparative advantage over fiscal policy in dealing with the balance of payments as compared with influencing aggregate demand, as has been emphasized by Mundell (1968).

The money supply in this framework has been assumed to be completely exogenous, so the frequently cited result that high mobility of capital will undercut the effectiveness of monetary measures under a regime of fixed exchange rates cannot be derived. Removal of the assumption of complete sterilization of reserve changes will yield this result.

A certain amount of empirical work on the Canadian economy provides general support for these results. Rhomberg (1964) confirmed the first result and found that capital mobility was sufficiently high that fiscal policy was more effective under fixed exchange rates. Caves and Reuber (1969), using a different method, got qualitatively similar results. Choudry et al. (1972) confirmed the first result but found capital mobility sufficiently low that fiscal measures would be stronger under flexible exchange rates. In each case the modeling incorporated response lags, so impact effects differ from subsequent effects. The Caves-Reuber results, shown in table 1, suggest the pattern.

Stock Equilibrium an Balance-Sheet Requirements

There are several important conceptual weaknesses in the kind of analysis represented by the Fleming model. The remainder of this article will be devoted to a discussion of some of these weaknesses and to suggestions on how they might alter the conclusions of the analysis.

The first problem is that capital movements have been cast exclusively in terms of flows, and the related point that no balance-sheet constraints have been imposed either on the public or on the monetary authorities of the country under examination. Under these circumstances, a given interest rate may lead to capital flows of a given magnitude for an indefinite period of time, and the country can run a balance-of-payments surplus or deficit for an indefinite period of time without having it affect the money supply.

It would be equally and for some purposes more appropriate to depict capital movements as changes in portfolio positions held by residents or nonresidents, and capital movements would cease when portfolio equilibrium was restored (or, in the context of a growing domestic and world economy, when all portions of the portfolio were growing at the same rate). Portfolio positions could be expected to change whenever there were changes in asset yields or in wealth. In addition, the monetary authorities would have a portfolio of domestic and foreign assets, and they could not sell either without limit. The major contribution of the "monetary" approach to balance-of-payments analysis is to focus attention on stock equilibrium and balance-sheet requirements, and to make the point that "equilibrium" is not reached so long as central-bank reserves or the public's holdings of bonds are changing in a nongrowing economy (or are changing in a way other than that dictated by steady-state growth in a growing economy). This is fundamentally an old idea; David Hume's analysis (1748) contained an endogenous money supply, changes in which were linked to balance-of-payments flows. Thus, according to this approach, Fleming has not provided an adequate characterization of the impact of policy measures so long as $dB \neq 0$. Moreover, by defining dG as a continuing change in government expenditure financed by sale or retirement of bonds, he has ensured continuing portfolio disequilibrium.

Equally important, formulation of the problem in terms of portfolio equilibrium draws attention to the transitional dynamics, since exogenous (or policy) changes lead to transitory stock adjustments in portfolios plus continuing debt-service payments.

It is very difficult to model portfolio equilibrium and stock adjustment satisfactorily without shedding much of what is of interest for stabilization policy. To avoid stock-flow complications and to emphasize the implications of full stock equilibrium, a number of authors have required continuous equilibrium in the balance of payments (even in a regime of fixed exchange rates), or assumed a stationary state or both (McKinnon in Mundell and Swoboda 1969; Swoboda 1972; Swoboda in Claassen and Salin 1972; Kenen 1976). As a consequence of these assumptions, a small country has no control at all over its money supply under fixed exchange rates, regardless of the degree of capital mobility, for any attempt to achieve a money supply differing from that required for total portfolio balance will evoke offsetting inflows or outflows from abroad. [Indeed, using basically the same kind of framework, Mundell (1969) has argued that a small, growing economy must have a balance-of-payments surplus to satisfy its growing demand for money if the monetary authorities are not increasing their purchases of domestic assets rapidly enough.] A commitment to fix the exchange rate *ipso facto* leads to loss of monetary autonomy, and the central bank can merely alter the composition of its domestic and foreign assets.

Kenen's model is illustrative of this approach. His system defines household wealth, requires that demand for money equal supply of money, stipulates that savings will occur only when actual wealth differs from desired wealth and that any such discrepancy must equal the trade balance, and defines the change in international reserves as equal to the balance of payments. Households cannot hold foreign bonds, but foreigners can (in the case of perfect capital mobility) hold our country's bonds and will do so at a constant yield. In equilibrium neither wealth nor reserves can be changing, and as a result the trade balance and the government budget must both be balanced. (Kenen's model is modestly flawed by failing to allow for service payments on external debt.) Fiscal policy must be defined in terms of a balanced-budget change in government expenditures or a once-for-all increase in bond-holdings by the public, in order to preserve the stock-equilibrium constraint.

Under these assumptions, monetary measures cannot influence domestic output at all under fixed exchange rates, but they can influence aggregate money demand under flexible rates. Thus, in a rough way, Fleming's first conclusion is confirmed, but with further restrictions. Fiscal action, as defined by Kenen, cannot influence aggregate demand under flexible rates if capital is perfectly mobile, but it can with immobility of capital—the same result Fleming got. In contrast, fiscal action cannot influence aggregate demand at all under fixed exchange rates in Kenen's world. (In Fleming's model the influence of fiscal action as defined by Kenen would remain positive.)

These kinds of results are not especially helpful to those concerned with stabilization policy. The need for stabilization policy is predicated on the assumption that from time to time the economy will be jostled off its full-employment equilibrium, perhaps with cumulative effect. Stabilization policy is designed to offset or at least mitigate these disturbances. But if stabilization policies will not work under fixed exchange rates, as indicated by this class of stock equilibrium models, neither will they be necessary, for exogenous disturbances will also lose their ability to affect aggregate demand. Adjustment of the economic system will automatically nullify them. Unfortunately, while a system of fixed exchange rates does under usual circumstances help to reduce the disturbances that impinge on an economy (as discussed below), the day is not yet at hand when we can rely on the economy to absorb them without effect. However good the adjustment of the system might be, in practice disturbances have important transitory effects—and so do stabilization measures. Short recognition and response lags are of course essential if stabilization measures are to help reduce variations in aggregate demand arising from exogenous disturbances.

An alternative to the stock equilibrium models is to require only flow equilibrium, but subject to balance-sheet consistency, as Borts and Hanson (1975) have done for the private sector. But that leaves the possibility of unresolved stock disequilibria. A complete model cannot avoid having both stock and flow equilibria, with explicit stock adjustment responses to disequilibria. This greatly complicates the model, and the results that are crucial for assessing the stabilization impact of monetary and fiscal measures depend critically on assumptions that are made about which markets clear instantaneously and which do not, and which markets clear in the short run by price adjustment as opposed to quantity adjustment. From the viewpoint of scientific analysis, these "dynamic" specifications, and tests of their validity, are of course desirable, however difficult they may be, for that is what economic stabilization is all about. With these more complicated models, the qualitative character of some of Fleming's results are likely to survive, for example that national monetary autonomy in the short or even the medium run exists even under fixed exchange rates, provided that capital is not highly mobile.

Dornbusch (1973) has emphasized the desirability of wedding flow equilibrium analysis to stock equilibrium through explicit stock adjustment in connection with assessing the impact of currency devaluation on an economy. More recently, Genberg and Kierzkowski (1975) have applied the "new" approach to devaluation to a model of employment and price fluctuations under flexible exchange rates. In this model, unlike Kenen's, the public is allowed to hold foreign bonds; but like Kenen's in equilibrium it allows no saving and no government deficit. Flexible exchange rates ensure that payments are always in balance, and in addition equilibrium requires no new acquisition of foreign assets, so the trade balance must equal any interest earnings on foreign investment. The economy is divided into two sectors, tradable and nontradable goods; labor is effectively the only factor of production (capital goods being specific to each sector and playing no role in the analysis), and the labor market always clears. But variations in employment, and hence in voluntary unemployment, occur through variations in the real wage rate.

An increase in the money supply through an open-market purchase of domestic bonds creates portfolio disequilibrium in this model both because of a reduced interest rate on domestic bonds and because the lower interest rate has raised the market value of the bonds, thus initially increasing total wealth. Provided that the elasticity of demand for foreign bonds with respect to the domestic interest rate is higher than the interest elasticity of demand for money, the percentage increase in demand for foreign bonds will be higher than the percentage increase in demand for money. And since the public holds neither stocks of tradable goods nor stocks of foreign money, the increased demand for foreign bonds can be "satisfied" in the short run only through a depreciation of the currency proportionately greater than the increase in the money supply. This is required to rebalance the portfolio in the short run. But at the newly depreciated rate, there will be an excess supply of tradable goods, a trade surplus will emerge, and gradually the currency will appreciate back toward (but not to) its initial level, as the public now adjusts its portfolio by purchasing new foreign bonds with the proceeds of its trade surplus. Employment during this process of adjustment to new stock equilibrium will fall at first, since the depreciation-induced increase in domestic prices will reduce total wealth and thereby induce net saving (the equivalent of the trade surplus), but then will gradually rise as portfolio balance is restored and in the final equilibrium will be above the initial level of employment prevailing before the increase in the money supply. Thus, in this model the initial impact on employment of an open-market operation is the opposite of the ultimate effect, and while the impact effect on the exchange rate is in the same direction as the ultimate effect, the exchange rate overshoots its final equilibrium position.

An increase in the money supply does not result in an equiproportionate increase in prices even in the long run in this model, because, as Patinkin (1965) showed in connection with government bonds, the existence of an outside asset other than money will break the proportionality. Here foreign bonds play the role of the second outside asset. Their presence causes real employment and output effects and even leads to changes in relative prices between the two sectors.

One has in the exchange rate of this model a variable that is analogous to the market valuation of physical assets in Tobin's analysis of incentives to invest. Movements in the exchange rate alter the real value of wealth and create discrepancies between the market valuation of foreign bonds in the bond-holding country and the long-run cost of foreign bonds purchasable through the net sale of tradable goods. Thus, the market for foreign bonds clears in the first instance through an adjustment of the exchange rate, but in the longer run quantities can adjust and the market price in domestic currency reverses course.

If this is the pattern, why is it not smoothed by currency speculation? Genberg and Kierzkowski do not allow foreign currencies to be held in anyone's portfolio, so in their model this complication is ruled out. But the possibility of speculation draws attention to the crucial role in dynamic adjustment processes that can be played by expectations. Speculation that is "stabilizing" in the sense of avoiding overreaction of the exchange rate would also greatly smooth the path of employment from its initial to its new equilibrium.

Before this type of portfolio-equilibrium model is accepted, however, we must explore more fully the reasons why households hold wealth, to ascertain what are sensible behavioral assumptions when it comes to adjustments in portfolios. In particular, under what circumstances is it plausible to assume that changes in the market valuation of households' wealth caused by changes in market interest rates will influence expenditure, as in Kenen's model, or that changes in the exchange rate will influence expenditure, as in the Genberg-Kierzkowski model? If either change is regarded as temporary, there has been no change in "permanent" (expected) wealth, and there may be no change in consumption (although expenditures on durable goods may be influenced even by the temporary change in relative prices).

Even if a change in the interest rate or the exchange rate is regarded as permanent, the pattern of desired future consumption may also be influenced in such a way as to neutralize or even reverse any apparent *ceteris paribus* effect of changes in wealth on current consumption. Thus, we need to know more about the formation of expectations and we need to combine portfolio-balance models with lifetime saving-consumption models to discover under what circumstances and in what ways changes in the market valuation of wealth will alter expenditure. If, for example, foreign bonds are held in part to backstop future anticipated consumption of foreign goods, the influence of a change in the exchange rate (regarded as permanent) on portfolio and consumption behavior will be quite different from the case in which foreign bonds are held merely as a yield-diversifying alterative to domestic bonds.

The latter motive would lead to results such as those in the Genberg-Kierzkowski model, but that is not the only possible outcome. A depreciation of the currency that reflects a "permanent" worsening in the country's terms of trade would increase the local-currency value of resident holdings of foreign assets, but it would generally lower the value of foreign assets in terms of imported goods. Under the former motive for holding foreign assets, therefore, domestic spending might fall rather than rise in response to the effects of depreciation on the "wealth" embodied in foreign bonds, to preserve its command over imports. However, if the change in relative prices substantially reduces the public's desire to consume imported goods in the future, the public may instead decide to spend more by liquidating some of its now redundant holdings of foreign bonds.

Flow Models of Capital Movements

A second weakness of the Fleming-type model concerns its specification of international capital movements, even when they are cast in terms of flows and when stock-adjustment considerations are deliberately neglected. The influence of changes in the exchange rate under flexible exchange rates is wholly neglected, and comparisons between regimes implicitly assume that the character of the regime itself does not influence the values of the structural parameters of the economy.

With the exchange rate free to move, capital movements should be specified to allow for (1) a possible price effect, since foreign securities are purchased or sold against domestic currency at different prices at different times, and (2) a speculative effect, since claims on foreigners may be held in anticipation of future increases in prices rather than just for current yield. In the latter instance it is of course necessary to specify how exchange-rate expectations are formed. If expectations are highly inelastic, a regime of flexible exchange rates differs little from a regime of fixed exchange rates; private speculative capital movements perform the function of official reserve movements under a fixed-exchange-rate regime. There is some evidence that this was the case in Canada during the 1950s; private speculation was strongly "stabilizing" around a one-for-one rate between the U.S. and Canadian dollars. But of course expectations might also be strongly elastic. In either case, $K_r dr$ might dominate $K_i di$ under a regime of flexible exchange rates, and this could either weaken (in the case of inelastic expectations) or strengthen (in the case of elastic expectations) the influence of monetary measures on aggregate demand under such a regime.

Moreover, alteration of regimes would in general be expected to alter the values of the parameters. In particular, both the marginal propensity to import (m) and the interest sensitivity of capital movements (K_i) might be expected to fall in value in moving from fixed to flexible exchange rates, because of the greater short-run uncertainty in foreign-currency dealings associated with flexible exchange rates. (Long-run uncertainty will be no greater, and possibly less, than under an adjustable peg regime of exchange rates.) If businesses are risk averse, at least as far as foreign-currency transactions are concerned, the possibility of wide week-to-week variations in rates will tilt transactions toward domestic customers and suppliers and away from foreign ones. (The Fleming analysis assumed that a change in interest rates will induce uncovered capital movements. The exchange-risk argument does not apply to covered movement, but changes in forward exchange rates may be assumed to eliminate any net covered interest incentive quickly.)

Making allowance for this likelihood does not alter the Fleming results formally, since the marginal propensity to import does not appear in the multipliers under flexible exchange rates and the interest sensitivity of capital movements, K_i, does not appear in the multipliers under fixed exchange rates because of the assumption of complete sterilization. But if sterilization is incomplete, that is, if reserve movements do have some effect on the money supply, then K_i will appear in the fixed-exchange-rate multipliers, and if initially $K_i > -mL_i/L_y$ under fixed exchange rates (so that fiscal expansion will produce a payments surplus), then a switch to flexible exchange rates which also lowers K_i may either increase or reduce the fiscal impact on income, depending on the extent of reduction of K_i. This is contrary to Fleming's second result.

Specification of the Demand for Money

The specification $L(Y, i) = M$ is a common one in simple macroeconomic models. But if the public can hold foreign money, what role should that play in the money-stock equation? Under what circumstances does foreign money satisfy the demand for money? If money is held only for transactions purposes and all transactions were denominated in the currency of the selling country, then one need not be concerned about holdings of foreign money in this context so long as trade is balanced. All holdings of domestic money, nonresident as well as resident, would be appropriate for the home country.

But if money is held for precautionary and speculative purposes, including precautions and speculation with respect to the exchange rate and the price of foreign bonds, then the appropriate concept of "money" is even less clear than it is in closed economies. Indeed, McKinnon (1963) has argued that the more open the economy, the more likely it is that residents will switch to the regular use of foreign money under a regime of flexible exchange rates, thereby denying the country the seigniorage gains arising from the issuance of money and denying it monetary control over aggregate demand, even under flexible exchange rates.

The question of holdings of foreign money has ceased to be of merely academic interest now that the Eurocurrency market contains over $200 billion in liabilities, mostly but by no means exclusively in U.S. dollars. To the extent that these liabilities represent money (the same controversy surrounds this that surrounds the appropriate classification of various highly liquid assets in domestic economies), in what country's model of financial and macroeconomic equilibrium should they be placed?

Whether or not allowance is made for the holding of foreign monies to satisfy the demand for money, in a regime of changeable exchange rates the demand for money surely should include the exchange rate as an argument, just as the demand for bonds does. This has been done by Dornbusch (1973) in his analysis of devaluation.

Macroeconomic Disturbances

In assessing the impact of openness and of exchange-rate regimes on stabilization policy, it is not sufficient to look only at the influence of policy instruments on aggregate demand; one must also look at the magnitude of the stabilization task. In general, that magnitude will be sensitive both to the degree of openness and to the exchange-rate regime. Openness of an economy exposes it to disturbances originating in the rest of the world, for example through variations in world demand for its export products. But openness also disperses disturbances originating at home, for example by permitting imports to satisfy a temporary boom in demand for goods and services. Thus, the choice for an economy with respect to the desired degree of openness is not a straightforward one of simply weighing the gains from trade against the losses with respect to stability.

In fact, the insurance principle is at work: If disturbances are widely distributed around the world with less than perfect correlation in their timing, the stability of the world economy will be enhanced by distributing them as widely as possible, so much offsetting of disturbances will occur and the task of stabilization policy will generally be reduced. But of course in "nature" some economies are more stable than others, so the stabilization gains from wide distribution of disturbances will be spread unevenly among countries, and some individual countries will find themselves experiencing greater instability than under autarky or with a lower exposure to the world economy. Moreover, an important source of disturbance is government policies, so if ineptitude in economic policy is greater abroad than at home, this too may increase the stabilization task for the domestic authorities in an open economy and tilt the balance of gains and losses toward greater autarky.

The main point can be made with a simple illustration. Consider a small economy in a Keynesian framework in which nonpolicy disturbances affect aggregate demand linearly, through shifts in home demand or shifts in export demand, with zero means and with standard deviations of w and w' respectively (see Cooper 1974). Then the standard deviation of aggregate demand (u) in the absence of stabilizing action (one measure of the task facing the stabilization authorities) will be w/s in a closed economy and

$$u^* = (w^2 + w'^2 + 2ww'\rho)^{1/2}/(s + m) \tag{5}$$

in a small open economy. Here s is the marginal propensity not to spend, m is the marginal propensity to import, and ρ is the correlation between disturbances at home and disturbances abroad in the presence of trade. The asterisk stands for the open economy. If the disturbances are perfectly correlated ($\rho = 1$), then $u > u^*$ if $w/s > w'/m$. That is, the unstabilized variation in aggregate demand will be reduced in moving from a closed to an open economy if the leakages through imports (as measured by m) exceed the imported disturbances (w'), relative to the multiplier effect on domestic disturbances in a closed economy. For $\rho < 1$ the conditions for a reduction in income variation in moving from a closed to an open economy will be less stringent.

A regime of flexible exchange rates is not the same as autarky, but it does reduce both the impact of disturbances abroad on domestic income and the leakage of domestic disturbances abroad. Thus, it is not obvious what the net impact will be. In general, the higher w' is relative to w, the more attractive will be some form of insulation from the world economy.

How much insulation does a floating exchange rate provide? The answer depends on the nature of the disturbance. In some cases a flexible exchange rate can neutralize completely a disturbance to aggregate demand that would take place under a fixed exchange rate, in others it can reduce but not eliminate the impact, and in still others a flexible rate may aggravate the impact of the disturbance as compared with a fixed exchange rate.

An example of complete neutralization is provided by a general rise in the world price level, which under a fixed exchange rate would stimulate demand in our small economy. But an appreciation of the currency proportionate to the increase in foreign prices will compensate at the border, preventing either relative price or wealth effects.

An example of mitigation is provided by a world increase in demand for our country's export products, which will raise incomes and stimulate domestic demand. With a flexible rate, the currency will appreciate and partially damp the sale of exports; it will also encourage a larger volume of imports, on both counts relieving pressure on the domestic economy. However, in contrast with the first example, relative prices will have changed, resources will be reallocated, and total wealth will have been increased. So the insulation is incomplete.

An example of aggravation is provided by an increase in foreign demand for our country's securities (at constant interest rates), which will lead to appreciation of the currency. That will diminish aggregate demand and will call for a reallocation of resources away from tradable goods to nontradable goods, possibly with transitional unemployment. Large movements of capital, in the absence of speculative countermovements, may therefore result in greater disturbance to aggregate demand than would be the case under fixed exchange rates, even when the monetary authorities cannot sterilize such flows and they result in changes in the money supply. Aggravation is especially likely if exchange-rate expectations are elastic and the exchange rate (rather than local-currency prices) represents the principal price which clears the market for holdings of foreign securities in the short run. Changes in exchange rates would be large under these circumstances, and they would play havoc with the profitability of foreign-trade transactions. Firms could be thrown into bankruptcy on a wide swing of the exchange rate, both creating damage to the economy and provoking risk-averting actions which increase costs. A movement in the exchange rate that persists will eventually evoke a corrective change in the trade balance, but only with a lag. Indeed, the "J-curve" effect of movements in the exchange rate on earnings from trade might in the short run (for a country that is not a price taker in its export markets) aggravate the swing. Under these circumstances, official stabilizing speculation, i.e. management of the exchange rate, will help stabilize aggregate demand (but of course it may increase the movement of capital). Part of the debate between fixers and flexers involves differing assessments of the importance of capital movements as a source of disturbance to the exchange rate (and, through it, to the economy) and differing assessments of the ability and willingness of private wealth holders to adopt speculative positions with the proper timing and magnitude to mitigate such disturbances.

All these categories have their counterparts in dealing with disturbances of domestic origin. Movements in a flexible exchange rate will offset fully a general monetary inflation, "bottling it up" in the originating economy and preventing both the relative price change between tradables and nontradables and the exportation of excess demand that would occur if the exchange rate were fixed. There is complete neutralization. But with a shift in the composition of demand, e.g. toward imports, currency depreciation will only mitigate the aggregate-demand and relative-price effects. And if residents want more foreign securities and the exchange rate is the short-run equilibrator of shifts in preference between foreign and domestic securities, its movement (in the absence of currency speculation) will aggravate domestic instability. If the shift in preference is durable, it will in time evoke the reallocation of resources toward tradables that will make the real transfer. Even then, the rate may overshoot, as in the Genberg-Kierzkowski model.

Thus, contrary to claims that have been made for it, a flexible exchange rate cannot insulate an economy completely from external disturbances, or even from purely "monetary" disturbances if by that term we encompass switches among financial assets. An open economy is open, no matter what its exchange-rate regime.

Flexible exchange rates do, however, have one further effect which may mitigate disturbances: They may reduce the correlation in timing between disturbances in different countries as compared with a regime of fixed exchange rates. Shifts in demand for goods or securities may be partly expectational in nature, and business activity is less likely to move in tandem in the presence of even the partial insulation provided by flexible exchange rates. (Canada's experience in the 1950s does not support this view, but in that case there was strongly stabilizing currency speculation plus a certain parallelism between Canadian and U.S. policies; i.e., the Canadian authorities did not use fully what autonomy a flexible exchange rate would have afforded them.)

Factor-Price Responses and "Money Illusion"

The Fleming analysis and much that has followed it assumes no change in the general level of factor prices (changes in exchange rates are assumed to affect real incomes), and indeed it is from this that they derive most of their influence. It has recently been argued that currency depreciation requires "money illusion" in order to influence real variables. This is not strictly true, since wealth effects will remain even if factor prices adjust to restore real income, but clearly the presence of "money illusion" helps the process of adjustment by introducing some flexibility into real factor prices. There may be sound reasons why an increase in goods prices brought about by currency devaluation will be accepted even though a general reduction in money incomes would not be acceptable. The first will be perceived as relatively impartial in its effects, whereas reductions in money incomes would be the subject of suspicions that some incomes were reduced more than others (e.g. because of differential protection through contracts)—that is, that the wage structure or the distribution of income would be altered. Thus, "money illusion" may be present without any illusion about it at all.

If money illusion is present, it is useful in facilitating adjustment. Hoarding or dishoarding to adjust actual to desired wealth following a change in the exchange rate is bound to be a prolonged process, and since it involves shifts in aggregate demand the adjustment may be frustrated by official action aimed at stabilizing employment. At best, therefore, exchange-rate flexibility may introduce some real factor-price flexibility into economies where nominal flexibility, at least in a downward direction, is rare. At worst, however, exchange-rate movements might trigger factor-price adjustments to compensate for them. Indeed, nominal factor prices might respond to a depreciation of the currency even more quickly than to other price changes because of the generality and the wide diffusion of the consequences of movements in the exchange rate. Moreover, if the exchange rate depreciates in response to shifts in portfolio preference, it may generate a price-wage-price spiral where none existed before, thereby confronting the monetary authorities with the difficult choice between validating the increase in prices and wages through monetary expansion and letting unemployment rise. It is thus possible that via this route inflation can be "imported" as much under flexible rates as it can under fixed rates.

Factor-price responses to changes in exchange rates, if they exist, may well not be symmetrical; a depreciation is more likely to trigger demands for increases in wages than an appreciation is for reductions in wages. Response may be rapid to depreciations, slow to appreciations. If so, fluctuating exchange rates will have an inflationary bias for the world economy as a whole. We have too little evidence so far to judge the presence or the extent of any such asymmetry, although it is noteworthy that wage settlements in recent years have been much more moderate in Germany and Switzerland, where currencies have appreciated, than in other European countries, where they have not. The causation between movements in wages and movements in exchange rates can of course run both ways, from wages to exchange rates as well as from exchange rates to wages, but at least a superficial look at the evidence offers no support for strong asymmetry in the response of money wages to changes in exchange rates.

We also have too little evidence on the presence and extent of money illusion with respect to movements in the exchange rate, but various estimates of the response of wages to increases in prices in the United States and Britain (summarized in Kwack 1974) suggest that, other things being equal, wages respond only partially to increases in expected prices (35–77 percent, averaging around 50 percent), where "expected" prices are a geometric weighted average of present and past price changes. Thus, an increase in price leaves a *ceteris paribus* reduction in real wages. Of course, Britain and the United States are rather large economies, and might not be representative of small ones.

The problem of factor-price response suggests another reason, in addition to the increase in certain kinds of disturbances, for managing a flexible exchange rate, at least to the extent of preventing large sudden changes in the rate except when they are clearly needed. The price to be paid for such management is some loss of monetary autonomy, but it may reduce the load on the monetary authorities more than enough to compensate for that loss.

Controls on Capital Movements

A principal source of difficulty under either fixed or flexible exchange rates seems to be capital movements. Movements of liquid funds can play havoc with domestic monetary control under a fixed rate and with the exchange rate under a flexible rate. This suggests that capital movements should be subject to direct control, and indeed many countries have some system of control. But direct controls confront three difficulties. First, it is difficult to separate socially desirable capital movements from potentially disruptive capital movements. Second, any limited set of controls is likely to prove temporary in its effectiveness, for one consequence of the increasing mobility of capital is its ability to discover new channels for movement. To be effective, therefore, controls must be extended to cover all capital movements and even trade transactions, since credit has become an inseparable part of much trade and changes in the terms of credit can move large amounts of capital from one country to another. Third, however, such a comprehensive set of controls, covering intracorporate transactions and trade, is bound to lead to major distortions in the allocation of resources and in many countries to foster corruption of the controlling officials and those who must deal with them.

The general move toward flexible exchange rates is motivated largely by a desire to provide some insulation without controls, but as noted above official management of the rates may be desirable if private speculation does not perform a stabilizing function.

Considerations in the Choice of an Exchange-Rate Regime

Countries now face a choice between floating and not floating, and if they do not float they must choose what currency or group of currencies they want to tie their own currency to. The theoretical work on flexible exchange rates is not well enough developed to answer these questions, even in principle, but the observations in this article, in addition to pointing to areas where more extensive analysis is needed, suggest that the choice of an exchange-rate regime for a small country should be influenced by the following:

the magnitude of external economic disturbances relative to internal ones, and the difficulty (e.g. in timing) the authorities have in coping with disturbances,

the responsiveness of nominal factor incomes to changes in the exchange rate,

the extent to which capital movements can be controlled successfully, and the costs of controlling them, and

the remaining tradeoff between the average level of real income and the stability of real income afforded by the relationship of the country to the world economy, and public preferences regarding this tradeoff.

References

Borts, G., and J. Hanson. "The Monetary Approach to the Balance of Payments." In J. Behrman, ed., *Short-Run Macroeconomic Policy in Latin America*. National Bureau for Economic Research.

Caves, R., and G. Reuber. 1969. *Canadian Economic Policy and the Impact of International Capital Flows*. University of Toronto Press.

Choudry, N., Y. Kotowitz, J. Sawyer, and J. Winder. 1972. *The TRACE Econometric Model of the Canadian Economy*. University of Toronto Press.

Claasen, E., and P. Salin, eds. 1972. *Stabilization Policies in Open Economies*. Amsterdam: North-Holland.

Cooper, R. N. 1974. "Economic Mobility and National Economic Policy." Article 4 in this volume.

Dornbusch, R. 1973. "Currency Depreciation, Hoarding, and Relative Prices." *Journal of Political Economy* 83 (July–August).

Fleming, M. 1969. "Domestic Financial Policies under Fixed and under Floating Exchange Rates." IMF *Staff Papers*, 1962. Reprinted in R. N. Cooper, ed., *International Finance* (New York: Penguin, 1969).

Genberg, H., and H. Kierzkowski. 1975. Short Run, Long Run, and Dynamics of Adjustment under Flexible Exchange Rates. Discussion paper, GIIS–Ford Foundation International Monetary Research Project, Graduate Institute of International Studies, Geneva.

Hume, D. "On the Balance of Trade." Reprinted in R. N. Cooper, *International Finance* (New York: Penguin, 1969).

Kenen, P. B. 1976. "International Capital Movements and the Integration of Capital Markets." In F. Machlup, ed., *Economic Integration: Worldwide, Regional, Sectional.* New York: St. Martin's.

Kwack, S. Y. 1974. The Effects of Foreign Inflation on Domestic Prices and the Relative Price Advantage of Exchange Rate Changes. Mimeo.

McKinnon, R. I. 1963. "Optimum Currency Areas." *American Economic Review* 53. Reprinted in R. N. Cooper, ed., *International Finance* (New York: Penguin, 1969).

Mundell, R. A. 1968. *International Economics.* New York: Macmillan.

Mundell, R. A. 1969. *Monetary Theory.* Pacific Palisades, Calif.

Mundell, R. A., and A. Swoboda, eds. 1969. *Monetary Problems of the International Economy.* University of Chicago Press.

Patinkin, D. 1965. *Money, Interest, and Prices,* second edition. Harper and Row.

Rhomberg, R. 1964. "A Model of the Canadian Economy under Fixed and Fluctuating Exchange Rates." *Journal of Political Economy* 72 (February).

Swoboda, A. 1972. "Equilibrium and Macro Policy under Fixed Exchange Rates." *Quarterly Journal of Economics* 86 (February).

9 An Analysis of Currency Devaluation in Developing Countries

Currency devaluation is one of the most dramatic—even traumatic—measures of economic policy that a government may undertake. It almost always generates cries of outrage and calls for the officials responsible to resign. For these reasons alone, governments are reluctant to devalue their currencies. Yet under the present rules of the international monetary system, laid down in the Articles of Agreement of the International Monetary Fund, devaluation is encouraged whenever a country's international payments position is in "fundamental disequilibrium," whether that disequilibrium is brought about by factors outside the country or by indigenous developments. Because of the associated trauma, which arises because so many economic adjustments to a discrete change in the exchange rate are crowded into a relatively short period, currency devaluation has come to be regarded as a measure of last resort, with countless partial substitutes adopted before it is finally undertaken. Despite this procrastination, over 200 devaluations occurred between the inauguration of the IMF in 1947 and the end of 1970 (to be sure, some were small, and many took place in the years of postwar readjustment, especially 1949). In addition, there were five upvaluations, or revaluations, of currencies before the significant revaluations of 1971.

By convention, changes in the value of a currency are measured against the American dollar, so a devaluation means a reduction in the dollar price of a unit of foreign currency or, what is the same thing, an increase in the number of units of foreign currency that can be purchased for a dollar. (The numerical measure of the extent of devaluation will always be higher with the latter measure than with the former; for example, the 1967 devaluation of the British pound from $2.80 to $2.40 was 14.3 percent and 16.7 percent on the two measures, respectively.) By law, changes in currency parities are against gold, but since the official dollar price of gold was unchanged from 1934 to 1971, these changes normally come to the same thing. Except when many currencies are devalued at the same time—as they were in September

1949, to a lesser extent in November 1967 (when over a dozen countries devalued with the pound), in August 1969 (when fourteen French African countries devalued their currencies along with the French franc), and in December 1971 (when over fifty countries devalued along with the U.S. dollar with respect to the currencies of other industrial countries)—a currency devaluation against the dollar is also against the rest of the global payments system, that is, against all other currencies.

Largely because they are so numerous, but partly also because they devalue on average somewhat more often than the developed countries, less-developed countries account for most currency devaluations. Yet the standard analysis of currency devaluation, which has advanced substantially during this period and is still being transformed and refined, fails to take into account many of the features that are typical of developing countries today and which influence substantially the impact of currency devaluation on their economies and on their payments positions.

This article attempts to do two things. First, it suggests how the standard analysis of currency devaluation has to be modified to take into account the diverse purposes to which the foreign-exchange system is put in many less-developed countries, and the extent to which these diverse purposes influence the nature of devaluation and its effects on the economy. Second, it draws on postwar experience with about two dozen devaluations to see to what extent the anxieties of government officials, bankers, and traders, and even some economists, about devaluation and its effects are justified, and interprets some of this experience in light of the earlier theoretical discussion.

An Analysis of Devaluation for Most Developing Countries

The foreign-exchange system of a country can be used to pursue many objectives other than clearance of the foreign-exchange market. Faced with inadequate instruments of policy to achieve the many objectives expected of them, the governments of many less-developed countries have called upon it to do so. These functions range from fostering industrialization, improving the terms of trade, and raising revenue to redistributing income between broad classes and even doling out favors to political supporters. A practice used frequently to accomplish all three of the first objectives, and also to redistribute income, is to give primary export products a rate of conversion into local currency lower than the rate that importers must pay to purchase foreign exchange (and that exporters of nontraditional products receive). Import-substituting investment is stimulated by the unfavorable rate on imports, foreign export prices are higher than they otherwise would be in the rare event that the country can influence world prices for its products, and the government gains revenue from the often substantial difference between the buying and selling prices of foreign exchange. Similarly, imported consumer goods are often charged a rate much higher than imported investment goods, in an effort to stimulate investment in manufacturing (and with the undesirable side effect of encouraging modes of production that use relatively more capital and relatively more imported ingredients or components). Finally, and not least, the exchange system can be used to redistribute income between broad classes, as for example in Argentina when the exchange rate applied to traditional exports (meat and wheat) was deliberately kept low for a number of years with a view to keeping down the cost of living for urban workers.

All these functions involve multiple exchange rates of some kind, either explicit or implicit, that is, charging different exchange rates according to the commodity or service, the origin or destination, or the persons involved in the transaction. As such, they inevitably invite arbitrage and require policing—but so, of course, do taxes, which they often replace in function.

Moreover, politicians have learned that an objective achieved indirectly is often socially acceptable when direct action would not be. This is not always because of an imperfect understanding of the indirect means in contrast to the direct means, although that plays an important role. It is much easier for an interest group to mobilize successfully against an export tax than it is to mobilize against an overvalued currency supplemented by high import tariffs and possibly accompanied by some export subsidies, even though the two systems might have precisely the same effects. As Fritz Machlup has said (in connection with Special Drawing Rights):

We have often seen how disagreements among scholars were resolved when ambiguous language was replaced by clear formulations not permitting different interpretations. The opposite is true in politics. Disagreements on political matters, national or international, can be resolved only if excessively clear language is avoided, so that each negotiating party can put its own interpretation on the provisions proposed and may claim victory in having its own point of view prevail in the final agreement.[1]

Machlup was speaking of language, but the same is true of action; a roundabout way of accomplishing a controversial objective will often succeed where direct action would fail, because it obscures, perhaps even from the policymakers themselves, who is really benefiting and who is being hurt.

The difficulty is that the pursuit of these diverse objectives too often leads to neglect of the function of the exchange rate in allocating the supply of foreign exchange. When balance-of-payments pressures develop (sometimes as a result of inflationary policies, which in the short run are often also a successfully ambiguous way to reconcile conflicting social objectives), officials engage in a series of patchwork efforts and marginal adjustments to make the problem go away (raising tariffs here, prohibiting payments there), which may disturb the original objectives as well as coping only inadequately with the payments difficulty. When devaluation finally occurs, in consequence, the occasion is also taken (sometimes under pressures from the IMF or from foreign-aid donors) to sweep away many of the *ad hoc* measures that have been instituted to avoid the necessity for devaluation. This fact makes currency devaluation in many developing countries (and some developed ones) a good deal more complex than a simple adjustment of the exchange rate, and the analysis must be modified to take these other adjustments into account. Broadly speaking, one can distinguish four types of devaluation "packages":

- straight devaluation (involving a discrete change in the principal exchange rate, as opposed to a freely depreciating rate or an administered "slide" in the rate, such as was adopted by Brazil, Chile, and Colombia in the late 1960s, when the rate was depreciated by a small amount every two to eight weeks),
- devaluation with a *stabilization* program of contractionary monetary and fiscal policy aimed at reducing the level of aggregate demand, or at least the rate of increase of demand,
- devaluation accompanied by *liberalization*, whereby imports and other international payments that were previously prohibited or subject to quota are allowed to take place freely under much less restraint than before the devaluation, and
- devaluation accompanied by partial or full *unification* of exchange rates, whereby a preexisting diversity of exchange rates is collapsed into a single, unified rate, or at most two rates, the lower one applying to traditional exports of primary products and in effect amounting to a tax on these exports.

It is obvious that these categories are not mutually exclusive. Devaluation may involve simultaneously a stabilization program, liberalization, and exchange-rate unification, and in fact at least some elements of all are often present in devaluation in developing countries. For example, of 24 devaluations studied in some detail (which will provide the basis for evidence cited below), ten involved a fairly substantial degree of trade liberalization, ten (partially overlapping) involved a major consolidation of rates, and virtually all were accompanied by at least token measures of stabilization.

These various simultaneous adjustments must be taken into account in analyzing the economic effects of devaluation. In particular, it is necessary to distinguish between devaluation from a position of open payments deficit and devaluation from a position in which a latent deficit is suppressed by import controls and related measures which are removed upon devaluation. An additional complication is that less-developed countries are more likely at the time of devaluation to be generating new money demand at a rate greater than can be accommodated by total domestic output plus foreign assistance and other long-term capital inflows from abroad; in short, they are pursuing inflationary policies, as opposed to merely having costs that have gotten out of line in the course of past inflation.

In fact, most devaluing countries have some combination of an open payments deficit and a suppressed one. However, for clarity of exposition, and to bring out the contrast with the standard analysis most clearly, we will consider devaluation from a position in which the payments deficit is fully suppressed by other measures, and where the devaluation is accompanied by liberalization and/or unification of the exchange system involving the removal of special taxes, subsidies, and prohibitions that have been installed earlier. In addition, we will suppose that the country is not pursuing inflationary policies at the time of devaluation.

Low Elasticities

The first point to note is that the elasticity of demand for imports is likely to be low when imports are concentrated on raw materials, semifabricated products, and capital goods, a structure prevalent in less-developed countries. With import substitution in an advanced stage, all the easy substitutions having already been made in the pursuit of industrialization, imports depend largely on output rather than income and are not very sensitive to relative price changes. There is more room for substituting home production for imports of foodstuffs, although it will usually take a season or longer to bring this about. Moreover, import liberalization and exchange-rate unification will actually result in a reduction of the prices of those imports most tightly restrained before the devaluation, so consumption of them will be encouraged.

There is greater diversity of experience with regard to exports. Some countries—producers of oil, copper, and cocoa, for instance—have virtually no domestic consumption of the export goods. In others, exports include the major wage good—beef in Argentina and fish in Iceland, for instance. In the former countries, increasing exports require enlarged output and development of new export products, and neither of these courses may be easy in the short run, although tree crops can sometimes be more intensively harvested. In the latter countries, there is more room for immediate increases in exports permitted by reductions in domestic consumption of the export products, but this gain is brought about only by courting a wage-price spiral, on which more will be said below. In developed countries, by contrast, there are many domestically consumed goods that are actual or potential exports, and hence there is much room for short-term increases in export supply by diverting output from the home to the foreign market.

When it comes to incentives to enlarge output and expand capacity, the principal reallocation here is between import-competing goods and exports, rather than between home goods and all foreign-trade goods as in the case of some developed economies. This is because, by assumption, imports have already been stringently limited by high tariffs, disadvantageous exchange rates, and quantitative restrictions, all of which create a strong price incentive for domestic production. Some exports may also have been subsidized, and where this is so devaluation accompanied by removal of the subsidy may leave no new incentive to increase production for export. Generally speaking, however, exports are heavily penalized under the regimes we are considering, and devaluation has the effect of reducing the premium for producing import-competing goods for the home market and increasing the premium for production for export, with the principal shift in incentives coming between these two sectors rather than with respect to the home-goods sector (although of course there will also be some incentive to shift resources into that sector from the import-competing sector and out of it to the export sector).

These points are shown in figure 1, which depicts a devaluing country's demand for imports, D_m, and a schedule of its receipts for exports, R_x. On the factually reasonable assumption that the foreign prices of their imports are beyond their influence, the import schedule reflects both quantities and foreign-exchange expenditure on imports; the export schedule, in contrast, reflects only foreign-currency receipts, this being a combination of quantity supplied for export and the foreign-currency price that any given quantity can fetch. It thus reflects both domestic supply conditions and foreign demand conditions.

We assume initially an exchange rate that leads to a domestic price P_0 per dollar of exports; this is also the price that importers pay for each dollar of foreign exchange. It results in export receipts X_0 and imports M_0, leaving a large trade deficit. The authorities may find it necessary to ration the foreign exchange to hold imports to M'_0, a level that is sustainable with X_0 in export

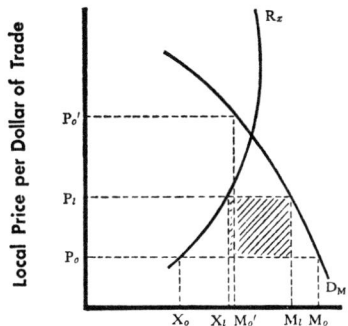

Figure 1

receipts and $M'_0 - X_0$ in capital inflow, say under a foreign-aid-program loan. Under these circumstances, the domestic market price of imported goods will rise to P'_0 and importers will earn a scarcity rent of $P'_0 - P_0$ per dollar of imports, brought about by the rationing system. (Auctioning the import licences would of course capture these rents in the absence of collusion among the importers, but auctioning in fact is rare.) Payments are in balance, taking into account the capital inflow.

Devaluation of the currency can supplant the rationing system by increasing the price of foreign currency to P_1. Export receipts will rise to X_1, and, as a result of the more favorable exchange rate, production of export goods will increase. If the rationing system is retained, the country will now find itself in payments surplus; but abandonment of the system will lead the local price of imports to *fall* to P_1 and imports will rise to M_1, preserving payments balance after allowing for the foreign assistance ($= M'_0 - X_0 = M_1 - X_1$). Thus, local production of import-competing goods will be discouraged by lower prices and a greater volume of imports. This marks a sharp contrast with straight devaluation from a position of open deficit, where production of import-competing as well as export goods is encouraged, since the local prices of both are raised relative to nontraded goods.

New investment in the capacity to export will require that investors expect the improvement in their position to last, i.e., that the devaluation and associated policies will establish a new regime that will not simply slide back into the old configuration of policies. Establishing these expectations is one of the most difficult tasks of those carrying out the reform. The same problem exists in principle in devaluation from open deficit too, but developing countries that have not relied on restriction of imports for payments reasons stand a better chance of success, because investors will expect any emerging disequilibrium to be corrected, rather than suppressed by controls.

Furthermore, the required investment may differ in character from that in developed countries. Where manufactures can be competitively exported under the new regime, conversion from domestic manufacturing may be relatively easy; but opening up export markets for manufactured goods for the first time is a drawn-out process, requiring the establishment of new marketing channels. The shift from domestic to export crops in agriculture or the opening of new lands is generally easier; however, for livestock and for tree crops the required gestation period may be several years.

For all these reasons, some pessimism with regard to price elasticities would be quite justified for many developing countries, at least in the short run, but, as we will see below, it does not usually go far enough to prevent devaluation from improving the trade balance.

Effects on Aggregate Demand

The absorption approach to devaluation suggests that a devaluation that merely substitutes for other measures, leading to no net improvement in the balance of goods and services, requires no cut in aggregate expenditure or increase in total output to "make room" for an improvement. But it is still worth asking what pressure devaluation in these circumstances might put on aggregate expenditure and output, since this will give some guide to the possible need for compensatory macroeconomic policy.

To provide a framework for discussion that captures several of the key elements, even though it does not do justice to them all, consider the following simple macroeconomic model:

$Y = E + D,$

$E = E(Y, i, r),$

$D = D(Y, r),$

$i = i(Y, p, L),$

$L = H + R,$

$\Delta R = D + K.$

Here Y is the level of output and income in the devaluing country, E is total domestic expenditure, D is the balance on goods and services, L is the money supply, H is domestic credit, R is international reserves, and K is capital inflow, all measured in domestic currency. In addition, r is the exchange rate measured as the dollar cost of a unit of local currency, i is the interest rate on financial assets other than money, and p is the domestic price level. We assume here that the local price of all domestic production, including production for export, is held constant—e.g. by the availability of unemployed resources at fixed money wages—so the only variation in p comes about through a devaluation-induced rise in local-currency import prices. Foreign prices of imports are assumed unchanged, so devaluation on these assumptions implies an equivalent worsening in the terms of trade. The function determining interest rates in turn reflects the equality of demand for real money balances with the supply.

In order to discover the impact effect on output, Y, we must ask what will be the effects of devaluation on its two components, the level of domestic expenditure and the external balance measured in domestic currency. The impact on output will in turn affect incomes, expenditure, imports, and output again in a multiplier process, but the impact effect will tell us the impetus to this multiplier process, and in particular whether it is expansionary or deflationary. Total differentiation of the model above and rearrangement of terms yields

$$dY = \frac{1}{s + m - E_i i_y} [D_r dr + E_r dr + E_i(i_L dL + i_p dp)],$$

where the subscripts indicate partial differentiation with respect to the indicated variable, $s = 1 - E_y$, and $m = -D_y$. Thus, the change in income, dY, is seen to depend upon a devaluation-induced change in the trade balance, a devaluation-induced shift in the level of expenditure, and a money-supply and price-induced shift in the level of expenditure, all augmented by an income multiplier. Let us consider the three terms within the brackets in turn, for these determine whether output will be increased or reduced as a result of devaluation.

To take the external balance first, for the reasons given above this might actually worsen in the period immediately following devaluation, when measured in foreign currency, and this by itself would have a deflationary impact upon the economy. The worsening would occur if import liberalization were to take effect immediately, giving rise to an increase in imports, while the stimulus to exports would occur only with a lag. In time, the stimulus to exports would also stimulate the domestic economy, but the immediate impact would be a deflationary one. Furthermore, any discrepancy between the local-currency value of a dollar's worth of imports and a dollar's worth of exports, for example due to tariffs, means that even a parallel expansion of imports and exports will be deflationary, provided the government does not spend the additional revenue at once.

Moreover, devaluation is deflationary to the extent that import quotas are replaced in their import-restricting effects by the depreciated exchange rate. Scarcity rents that went to privileged importers before the devaluation would now accrue to the central bank as it sells foreign exchange. In effect, price rationing will have replaced quantitative rationing, with no ultimate effect on the final market price but with a higher domestic-currency price to the importer or firm enjoying the licence.

Finally, the inelasticity of demand for imports suggests that a sharp rise in their local-currency price will lead to an increase in expenditure upon them, even if the quantity and the foreign-exchange value of imports fall. In this respect devaluation is like an efficient revenue-oriented excise tax, increasing the price far more than it reduces the quantity purchased. Since inflows of foreign grants and capital generally cause imports to exceed exports, sometimes by a substantial margin, exports will have to expand a great deal before the increased local-currency income from their sale exceeds the increased local-currency expenditure on imports. Thus, in figure 1, which is drawn on the assumption that exports and imports increase by the same amount in terms of foreign currency, total local-currency expenditure on imports increases by $P_1 M_1 - P_0 M_0'$, while local-currency receipts rise by only the L-shaped area $P_1 X_1 - P_0 X_0$. The difference is the shaded rectangle, representing the increased local-currency value of the capital inflow, which if the government does not spend it promptly represents a deflationary force, like additional tax receipts. A greater devaluation would have led to imports lower than M_1, but an inelastic demand for imports would lead to a still further increase in total domestic expenditure on them. Thus, even though the trade balance would have improved in terms of foreign currency, the devaluation would have had a deflationary impact on this account. For some (possibly excessive) degree of devaluation, however, increased receipts from exports would overtake the increased expenditures on imports, and the conventional assumption that successful devaluation is expansionary would prevail.

The exact conditions under which the trade-balance effect of devaluation will be deflationary have been set down elsewhere.[2] They may be summarized briefly by noting that $B = rD$, where B is the trade balance measured in foreign currency. Taking differentials yields

$$dB = r(1 + k)dD + kB,$$

where k is the proportionate devaluation and is negative. Thus, for an initial

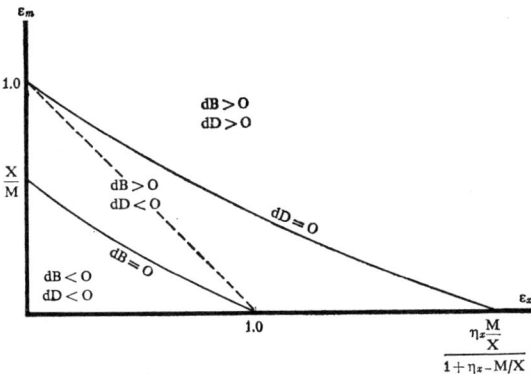

Figure 2

trade deficit the second term on the right is positive, giving rise to the possibility that dD is negative even when the trade balance in foreign currency has improved. This will in fact happen provided the elasticity of demand for imports (ε_m) is below unity and the foreign elasticity of demand for exports (ε_x) is sufficiently low, though it may be above unity.

The point can be made geometrically in terms of demand elasticities, indicating whether the balance improves or deteriorates in domestic and foreign currency. This is shown in figure 2, where $dB = 0$ and $dD = 0$ result in two boundaries marking off three regions. Between the boundaries, which are also influenced by the initial trade imbalance (X/M) and by the elasticity of supply of exports (η_x, which determines the curvature of the boundaries; they are straight lines if domestic costs are constant, as in the model above), the trade balance will improve in terms of foreign currency and deteriorate in terms of domestic currency, thereby exerting deflationary pressure on the economy. If trade is initially in balance, the two boundaries will coincide and a devaluation that improves the balance will also be expansionary. (The dashed straight line joining the unity positions on each axis represents the celebrated Marshall-Lerner condition, under which for infinite supply elasticities devaluation will improve the trade balance—and be expansionary in its domestic effects—if the sum of the two demand elasticities exceeds unity.) But many developing countries meet the conditions for falling into the middle region, with continuing aid-financed trade deficits, low elasticities of demand for imports, and moderate foreign elasticities of demand for their exports, at least in the short run that is relevant for considering the impact effect on income. Therefore, the foreign sector may well exert a deflationary impact on the economy following devaluation, and indeed did so in 14 of the 24 devaluations examined below.

The external sector, however, is only one component of demand. It is necessary also to ask how devaluation may affect the level of total domestic expenditure, E. Refined analysis is required to discuss the possible effects satisfactorily, but here it will be sufficient to identify six effects that are likely to be important in developing countries, some arising directly from the change in exchange rate others from monetary effects induced by the devaluation.

(1) There is first the *speculative effect*, which is also important in devaluations from open deficits. If devaluation has been anticipated and is expected to lead to a general increase in prices, there will be anticipatory buying before the devaluation. The post-devaluation period will therefore commence with larger-than-usual holdings of goods. Total expenditure by the public may therefore drop in the period immediately following devaluation, until these inventories are worked off. (This effect would also lead to a rise in imports before and a drop after the devaluation, insofar as this is permitted by the system of licensing or other controls.) Though the speculative effect will normally lead to a drop in expenditure, it may also lead to an increase if the price increases following devaluation are expected to lead to general inflation, or if another devaluation is in prospect.

(2) Devaluation will generally lead to a redistribution of income, and this *distributive effect*, while present for any devaluation, is likely to be especially important in developing countries with heavy reliance on primary products for export. Unless checked by special export taxes, a devaluation will lead to a sharp increase in rewards to those in the export industry, who are often landowners. Whether large or small, landowners are likely to have different saving and consumption patterns from urban dwellers, generally saving more out of marginal changes in income, at least in the short run. Thus, a redistribution of real income from workers to businessmen and from urban to rural dwellers is likely, in the first instance, to lead to a drop in total expenditure out of a given aggregate income, and this drop will be deflationary. But of course the redistributional effect could also go the other way, if as a result of devaluation the real income of those with a low marginal propensity to save is increased at the expense of others. The redistributional effect will also affect the level of imports out of a given total income, since the consumption pattern of those who gain may differ from that of losers. But this effect is likely to be less marked than the total expenditure effect, partly because much of the import bill of developing countries represents inputs into domestically produced goods and services, so they are somewhat

more widely diffused throughout the economy than would be the case for direct imports of manufactured consumer goods. Díaz-Alejandro has documented well the dominating importance of the redistributive effect following the Argentine devaluation of 1959, where the shift of income to the landowners led to a sharp drop in domestic spending and therefore to a secondary drop in imports.[3]

(3) A devaluation will lead to a rise in the domestic costs of servicing *external debt* denominated in foreign currency. These are implicitly included in our calculation of *dD* above. But where the liabilities are those of businessmen who do not benefit much from the devaluation, it may lead to bankruptcy, even when businesses are otherwise sound, and to an attendant decline in business spending, both by the bankrupt firms and by others affected adversely or merely made anxious. This factor allegedly figured in the decline in investment following the Argentine devaluation of 1962. Even where the debt is held officially, the problem of raising the local-currency counterpart of external servicing charges often poses a serious problem and sometimes represents a serious inhibition to devaluation.

Indeed (to digress for a moment), these "accounting" relationships, usually ignored by economists, often preoccupy officials and bankers. Local development banks that have borrowed abroad (for instance, from the World Bank or the IDA) in foreign currencies and re-lent to local business in domestic currency have accepted an exchange risk that has occasionally provided the major barrier to devaluation: to allow its development bank to fail might psychologically undermine the government's development plans. But if the bank is to be saved, who is to absorb the devaluation loss, and how? (The obvious retrospective answer is that local borrowers should be charged interest rates sufficiently above what the development bank pays on its foreign debt to cover the exchange risk—with the added advantage that such rates will more closely approximate the true cost of capital in the developing country. But development banks have often failed to do this. Or, if they have done it, they have failed to set aside a sufficiently large reserve out of the difference in rates.)

A similar problem arises for net *creditors* when the value of their foreign claims is reduced in terms of local currency by devaluation abroad or revaluation of the home currency. Thus, Hong Kong inadvisedly devalued its currency following the 1967 devaluation of sterling, apparently because the commercial banks in Hong Kong held large sterling assets against their local-currency deposits, and the banking system would have been threatened if the relationship between sterling and Hong Kong dollars had not been preserved. But the government thought better of this decision and revalued again four days later, in the meantime having worked out a way to indemnify the banks out of official reserves. By the same token, the German Bundesbank showed substantial paper losses (in marks) on its assets held in gold and dollars following the revaluations of 1961 and 1969. The 1961 revaluation was delayed until the German government would agree to indemnify the bank for its "losses" (which were entirely paper losses arising from double-entry bookkeeping conventions) out of the budget over a period of seven years. Where private parties have incurred foreign debt, of course, the loss is real to the firm or bank, and that may have undesirable consequences for the economy as a whole. But a thorough discussion of this important issue is beyond the scope of the present article.

(4) When the balance of goods and services has turned adverse in terms of domestic currency—which, as we have seen above, may frequently be expected—then in the absence of countervailing monetary action a domestic *credit squeeze* may result, since importers and others will be paying more into the central bank for foreign exchange than exporters are receiving.[4] This credit stringency in turn may lead to higher interest rates and a reduction in domestic expenditure.

(5) In addition to affecting the money stock, devaluation may also influence the *demand for real money balances*. By raising the local prices of imports and (in general, outside our formal framework) of export products, devaluation will reduce the real value of a given money stock. Indeed, a monetary interpretation of balance-of-payments difficulties and their correction focuses on the excess of money holdings as a source of the deficit, and on the devaluation-induced reduction in real balances as the corrective, leading to a reduction in spending. In the case of devaluation from a suppressed deficit, however, this money demand effect is more complicated and may not be present at all. A devaluation that simply displaces other instruments of policy, with no effect on domestic prices, will not alter the real value of money balances. If, as is more typically the case, devaluation displaces restraints on imports but also raises the local prices of exports, the effect on the real value of money holdings will depend upon the importance of export products in local expenditure. When export products are extensively purchased by residents, the monetary effect will tend to reduce domestic spending. Import liberalization, on the other hand, cuts the other way insofar as import prices actually fall.[5]

(6) In the long run another factor comes into play: To the extent that devaluation displaces measures that led to a less efficient use of resources, the devaluation package will lead (after the necessary reallocation of resources has taken place) to an increase in real income, and this *resource efficiency effect*

in turn will require a supporting increase in real money holdings. Unless it is supplied by the monetary authorities, this demand for money balances will depress expenditure relative to potential income.[6]

The upshot of these various considerations is that devaluation in developing countries is likely to be deflationary in the first instance, and thus may "make room" for any improvement in the balance on goods and services, without active reinforcement from monetary and fiscal policy. Indeed, for reasons given below, it may sometimes be desirable to accompany devaluation with modestly *expansionary* policies. Frequently, however, the devaluation will take place against a background of excessively expansionary policies. In this case the devaluation-induced deflation will be helpful in bringing the economy under control, but these effects must be taken into account if the government is to avoid overshooting the target with deliberately contractionary measures.

In short, unless the devaluation is very successful in stimulating exports or in stimulating investment, the absorption approach to devaluation is of less relevance to devaluation in developing countries except in manifestly inflationary situations. The real problem will often be getting adequate capacity in the export sector, not releasing resources overall.

Before we turn to the actual experience of devaluations in developing countries, it should be noted that a devaluation will have powerful short-run distributive effects (alluded to above in the discussion of the impact of devaluation on expenditure). When tariffs are reduced (unless they are offset by a reduction in subsidies), the government loses revenue; when quotas are eliminated, quota holders lose the quasi-rents they enjoyed by getting a scarce resource (the right to import) at a price below its social value. When prices rise, all those on fixed money incomes suffer. Petty officials responsible for licensing or tariff collection may also lose the "fees" they can collect by virtue of their position of control. The gainers are those in the actual and potential export industries and, where a quota system is replaced by a dual-exchange-rate system (the lower rate usually applying to traditional exports), the government. These prospective gains and losses influence sectional attitudes toward devaluation and their willingness to help make it succeed.

Some Evidence on the Impact of Devaluation

Having set out how the conventional analysis of devaluation may have to be adapted to devaluations in developing countries, we turn now to the actual experience of these countries with devaluation. As noted in the introduction, currency devaluations have occurred with some frequency in the last 25 years despite widespread reluctance to engage in them. Many of these were small, or were by countries with inadequate statistics, or were by developed countries, or were part of a larger movement of exchange rates of one block of countries as against another. (The last kind of devaluation raises rather different issues for analysis than have been considered above.) The evidence drawn on here derives from a study of 23 devaluations occurring over the period 1953–1966 and including most of the major devaluations in developing countries in the early 1960s.[7]

There are many questions that one can ask about the consequences of devaluation and its associated package of policies, which may have profound effects upon the allocation of resources, growth, and the distribution of income in developing economies. We are not concerned with these ultimate effects (although empirical work on them is all too rare), but with the immediate impact effects of devaluation. These start the transition to the longer-term effects, if they are given a chance to work themselves out. The reason for focusing on impact effects is that they often determine whether the longer-term effects will be given a chance to work themselves out. Officials have notoriously short planning horizons, and their anxieties about the impact effects of devaluation often lead to a postponement of devaluation and the substitution in its place of numerous *ad hoc* measures, imposing substantial costs by impeding the efficient operation of the economy.

The reluctance of officials arises in large measure from the considerations adduced in the introduction: Devaluation will disturb an implicit social contract among different segments of society—or at least will jar some groups out of their acquiescence in the existing state of affairs, with its numerous implicit compromises—and officials are understandably anxious about rocking an overloaded and delicately balanced boat. But sooner or later the decision may be forced upon them, when for external or internal reasons the external disequilibrium deepens and a suppressed deficit becomes an open deficit which can be corrected only by disturbing the social equilibrium anyway.

However, more specific anxieties are also expressed about the consequences of devaluation:

• Devaluation, it is feared, will not achieve the desired improvement in the balance of payments, because neither imports nor exports are sufficiently sensitive to relative price changes within the acceptable range of such changes—in a phrase, elasticity pessimism.

• Devaluation will worsen the terms of trade of the country and thus will impose real costs on it.

- By raising domestic prices, devaluation will set in motion a wage-price spiral that will rapidly undercut the improved competitiveness that the devaluation is designed to achieve.
- Whatever its economic effects, it is thought that devaluation will be politically disastrous for those officials responsible for it.

Let us see to what extent these fears are justified by experience, adopting the short-run (one year, say) perspective of the official.

Impact on Trade and Payments

In nearly two-thirds of the 23 devaluations examined (see table 1) the balance on goods and services, measured in foreign currency (as is appropriate for balance-of-payments analysis, although a number of countries record their payments positions in domestic currency), improved in the year following devaluation. In over 80 percent of the cases either this or the overall monetary balance (often both) improved in the year following devaluation. Of the four countries that showed a worsening on both counts, two involved important import liberalization resulting in a rise in imports.

Of course, these actual improvements could have taken place for reasons quite independent of the devaluation, for example an increase in world demand for the country's products or a drop in domestic expenditure due to a crop failure. Adjustment of the trade data to allow for movements in world demand and for changes in the level of domestic activity reveals a slight increase in the number of countries that improve their trade balance following devaluation.

These improvements occurred despite good reasons for being an elasticity pessimist about developing countries, for the reasons already given above. No doubt some part of the improvement in trade and in overall payments can be explained by the speculative considerations already mentioned—a reversal of flows after the devaluation occurred. But not all of it can be explained in this way, for the second year following devaluation usually showed a preservation of, and sometimes a substantial increase in, the gains. The fact that supply elasticities are low in the short run helps in theory to ensure that there is little or no loss in export receipts such as would arise if supply could be increased rapidly at unchanged *domestic* prices. A steadiness in export earnings combined with some reduction in imports will ensure some improvement in the trade balance, but only a modest one. In only three of the cases examined did the improvement in the trade balance exceed the initial trade deficit, thereby swinging the country into trade

Table 1
Selected currency devaluations, 1953–1966.

	Time of devaluation	Nominal devaluation[a]	Effective devaluation for imports[b]	Change in balance on goods and services from previous year ($ million)	Monetary balance in following year ($ million)	Percent change in real wages in manufacturing in following 12 months
Argentina	Jan. 1959	66	61	270	199	−25
Brazil	Sept. 1964	66[c]	61[c]	159	458	−3
Colombia	Nov. 1962	26	23	30	−29	−3
Colombia	Sept. 1965	33	25	−253	−39	−5
Costa Rica	Sept. 1961	15	6	−2	7	8
Ecuador	July 1961	17	16	18	12	5
Greece	Apr. 1953	50	41	60	56	n.a.
Iceland	Feb. 1960	57	41	2	6	n.a.
Iceland	Aug. 1961	12	11	3	20	n.a.
India	June 1966	37	30	−35	−10	n.a.
Israel	Feb. 1962	40	26	−33	164	1
Korea	Feb. 1960	25	34	−34	1	2
Korea	Feb. 1961	50	36	64	47	8
Korea	May 1964	49	50	112	−30	5
Mexico	Apr. 1954	31	31	98	−40	−1
Morocco	Oct. 1959	17	12	−94	65	−1
Pakistan	July 1955	30	28	−21	18	0

Country	Date					
Peru	Jan. 1958– Apr. 1959	31	31	78	18	−12
Philippines	Jan. 1962	40	16	99	36	3
Philippines	Nov. 1965	10	0	46	−29	−3
Spain	July 1959	30	26	404	465	n.a.
Tunisia	Sept. 1964	20	17	−56	−3	n.a.
Turkey	Aug. 1958	56	39	−31	−2	−8

a. Parity or principal import rate (percent change in dollars per unit of local currency).

b. Percent change in dollars per unit of local currency, excluding effects of relaxation of import quotas.

c. During calendar year 1964.

Note: For definitions, explanations, and qualifications, see R. N. Cooper, "An Assessment of Currency Devaluation in Developing Countries," in G. Ranis, ed., *Government and Economic Development* (New Haven, Conn.: Yale University Press, 1971).

surplus—a fact that should not be surprising for countries that normally import capital from the rest of the world.

Most of the countries that liberalized imports experienced a reduction in the volume of imports in the year following devaluation—partly because of a decline in activity and a switching away from imports to domestic sources of supply, but even more because import liberalization was often delayed from three to nine months following the devaluation, apparently reflecting a wait-and-see attitude on the part of the authorities toward the devaluation. In delaying, however, they increased the risk of a wage-price spiral.

Impact on the Terms of Trade

Many countries do not have even reasonably comprehensive data on the prices they pay for imports and receive for their exports, hence on their terms of trade. Among those that do, somewhat under one-half showed a deterioration in the terms of trade following devaluation. But some of these deteriorations were independent of the devaluation, and in any case all were small relative to the size of the devaluation—1 or 2 percent, compared with nominal devaluations ranging from 10 to nearly 70 percent.

The negligible deterioration observed in the terms of trade may of course have been due to preventive measures taken by the devaluing countries. Most of them imposed special taxes (or a disadvantageous exchange rate, lower than the new principal rate) on certain exports of primary products. But usually these taxes were imposed for distributive or revenue reasons and not to prevent a deterioration in the terms of trade through a fall in foreign-currency prices of exports. A standard pattern, for example, is to impose a tax roughly equivalent to the amount of devaluation on exports out of the current harvest, on the ground that the quantity of such exports can be increased only marginally (unless domestic consumption is substantial) and there is no reason to pass windfall gains on to the farmers. The new exchange rate is applied to subsequent harvests. In other instances the tax has been imposed to prevent an immediate rise in the domestic price of an export product important in local consumption, such as olive oil in Greece. In both cases it is a rise in domestic prices, not a fall in foreign ones, that the authorities are guarding against. Where only one or two foreign marketing organizations dominate a country's export sales, however, these buyers may retain their pre-devaluation buying price for domestic produce, which of course implies a decline in the price in terms of foreign currency. Thus, existing institutional arrangements may permit foreign buyers, in the short run, to improve their terms of trade at the expense of the devaluing country, and a tax will help to prevent this. In the long run, competition from potential foreign buyers will also prevent it, but by that time domestic supplies may also have increased. Finally, there are some commodities—such as hazel nuts in Turkey, jute in Pakistan, cocoa in Ghana—where one country does have a dominant position in the world market, and in these cases too the imposition of an export tax or its equivalent will prevent a deterioration in the terms of trade.

But preoccupation with the terms-of-trade effects of devaluation in fact reflects a misunderstanding of the purposes of devaluation, or at best confuses devaluation theory with optimal-tariff theory. A country that dominates world markets in one or more of its export products can increase its welfare by imposing a tax on those exports up to the point at which the additional gains from further increases in the foreign-currency price (arising from the willingness of foreign buyers to pay part of the tax) just compensate for the additional welfare losses arising from the tax-induced reduction in trade. If the devaluing country has already imposed such optimizing export tariffs (import tariffs alone will not do here, because in equilibrium they also discourage manufactured exports, on which the optimal export tax is surely zero for developing countries), then devaluation will not require their alteration unless the cause of the payments imbalance also happens to have altered the optimum export tax. A pre-devaluation rise in domestic costs and prices, leading indeed to the need for devaluation, will have improved the country's terms of trade beyond the optimal point. The objective should be to maximize net returns on exporting, not merely to prevent a deterioration in the terms of trade, and in these circumstances some lowering of export prices in terms of foreign currency will be desirable to stimulate foreign purchases.

Impact on Wages and Prices

Assessing the impact of devaluation on domestic prices and wages is exceptionally difficult, and only partly because price and wage data are sparse and of dubious quality for most developing countries. It is difficult also because exogenous events, expectational patterns based on the same history that led to the devaluation, and policies associated with but sometimes also at variance with the devaluation may all have important influences on both wages and prices.

It is useful first of all to distinguish between demand-induced and cost-induced increases in prices and wages. By conventional analysis, both should be present following a successful devaluation, for the improved trade balance will increase the claims on domestic output and the devaluation will lead directly to an increase in the local prices of imports and other foreign-trade goods. We have seen, however, that devaluation may lead to a decline rather than an increase in demand for domestic output, and this alone would tend to depress prices. The extent to which devaluing countries have taken the advice normally tendered to pursue deflationary monetary and fiscal policies will reinforce these devaluation-induced pressures. There is of course no contradiction between deflationary pressures and observed price increases; the devaluation here is very much like an excise tax, which reduces demand by withdrawing purchasing power from circulation but also raises prices. Where the devaluation merely substitutes for other measures to restrict imports, such as quotas or special tariffs, there need, of course, be no rise in these prices following devaluation, for under competitive conditions the local market prices will have already risen to reflect scarcity values.

In fact, some depression in economic activity is often found following devaluation in developing countries, sometimes lasting only a few months but not infrequently lasting more than a year. While it is impossible to disentangle the deflationary effects of devaluation from those of autonomous policy measures designed to facilitate success of the devaluation, there is much circumstantial evidence to suggest that the extent of depression is a surprise to the authorities in the devaluing countries, that they have not adequately taken into account the depressing effects of the devaluation itself or that they have exaggerated its expansionary impetus. In too many cases, of course, the need to devalue arises from pre-devaluation inflation that has not been brought fully under control even after devaluation, and these cases reinforce the views of those who insist on strongly deflationary measures to accompany devaluation; in those cases further deflation is necessary to make the devaluation work. But in other cases further deflation is not necessary, and on the contrary may aggravate the difficulties of the authorities in keeping the situation under control just as exports are expanding most rapidly. We return to this possibility below.

Despite the theoretical argument that under some circumstances domestic prices need not rise following devaluation, in fact they invariably do. This is partly because there is normally some effective devaluation for imports and export products, even when export subsidies are removed and imports are liberalized, and partly because the instinctive reaction of importers is to pass along to their customers any increase in costs that they have incurred. If they are already charging what the market will bear, however, as shown earlier in figure 1, these higher prices are not sustainable in a given monetary environment, and in the course of time competition among importers will

Currency Devaluation in Developing Countries

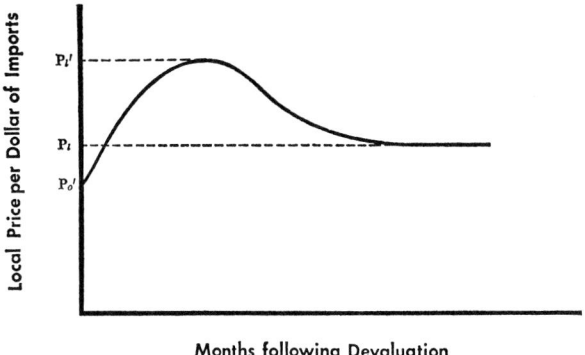

Months following Devaluation

Figure 3

result in a subsequent drop in prices—not to below the pre-devaluation level, but toward it to an extent governed by the degree to which devaluation substitutes for import quotas as a restraint on imports. Such a pattern can be observed for about half of the few countries for which adequate monthly data on local prices of imports are available: prices rise sharply following devaluation, reach a peak three or four months later, and then gradually drop back, sometimes substantially as depicted in figure 3. In an inflationary monetary environment, of course, one does not observe a post-devaluation decline in prices, but the rate of increase is reduced temporarily.

Higher prices will raise costs directly (especially since most imports are intermediate products and capital goods) and will also stimulate demands for higher money incomes by local factors of production, especially wage and salary employees. But the cycle of wage and price increases should be self-limiting, unless all parties (including the goverment) attempt to maintain their real incomes in the face of rising import prices, or unless the devaluation stimulates price increases that are quite unrelated to increases in costs. In addition, for either case the monetary authorities must support the increase in money incomes with domestic credit expansion if domestic prices and incomes are to rise by the full amount of the devaluation without generating unemployment.

An open deficit will reflect a level of expenditure and a distribution of income that are not sustainable at the existing level of output and with the existing structure of taxation and expenditures insofar as they affect distribution. Devaluation requires that some real incomes go down and that total expenditure go down, even though aggregate income need not drop. If, however, those who benefited from the initial disequilibrium insist on retaining the same level of real income, and if they have the market power (through administered prices or through wage bargaining) to stake out that claim in monetary terms, then the devaluation cannot succeed without general deflation leading to unemployment—unless, of course, there is some unutillized capacity and the tax system can be so altered as to ensure that enough of the increased output will go to the powerful factors in the post-devaluation period. Even this will not work if these factors insist on maintaining their pre-devaluation share of income.

Second, the devaluation may stimulate price increases that were overdue but that for reasons of law, custom, fear of public opprobrium, or simply inertia were not made earlier—the liquidation of unliquidated monopoly gains, to use Galbraith's term. This problem arises especially with public utilities subjected to an inflationary environment in the past. Being highly visible to the public, electric companies and bus companies do not readily raise their rates, and they are frequently under substantial government pressure not to do so. A currency devaluation, being little understood by the public, presents a natural occasion to raise such prices and lay responsibility on the devaluation. Several devaluations led to rioting in the streets—as well as larger wage claims—when an economically unrelated but psychologically related increase in urban bus fares occurred shortly afterward.

In either case the monetary authorities are confronted with a dilemma; it is here that management of a devaluation is trickiest. Economists have been too little interested in these matters of management, even though they affect the final result (that is, the path is important for determining the equilibrium, or indeed whether equilibrium is achieved). If the authorities do not allow some monetary expansion, unemployment and underutilization will result; if they do allow it, the effects of the devaluation will be weakened and perhaps undermined. That various groups attempt to maintain their pre-devaluation income poses a more acute problem in the case of devaluation from open deficit than devaluation from suppressed deficit, since in the latter case much of the adjustment toward equilibrium income distribution will already have been made, except insofar as some firms and individuals are profiting from quantitative restrictions. Since developing countries generally do rely on quantitative restrictions before devaluation, and since they also generally have some open deficit in spite of their *ad hoc* adjustments, the problem remains a practical one.

In the event, price-wage spiraling does not generally get out of control, at least within the year or so following devaluation. Twelve months after devaluation, wholesale prices of imported goods will generally have risen, but by less than the devaluation (after having fallen from a peak reached three or four months after devaluation, as noted earlier), general wholesale prices will have risen less than this, consumer prices will have risen by about the same as wholesale prices, and (except where devaluations are small) manufacturing wages will have risen by less than consumer prices, showing a decline in real wages following the devaluation (see the last column of table 1, which shows a decline in real wages for half the countries for which data are available, and negligible increases in several others despite continued growth in output). Thus, nonwage incomes of employed factors—mostly profits and rents—show an increase in real terms a year later, and it is this increase that provides the incentive for the necessary reallocation of resources, which reallocation may ultimately restore and even raise real wages, depending on the relative factor intensities in the export industries as opposed to the protected industries.

Thus, to sum up briefly the experience following devaluations in less-developed countries, it seems that official anxieties concerning the economic effects are exaggerated. The firmest generalization that can be made is that country experiences are highly diverse. That may be unsettling to cautious officials. However, for a hypothetical "representative" country, devaluation seems to improve both the trade balance and the payments position within the first year; it does not seem to lead to deterioration in the terms of trade of any consequence; it does lead to price increases, but not by amounts great enough to undermine the devaluation; price increases of imports are substantially less than the devaluation, suggesting that importer margins have been reduced; real wages fall; and there is a slump in economic activity following the devaluation.

The Political Impact

The fourth apprehension concerns the political fate of those responsible for the decision to devalue, and here the experience is not nearly so encouraging. A naive test is whether the government fell within a year of the devaluation. In nearly 30 percent of the cases examined it did. Some of these changes in government were clearly unrelated to the devaluation—Costa Rica and Colombia each happened to have elections within the year, for example, and both countries have quite regularly voted out the incumbent government in recent history, devaluation or not. But in other cases the devaluation and associated policies for managing the economy were the main issue on which the government fell. And there were near misses in both Israel (1962) and India (1966), where the ruling government came under severe criticism for its decision to devalue but survived the crisis for more than a year.

A check was provided by examining a random control group of similar countries that did not devalue. Governments changed within the year in only 14 percent of the control sample. Thus, it appears that devaluation—or the policies that led to the need for devaluation, or the policies that followed it—roughly doubles the chance that a ruling group will be removed from power. But the test will have to be refined considerably before it can be regarded as anything more than suggestive, in particular by selecting a control group from countries that seem to be in some balance-of-payments difficulty (of either an open or a suppressed type) rather than just from all developing countries.

Ministers of finance fared much worse. Nearly 60 percent of them lost their jobs in the year following devaluation—half of them when their government fell—compared with a turnover in a control group of only 18 percent. So the chances of ouster for the official immediately responsible seems to increase by a factor of 3 as a result of devaluation. Again the test should be refined. In any case, losing one's job as finance minister does not necessarily end a political career; James Callaghan of Britain felt obliged to resign after devaluing sterling, but was immediately made Home Secretary.

Conclusions

Managing a devaluation through the transition phase to final success requires judgment and delicacy. Consider first the problem of aggregate demand. As noted, this frequently falls following a devaluation, and unless the economy was badly overheated beforehand it may lead to a drop in profits and employment. If the slump is sufficiently severe and prolonged, it will evoke calls for expansionary action by the government, for few governments these days can escape responsibility for developments in their economies. If the government then yields to these pressures, the expansionary policies may come when devaluation-induced export expansion is also taking hold with a lag, and thereby increase demand pressures on the economy at just the wrong time. The better course of action, on these grounds, would be to mitigate the slump—that is, to take some modest expansionary action with or immediately following the devaluation, contrary to the usual advice, and then to draw back with monetary and fiscal policy when new export demand is becoming important. Properly timed, this would reduce the social and economic costs of the slump and would prevent belated expansionary action, in response to political pressure, from undermining the effects of the devaluations on the trade balance.

On the other hand, we have also seen that there is often a sharp increase in prices in the period immediately following devaluation, as importers attempt to pass on to their customers all or most of the increased cost of foreign goods. To the extent that these price increases (some of which are not otherwise sustainable) get built into wages and other local costs, they will undermine the devaluation. Timing here becomes crucial. The authorities should do what they can to reduce the temporary increase in prices (lest it become permanent), to make sure that it comes quickly and is brief, and to delay any wage settlements or administered price increases until after the peak of import prices has been reached and they are falling.

The size of the temporary increase in prices can be influenced by the speed and extent of import liberalization, and this argues for liberalizing imports at once with devaluation (or even before, if that can be done without signaling the intention to devalue), instead of waiting for several months as most countries have done. With respect to the promptness with which prices of imported goods begin to fall after their initial rise, the slump in total demand reinforces the desired outcome, and this factor cuts against the suggestion above that the slump should be mitigated. The timing of prospective wage settlements should if possible be taken into account in choosing the time to devalue, the aim being to allow a considerable lapse of time between devaluation and major wage settlements. Necessary increases in administered prices, such as those of public utilities or of industries in the public sector, should also be delayed until the temporary rise is past and some prices are falling. Finally, the seasonality of food prices should also be taken into account; devaluations immediately after a good harvest are more likely to achieve prolonged success than are devaluations after a poor harvest or before the new harvest is in, when food stocks are low and food prices are rising. Bad harvests have greatly weakened the impact of several devaluations, notably those of India in 1966 and Colombia in 1962.

New investment in the export sector will take place only if investors believe that the change in relative prices achieved through devaluation is a reasonably durable one. Thus, in terms of the timing of export response, expectations about the capacity and the will of the authorities to keep the economy under control are as important as their actual success in doing so. Here history lives in the present. A country with a poor record of monetary and fiscal management and a history of inflation is likely to have greater difficulty in bringing about the required reallocation of resources than one with more favorable experience in these respects. A slump, deep if not prolonged, may (regrettably) be necessary in such a country in order to establish a new pattern of expectations.

Thus, there is a dilemma with respect to macroeconomic management in the period immediately following a devaluation. In the end, the authorities must tailor their policies to the particular requirements of the country, to some extent even playing by ear. Short-term economic management of this type remains very much an art.

At the same time, the apparent political consequences of devaluation (an increased probability that governments will lose their positions and ministers their jobs) are unsettling, for there may be a sharp conflict between the personal interests of those in authority and the interests of the country—a conflict that has to be resolved by those same persons and which too often may be resolved at the expense of the country. This conflict may play an even greater role than the "social contract" considerations outlined earlier in leading to procrastination over devaluation and an attempt to substitute *ad hoc* restrictions and subventions.

It would thus be desirable to depoliticize the whole question of devaluation by making it less traumatic both for the officials and for the public. This suggests another reason, in addition to the economic ones, for moving toward greater flexibility of exchange rates, along the lines of the gliding parity, as Brazil and Colombia have done. Gradual changes in exchange rates would not only eliminate the political jolt and major economic dislocations following a large discrete devaluation, with its sharp alteration of relative prices and hence of factor incomes, but would also avoid the major misallocation of resources that takes place as a disequilibrium builds up under a fixed exchange rate. Taking exchange-rate changes in small, frequent steps would also help to resolve the dilemma posed above; a slump would not be necessary to redirect resources into export industries.

Notes

1. F. Machlup, *Remaking the International Monetary System* (Baltimore: Johns Hopkins University Press, 1968), p. 7.

2. R. N. Cooper, "Devaluation and Aggregate Demand in Aid-Receiving Countries," in J. Bhagwati et al., eds., *Trade, Balance of Payments, and Growth* (Amsterdam: North-Holland, 1971), pp. 335–376.

3. C. F. Díaz-Alejandro, *Exchange-Rate Devaluation in a Semi-Industrialized Country* (Cambridge, Mass.: MIT Press, 1965).

4. In most developing countries the distinction between monetary and fiscal policy does not have the same meaning it has in more advanced countries. Since capital markets are little developed and access to foreign capital markets is limited, budget deficits, after allowing for foreign assistance, must be financed by the banking system, which results directly or indirectly in monetary expansion. Thus, the usual focus on eliminating government deficits is merely an indirect way to limit the rate

of monetary expansion, provided, of course, that bank credit to the private sector is also kept under control. Similarly, increased government receipts from the local sale of foreign-aid funds or goods will lead to repayment of the central bank and a resulting contraction in the money supply.

5. Murray Kemp has argued that a small currency devaluation from equilibrium will have no net effects on expenditure levels, apart from the effect on the trade balance, with the real money balance effect just offsetting any other tendencies, and in particular offsetting the Laursen-Metzler effect, whereby a reduction in real income arising from a devaluation-induced deterioration in the terms of trade will give rise to an upward shift in money expenditure out of a given money income. But Kemp's finding derives from a model at a higher level of generalization than is being considered here, and it therefore leaves no room for most of the influences identified in the text. See his *Pure Theory of International Trade* (Englewood Cliffs, N.J.: Prentice-Hall, 1964), pp. 277–280.

6. This source of deflationary pressure has been emphasized by Egon Sohmon in "The Effect of Devaluation on the Price Level," *Quarterly Journal of Economics* 72, no. 2 (1958): 273–283.

7. A more nearly complete description and analysis of these cases is found in chapter 13 of G. Ranis, ed., *Government and Economic Development* (New Haven, Conn.: Yale University Press, 1971).

10

Borrowing Abroad: The Debtor's Perspective

Richard N. Cooper and
Jeffrey D. Sachs

External debt has risen to the top of the agenda of international monetary economics in recent years. This is partly because developing countries have become much more dependent on external funding for their economic development during the past decade than they were before, and partly because a growing number of countries have experienced difficulties in servicing their external debts since 1981. This article addresses the question of external borrowing from the perspective of the borrowing country, with a view to discovering principles or guidelines that might be helpful to such countries in managing the level and the character of their external debt.

The first section sketches a formal framework for optimal borrowing by a developing country, as seen from a planner's point of view. The next three sections use this framework for the development of three important limits on external borrowing: the problem of solvency, the problem of liquidity, and the problem created by the possibility of repudiation. The fifth section relates external borrowing to macroeconomic management of the borrowing country, and the sixth section pulls together the many factors that suggest that external debt of a country should be subject to central management or at least surveillance. Following that, we offer some guidelines for limits to the magnitude of external debt, and then discuss the character or mix of external debt. A brief concluding section pulls some of the strands together.

The first four sections are more formal and algebraic in their approach to the subject. That will appeal to some readers and offend others. It is not offered here merely to appeal to those who prefer a formal approach to a subject that lends itself to formal analysis. It also suggests a format that can be adapted to the formal planning models used by many developing countries. An appendix offers a numerical illustration of how the framework can be used. The final four sections are written to be accessible to a wider audience and to offer some judgments on issues that are not fully covered in the more formal treatment. Our discussion throughout on the links between borrowing and monetary policies is necessarily brief, and we point the reader to Dornbusch 1985 for a detailed treatment.

Strategies for International Borrowing

We approach the management of international borrowing as a formal problem of dynamic resource allocation. (The formal approach taken here follows closely the treatment in Sachs 1982a and 1984, wherein further details may be found.) Admittedly, a formal approach may neglect some aspects of the borrowing decision; we take up some of these in later sections. The formal approach, however, has the advantage of showing how a quantitative assessment of borrowing may be made using standard models of development planning. This section illustrates how such development models can be used.

All models of optimal borrowing have two features. First, they set out a dynamic budget constraint, which describes the country's long-term options with respect to foreign borrowing. Second, they specify a planning function or social-welfare function, which describes in a dynamic setting the desirability of various possible paths for consumption and output over time. The borrowing problem is solved in a formal way by maximizing the social-welfare function subject to the dynamic budget constraint.

We shall also insist upon a third feature, which is sometimes missing in borrowing models, namely optimal implementation of a borrowing strategy. The solution of a borrowing model typically yields a path of investment, consumption, and foreign indebtedness that maximizes the social-welfare function. However, it may remain silent on what policies are needed to achieve that path. Will the path result from decentralized market forces, with direct private-sector access to foreign capital? Or does the path require active government intervention in the borrowing process? In sum, in addition to studying the correct path for borrowing, we must ask how that path may in fact be reached.

This section sets out the three key elements of the formal borrowing problem: the budget constraint, the welfare function, and the instruments for policy implementation. Later sections are devoted to a more refined treatment of these elements that address special features of the actual borrowing process.

The Dynamic Budget Constraint

Many features of an economy determine how much and on what terms it may borrow from the rest of the world. Potential lenders as well as equity investors must assess the country's future ability and willingness to service its external obligations. New credit may be limited because creditors doubt that the economy can ever earn sufficient foreign exchange to repay a new loan. In this case, the country is said to be rationed by a *solvency constraint*. Alternatively, the country may be deemed unsuitable for loans because of short-run difficulties, even though its long-run prospects are bright. In this case, the lending is bound by a *liquidity constraint*. Finally, the country may have foreign-exchange earnings sufficient to honor its obligations, but may be deemed unwilling to do so because debt repayment is too onerous or because it is holding out for some sort of debt relief. Lending may therefore be constrained by *repudiation risk*.

The country's capacity to borrow will therefore reflect creditors' concerns about solvency, liquidity, and repudiation risk. The interaction of these constraints determines the dynamic budget constraint facing an economy. For analytical simplicity, we consider each of these factors in turn. In truth, a full model of optimal borrowing must consider them together.

The Solvency Constraint

Even assuming no liquidity or repudiation risks, a country's borrowing is bound by its long-run capacity to service its debt. From the creditors' point of view, long-run solvency does not mean that the debtor nation must have the prospect of becoming a creditor nation in the long run (i.e., actually repaying its debt). All that is required is that the debtor have the future resources to service its debt, without the need to borrow forever in order to make interest payments. To take two extreme cases, a $1 million loan has a market value of zero if the debtor must forever borrow new money to service the loan, whereas the loan is worth a $1 million if the country always services the debt out of its own earnings, even though it never repays the principal.

A country's resources for external debt servicing each period may be measured by its trade surplus, TB_t (when $TB_t < 0$, the country is running a trade deficit). If the maximum discounted sum of current and future trade balances, $\max \sum_{i=t}^{\infty} (1 + r)^{-(i-t)} TB_i$, is less than the current debt, the country can never service the debt out of its own resources (r is the real interest rate, assumed to be constant unless otherwise specified). It will have to borrow forever, and in an amount growing at the real interest rate, in order to continue debt servicing. Let D_t be the stock of debt at the end of period $t - 1$, so that $(1 + r)D_t$ is the debt due as of period t. The solvency constraint can be stated simply as the requirement that

$$(1+r)D_t \leq \max \sum_{i=t}^{\infty} (1+r)^{-(i-t)} TB_i. \tag{1}$$

To gain some insight into equation 1, let us turn to the goods market. Suppose as a first illustration that the country produces a single tradeable good, with real GDP given by Q_t. Output is a function of the capital stock K_t, with $Q_t = F(K_t)$. K_t evolves according to the path of investment, with $K_{t+1} = (1-d)K_t + I_t$, where d is the rate of depreciation and I_t is gross capital formation (public plus private). The trade balance is $TB_t = Q_t - I_t - C_t$, where C_t is gross domestic consumption (public plus private). Let $\bar{C}_t$ be the subsistence or minimal level of consumption possible in period t, so that TB_t is maximized with $C_t = \bar{C}_t$.[1] Then, from equation 1,

$$(1+r)D_t \leq \max \sum_{i=t}^{\infty} (1+r)^{-(i-t)}(Q_i - I_i) - \sum_{i=t}^{\infty} (1+r)^{-(i-t)} \bar{C}_i. \tag{2}$$

The first term on the right-hand side of equation 2 is the maximum discounted sum of $Q_i - I_i$, and may be considered the productive wealth of the economy, in dynamic terms. The second expression is the discounted sum of minimum consumption expenditure. In words, the solvency constraint is that the economy's debt D_t must be less than or equal to productive wealth net of minimum consumption expenditure. For simplicity in the discussion that follows, we set $\bar{C}_t = 0$ in equation 2 and simply compare the external debt with the economy's productive wealth. Reintroducing $\bar{C}_t$ in the later discussion is straightforward.

If a country is always willing to repay its debt if it can, and if it can always borrow freely subject to the condition that it remain solvent, then equation 1 or equation 2 defines the loan supply schedule to the country. In particular, it can borrow to the point where $(1+r)D_t$ just equals

$$\max \sum_{i=t}^{\infty} (1+r)^{-(i-t)}(Q_i - I_i)$$

(ignoring $\bar{C}_i$). This loan supply schedule is shown in figure 1. We return later to more refined measures of solvency, that take into account traded versus nontraded goods and the public versus the private sector.

Two important qualifications must be added to equation 2 and figure 1. If $Q_i - I_i$ grows in the steady state at a rate n greater than r, then the economy faces no solvency constraint. The sum

$$\sum_{i=t}^{\infty} (1+r)^{-(i-t)}(Q_i - I_i)$$

Borrowing Abroad: The Debtor's Perspective

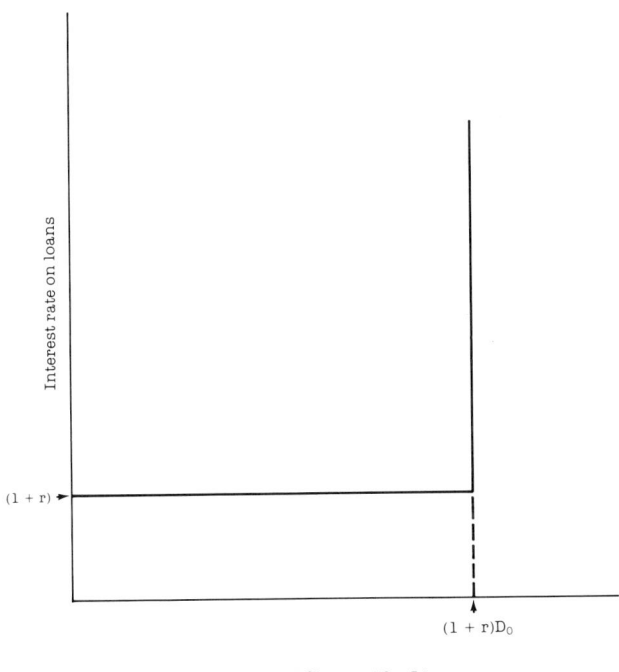

$$\max \Sigma_{t=0}^{\infty}(1 + r)^{-t}(Q_t - I_t)$$

Figure 1
Loan supply with no liquidity or repudiation risk.

is infinite (i.e., the economy's productive wealth is infinite). Starting from any level of debt D_t, the economy has the future resources to repay the debt. Curiously, even if the borrowing country is not growing at a rate n greater than r, there may be no solvency constraint if lender countries are growing at n greater than r. This situation can arise if creditors are always willing to make new loans to debtors to enable the debtor to service its debt. In such a Ponzi scheme, the borrower's debt grows at the rate of interest (and becomes infinite), but since the lenders' economies are growing even faster the debt remains a small (and even decreasing) fraction of the creditors' wealth. As long as the creditors' economies are always growing at $n > r$, such a Ponzi scheme is viable forever. The debtor cannot repay its debt, but never has to. No creditor calls in his loan, on the belief that future lenders will keep the debtor afloat.[2] Therefore, a rise in the real interest rate r above the growth rates of debtor and creditor countries can have a profound effect on the debtor's solvency constraint. When r is low, there may be no solvency constraint on borrowing; when r is high there surely is one. Thus, the rise in real interest rates after 1979 may have severely jolted long-term expectations about the debtor countries' capacity to repay debt.

The Liquidity Constraint

In some theories, solvent countries can always borrow up to the point of the solvency constraint. We suspect that a borrowing limit may be reached far below the solvency limit, because creditors fear liquidity problems of heavily indebted countries and because they fear debt repudiation by these countries. A liquidity constraint may (but need not always) occur when a country owes more in a given period then it can service in the absence of new loans. Specifically, if α percent of outstanding debt is coming due to period t, amortization payments are αD_t and interest payments are rD_t, so that total debt servicing is $(r + \alpha)D_t$. It may well happen that $(r + \alpha)D_t$ exceeds Q_t (especially when Q_t represents tradeable goods alone rather than total GDP), even though

$$(1 + r)D_t \leqslant \max \sum_{i=t}^{\infty} (1 + r)^{-(i-t)}(Q_i - I_i).$$

That is, the country faces a cash-flow problem, though it is solvent by long-run criteria.

In normal periods, such a country will be able to borrow $(r + \alpha)D_t - Q_t$ in order to honor its current debt-service obligations. However, the loan markets may not function well under a variety of circumstances, and the country may find itself unable to borrow. This rationing may result when each bank's lending decisions are importantly affected by the actions of other banks. For example, suppose that bank-capital regulations restrict each bank to make loans to the country in amounts L less than $\bar{L}$, where $\bar{L} < (r + \alpha)D_t - Q_t$. Then, no single bank can lend enough to the country to allow the country to honor its current debt servicing. Two things can happen. Perhaps n banks will each make loans L such that $nL \geqslant (r + \alpha)D_t - Q_t$. They should be happy to do so, because the country is fundamentally healthy (i.e. solvent). On the other hand, if each bank suspects that other banks are not going to make new loans, a panic may ensue. Assuming that no other banks are extending loans, it is rational for each individual bank to stop as well, since its loan of size $\bar{L}$ is not big enough to keep the country solvent. Thus, two equilibria are possible, one in which the country is able to refinance its debt and one in which it is forced into arrears by the inability to obtain new lending. Once the arrears appear, the banks may feel vindicated in their decisions to pull out of new lending. It may become ever more difficult for the country to attract new loans, and an eventual debt rescheduling or moratorium—injurious to creditor and debtor alike—may in time be necessary.

There are several reasons other than bank-capital restrictions on new loans why a panic might arise, some of which have been spelled out in other papers (see Sachs 1984). A bank might be willing, individually, to lend the requisite amount $(r + \alpha)D_t - Q_t$, but only at a new interest rate $\tilde{r}$ much above the existing rate r. The spread $\tilde{r} - r$ would be necessary to compensate a new lender for tying up a large fraction of bank capital. The rate $\tilde{r}$ might be so high, therefore, that a new loan at rate $\tilde{r}$ pushes the country over the brink of insolvency. Specifically, with a new loan $L_t = (r + \alpha)D_t - Q_t$ at rate $\tilde{r}$, indebtedness might rapidly rise above productive wealth. Once again, the individual bank would be unwilling to lend in the event that the other banks also stopped making loans.

It is not hard to think of other reasons why banks may be happy to make small loans as part of a group but not large loans when standing alone. For example, a syndicate may have stronger bargaining with respect to a debtor country than a single bank. A bank may therefore fear to be the only lender because it realizes that its future bargaining position with respect to the debtor may be weak. Also, banks may feel that they are more likely to enjoy central-bank protection from default risk if other banks are also involved in loans to a defaulting country. The central bank might be content to let a single irresponsible bank fail, as an example to others, but not to jeopardize the banking system by letting several banks fail.

The upshot of liquidity risk is that credit rationing may be far more restrictive than the limits of figure 1. Healthy countries with heavy debt-servicing obligations can suddenly find the spigot turned off, perhaps requiring them to make rather drastic short-run adjustments.

Repudiation Risk

Countries may be unable to obtain new loans because there is little confidence that the debtor will choose to repay the debt. To fix ideas, suppose that the debtor country owes D_t and has productive wealth $W_t > D_t$. If the country defaults, the creditors receive a fraction γ of W_t, perhaps by direct confiscation of the debtor country's assets. Moreover, the creditors can impose sanctions on the defaulting country in the amount θW_t. These sanctions include the direct seizure of assets, γW_t, and other penalties that may be costly to the debtor without yielding direct benefits to the creditors. Generally, then, we may assume that the sanctions exceed the payments to the creditors $(\theta > \gamma)$.

Consider the default decision. A repudiation of debt yields a gain of D_t and a loss of θW_t to the debtor, and a net loss to the creditor of $D_t(1 - \gamma)$. For debtors and creditors within a closed economy, θ is generally near 1.0, since creditors can use the legal system to seize much of their debtors' assets in the event of a repudiation. When $\theta = 1$, debt repudiation will make sense only when $D_t > W_t$, i.e. when the debtor is insolvent. In the international setting, the seizure of assets on a large scale is very difficult and sanctions such as trade embargoes against a defaulting country may have only limited effect. Thus, θ is generally much smaller than 1.0, so it may be true that $D_t > \theta W_t$ even when $D_t \ll W_t$.

The penalty function and the institutional setting together determine the loan supply schedule to a debtor country. In one extreme case, closer to nineteenth-century bond financing than to twentieth-century bank financing of LDC loans, there is little negotiation between creditors and debtors before a loan is defaulted. Debtors simply compare D_t and θW_t and repudiate when $D_t > \theta W_t$. Farsighted creditors therefore restrict loans to ensure that $D_t \leqslant \theta W_t$, and therefore shrink the loan supply relative to that of figure 1.

When active negotiation is possible between creditors and debtors, the situation is far more complicated. Suppose that $D_t > \theta W_t$, so that the debtor has an incentive to repudiate the debt. Both creditors and debtors also have an incentive to agree to debt relief in lieu of complete debt repudiation, since both sides can be left better off with debt relief instead of default. In the event of default, the creditor receives γW_t and the debtor loses θW_t, with $\theta > \gamma$. Clearly, if instead of default an agreement is reached in which the debtor pays θW_t of the debt while the creditors agree to forgo retaliation, the creditors are better off by $(\theta - \gamma) W_t$ and the debtor is left as well off. Alternatively, if the debtor agrees to pay γW_t to the creditor in exchange for no retaliation, the creditor is as well off as with repudiation, while the debtor is better off by the amount $(\theta - \gamma) W_t$. Any payoff by debtor to creditor between γW_t and θW_t, with no sanctions imposed by the creditors, therefore leaves both sides better off than with an outright repudiation.

Inevitably, then, in the event that indebtedness approaches or exceeds the repudiation threshold θW_t, there will be a strong incentive to negotiate. In general, economic theory cannot precisely specify the outcome of these negotiations, but standard models of bargaining can give us some indication of likely results. In the Nash bargaining solution, for example, there exists a so-called threat point, which is the outcome if negotiations break down. Let us assume that debt repudiation occurs in the absence of successful negotiation, so that the creditor gets γW_t and the debtor ends up with $(1 - \theta) W_t$. A successful bargaining outcome is a payoff P, that leaves the creditor with P and the debtor with $W_t - P$, and in which the creditor agrees to impose no

Borrowing Abroad: The Debtor's Perspective

sanctions on the debtor. Let U be the utility level of the creditor and V be the utility level of the debtor. The creditor's gain in utility from a successful negotiation is $U(P) - U(\gamma W_t)$, and the debtor's gain is $V(W_t - P) - V[(1 - \theta)W_t]$. In the Nash bargaining solution, the product of the gains to the debtor and creditor is maximized, subject to $P \leq D_t$. That is,

$$P \text{ maximizes } [U(P) - U(\gamma W_t)] \cdot \{V(W_t - P) - V[(1 - \theta)W_t]\}. \quad (3)$$

Suppose, for example, that both creditor and debtor are risk neutral, so that $U(P) = P$, $V(W_t - P) = W_t - P$, and so on. Then, we maximize $(P - \gamma W_t)(\theta W_t - P)$ subject to $P \leq D_t$. The payoff schedule is then

$$\begin{aligned} P &= D_t & \text{for } D_t &\leq (\theta + \gamma)W_t/2, \\ P &= (\theta + \gamma)W_t/2 & \text{for } D_t &> (\theta + \gamma)W_t/2. \end{aligned} \quad (4)$$

Thus, for small levels of debt, the country has no bargaining power, and the payoff equals the entire debt due. However, as D_t rises above $\theta W_t/2$, the country ends up paying only $(\theta + \gamma)W_t/2$. The payoff rises with θ and γ. Thus, as the creditor is able to impose large penalties on the debtor (high θ) and to seize a large amount of assets (high γ), the creditor's bargaining power and ultimate payoff are raised.

Now, it makes sense to suppose that a potential creditor understands its prospects in the event of negotiations, so that it limits its debt exposure to levels that the country will choose to repay. In this case, the required debt servicing will be kept below $(\theta + \gamma)W_t/2$. The lower the creditor's ability to retaliate in the event of repudiation, as measured by θ and γ, the tighter is the lending limit that creditors will impose. At least in the absence of uncertainty, borrowers are better off with higher θ and γ, since the existence of large penalties for repudiation frees up capital inflows.

The Planner's Problem

We have so far discussed three aspects of loan supply to a borrowing country. While a country's ability to repay debt is probably a necessary condition for it to attract new loans, its willingness to repay and its ability to do so on a short-term basis are probably even more important. Our next task is to study the optimal borrowing choice in light of these constraints.

Suppose that the goal of debt policy is to maximize a social-welfare function that depends on the consumption flow over time. Specifically, we write debtor utility V as

$$V = \sum_{i=0}^{\infty} (1 + \delta)^{-i} U(C_i). \tag{5}$$

C_i is real consumption (either per capita or aggregate) in period i, and $U(C_t)$ is an instantaneous utility in period t, with $U' > 0$ and $U'' \leq 0$. Intertemporal utility is given by a discounted sum of instantaneous utilities, where δ measures the rate of subjective time discount. A function like 5 is really an economist's presumption about what borrowing policy should be about, and much less a statement about the actual determinants of borrowing policies. The goals of planners or economic authorities might be much more concerned with the growth of GDP, the use of debt to stabilize a political regime, or even nationalist sentiments against foreign indebtedness, than about a careful calculation of intertemporal consumption possibilities. Since our topic is an analysis of appropriate borrowing strategies rather than an empirical account of actual borrowing behavior, we choose to proceed with equation 5.

Under certainty, and with no liquidity or repudiation risk, the optimal borrowing problem is

$$\max V = \sum_{i=0}^{\infty} (1 + \delta)^{-i} U(C_i) \tag{6}$$

subject to

(a) $K_{t+1} = K_t(1 - d) + I_t,$

(b) $Q_t = F(K_t),$

(c) $D_{t+1} = (1 + r)D_t + (I_t + C_t) - Q_t,$

(d) $\lim_{t \to \infty} (1 + r)^{-t} D_t = 0,$

(e) K_0, D_0 given.

Condition d is a convenient way to impose the solvency constraint on borrowing. Implicitly, we are taking the case in which $n < r$, so that foreign borrowing is limited by the future capacity to repay debt. In that case, condition d is equivalent to the condition described by equation 2. Rather than proceed to a complete solution of equation 6, we shall simplify the problem further. (The complete numerical solution is found in the appendix.) With optimal policies, the maximum value V is implicitly a function of K_0 and D_0. We write this value at time 0 as $V = V(K_0, D_0)$. Similarly, if the economy enters any period t with an inherited capital stock K_t and debt D_t, optimal policies from that period onward will yield intertemporal utility of $V(K_t, D_t)$. Now, consider the planner's problem at time 0. He will choose values of C_0 and I_0, which then yield K_1 and D_1 via conditions a–c. Thereafter, he will continue to borrow optimally, so that from period 1 onward the economy achieves $V(K_1, D_1)$. From the perspective of period 0, utility is therefore

$$V(K_0, D_0) = U(C_0) + V(K_1, D_1)/(1 + \delta).$$

The infinite-horizon problem becomes a one-period problem as long as $V(K_1, D_1)$ is known.

More usefully, we shall work with a two-period variant of the problem in equation 6. We rewrite the planner's problem as

$$\max V(K_0, D_0) = U(C_0) + U(C_1)/(1 + \delta) + V(K_2, D_2)/(1 + \delta)^2 \quad (7)$$

subject to

(a) $K_{t+1} = K_t(1 - d) + I_t, \quad t = 0, 1$

(b) $Q_t = F(K_t)$,

(c) $D_{t+1} = (1 + r)D_t + (I_t + C_t) - Q_t$,

(d) K_0, D_0 given.

We shall assume that the function $V(K_2, D_2)$ is known, and study the optimal choices in periods 0 and 1. In fact, for many of our results we will not need to know $V(K_2, D_2)$. In general, $V(K_2, D_2)$ may be found by more powerful methods of optimal control or dynamic programming, or the infinite-horizon problem may be tackled head on, as in the appendix.

Optimal Borrowing Without Liquidity or Repudiation Risks

In this section we study the optimal borrowing decision when borrowing is limited only by a solvency constraint. The solvency constraint is implicitly built into the $V(K_2, D_2)$ function. Let

$$W_2 = \max \sum_{i=2}^{\infty} (1 + r)^{-(i-2)}(Q_i - I_i).$$

W_2 is implicitly a function of K_2, so the solvency constraint $(1 + r)D_2 \leq W_2(K_2)$ is a constraint on debt relative to the capital stock. When $(1 + r)D_2 = W_2(K_2)$, consumption must be zero forever into the future in order to service the debt, so that

$$V[K_2, W_2(K_2)] = \sum_{i=2}^{\infty} (1 + \delta)^{-(i-2)} U(0),$$

which is obviously a lower limit for V.

The optimal borrowing strategy is found by direct optimization of equation 7. The first-order conditions are

(a) $U_0(C_0) = \lambda$,

(b) $U_1(C_1)/(1 + \delta) = \lambda/(1 + r)$,

(c) $F_K(K_1) = (r + d)$,

(8)

(d) λ is the marginal utility of wealth.

The results of the optimization are straightforward and well known. With a perfect world capital market, borrowing and lending should be undertaken to smooth the marginal utility of consumption over time. The marginal utility of consumption in period i (MUC_i) is given by $U_i(C_i)/(1 + \delta)^i$, where $U_i(C_i)$ denotes $\partial U(C_i)/\partial C_i$. The present-value price of output in period i is $\pi_i = (1 + r)^{-i}$, where π_i is the number of units of output that must be saved at time 0 in order to yield one unit of the good in period i. The consumption smoothing rule is then

$$MUC_i/\pi_i = \lambda \quad \text{for all periods } i. \tag{9}$$

The major implication of equation 9 has been described in Sachs 1982b and Sachs 1984. Basically, it captures the old dictum "Finance a temporary shock, adjust to a permanent shock." When output is *temporarily* depressed, λ does not change much and according to equation 9 the MUC should also remain unchanged. This involves maintaining a high rate of consumption in spite of temporarily low output, by accumulating debt. When output is *permanently* reduced, λ rises, so the MUC in every period should also rise. In effect, consumption is reduced in line with lower permanent income, and the country should not borrow in order to maintain a high rate of consumption.

Equation 8c expresses the second half of the standard borrowing strategy. Investments should be undertaken to the point where the marginal product of capital equals the world cost of capital, where the latter is measured as a world real interest rate plus the rate of depreciation. In more complex investment environments, this rule would be restated as a rule to undertake all investment projects with positive present value at the world interest rate.

Suppose that these guidelines are to be adopted. By what set of policy rules can they be implemented? Under a set of restrictive conditions, the guidelines are those that would be adopted by value-maximizing firms and utility-maximizing households in a fully decentralized economy. The necessary assumptions are

perfect foresight (or rational expectations under uncertainty),

a social-welfare function V that is also the representative household's utility function,

unrestricted access of households and firms to the world capital market,

no taxes or other distortions that cause the private marginal product of capital to diverge from the social marginal product of capital (F_K), and

no taxes or other distortions that cause the post-tax real interest rate to diverge from the world real interest rate.

If these conditions hold, then the laissez faire approach to foreign borrowing will yield an optimal path of external indebtedness. When any of these conditions is violated, the case for laissez faire is substantially weakened. Though much of the rest of the paper involves relaxing the assumptions needed to justify laissez faire, it is useful to mention a few examples of how these assumptions may be violated. Some illustrative cases are described in table 1.

We now turn to some key extensions of the basic model, still assuming the absence of liquidity and repudiation risk.

Traded versus Nontraded Goods

Suppose, now, that the economy produces nontraded as well as traded goods. Sectoral output is written as a function of sectoral capital stocks (labor input is suppressed, but could be added easily): $Q^T = F^T(K^T)$ and $Q^N = F^N(K^N)$. Let P_t^N signify the relative price of nontradeables in terms of tradeables in period t. Consumption is divided between N and T subject to an intertemporal social-welfare function of the form

$$V = \sum_{i=0}^{\infty} (1 + \delta)^{-i} U(C_i^T, C_i^N).$$

For simplicity, all investment is assumed to use the traded good (here, too, extension to the general case is straightforward). Let I^N be investment made in the nontraded-goods sector (using tradeable output) and I^T be investment in tradeable-goods production, so that

$$K_{t+1}^T = K_t^T(1 - d) + I_t^T$$

and $K_{t+1}^N = K_t^N(1 - d) + I_t^N.$

Table 1
Assumptions underlying the case for laissez faire, and examples of violation.

Assumption	Examples of violation
Perfect foresight or rational expectations	Households or firms may incorrectly extrapolate current exchange rates and interest rates into the future, particularly since governments are fond of promising that there will be no exchange-rate changes.
Social-welfare function	The government's planning horizon and rate of time preference may differ from that of a "typical household." Ideally, governments may represent future generations that are underrepresented in the interests of current households.
Access to world capital markets	Most LDC capital markets are highly segmented, so that "free" access to the world market may imply a sharply different degree of access for different groups within the economy and may therefore have perverse effects on resource allocation.
Equality of social and private marginal products of capital	This assumption will be violated for public goods (e.g. physical infrastructure), providing a crucial reason for direct government intervention in the investment process. Similarly, tariffs and domestic taxes may drive a wedge between market and shadow prices.
Equality of domestic and world interest rates	Taxes and subsidies on capital, market segmentation, and a noncompetitive financial sector may all contribute to a major divergence between the world cost of capital and the domestic interest rate. Also, there may exist externalities in the borrowing process so that individual borrowers drive up the external cost of funds for others. In this case, interest rates will not equal the marginal cost of funds to the country as a whole.

The trade balance is $Q^T - C^T - (I^T + I^N)$, and the nontraded-good equilibrium is $Q^N = C^N$.

From the point of view of the solvency condition, productive wealth must be redefined as productive *tradeables* wealth,

$$\max \sum_{i=0}^{\infty} (1 + r)^{-i}(Q_i^T - I_i^T - I_i^N).$$

External debt cannot exceed the present discounted value of net tradeables production, since by definition only tradeable goods can be used for exports to service the external debt.

Let us now consider the two-period borrowing problem with tradeables and nontradeables:

$$\max U(C_0^T, C_0^N) + \frac{U(C_1^T, C_1^N)}{1+\delta} + V(K_2^N, K_2^T, D_2)/(1+\delta)^2 \qquad (10)$$

subject to

$$D_{t+1} = (1+r)D_t + Q_t^T - C_t^T - (I_t^T + I_t^N),$$

$$Q_t^N = C_t^N,$$

$$K_{t+1}^T = K_t^T(1-d) + I_t^T,$$

$$K_{t+1}^N = K_t^N(1-d) + I_t^N,$$

$$Q_t^T = F^T(K_t^T),$$

$$Q_t^N = F^N(K_t^N).$$

The solution to this problem is easily shown to be

$$U_{0T} = \lambda,$$

$$U_{0N} = \lambda P_0^N,$$

$$U_{1T} = \lambda(1+\delta)/(1+r), \qquad (11a)$$

$$U_{1N} = \lambda P_1^N(1+\delta)/(1+r),$$

$$F_K^T(K_1^T) = (r+d), \qquad (11b)$$

$$P_1^N F_K^N(K_1^N) = (r+d).$$

The main insight from this optimization is that current decisions regarding consumption and investment must involve forecasts of the future relative price of nontradeables. At time 0, for example, the investment in nontraded goods should equate $P_1^N F_K^N(K_1^N)$ with $(r+d)$. It will likely be the case that P_1^N will not equal P_0^N, with the result that myopic expectations regarding P^N will result in a misallocation of investment expenditure. We provide a quantitative illustration of this point in the appendix.

Official Borrowing to Augment Private Savings

In many economies, private investment is deemed insufficient to generate desired growth rates in the economy, and the public sector is regarded as an "engine of growth" through the role of augmenting the rate of capital accumulation. Underdeveloped domestic capital markets may cause private savings, and hence private investment, to remain low. Fiscal expenditures on investment goods may then form a significant share of total capital formation, with foreign official borrowing playing an important role in the finance of government investment and taxes playing a crucial role in generating official resources for debt servicing. The optimal borrowing strategy must be recomputed under these circumstances, for debt-servicing capacity depends not only on national wealth but also on the public sector's ability to tax that wealth. When there are weaknesses (either political or economic) in the government's authority to raise taxes, the government must be especially cautious in its foreign borrowing. The following illustration underlines this need for caution. (This section relies heavily on Sachs 1984.)

Suppose that, because of an underdeveloped capital market, the private sector in a developing country saves a fixed fraction of post-tax income rather than optimizing intertemporarlly. The government uses its taxing and borrowing authority to supplement private saving. (See chapter 6 of Arrow and Kurz 1970 for a similar model of imperfect capital markets.) Private investors have no direct access to the international loan market. The government taxes domestic output at rate τ_t, which may change over time. This rate must be less than 1.0, and may be less than zero if the government is making net income transfers to the private sector. There is no public consumption.

With domestic output given by Q_t, tax revenues are $\tau_t Q_t$ and private-sector savings are $s(1 - \tau_t)Q_t$. Private consumption is given by $C_t = (1 - s)(1 - \tau_t)Q_t$. In any period, the government borrows D_{t+1} and repays $(1 + r)D_t$. Total investment in the economy is given by

$$I_t = s(1 - \tau_t)Q_t + \tau_t Q_t + [D_{t+1} - (1 + r)D_t],$$

where the first term on the right-hand side represents private savings, the second represents tax revenue, and the third represents net foreign resource inflow. As written, it appears that all foreign borrowing is used for investment rather than consumption; however this is true only as an accounting matter. Suppose, for example, that the government wants to raise private consumption while holding investment levels fixed. It merely raises D_{t+1} while reducing τ_t sufficiently to keep I_t constant; in that case the borrowing finances consumption 100 percent on the margin.

Now, let us calculate the optimal financial policy of the government, assuming again that it tries to maximize an intertemporal utility function of the form

$$U(C_0) + U(C_1)/(1 + \delta) + V(K_2, D_2)/(1 + \delta)^2.$$

The basic public finance problem with international borrowing is

$$\max_{I_0, I_1, \tau_0, \tau_1} U(C_0) + \frac{U(C_1)}{(1 + \delta)} + \frac{V(K_2, D_2)}{(1 + \delta)^2} \qquad (13)$$

subject to

$$Q_t = F(K_t),$$

$$K_{t+1} = K_t(1-d) + I_t,$$

$$C_t = (1-s)(1-\tau_t)Q_t,$$

$$I_t = s(1-\tau_t)Q_t + \tau_t Q_t + D_{t+1} - (1+r)D_t.$$

As long as tax rates are completely flexible, the solution to this problem is identical to the solution to equation 7, since the dynamic budget constraint facing the government is no different whether it chooses C_t and I_t (as before) or τ_t and I_t (as here).

To find the tax rates corresponding to this optimal plan, note that

$$C_i = (1-s)(1-\tau_i)F(K_i),$$

so that

$$\tau_i = 1 - [C_i/F(K_i)][1/(1-s)].$$

If s is fixed, a typical optimal growth path will involve a rising τ. Low tax rates in the early period allow households to benefit early on from the growth that will be achieved in periods 1 and 2. Higher taxes later on are necessary to service the international debt.

Now let us introduce a simple yet crucial hitch into the model. Suppose that the government can raise tax rates only to a limit $\bar{\tau} < 1$, and that the constraint is binding in the sense that the optimal τ_0 and/or τ_1 exceeds $\bar{\tau}$. The first effect of the tax ceiling is to tighten significantly the solvency constraint in equation 2. Debt repayment now depends on taxing authority as well as national wealth. The new constraint is that D_t must be less than or equal to the maximum level of tax revenues net of government investment. Government investment is I_t minus private investment, $s(1-\tau_t)Q_t$. Thus,

$$D_t(1+r) \leq \max_{\tau,I} \sum_{i=t}^{\infty} (1+r)^{-(i-t)}[\tau_t Q_t - I_t + s(1-\tau_t)Q_t]. \tag{14}$$

It is more likely that equation 14 rather than equation 2 holds as a binding constraint, since equation 14 does not imply that future consumption must equal zero when the constraint binds. Nonetheless, in the examples that follow, we do not consider the case in which equation 14 binds. We focus rather on the constraint $\tau = \bar{\tau}$, assuming that D_t remains below the maximum level in equation 14.

Since the optimal tax path tends to involve rising τ, a natural case to consider is one in which the tax constraint does not bind in period 0 while it does bind in period 1. Thus, we assume $\tau_0 < \bar{\tau}$ and $\tau_1 = \bar{\tau}$. What are the implications of the tax constraint? Basically, first-period consumption C_1 remains "too high" relative to the plan that an unconstrained government would choose, since the fiscal authority would like to raise taxes in the first period but cannot do so. Therefore, the marginal utility of income in the first period is too low, and the returns to investment in period 1, namely $F_K(K_1)$, should be given a weight less than 1.0 in project analysis. After some algebra, we can prove

$$F_K(K_1) = (r + d) \cdot \varepsilon, \quad \varepsilon > 1. \tag{14}$$

We have the key result:

Under a regime of constrained tax levies, the marginal product of capital should no longer be equated with the world market cost of capital, but rather should be kept higher to reflect a lower shadow value of first-period output.

If the government follows the standard rule $F_K(K_1) = r + d$, the country is led to overborrow, with the result that social welfare is reduced.

Let us consider a graphic case of this issue that follows the analysis of Kharas (1981). Suppose that the government cares only about growth, in the sense that $u(C_0) \equiv u(C_1) \equiv 0$ and $V(K_2, D_2) = F(K_2) - (1 + r)D_2$. The government is trying to maximize second-period national income (net of international indebtedness). If τ_t is not constrained, τ_0 and τ_1 should be set at 1.0, with government revenue plus net foreign borrowing used to equate $F_K(K_2)$ with $r + d$, according to the classical policy prescription.

Now suppose that $\tau_0, \tau_1 \leq \bar{\tau} < 1$. Since consumption has no weight in utility, it is optimal to set taxes at their maximum rate: $\tau_0 = \tau_1 = \bar{\tau}$. Then D_2 and K_2 are given by

$$D_2 = (1 + r)\{I_0 - [s(1 - \bar{\tau}) + \bar{\tau}]F(K_0)\}$$
$$+ \{I_1 - [s(1 - \bar{\tau}) + \bar{\tau}]F[K_0(1 - d) + I_1]\}, \tag{15}$$

$$K_2 = K_0(1 - d)^2 + I_0(1 - d) + I_1.$$

By setting $\partial V/\partial I_0 = \partial V/\partial I_1 = 0$, we find the optimal investment policy. After some algebra, we find

$$F_K(K_1) = \frac{r + d}{s(1 - \bar{\tau}) + \bar{\tau}} > r + d,$$

$$F_K(K_2) = r + d. \tag{16}$$

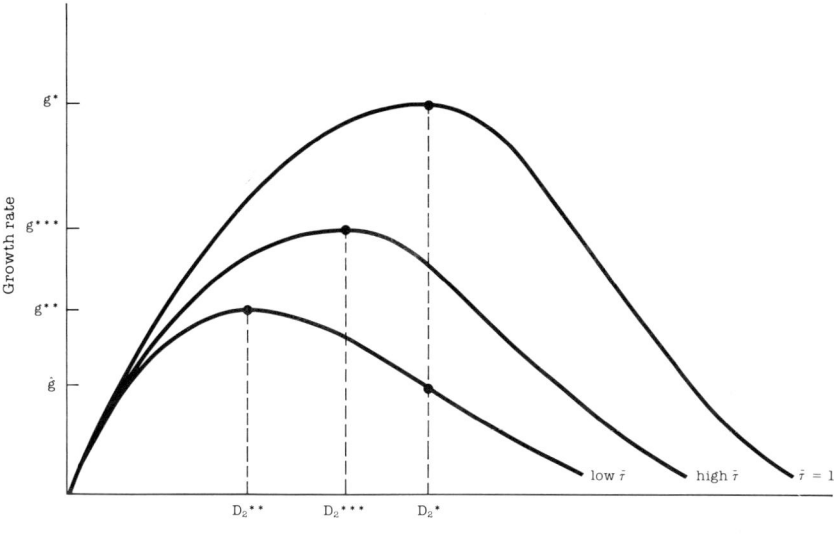

Figure 2
Foreign borrowing and growth in a tax-constrained regime. Growth is measured by $F(K_3) - (1 + r)D_3$, as in text.

Once again, the country should not invest enough to equate $F_K(K_1)$ and $r + d$.

This model provides a powerful indictment against foreign borrowing, even for productive investment projects, if the domestic fiscal system is not equipped to handle rising debt-service ratios. Figure 2 illustrates how aggregate growth is slowed by excessive borrowing in a tax-constrained regime, for specific parameter values of the model. In the unconstrained regime, optimal borrowing is at D_2^*, with growth at g^*. In the constrained case, with a low $\bar{\tau}$, the optimum is at $D_2^{**} < D_2^*$, with growth at $g^{**} < g^*$; in the constrained case with a high $\bar{\tau}$, the optimum is at D_2^{***}, with growth at g^{***}. If the borrower with low $\bar{\tau}$ equates $F_K(K_1)$ with $r + d$, in spite of the tax constraint, the growth rate ends up at $\hat{g}$ (corresponding to D_2^*), which is lower than can be achieved with less foreign borrowing, g^{**}.

Optimal Borrowing with Liquidity Constraints

Debt crises almost never involve the strict solvency constraint in foreign borrowing. Well before consumption levels are driven to subsistence, countries typically repudiate their foreign debt or succeed in gaining debt relief.

Often a debt crisis has little to do with fundamental solvency considerations but rather turns on the short-run difficulties of debt servicing. In this section, we explore how borrowing strategies should be modified when short-run liquidity risks are present. We establish two principal results. First, the optimal level of borrowing depends importantly on the probability of a cutoff in lending. Second, the possibility of a lending cutoff increases the importance of the maturity structure of the debt. The standard prescription that long-term projects should be financed with long-term loans grows in importance as the probability of a lending cutoff rises.

We begin with an extremely simple version of the two-period model, with physical investment ignored. The goal of borrowing is to maximize expected utility,

$$\max E(V) = E[U(C_0) + U(C_1)/(1 + \delta) + V(D_2)/(1 + \delta)^2], \tag{17}$$

subject to

$$C_0 = Q_0 + D_1,$$
$$C_1 = Q_1 + D_2 - (1 + r)D_1$$

with the borrowing constraint that, with probability π, $D_2 \leq 0$ (i.e. no foreign borrowing), whereas with probability $(1 - \pi)$, D_2 is not restricted.

With probability π, the country is unable to obtain new finance D_2 in period 1, and the country must borrow D_1 without knowing whether D_2 will in fact be available. At this point, we assume that π is independent of the level of debt. Below, we introduce the more realistic assumption that π rises with D_1, i.e. that high debt levels make potential creditors less likely to extend new debt.

Consider first the case when $\pi = 0$. From our earlier results we know that

$$U_0(C_0) = U_1(C_1)(1 + r)/(1 + \delta)$$

and that

$$U_1(C_1) = -V_D/(1 + \delta).$$

When $\pi > 0$, we must consider two outcomes: either the economy is liquidity constrained (denoted by superscript L) or it is not (denoted by superscript N). D_1 is borrowed without knowledge of the outcome in the next period. Consumption turns out to be

$$C_1^L = Q_1 - (1 + r)D_1$$

if the borrowing constraint holds and

$$C_1^N = Q_1 - (1 + r)D_1 + D_2^N$$

if it does not.[3] Clearly $C_1^N > C_1^L$. In case N, D_2^N is selected according to the standard criterion

$$U_1^N(C_1^N) = -V_D(D_2^N)/(1 + \delta).$$

In case L, we have

$$U_1^L(C_1^L) > -V_D(0)/(1 + \delta).$$

Parenthetically, D_2^N is an increasing function of D_1.[4]

By writing EV as

$$U(C_0) + \pi[U(C_1^L)/(1 + \delta) + V(0)/(1 + \delta)^2]$$
$$+ (1 - \pi)[U(C_1^N)/(1 + \delta) + V(D_2^N)/(1 + \delta)^2],$$

we find the optimal borrowing level D_1 as the solution to $d(EV)/dD_1 = 0$:

$$\frac{d(EV)}{dD_1} = 0 \Rightarrow U_0 = [(1 + r)/(1 + \delta)][\pi U_1^L + (1 - \pi)U_1^N]. \tag{18}$$

By totally differentiating this equation with respect to D_1, D_2^N, and π, we can find the dependence of D_1 on π. After some algebra, we can show[5]

$$\frac{dD_1}{d\pi} < 0. \tag{19}$$

Thus, as the probability of a second-period lending cutoff rises, optimum first-period borrowing should decline.

Liquidity Crises and Borrowing Externalities

Should governments regulate foreign borrowing if liquidity crises are possible? Under some special circumstances, the answer is no, though more generally this form of market failure does provide a case for intervention. The model we have just explored can justify laissez faire if the following assumptions hold:

The private sector has rational expectations of a liquidity crisis.

The probability π is not a function of the overall level of borrowing.

The government can credibly commit itself to refuse to bail out private agents who find their credit cut off.

The liquidity crisis causes no widespread bankruptcies, or if bankruptcies occur they are handled efficiently, without social cost.

If these assumptions are maintained, then individual agents will choose their intertemporal plans such that

$$U_0 = E(U_1)[(1 + r)/(1 + \delta)],$$

where

$$E(U_1) = \pi U_1^L + (1 - \pi)U_1^N.$$

This is precisely the first-order condition found in equation 18.

All these assumptions are highly suspect. Borrowers probably do not have a good understanding of financial crises (neither do economists or governments!), much less an ability to predict their occurrence. Moreover, though π is hard to forecast, it is likely that the frequency of a loan cutoff increases with the amount of debt outstanding. We have already argued that such a crisis arises when no single lender is willing to lend the country as much as it needs to remain current on debt servicing. That possibility cannot arise when D_1 is very low. Furthermore, when liquidity crises arise, governments are almost inevitably called upon to act to bail out debt-ridden firms. As Díaz-Alejandro has recently argued (1984, pp. 19 and 22), based on the experience of Argentina, Uruguay, and Chile,

> Whether or not deposits are explicitly insured, the public expects governments to intervene to save most depositors from losses when financial intermediaries run into trouble. Warnings that intervention will not be forthcoming appear to be simply not believable....
>
> Foreign lenders take government announcements that it will not rescue local private debtors, especially banks, with non-guaranteed external (or domestic) liabilities even less seriously than depositors take the threat of a loss of their money.... Foreign bank lending to both the public and private sectors of a country have considerable leverage to convince governments to take over *ex-post* bad private debts, especially those of financial intermediaries.

If the government is always expected to bail out bad debts, moral hazard problems are rife. Debtors will no longer expect to feel the full brunt of the crisis, since losses will be socialized (i.e. spread among borrowers and nonborrowers throughout the economy). Obviously, overborrowing may then arise.

The fourth assumption, that bankruptcies impose no social costs, is also likely to be far off the mark. In an ideal legal system, overextended debtors would simply transfer their equity claims to creditors without a loss of production in those firms still covering variable costs. In practice, when firms go bankrupt they often cease operations in the short or the long run, leading to unemployment of resources. Indeed, it is precisely because bankruptcies impose heavy social costs that governments are obliged to extend debt relief.

It is not very easy to specify the appropriate borrowing strategy given the above complexities. It is, however, worthwhile to take just one of the issues and develop its implications analytically. Suppose that the model remains as in equation 17, but now with π an increasing function of D_1. When we recalculate the optimal borrowing level by setting $d(EV)/dD_1 = 0$, we find

$$U_0 = \frac{1+r}{1+\delta}[\pi U_1^L + (1-\pi)U_1^N] + \frac{d\pi}{dD_1} \frac{V_1^N - V_1^L}{1+\delta}, \tag{20}$$

where

$V_1^N = U(C_1^N) + V(D_2^N)/(1+\delta),$

$V_1^L = U(C_1^L) + V(0)/(1+\delta),$

$V_1^N - V_1^L > 0.$

Compare the expressions for U_0 in equations 18 and 20. We see in equation 20 that U_0 is greater than $[(1+r)/(1+\delta)][\pi U_1^L + (1-\pi)U_1^N]$ by a term that reflects the effect of D_1 on π. Basically, equation 20 holds that r does not reflect the marginal cost of external funds, since an increase in D_1 also makes more likely a welfare-reducing liquidity crisis.

If the marginal borrower behaves as if π is given, the private marginal cost of funds (r) will fall short of the social cost and overborrowing will occur. Laissez faire is no longer first best, even if all of the other necessary assumptions hold true. The optimal borrowing strategy is then to tax foreign borrowing so that private and social costs are aligned. The situation is formally equivalent to the Bhagwati-Srinivasan (1975) argument for a disruption tariff when high export levels raise the possibility of foreign-trade retaliation.

Liquidity Crises and Debt Maturities

The possibility of a loan supply cutoff provides an important reason for matching the maturity structure of the debt with the gestation period of physical capital investment. Suppose that an incremental investment opportunity dI_1 becomes available in the problem illustrated by equation 20. We call the investment short-term if it pays off in the next period and long-term if it pays off in two periods. For the short-term case, we assume that the yield is $(1+\theta)dI_1$, with $\theta > r$. For the long-term case the yield after two periods is

$(1 + \theta)^2 dI_1$, again with $\theta > r$. We also assume the existence of short- and long-term loans, with the same interest rate per period. A short-term loan D_1^S requires repayment $(1 + r)D_1^S$ in the next period. A long-term loan D_1^L requires repayment $(1 + r)^2 D_1^L$ in two periods.

It is easy to prove the following results:

- For any π, the short-term project should be undertaken with short-term finance.
- For any π, the long-term project should be undertaken with long-term finance.
- The long-term project should not necessarily be undertaken with short-term finance. This is true even though the project has positive present value at the world interest rate. The project becomes more desirable the lower is π and the greater is θ relative to r.

The proof of these propositions is simple. Start at an equilibrium with no investment. When maturities of I and D are matched, it is easy to show that consumption plans can be left unchanged, and final indebtedness D_2 can be lowered, by undertaking the investment project. For the case of short-term finance for a long-term project, the demonstration is a little more involved. Basically, a liquidity crisis is more severe the larger is D_1. If $\theta = r$, then undertaking the investment yields no net benefits, but it does impose a cost by raising D_1 (and therefore raising the welfare loss in the event of a liquidity crisis). Therefore, θ must be sufficiently above r to justify new borrowing.[6]

Generally, long-term debt reduces the costs of a possible lending cutoff. This is for two reasons. The first and the more obvious reason is that, for a given external debt, the shorter the maturity structure, the greater on average is the amount of principal repayment in a given period. Therefore, the larger is the required short-run cut in domestic spending if new lending suddenly ceases. Second, and perhaps more important, a judicious use of long-term borrowing with short-term lending (i.e., reserve accumulation) can help to obviate liquidity crises by reducing the need to borrow in a given period. Suppose that without fear of a debt cutoff the optimal path of short-term borrowing would be D_1 in the first period and D_2 in the next. Using long-term loans, this pattern can be replicated without any second-period borrowing (assuming, as we have done, that both short-term and long-term loans have the same interest rate per period). The economy simply borrows $D_1 + D_2/(1 + r)$ in long-term funds and puts $D_2/(1 + r)$ into reserves. The reserves have value D_2 in the next period, and these reserves are then drawn down to zero in the next period. Thus, it becomes irrelevant whether new lending is or is not available in that period.

The fact that countries hold substantial reserves provides good evidence that liquidity can be a serious concern. Governments borrow over the long term to hold reserves even though the cost of long-term finance is higher than the returns to official reserves. This behavior makes sense if governments are willing to pay a premium to ensure the availability of foreign exchange in a given period. Other evidence in this regard is that countries often pay commitment fees to guarantee the availability of loans at a future date.

Borrowing Strategies When Debt Repudiation Is Feasible

Now we turn to the case in which countries can repay debt in both the short and the long term but may be unwilling to do so. (This section relies heavily on Sachs and Cohen 1982.) The key to modeling debt repudiation is an explicit assumption regarding its benefits and costs. The benefits are straightforward: The borrower saves the real value of the outstanding debt, which it no longer services. The costs are far more difficult to specify. (See Sachs 1982 for a discussion of the historical experience.) One aspect of the costs may be a partial or complete inability to obtain new loans in the world capital markets, at least for some time after the repudiation occurs. Another aspect of the costs may be a direct seizure of the country's overseas assets, including bank accounts, foreign direct investments, ships, and aircraft. A third and even more important cost may be a dramatic decline in the country's capacity to engage in trade, even if no net new borrowing is involved. Modern trade is built on a sophisticated system of revolving trade credits. Even if a country's net debt is zero, its gross stocks of trade-related financial assets and liabilities are likely to be large. Because a borrower would have difficulty arranging trade credits after a repudiation, the mechanics of trade would be made onerous. Moreover, merchandise at ports ready to be dispatched to the debtor country could be subject to seizure by creditors.

To introduce these elements, we assume that when a debt is repudiated the creditors retaliate by imposing two costs. First, in all future periods the borrower's production is reduced, for a given K, by a fixed fraction θ; second, the borrower is excluded from all further borrowing. We now assume that this retaliation yields neither costs nor benefits to the creditors (or that the costs and the benefits cancel). In terms of the discussion in the first section, we set $\gamma = 0$.

As an easy start, we begin with a simplified version of the international borrowing model; we simply drop $V(K_2, D_2)$. The tax considerations are ignored, so we implicitly assume that domestic tax levies are not constrained. Loans are made to the sovereign borrower in period 0. If they are not repaid in period 1, the penalty is enforced and output is reduced by θQ_1. The borrower makes the repudiation decision in period 1; there is no way that it can precommit itself to a decision before the period arrives. Moreover, in this section the possibility of a negotiated settlement is ignored. (The general principles of credit rationing are the same when *ex post facto* negotiations are allowed.) Since second-period utility is simply $U(C_1)$, the borrower compares consumption levels with and without repudiation. With repudiation, C_1 equals $Q_1 - \theta Q_1$, which equals $(1-\theta)Q_1$. (We denote this level as C_1^R.) With no repudiation, C_1 equals $Q_1 - (1+r)D_1$, which we denote C_1^N. The borrower defaults whenever C_1^R exceeds C_1^N, and thus whenever $(1+r)D_1 > \theta Q_1$.

There are two choices with respect to the timing of loans. The level of credit D_1 may be extended before or after the investment decision I_0 is made. (We shall see shortly that it is a great advantage to the country to be able to choose I_0 before going to the capital markets, since I_0 may then be chosen to make the credit terms on a given loan more favorable or to increase the total amount that the country can borrow.) A more natural assumption, however, is that loans are arranged first and that the government then allocates them to consumption and investment. In this case the government will generally have an incentive to renege on a promised level of I_0 once a loan has been arranged, even if *ex ante* it would be better off to fix I_0. Thus, promises concerning I_0 will be unconvincing. We term the case in which I_0 is set first the precommitment equilibrium, and regard the other case as the standard assumption.

A linear model offers a vivid illustration of the effects of repudiation risk and of investment precommitment. Let

$$Q_0 = \bar{Q},$$
$$Q_1 = \bar{Q} + (1+\gamma)I_0, \quad I \leq \bar{I}$$
$$V = C_0 + C_1/(1+\delta),$$
$$\delta > \gamma > r.$$

(21)

According to these expressions, there is a quantity $\bar{I}$ of investment projects with a rate of return γ exceeding the world interest rate r. The rate of time discount δ is assumed to be greater than the world interest rate. In the no-repudiation model, utility V is maximized by setting $I_0 = \bar{I}$. (All investment projects are undertaken.) Consumption is shifted entirely to the first period, with no consumption in the second (since $\delta > r$ and utility is linear). In sum, in the case of no repudiation we have

$$C_0 = \bar{Q} + \frac{\bar{Q} + (1 + \gamma)\bar{I}}{1 + r},$$

$$I_0 = \bar{I},$$

$$C_1 = 0,$$

$$D_1 = C_0 + I_0 - \bar{Q}.$$

(22)

Now we turn to the "standard" case of the repudiation model. Once a loan D_1 is arranged, the borrower will choose to set $I_0 = 0$, since $\delta > \gamma$. Therefore $Q_1 = \bar{Q}$, and the debt ceiling is given by $\bar{D}_1 = \theta\bar{Q}/(1 + r)$. The complete solution in the standard repudiation case is

$$C_0 = \bar{Q} + \theta\bar{Q}(1 + r),$$

$$I_0 = 0,$$

$$C_1 = \bar{Q} - \theta\bar{Q},$$

$$D_1 = \theta\bar{Q}/(1 + r).$$

(23)

Therefore, the presence of repudiation risk causes rationing of the borrower. (Note that D_1 is lower in equation 23 than in the previous equation.) Investment is reduced (all the way to zero in this example), and consumption is pushed to the second period. The presence of repudiation risk reduces the borrower's welfare by restricting capital inflows.

Finally, we turn to the precommitment case. It turns out that the borrower may be able to raise its welfare by promising a high level of investment I_0. Higher I_0 raises Q_1 and thus raises the penalty for repudiation, which equals θQ_1. When I_0 is high, creditors are therefore more willing to lend, and the credit constraint is eased. In this version, the borrowing country will choose to precommit to $I_0 = \bar{I}$ when γ is close to δ and when δ is much greater than r. Specifically, we find in the precommitment, repudiation case

$$C_0 = \bar{Q} + D_1 - I_0,$$

$$I_0 = 0 \text{ for } (\delta - r)\theta(1 + \gamma) < (\delta - \gamma)(1 + r),$$

$$I_0 = \bar{I} \text{ for } (\delta - r)\theta(1 + \gamma) > (\delta - \gamma)(1 + r),$$

$$C_1 = Q_1 - \theta Q_1,$$

$$D_1 = \theta Q_1/(1 + r).$$

(24)

Thus, the precommitment case may be the same as the no-precommitment case, but may (and generally will) result in an equilibrium somewhere between the textbook model and the standard repudiation model. Precommitment makes sense when $\delta \approx r$ (that is, the rate of time discount is not too high), and when $\gamma \gg r$ (that is, investment is quite profitable). Precommitment allows greater borrowing, greater investment in profitable projects, and higher first-period consumption.

Repudiation Risk with Uncertainty

So far, an actual default never occurs in the model, though the threat of default has a profound effect on economic welfare and the nature of macroeconomic equilibrium. Once uncertainty is introduced into the model, debt repudiations will actually occur as random events. The presence of uncertainty has several effects. First, the loan supply schedule becomes upward sloping, rather than perfectly elastic, up to a maximum debt level $\bar{D}$. Second, and even more important, the incentive structure for macroeconomic management may become perverse in ways now described. (A more complete treatment of debt repudiation under uncertainty may be found in Sachs and Cohen 1982 and Sachs 1984.)

A recent theme of financial economics is that the various claimants on a firm's income stream (e.g. shareholders, bondholders, workers) have differing interests regarding the firm's policies because alternative policies affect the relative valuation of the different claims. Thus, the shareholders may urge policies that raise shareholder wealth at the expense of bondholder wealth, as described by Jensen and Meckling (1976). Or coalitions of the shareholders and banks may engage in policies at the expense of bondholders, especially in the context of bankruptcy actions (see Bulow and Shoven 1978). A notable feature of these examples is that the firm may pursue inefficient policies that reduce the overall value of the firm, because some groups will benefit even though other groups will be hurt more. A related theme is that all groups are generally left better off, *ex ante*, if the firm can be constrained from pursuing inefficient policies.

Several direct analogies can be made to macroeconomic behavior by the borrowing country. Like a firm, the country also has various claimants on the income stream, including the government, domestic citizens, and international creditors. Like a firm, a country may be led to select inefficient policies to transfer income from the creditors to the "shareholders" (the government and domestic private sector). Generally, the country would like to forswear these policies *ex ante* but may find it difficult to do so.

There are several areas of behavior in which timing and default risk interact to produce bad macroeconomic choices. The earlier discussion of investment precommitment can be thought of precisely in these terms. From an *ex ante* point of view it is best for the country to choose a high level of investment, because high investment relaxes credit ceilings. However, once a loan package is arranged, the country prefers to raise first-period consumption at the expense of investment. Since creditors understand this, they will tend to discount initial promises of high investment plans, and indeed they will be right.

A similar phenomenon occurs when countries borrow with long-term debt. When a country owes long-term debt, each new amount of borrowing tends to reduce the expected value of the original debt by making its eventual repudiation more likely. In many cases, the borrowing country would like to be able to promise a potential long-term creditor that it will not overborrow once the long-term debt is arranged. Such a promise would reduce the risk premium on the long-term debt. However, there will generally be strong incentives, *ex post*, to do precisely the contrary. The results are, in general, that long-term debt will command a high risk premium and that, as expected, overborrowing will occur.

Market participants search for ways to reduce these deleterious incentives. It may be the case that countries can establish reputations for maintaining macroeconomic policies in line with announced plans. The growing literature on establishing a reputation may well give some insights in this direction. Other specific actions, such as relying on short-term rather than long-term borrowing, may reduce some of the incentive problems. In domestic capital markets, and to a much smaller extent in international lending, bond covenants can be used to precommit the borrower to a future line of action. Smith and Warner (1979) provide an excellent survey of such covenants, indicating how they help to enforce an efficient borrowing and investment plan by corporate borrowers. For example, covenants often directly restrict dividend payments, which may be tantamount to requiring the shareholders to invest rather than "consume" their loans. Other types of provisions include restrictions on new borrowing, maintenance of the firm's existing assets, financial disclosure requirements, and restrictions on merger activity. Such provisions are typically unenforceable when foreign sovereign borrowers are involved, and thus are not part of most (international) syndicated loan agreements.

Further Aspects of Managing Repudiation Risk

So far, we have derived the optimal borrowing behavior for an economy that has the option of repudiating its debt. As in earlier sections, we should now ask how these optimal borrowing policies can be implemented. What is the role of the government in managing repudiation risk?

There is a profound externality in the borrowing process under repudiation risk that leads governments into a central policy role. In many cases, a default or debt repudiation by an individual agent affects market judgments regarding the creditworthiness of the country as a whole. Most potential creditors are unable to discern the ultimate causes of a default and, in particular, whether the action reflects a weakness of a particular debtor or is instead a signal about government policy and economic health in the whole debtor economy. An individual default raises subjective probabilities of structural weaknesses or widespread mismanagement in an economy and so causes credit to tighten for all borrowers.

The implications of this spillover are immediate. First, governments—even the most laissez faire—must assume some responsibility for honoring the external obligations of bankrupt firms in the private sector. Second, creditors act on the expectation of such actions, and indeed may withdraw credits from countries when such actions are not forthcoming. Naturally, therefore, a government must at the minimum undertake the prudential supervision of private-sector foreign borrowing in order to safeguard the economy's international creditworthiness. In some cases, it may be necessary to make government backing explicit to facilitate the appropriate levels of inflow.

Even when all lending is to the private sector of an economy, creditors will still be correct to aggregate the country's debt in assessing an economy's incentive to repudiate. This is because a government always has ability to nationalize a substantial part of the external debt and bargain for the country as a whole with respect to foreign creditors. This has been the experience of several Latin American countries in recent years.

Since the risk of repudiation puts a limit on overall borrowing, the interest rate on international loans may be a poor measure of the marginal cost of funds to a borrowing country. Suppose that total lending is rationed at the point $D = \theta Q/(1 + r)$. Those lucky enough to borrow at the world market rate will pay a price r, whereas borrowers on the domestic market will be forced to pay a higher price. The shadow price of capital appropriate for the marginal investment decision will be the higher rate. An interest-equalization tax on foreign borrowing, raising its costs to domestic levels, would improve the microeconomic allocation of investment funds without necessarily increasing the overall supply of external credits.

We have already noted additional scope for active policies. Governments may have an incentive to spur investment projects for the purpose of enhancing creditworthiness. Another possibility is that governments act to change θ, the cost of repudiation. Outward-looking trade policies probably raise the costs of repudiation by making the country more vulnerable to trade embargoes, credit cutoffs, and the like. Thus, a bonus to export-promotion policies may well be enhanced access to world credit markets. To a limited extent, governments may also be able to raise θ by offering to collateralize loans. There are cases in which airplanes and ships have been offered as collateral on trade financing.

The welfare effects of policy-induced changes in θ are not easy to discern. On the one hand, higher θ stimulates the inflow of capital by reducing the likelihood of repudiation. On the other hand, if an economy runs into severe macroeconomic difficulties, the benefit of default is compromised by a high value of θ. Analytical work suggests that there is likely to be an intermediate value $0 < \theta^* < 1$ that maximizes the debtor's expected utility under repudiation risk.

External Debt and Macroeconomic Policy

This topic is covered in detail by Dornbusch (1985). Here we will focus on the possible complications for macroeconomic policy that are created by the buildup of external debt and by the presence of large external debt.

Despite the freedom that countries have to float their currencies under present international arrangements, most borrowing countries in fact fix their exchange rates to another currency or to a weighted average of other currencies. Often there are periodic adjustments of the central rate, but in the short run the exchange rate is fixed by the central bank.

Under these circumstances, external borrowing for local expenditure will lead to monetary expansion. If undertaken freely and extensively, either by the government or by private economic agents, it interferes with monetary control, since borrowing countries typically have little opportunity to "sterilize" inflows of foreign exchange through domestic sales of securities or by other means. Thus, new external borrowing more or less directly increases the money supply. External debt that is acquired to cover directly the import of foreign goods or services does not have these internal monetary effects. It is the conversion to local currency at a fixed exchange rate that creates the complication.

Of course, the counterpart in the short run to external borrowing for local expenditure is an increase in international reserves, and these reserves are available to finance imports. As monetary and income effects work their way through the economy, the demand for imports will increase and the reserves will be drawn down, reversing the monetary expansion that initially took place. But this corrective process is brought about by the monetary expansion itself, which it might have been desirable to avoid under some circumstances. For this reason, many developing countries operating under fixed exchange rates have found it desirable to limit the inflow of foreign capital, especially that which comes through the banking system. Unless their access to international credit is restricted, banks and private firms with access to the international market can escape the rigors of a tight domestic monetary policy. For example, a multinational corporation that is denied credit at the local bank because of monetary restriction can resort to borrowing from its head office or directly from the international market and thereby bypass the local restrictions. In sum, a commitment to a fixed exchange rate under these circumstances weakens monetary control; its restoration may require limitations on capital flows.

A high *level* of debt, not just its rate of change, can also create problems for monetary policy. This is especially true when it comes to rolling over a large external debt or correcting a misalignment in the exchange rate. Changes in the exchange rate under such circumstances can have important effects on the balance sheets of business and financial firms. In particular, a currency devaluation can transmute overnight a solvent firm into a technically insolvent one as the local-currency value of external debt is raised.

This process is sometimes necessary and even useful. Firms may have overextended themselves with foreign credit on the basis of an overvalued currency. Their operating costs may have been artificially reduced, insofar as they have imported inputs, by the overvalued currency. Currency devaluation puts a halt to the process and introduces some useful economic discipline both for the debtors and for the foreign creditors, who under bankruptcy proceedings would normally share in some of the losses.

Governments are typically reluctant, however, to take steps that will throw firms (especially major firms) into bankruptcy. The presence of extensive external debt may therefore inhibit or force changes in exchange rates in order to limit the financial difficulties of large firms. In 1967, for instance, after the devaluation of sterling, Hong Kong at first devalued its dollar. Not to have done so would have badly weakened the balance sheets of some leading banks, which had assets in sterling, even though on other economic grounds the devaluation was not justified (and, indeed, the action was reversed after a few days when alternative methods for protecting the banks were worked out). Similarly, some countries have put their local development banks into technical insolvency by devaluing the currency. In this way also the presence of external debt serves to limit macroeconomic policy.

Finally, a large external debt of the government itself reduces the flexibility of fiscal policy. Large interest payments cannot be cut if the government desires to retrench. A government that has made total budget expenditures or the total budget deficit a target of economic policy will have to put all the more pressure on domestic expenditures to the extent that external debt servicing is large. This is especially true after a currency devaluation, when the local-currency counterpart of external debt denominated in foreign currency will rise in proportion to the devaluation. In the framing of national stabilization programs, on the other hand, it must be recognized that interest payments to foreigners do not stimulate the domestic economy. Thus, interest on foreign debt should be treated differently from normal government expenditures.

Is Laissez Faire a Desirable Borrowing Strategy?

A useful reference point for evaluating a debtor's policies toward external borrowing is the complete freedom of all economic agents to borrow abroad without restriction by the borrowing country. This regime existed generally in the nineteenth century and continues to exist in some advanced countries, including Canada and the United States. Under these circumstances, creditors must assess and take the risks borrower by borrower, just as they do with domestic loans. If a particular loan cannot be repaid, the external creditors share the loss through bankruptcy without, in principle, affecting the creditworthiness of other (independent) borrowers in the same country.

There are a number of reasons why the laissez faire approach is not at present likely to be suitable for most developing countries. First, their governments have almost universally taken a strong hand in economic management, including economic development. Government influence—not only on the macroeconomic environment but also on resource allocation—is pervasive, to the point where it is often difficult to say whether an enterprise's insolvency is due to bad judgment on the part of management or due to government actions. Under these circumstances, creditors will not view the individual projects as independent but will attach a heavy weight to the "country factor."

Second, even under true laissez faire, creditors may find it prudent to ration credit to individual borrowers because of the problem of adverse selection in the presence of imperfect information (Stiglitz and Weiss 1981). If the borrowing is truly and persuasively decentralized, the rationing will be by individual borrower, not (in general) by country except insofar as there is identifiable countrywide risk. But insofar as there is country risk, as there is bound to be for the first reason above, prospective debtors can enlarge their access to credit by taking steps to reduce the perception of country risk. One part of this may be, paradoxically, to exert closer control over the external borrowing of economic agents.

Furthermore, many of the potential foreign borrowers in a country may be so important for the continuing functioning of the national economy that bankruptcy—involving a writedown of the foreign debt—cannot be contemplated. This is especially true of banks and of some other financial intermediaries, as we have already seen. Both the external reputation of the country and the internal confidence in its institutions may be so closely tied to particular firms that in practice the government must guarantee their external debt or else avoid any actions that bring its servicing into question. External creditors of the leading banks are thus guaranteed (formally or informally) by the national government, and their expectations reflect this fact. The same may be true of other important commercial enterprises, especially government-owned enterprises. In short, bankruptcy of certain institutions would have strong negative reputational externalities for the debtor country. Knowing this, the government should monitor closely and perhaps even limit the external indebtedness of these institutions.

The general point is that countries acquire reputations—for prudence or foolhardiness, for caution or boldness in economic planning, for market orientation or dirigisme, and so on—that are important to creditors in assessing creditworthiness. Thus, difficulties by some borrowers affect the supply-of-funds schedule of the entire country (and, in periods of exceptional uncertainty, of neighboring countries as well). In short, there is an informational or reputational externality arising from the inability or unwillingness of lenders to make fine distinctions among borrowers. This occurs in domestic markets as well. For example, the fact that virtually all utility stocks are depressed in the United States is due in part to the difficulties of those relatively few utilities with nuclear power plants under construction. These "pigeonhole effects" dissipate over time as more information becomes available, but perhaps only after a liquidity crisis has occurred and much damage has been done—which in turn can lead to the self-fulfillment of pessimistic prophecies.

Direct Responsibility

There are three areas in particular where a government cannot really escape responsibility for external borrowing and therefore must make decisions on both the level and the character of external borrowing.

The first is the area of borrowing by the government itself for the provision of public goods and services. Much traditional external borrowing has been for such purposes; indeed, the World Bank was created as a mediating lender in part for the provision of funds for public investments. Some parts of the public infrastructure, such as railroads, are potentially revenue-producing, but most are not. The government must raise the debt service through general taxation, with all the implications discussed above. Although the old borrower's guideline to match the maturity of the loan to the life of the project does not strictly hold when the project is not revenue-producing, it is a good rule nonetheless; a long-term project whose contribution to the GNP and hence to taxable income is spread over many years should if possible be financed by long-term borrowing. Not doing so places more pressure on the internal terms of trade to generate the trade surplus necessary to amortize the debt rapidly. The main point is that governments of developing countries are likely to be borrowing abroad to finance public infrastructure, and perhaps operating expenses as well, and they must take a position on the amount and character of their external debt.

The second area is that of widespread government ownership of revenue-generating commercial enterprises—the so-called parastatals. Rare is the country that does not have some parastatals, and in many countries they generate over half the output of the modern sectors of the economy. The government, as chief or sole stockholder, cannot ultimately dissociate itself from the parastatals, although varying degrees of association are possible. At one end of the spectrum, parastatals can be chartered with a high degree of independence with respect to all business decisions, with a top management that has independent standing and is compensated in relation to profitability of the enterprise. Some British firms approach this model. It would make as clear as possible to lenders that they are dealing with a commercial enterprise, with all the attendant risks, and that the enterprise does not have the full credit backing of the government. Even in such extreme circumstances, it is unlikely that a government-owner could allow such a firm to go into bankruptcy—at some loss to its foreign creditors—without damaging the reputation of the country and especially the government as a borrower. This kind of linkage is not limited to government-owned enterprises. Several U.S. banks went to considerable expense in the mid 1970s to bail out insolvent or weak real-estate investment trusts under their sponsorship—which were legally separate and could have been allowed to fail, as many did—for the sake of preserving their overall reputation with both creditors and customers. In any case, most parastatals are not put at arm's length from the government that owns them, managers are not given full autonomy, and managers are not typically compensated on the basis of the profitability of the firm. These factors make it all the more difficult for a government to dissociate fully from the economic performance of its state enterprises. In the first place, government often uses parastatals to pursue social goals other than profitability, so it is inappropriate to hold management responsible for profitability, as would be the case with a privately owned firm. Major investment plans must typically be approved by the relevant ministry, and employment levels and practices are subject to government guidance (as is also true, in lesser degree, of privately owned firms in many countries). Second, management is typically on salary—often very low salary in comparison with compensation in privately owned enterprises of comparable size—and though salaries are occasionally augmented by incentive bonuses, the bonuses are typically not related to profitability. For these reasons, managers have no direct incentive to gauge their borrowing to the requirements of profitability. Indeed, since the main motivations of managers in parastatals in many countries is some combination of personal enrichment (other than through direct compensation) and political advancement, the principal incentive is toward enlargement of scale rather than profitability. Yet enlargement of scale, if not limited, is likely to lead to excessive external borrowing by the enterprise. The classic case is the rapid expansion and diversification of the Indonesian national oil firm, Pertamina, in the wake of its enhanced borrowing power after the 1974 oil-price increase (Wellons 1977). The divergence of interest between managers and owners is of course not limited to state-owned enterprises; it can be found in large privately owned firms as well. One study has shown that U.S. firms managed by or under the close control of owners tend to be more profitable than those in which the role of owners is more remote (McEachern 1975). For this reason too, therefore, governments will want to monitor closely and perhaps even control directly the external borrowings of their parastatals. Their managers under prevalent arrangements cannot be assumed to borrow abroad to the socially optimal degree; in general, they will tend to overborrow if left unrestrained.

A third area where a government cannot in practice escape responsibility for the level and character of external borrowing is that of local banks, and perhaps similar financial institutions. Banks are typically under heavy regulation, presumably for the protection of the public. Banks are, furthermore, the repositories of public confidence in the functioning of an economic system. If a major bank fails, it has potential ramifications going far beyond the failure of one enterprise; both borrowers and lenders become much more cautious, a development that on occasion is welcome but that generally results in recession and economic hardship. For this reason, governments must take an active interest in the smooth functioning of the major banks under their jurisdiction. This does not mean that they must protect bank managers against their mistaken judgments; management can be dismissed. It does mean that the mistaken judgments of bank management cannot be allowed to weaken the institution at the expense of depositors and creditors except at a cost that may go far beyond the institution in question. We are speaking here of the financial system as a whole and its major components. Minor banks whose fate can be clearly separated from the financial system as a whole may be allowed to fail.

The reputation and fate of the banks can influence a country's reputation with foreign creditors as well. In the late 1970s, Chile was widely applauded in some circles for its return to a relatively unregulated free-enterprise system. Chilean banks had borrowed heavily in international markets for relending in the local economy. When in 1982 a private bank became insolvent, the government let it be known that the bank was private and that creditors had lent to it at their own risk. External credits to Chile immediately dried up. Within a short interval the government felt obliged to reverse itself and guarantee the external liabilities of the bank. Creditors did not accept the dissociation of the government from the banks. Consequently, a government must perforce be concerned with both the internal and the external exposure of the banks. (Even a country as averse to government interference as Switzerland has let it be known that the three largest banks cannot be allowed to fail.)

Guidelines for External Borrowing

Given that a government should take a strong interest in the total level and character of external indebtedness, what should be its guiding principles? It is difficult to lay down universally applicable quantitative guidelines for external debt. Because reputation so heavily influences the possibilities a country faces and the difficulties it is likely to encounter in international financial markets, and because reputation is based on history, experience, and prevailing ideological views in the borrowing country, each country confronts a distinctive set of issues and problems.

Indicators such as the debt/GDP ratio or the debt-servicing ratio are often used to signal when external debt is reaching dangerous levels. So long as such indicators are widely used, they of course become important in establishing creditworthiness. However, such indicators have little objective basis; they can vary widely with safety, depending on the circumstances. For

Table 2
Debt, GDP, GNP, and debt service in a steady state.

Debt/GDP	Exports/GDP	Debt service/Exports	GDP	GNP	Debt
0	0.2	0	1.0	1.0	0
0.5	0.25	0.2	1.08	1.03	0.54
1	0.3	0.33	1.18	1.06	1.18
2	0.4	0.5	1.43	1.14	2.86
3	0.5	0.6	1.82	1.25	5.46
4	0.6	0.67	2.50	1.50	10.0

GDP, GNP, and debt are relative to pre-debt GDP.
Quantitative assumptions: return on investment $=0.15$, interest on debt $=0.1$.

instance, table 2 sets out a series of debt/GDP ratios and their implied debt-servicing requirements, all on the assumption that the (constant) rate of return on investment is 15 percent and the (constant) cost of borrowing in world capital markets is 10 percent—numbers that were plausible, even conservative, for many countries in the late 1970s.

The advantages of external borrowing so long as the return to investment exceeds the servicing requirements are quite dramatic. For instance, if the yield on investment is 15 percent and the cost of borrowing is 10 percent a year, and if external borrowing is the sole source of growth in output, a country can increase its output to 2.5 times its initial level in steady-state equilibrium (where the debt remains outstanding but does not grow further) by borrowing an amount equal to 4 times its postborrowing GDP. Of course, under these circumstances interest payments on outstanding debt will be very high: 40 percent of total output. Moreover, if import requirements are 20 percent of GDP, the interest-servicing ratio (interest payments/total exports) will be 2/3. However, even after these large payments of interest to foreigners, the output available for the residents of the borrowing country (GNP) will be 1.5 times the initial, predebt level of GNP. This represents the net gains from borrowing abroad. In this example, while the final debt to GDP ratio is 4, total borrowings will be 10 times the initial level of GDP. Lower levels of borrowing will of course result in lower debt/GDP ratios and lower debt-servicing ratios (see table 2). The general point is that quite high debt ratios are sustainable in long-run equilibrium if the country is not subjected to large uncertainty in output or exports.

A debt/GDP ratio of 4, although sustainable on the assumptions given, is far higher than anything we actually observe. Actual debt/GDP ratios even of countries heavily in debt are in the vicinity of 0.6. Israel has the highest observed debt/GDP ratio, 1.6, and much of Israel's external debt is on concessional terms. Interest-service ratios as high as 50 percent can be observed, but these are still well below the 2/3 given in the illustration.

We may well ask why countries do not borrow even more, for the illustration suggests much higher sustainable debt than we observe. One possible answer is that debt on a much larger scale would depress returns to investment, so that the assumption made here of a constant return is unrealistic. In fact, however, we have observed roughly constant returns to investment (abstracting from economic cycles) over a long period of time. If the debt is acquired quickly, diminishing returns are indeed likely to set in. But that is less likely to be true of investments made over several decades, unless the investment itself depresses the external terms of trade of the borrowing country.

A second possible answer is that the cost of borrowing will rise with the amount of outstanding indebtedness, or, more generally, that countries are rationed in their total borrowing well before the solvency constraint is reached. This is particularly true if repudiation risk is a major concern of the creditors. Again the *pace* of borrowing is important; a rapid increase in debt is very likely to increase the cost to the borrowing country, but a slower, more gradual increase is less likely to do so. Nonetheless, for debt/GDP ratios much higher than is normal, a risk premium is likely to be added to interest rates even if the buildup is gradual, and after a given debt/GDP ratio is reached the borrower may be frozen out of further borrowing.

A third possible reason is that debt must be serviced in tradeables but is often acquired to finance investment in nontradeables. (To be sure, some infrastructure investments, such as feeder roads or port facilities, are indirectly in tradeables, by lowering the domestic cost of getting exportables to market.) Several factors are important in determining the amount of investment of external debt in nontradeables that is sustainable: the return on investment in tradeables relative to the cost of investment, the share of investment in tradeables as opposed to nontradeables, and the ability of the government to raise revenues in tradeables in order to service debt acquired to invest in nontradeables. If, as is likely, the investment in nontradeables will require a decline in the domestic prices of nontradeables relative to tradeables, the extent of decline that is tolerable may also influence the amount of debt that can be acquired for this kind of investment.

These points can be illustrated with a numerical example. Suppose, as was the case in table 2, that the yield on investment is 15 percent in both the tradeable sector and the nontradeable sector of the economy, and that the

Table 3

Share of investment in nontradeables (percent)	Required fall in relative price of tradeables (percent)
0	−7
20	2
40	8
60	13
80	18
100	22

See text and note 7 for assumptions.

cost of foreign borrowing is 10 percent a year. Suppose further that import requirements are 20 percent of GDP, domestic expenditure out of disposable income is initially evenly divided between tradeables and nontradeables, and the price elasticity of substitution between tradeables and nontradeables in domestic demand is −2, but that the structure of production is not influenced by relative prices. The government must raise revenues to service the external debt invested in nontradeables, and it does so through lumpsum taxation. On these assumptions, and for the case in which external debt is twice GDP, table 3 shows the fall in the relative domestic price of nontradeables that must occur in order to service the external debt (the overall debt-service ratio is 0.5, from table 2), given different shares of investment in nontradeables.[7] For instance, if 60 percent of the external funds are used for investment in nontradeables, the relative price of tradeables will have to rise by 13 percent to release enough tradeables from domestic consumption to pay interest on the external debt. (An illustration of the time profile of the relative price of nontradeables in an optimizing model is given in the appendix.)

Political limits to the permissible change in relative prices may limit the amount of external debt that can be invested in nontradeables. On the assumptions here, the world prices of exports and imports are unchanged. Therefore, alteration of the internal terms of trade will require either a currency devaluation, which will raise the local-currency prices of tradeable goods, or a decline in the local prices of nontradeables. Either course poses difficulties.

This illustration has asumed a debt/GDP ratio of 2. A lower debt ratio will reduce the required change in relative prices, simply because it requires a smaller increase in exports. This may be another reason for limiting external borrowing for investment in nontradeables even when it augments GNP. A lower demand elasticity of substitution will call for a larger change in relative prices, whereas allowing the composition of output to respond to relative prices (assuming that investment decisions are made over a period of time) will work in the other direction.

Finally, any practical limit to the taxing powers of government may limit the amount of investment in nontradeables. For instance, if 100 percent of investment is in nontradeables in the example offered in table 3, the government must tax 20 percent of GDP (and 25 percent of GNP), valued at predebt prices, in order to service the debt. If the practical limit on taxation is 10 percent of GDP, the country will be unable to service external debt if more than 50 percent is invested in the nontradeable sector.

A fourth possible answer to the question of why actual debt/GDP ratios are not higher than they are is that countries face uncertainty in their output and export receipts. If debt service takes priority and the country has exhausted its reserves and lines of credit, any shortfall in exports must be met by squeezing imports. In many developing countries this can be accomplished in the short run only by cutting production. The necessity of cutting production from time to time in response to unforeseen shortfalls in net exports will reduce the optimal level of foreign indebtedness. Usually a less costly way of absorbing these shocks is to hold sufficient reserves to cover normal and even some extraordinary variations in net exports. Such reserves typically will earn a lower rate of return than could real investment under stable conditions, but they protect the country from large losses when conditions are not stable.

One method for hedging against uncertainty in output and export receipts is for foreign creditors to share the risks directly, as they would do with equity investments. We believe that most developing countries have paid too little attention to the advantages of foreign direct investment—not only for the sharing of risks but also for the technology transfer that they normally bring. More accurate, many countries have been equivocal in their official stance toward direct investment, and ambivalence—which is often understandable in historic terms—does not provide the stable business environment in which foreign investment thrives. Political ambivalence is a reality in many countries, however, and so long as it is present the scope for proportionately large inflows of direct investment will be limited.

The Mix of External Obligations

The discussion so far has been in terms of external debt in a conventional form: interest-bearing debt with a fixed foreign-currency value at maturity.

In practice, a borrower may face several different kinds of opportunity for drawing capital from the rest of the world: concessional aid, including grants; equity investment by foreigners, which may involve some managerial control by foreigners (direct investment) or simply minority foreign shareholders; and interest-bearing fixed-value obligations, which in turn may be directly linked with imports (trade credits), may involve shorter or longer maturities, and may be denominated in local or foreign currency. We offer some observations on each of these forms of obligation and on the mix among them.

So long as domestic investment opportunities with expected rates of return exceeding the cost of foreign capital are available, a country can always raise its expected level of income by borrowing abroad. However, it should be cognizant of the constraints that we have discussed in previous sections. In particular, it should take as much concessional aid as possible, provided certain conditions are met and leaving aside the question of political overtones that often pervade bilateral aid. First, the country is able to service the debt adequately from tax and other government revenues. Second, supplementary domestic financing of the aid-supported projects does not draw domestic savings away from investments that offer far greater returns to the country. Third, the aid is not so tied up with procurement and other restrictions that it turns out to be much less concessional than it seemed at first glance. Many governments seem to give much greater weight to obtaining low interest rates, if necessary at the expense of higher purchase prices or lower-quality products, than is economically warranted. This preoccupation with the interest rate, to the virtual exclusion of other features of the purchase, can be a serious mistake.

Foreign equity investments have the obvious advantages over interest-bearing obligations that they do not have to be amortized and that earnings are likely to be positively correlated with the general economic performance of the country. We believe that countries would be well advised to encourage direct foreign investment so long as the attraction to foreign investors is not due mainly to price distortions in the economy. In the presence of severe price distortions, however, foreign investment can actually make the country worse off (Brecher and Díaz-Alejandro 1977). Given the high, selective import tariffs and other price distortions in many developing countries, this is a serious problem in evaluating all projects, not merely those undertaken by foreign investors.

Direct investment in general has advantages that go beyond the provision of foreign capital. It introduces technical know-how and useful managerial and marketing skills. It may also, in a world of imperfect capital markets, provide access to additional debt capital for the country. It has the final advantage that if the activity fails economically, there is no need to repay the capital, since the foreign investor bears the commercial risk.

Equity investments also have some disadvantages. First, while earnings will generally be high when the economy is doing well, remittances of earnings may not be so strongly correlated with domestic or export performance. They may actually be somewhat perverse, since earnings tend to be reinvested more readily when the economy is going well. More important, foreign investors' behavior—like that of domestic firms engaged in foreign trade—may aggravate a liquidity crisis by exporting capital if a devaluation of the currency (or the introduction of exchange controls) is thought to be imminent. This can be done either directly or by manipulating the timing of receipts and payments associated with exporting and importing. These swings can often be large relative to the equity stake of the foreign investor. The host country then faces a dilemma. Absence of exchange controls invites the speculative movement of capital, but the imposition of exchange controls damages the country's reputation as a debtor. If exchange controls are in place they can be used to discourage speculative withdrawals of capital, but it is difficult to control firms that are heavily engaged in foreign trade.

Finally, it is a fact of life that foreign direct investment, involving management control and foreign ownership of land, is politically sensitive in many countries. Too much foreign investment may result in a political reaction that damages the country's overall reputation as a borrower. In some countries, fear of arousing political sensibilities may be the most significant restraint on direct investment. And, of course, fear of expropriation is one of the factors inhibiting investment by prospective foreign investors.

Foreign purchases of noncontrolling equity interests in indigenous firms carries some but not all of the disadvantages of foreign direct investment, and joint ventures are actively encouraged by many countries. However, for a variety of reasons, including the lack of well-developed equity markets, the scope of equity investment in developing countries that does not involve some foreign influence on management is quite limited.

Our principal focus above has been on interest-bearing obligations, and there is little more to be said here. Trade credits, whether officially guaranteed by the government of the exporting country or not, are often considered as separate and distinct from bank term loans or other forms of interest-bearing investment. They represent, as it were, a somewhat separate "pool" from which borrowing can take place. Because they tend to be less centralized in the borrowing country, however, they can offer a troublesome surprise when they begin to dry up during a liquidity crisis. The country then senses, perhaps for the first time, how large the total of trade credit is and how difficult it is for the economy to function if such credits suddenly disappear. For this reason, countries that have heavy debt obligations should monitor their trade credits closely.

When it comes to debt maturity, we observed earlier that a serious mismatch between the maturity of credits and the maturity of the projects they are financing increases the exposure of a country to liquidity crisis. Having to repay a debt before the returns to the project can be realized can be costly. For this reason, the old banker's rule of thumb that debt maturity should be matched to the maturity of the underlying investment is a sound one.

In principle, countries have the choice of borrowing in their own currency or in some foreign currency. Borrowing in the home currency shifts to the lender not only the convertibility risk but also the exchange risk, and he will extract a price for that. In reality, few developing countries have a practical possibility of borrowing abroad in their home currency on any scale in the absence of exchange-rate guarantees. Even most developed countries are limited to borrowing abroad in one of the four or five leading currencies rather than their own.

Concluding Remarks

Actual levels of external borrowing by developing countries are considerably lower than could in principle be serviced from productive investments. This may reflect restraint on the part of borrowers arising from concerns about their ability to raise the funds required for debt servicing when the projects are government-sponsored or are in sectors of the economy that do not directly save or generate foreign exchange. It may also reflect concern about taking on fixed external obligations in an uncertain world when the capacity of the domestic economy to absorb shocks at low cost is limited.

However, much of the reason for lower-than-sustainable external borrowing is no doubt due to constraints imposed by lenders who fear that mismanagement of the borrowing economy may reduce returns on investments; that future difficulties may lead the authorities to repudiate the debt, in whole or in part, openly or (more likely) tacitly; or that waves of sentiment in world financial markets may lead to periodic liquidity crises that prevent an otherwise viable economy from servicing its debt. All these factors lead to a supply-of-funds schedule confronting each borrower that reflects borrowing costs that increase as a function of outstanding debt and current borrowing levels. Beyond some (on our calculation, modest) level, higher interest rates elicit no new lending at all.

From the perspective of debtors, with many productive investment opportunities, the task is to lower and to flatten the supply of external funds schedule that the debtor faces. A debtor can thereby increase its gross national product and per capita income after servicing external debt. How can it do this?

Since the main restraints on further borrowing seem to be concerns by lenders, borrowers must pay attention to these concerns. We offer some observations which flow from our earlier analysis of external debt.

First, the debtor can improve lenders' perceptions of its ability to pay by concentrating its external borrowing on productive investments rather than on consumption (even though, as we have seen, consumption loans are sometimes perfectly sensible), especially on investments that will generate foreign exchange. To accomplish the latter aim, the pricing structure of the economy cannot be too far out of line with that prevailing in world markets. Where possible, the debtor should become thoroughly committed to the investments in question so that the scope for diversion of funds away from the project is limited. From this point of view, World Bank or regional development bank loans and even medium-term trade credits are seen as being in a different and (to the lender) more comforting category than are straight term bank loans not linked to projects or to the procurement of project-related equipment.

Second, the debtor can improve lenders' perceptions concerning its willingness to pay by raising the visible costs to itself that would be incurred on nonpayment. That could involve such traditional steps as offering central-government guarantees, posting collateral (e.g. reserves), pledging particular export revenues, and agreeing to third-party arbitration or even to jurisdiction of courts in the lending countries.

Receptivity to foreign direct investment is taken as a positive general attitude toward foreign capital even when direct investment flows themselves are small. A country can, over time, establish a reputation for punctiliousness in servicing its debts. Since a good reputation is itself an important asset, especially in the world of finance, loss of reputation is one of the visible costs associated with nonpayment. Cooperation of international institutions such as the World Bank and the regional development banks in investment planning and financing can also improve the peceived willingness to pay, since each country's relationships with these institutions is a continuing one, and no government likes to be a pariah to organizations with which it must deal on a regular basis.

Finally, to reduce the harm from a liquidity crisis, and hence also the probability of such a crisis, a country should recognize the advantages of longer maturities of debt and should balance these advantages against the higher costs of long-term debt. Similarly, the debtor should recognize the gains from diversifying the sources and character of its external financial support as much as possible. Although trade credits and direct investment are not immune to the forces involved in a liquidity crisis, as we have seen, they are influenced by somewhat different factors, and thus they may help to forestall a liquidity crisis.

When it comes to bank term lending, on the other hand, having a strong lead bank whose leadership is accepted by other banks may offer better assurance against a liquidity crisis than does borrowing from a larger number of unrelated banks. The former arrangement internalizes to some extent the externality that generates liquidity crises.

The conventional indicators of capacity to handle external debt, such as the debt-servicing ratio or the debt/GDP ratio, have little theoretical basis, at least in the vicinity where they are generally observed. Nonetheless, they have become important indicators in the eyes of lenders, with each borrowing country measured both against other countries and against the borrowing country's own past, and that makes them important to borrowers. A sharp increase in these indicators is taken as a warning signal even when they are relatively low. Expectations concerning appropriate levels can be altered only gradually and in the context of other actions that persuade lenders of the soundness of the borrowing.

Appendix: Simulation Models for Optimal Borrowing

This appendix illustrates the use of simulation techniques to calculate optimal borrowing paths. Although we rely on fairly simply dynamic models, the methods may be directly extended to more complicated, multisector models. Earlier studies using the techniques in this appendix include Blanchard 1983, Sachs 1983, Bruno and Sachs 1982, Lipton and Sachs 1983, and Blanchard and Sachs 1982.

We illustrate three models from the text: the one-sector optimal-borrowing model, the two-sector (traded and nontraded goods) optimal-borrowing model, and the one-sector model with a public sector facing tax constraints.

We make only one amendment to the models in the text: that investment imposes adjustment costs on the economy, so that the marginal product of capital F_K should adjust slowly rather than instantaneously to equal the world cost of capital. In particular, following Hayashi (1982), we distinguish between gross capital formation J_t and total investment expenditure I_t (which includes adjustment costs as well as the direct cost of capital goods). Specifically, let ψ be the per-unit adjustment cost, so that $I_t = J_t + \psi J_t$. Now, assume that ψ is not constant but rather is a linear function of the rate of capital formation, $\psi = (\phi/2)(J/K)$. Thus, rapid investment rates impose higher per-unit costs of adjustment than slow investment rates. The accumulation equation is

$$K_{t+1} = K_t(1-d) + J_t,$$

where d is the rate of geometric depreciation. Since

$$I_t = J[1 + (\phi/2)(J/K)],$$

we may derive

$$J_t = -(K_t/\phi) + (K_t/\phi)\sqrt{1 + 2\phi(I_t/K_t)}.$$

Plugging this into the accumulation equation yields

$$K_{t+1} = K_t(1-d) + f(I_t, K_t), \tag{A1}$$

where

$$f_t = -(K_t/\phi) + (K_t/\phi)\sqrt{1 + 2\phi(I_t/K_t)}.$$

For later reference, we note that

$$f_{K_t} = -(1/\phi) + (1/\phi)\sqrt{1 + 2\phi(I_t/K_t)} + (I_t/K_t)/\sqrt{1 + 2\phi(I_t/K_t)}.$$

When I_t/K_t is small, $f_{K_t} \approx 0$.

The infinite-horizon, one-sector borrowing problem is shown in table A1. The aggregate production function is $Q_t(K_t)$. Implicitly, labor is held fixed at $L_t = 1$. For completeness, government expenditure has been placed in the utility function. The entire system is set up as a Lagrangian, and the first-order conditions are solved in part III of the table. μ_t is the co-state variable (or dynamic Lagrange multiplier) attached to D_t, so it represents the marginal utility of wealth. λ_t is the shadow value of installed capital. In all, the system is a four-dimensional nonlinear difference equation system in λ_t, μ_t, K_t, and D_t. We solve the system below for particular numerical values.

It is easy to extend the model to include nontraded goods, with sector-specific capital and freely mobile labor. Thus, we introduce the production functions $Q^T = F^T(K^T, L^T)$ and $Q^N = F^N(K^N, L^N)$. Full employment of labor requires $\bar{L} = L^T + L^N$. Capital in each sector is governed by an accumulation equation of the form

Table A1
The one-sector model.

I. **Problem**

$$\max_{G_t, C_t, I_t} \sum_0^\infty (1+\delta)^{-t} U(C_t, G_t)$$

such that

(a) $D_{t+1} = D_t(1+r) + I_t + G_t + C_t - Q_t(K_t)$
(b) $K_{t+1} = K_t(1-d) + f(I_t, K_t)$
(c) $\lim D_t(1+r)^{-t} = 0$
(d) K_0, D_0 given

II. **Lagrangian**

$$\mathcal{L} = \sum_0^\infty (1+\delta)^{-t}\{U(C_t, G_t) + \mu_t[D_{t+1} - D_t(1+r) - I_t - G_t - C_t + Q_t(K_t)] \\ + \lambda_t[K_{t+1} - K_t(1-d) - f(I_t, K_t)]\}$$

III. **First-order conditions**

(a) $\dfrac{\partial \mathcal{L}}{\partial C_t} = 0 \Rightarrow U_C = \mu_t$

(b) $\dfrac{\partial \mathcal{L}}{\partial D_t} = 0 \Rightarrow (1+r)\mu_t = (1+\delta)\mu_{t-1}$

(c) $\dfrac{\partial \mathcal{L}}{\partial I_t} = 0 \Rightarrow \lambda_t f_{I_t}(I_t, K_t) = -\mu_t$

(d) $\dfrac{\partial \mathcal{L}}{\partial K_t} = 0 \Rightarrow \lambda_t[1 - d + f_{K_t}(I_t, K_t)] = \lambda_{t-1}(1+\delta) + \mu_t Q_{K_t}$

(e) $\dfrac{\partial \mathcal{L}}{\partial G_t} = 0 \Rightarrow U_G = \mu_t$

$$K^i_{t+1} = K^i_t(1-d) + f(I^i_t, K^i_t), \quad i = T, N.$$

For simplicity, we treat all investment expenditure as drawing on the traded good (this can easily be modified). Thus, the market-clearing condition for nontraded goods is $Q^N = C^N + G^N$, where C^N and G^N are real consumption expenditures falling on N. The debt-accumulation equation is

$$D_{t+1} = D_t(1+r) + C^T_t + G^T_t + (I^T_t + I^N_t) - Q^T_t(K^T_t, L^T_t).$$

The entire model, including Lagrangian and first-order conditions, is shown in table A2.

Note that θ_t is the co-state variable for the constraint that the nontraded-goods sector clears. It is easy to show that θ_t/μ_t is the shadow price of nontraded goods relative to traded goods in the model. If the optimal solution is to be decentralized via market forces, θ_t/μ_t will be the ratio P^N_t/P^T_t.

Table A2
The two-sector model.

I. Problem

$$\max_{G_t^N, G_t^T, C_t^N, C_t^T, I_t^N, I_t^T} \sum_0^\infty (1+\delta)^{-t} U(C_t^N, C_t^T, G_t^N, G_t^T)$$

such that
(a) $D_{t+1} = D_t(1+r) + (I_t^N + I_t^T) + G_t^T + C_t^T - Q_t^T(K_t^T, L_t^T)$
(b) $Q_t^N(K_t^N, 1 - L_t^T) = C_t^N + G_t^N$
(c) $K_{t+1}^i = K_t^i(1-d) + f(I_t^i, K_t^i)$, $i = N, T$
(d) $\lim D_t(1+r)^{-t} = 0$
(e) D_0, K_0^T, K_0^N given

II. Lagrangian

$$\mathcal{L} = \sum_0^\infty (1+\delta)^{-t} \{ U(C_t^N, C_t^T, G_t^N, G_t^T)$$
$$+ \mu_t[D_{t+1} - D_t(1+r) - (I_t^N + I_t^T) - G_t^T - C_t^T + Q_t^T(K_t^T, L_t^T)]$$
$$+ \theta_t[Q_t^N(K_t^N, 1 - L_t^T) - C_t^N - G_t^N] + \lambda_t^T[K_{t+1}^T - K_t^T(1-d)$$
$$- f(I_t^T, K_t^T)] + \lambda_t^N[K_{t+1}^N - K_t^N(1-d) - f(I_t^N, K_t^N)] \}$$

III. First-order conditions

(a) $\dfrac{\partial \mathcal{L}}{\partial C_t^N} = 0 \Rightarrow U_{C^N} = \theta_t$

(b) $\dfrac{\partial \mathcal{L}}{\partial C_t^T} = 0 \Rightarrow U_{C^T} = \mu_t$

(c) $\dfrac{\partial \mathcal{L}}{\partial G_t^N} = 0 \Rightarrow U_{G^N} = \theta_t$

(d) $\dfrac{\partial \mathcal{L}}{\partial G_t^T} = 0 \Rightarrow U_{G^T} = \mu_t$

(e) $\dfrac{\partial \mathcal{L}}{\partial D_t} = 0 \Rightarrow (1+r)\mu_t = (1+\delta)\mu_{t-1}$

(f) $\dfrac{\partial \mathcal{L}}{\partial K_t^i} = 0 \Rightarrow \lambda_t^i[1 - d + f_{K_t}(I_t^i, K_t^i)] = \lambda_{t-1}^i(1+\delta) + \mu_t Q_{K_t}^i$, $i = T, N$

(g) $\dfrac{\partial \mathcal{L}}{\partial I_t^i} = 0 \Rightarrow \lambda_t^i f_I(I_t^i, K_t^i) = -\mu_t$, $i = T, N$

(h) $\dfrac{\partial \mathcal{L}}{\partial L_t^T} = 0 \Rightarrow \mu_t Q_{L^T}(K_t^T, L_t^T) = \theta_t Q_{L^N}(K_t^N, L_t^N)$

The entire system is now implicitly a six-dimensional nonlinear difference equation system in the variables K_t^N, K_t^T, D_t, λ_t^N, λ_t^T, and μ_t. All the other variables may be expressed in terms of these six variables.

The final model we consider is the one-sector, tax-constrained economy, in which official borrowing is used to augment suboptimal private savings but in which the maximum tax rate is constrained to be below some rate $\bar{\tau}$. As explained in the text, private saving is assumed to be a constant fraction s of after-tax income $(1 - \tau)Q_t$, so private consumption expenditure is $C_t = (1 - s)(1 - \tau)Q_t$. Total investment expenditure is equal to private savings, $s(1 - \tau)Q_t$, plus public savings, $\tau Q_t - G_t - rD_t$, plus new borrowing, $D_{t+1} - D_t$. (In the text, government consumption expenditure was ignored.) Thus,

$$I_t = s(1 - \tau)Q_t + (\tau Q_t - G_t - rD_t) + (D_{t+1} - D_t).$$

Since

$$s(1 - \tau)Q_t = Q_t(1 - \tau) - C_t,$$

we have

$$I_t = [Q_t(1 - \tau) - C_t] + (\tau Q_t - G_t - rD_t) + (D_{t+1} - D_t),$$

which after rearrangement yields the standard balance-of-payments identity

$$D_{t+1} = (1 + r)D_t + C_t + I_t + G_t - Q_t.$$

It is easy to demonstrate that if $\bar{\tau} = 1$ (in other words, if tax rates are unconstrained), the optimization problem in which the government controls τ_t, G_t, and $D_{t+1} - D_t$ amounts to precisely the same problem as in table A1, where the government controls C, I, and G. In other words, when taxes are unconstrained, the economy can reach the first-best optimum of table A1 even though private savings are set in an *ad hoc* way as a fixed fraction of disposable income.

The more interesting case occurs when the tax constraint $\bar{\tau}$ is binding. Let C_t^* and Q_t^* be optimal in the solution to the problem in table A1. If C is controlled directly, C_t is simply set at C_t^*. If C is controlled via taxes, $\tau_t^* = 1 - [C_t^*/(1 - s)Q_t^*]$. If $\tau_t^* > \bar{\tau}$, the first-best solution is no longer feasible when taxes are the control instrument. We now assume that, for some period t, $\tau_t^* > \bar{\tau}$. Thus, we must find a second-best solution.

The tax-management problem is show in table A3. It is convenient to rewrite the tax constraint as a constraint on consumption: $C_t \geq \bar{C}_t$, where $\bar{C}_t = (1 - s)(1 - \bar{\tau})Q_t$. Then we rewrite the first-order conditions a and e of table A3 and define a "notional" demand C^D such that $U_C(C_t^D, G_t) = \mu_t$. C_t^D

Table A3
Optimal borrowing with tax constraints.

$$\max_{G_t, \tau_t, D_t} \sum_{0}^{\infty} (1+\delta)^{-t} U(C_t, G_t)$$

such that

(a) $D_{t+1} = (1+r)D_t + I_t + G_t + C_t - Q(K_t)$
(b) $C_t \geq \bar{C}$
(c) $\bar{C}_t = (1-s)(1-\bar{\tau})Q_t$
(d) $K_{t+1} = K_t(1-d) + f(I_t, K_t)$
(e) D_0, K_0 given

Lagrangian

$$\mathscr{L} = \sum_{0}^{\infty}(1+\delta)^{-t}\{U(C_t, G_t) + \mu_t[D_{t+1} - (1+r)D_t - I_t - G_t - C_t + Q(K_t)]$$
$$+ \lambda_t[K_{t+1} - K_t(1-d) - f(I_t, K_t)] + \gamma_t[C_t - (1-s)(1-\bar{\tau})Q(K_t)]\}$$

First-order conditions

(a) $\dfrac{\partial \mathscr{L}}{\partial C_t} = 0 \Rightarrow U_C(C_t, G_t) = \mu_t - \gamma_t$

(b) $\dfrac{\partial \mathscr{L}}{\partial G_t} = 0 \Rightarrow U_G(C_t, G_t) = \mu_t$

(c) $\dfrac{\partial \mathscr{L}}{\partial D_t} = 0 \Rightarrow (1+r)\mu_t = (1+\delta)\mu_{t-1}$

(d) $\dfrac{\partial \mathscr{L}}{\partial K_t} = 0 \Rightarrow \lambda_t(1-d)f_{K_t}(I_t, K_t) = \lambda_{t-1}(1+\delta) + \mu_t Q_{K_t} - \gamma_t(1-s)(1-\bar{\tau})Q_{K_t}$

(e) $\gamma_t = 0$ when $C_t < \bar{C}_t$ and $\gamma_t > 0$ when $C_t = \bar{C}_t$

---

is the level of consumption that will be chosen if the tax constraint is not binding in the current period. Actual consumption is given by $C_t = \min(C_t^D, \bar{C}_t)$.

The problem in table A3 presents a highly nonlinear difference equation system in four variables: $D_t, K_t, \mu_t,$ and λ_t. The other variables can all be expressed as functions of these four variables.

Numerical Simulations

We now proceed to numerical simulations of these optimal borrowing models. For purposes of the simulations, we assume the following.

In the one-sector model:

$$Q_t = K_t^\alpha,$$
$$U(C_t, G_t) = \log(C_t^\beta G_t^{1-\beta}),$$

$\alpha = 0.5$,

$\beta = 0.67$,

$\phi = 10.0$,

$d = 0.10$,

$r = 0.12$,

$\delta = 0.12$,

$\bar{\tau} = 0.45$.

In the two-sector model:

$Q_t^T = (K_t^T)^\alpha (L_t^T)^{1-\alpha}$,

$Q_t^N = (K_t^N)^\alpha (L_t^N)^{1-\alpha}$,

$1 = L_t^T + L_t^N$,

$U(C_t^T, C_t^N, G_t^T, G_t^N) = \log[(C_t^T)^{a_1}(C_t^N)^{a_2}(G_t^T)^{a_3}(G_t^N)^{1-a_1-a_2-a_3}]$,

$\alpha = 0.5$,

$\phi = 10.0$,

$r = 0.12$,

$\delta = 0.12$,

$d = 0.10$,

$a_1 = 0.25$,

$a_2 = 0.41$,

$a_3 = 0.13$,

$a_4 = 0.21$.

Two simulations are performed. In the first, we begin with K_0 below the steady-state level in the one-sector model and compare the adjustment costs in the tax-constrained model ($\bar{\tau} = 0.45$) with those in the tax-unconstrained model ($\bar{\tau} = 1.0$). Remember that the case $\bar{\tau} = 1.0$ in the model of table A3 will give exactly the same outcome as the solution to the model of table A1. In the second simulation, the process of capital accumulation in the traded/nontraded goods model is studied.

Figure A1 illustrates the basic proposition with respect to the fiscal constraint: With low $\bar{\tau}$, the country should not borrow as rapidly as on the unconstrained path. The solid line is the debt/GDP ratio for the unconstrained case, and the dotted line is the optimum path in the constrained case. (The economy is assumed to begin in 1970 with D/Q equal to 0.38.) When taxes are unconstrained, foreign borrowing is more rapid and stabilizes at a much higher level of debt than in the tax-constrained case. Note that the optimal path in the unconstrained case involves a very high D/Q ratio, a point we made in the text in a static context. Figure A2 illustrates the path of physical capital in the two economies. The counterpart of the larger foreign borrowing in the unconstraind economy is more rapid capital formation and a higher steady-state capital stock.

The two-sector model simulation is illustrated in part in figure A3. Once again, we assume that capital stocks (in this case both K_0^T and K_0^N) are sufficiently low that rapid accumulation of capital should take place in both sectors. As shown in figure A3, the relative price of nontraded goods declines over time, as the initial current account turns into eventual balance and the initial trade deficit turns into long-run surplus. Figure A4 shows the paths of K^N and K^T. In the simulation shown, the optimal planner (or the market, in its decentralized interpretation) has perfect foresight of the long-run changes in P^N/P^T. In practice, however, it is likely that many agents will underestimate the necessary long-run decline in P^N/P^T and thereby overinvest in the nontraded-goods sector in the initial phase of adjustment. Such overinvestment would eventually necessitate even larger declines in P^N/P^T along the adjustment path, in order to move capital and labor back to the traded-goods sector.

The simulation techniques outlined here can be extended to larger and more realistic models that include Keynesian and monetary features not explored in this article. (See, e.g., Blanchard and Sachs 1982.) Such models should prove fruitful in improving medium-term assessments of an economy's debt-servicing capacity and creditworthiness.

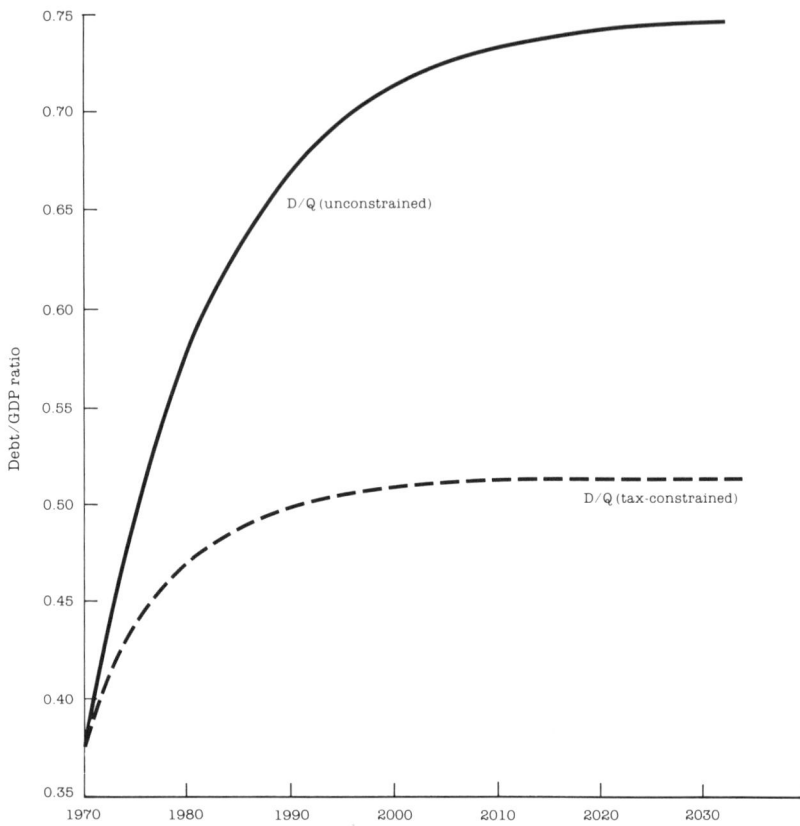

Figure A1
Comparison of optimal foreign-debt accumulation in tax-constrained and unconstrained models.

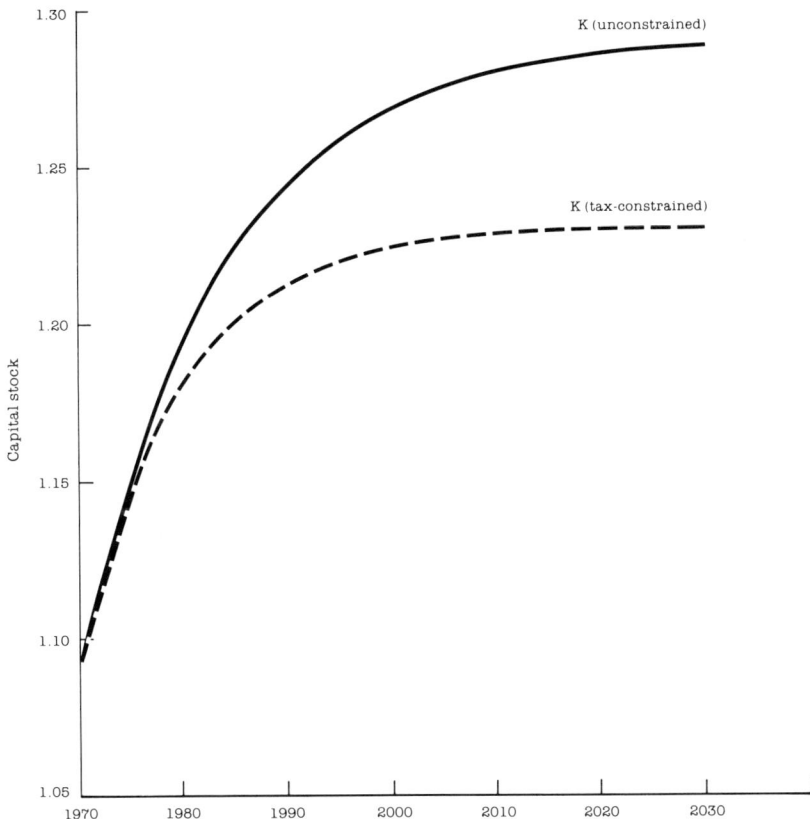

Figure A2
Comparison of capital accumulation in tax-constrained and unconstrained models.

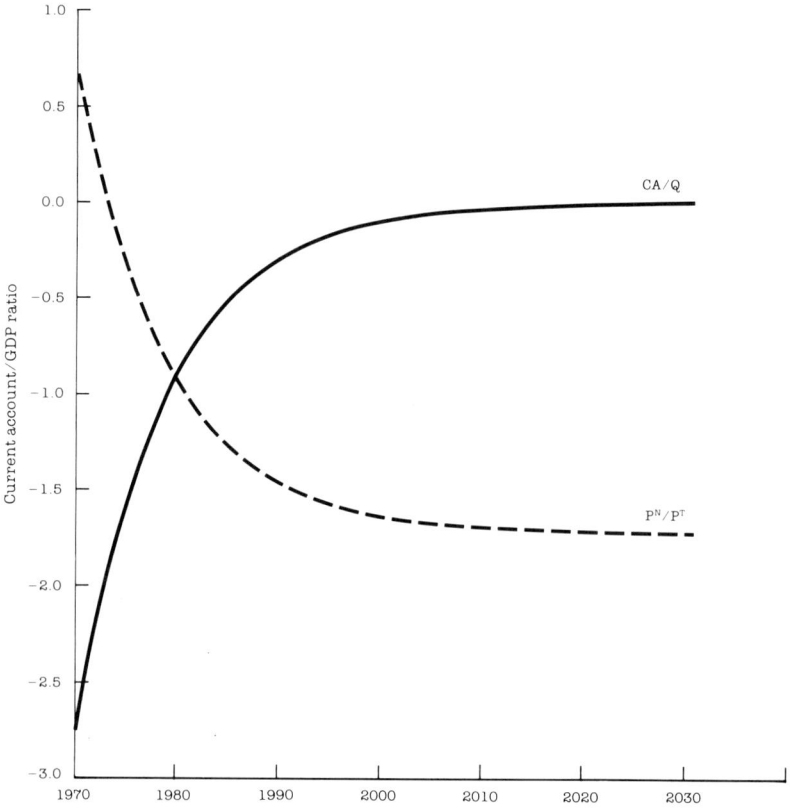

Figure A3
Paths of current account/GDP ratio and P^N/P^T (percentage deviations from constant baseline).

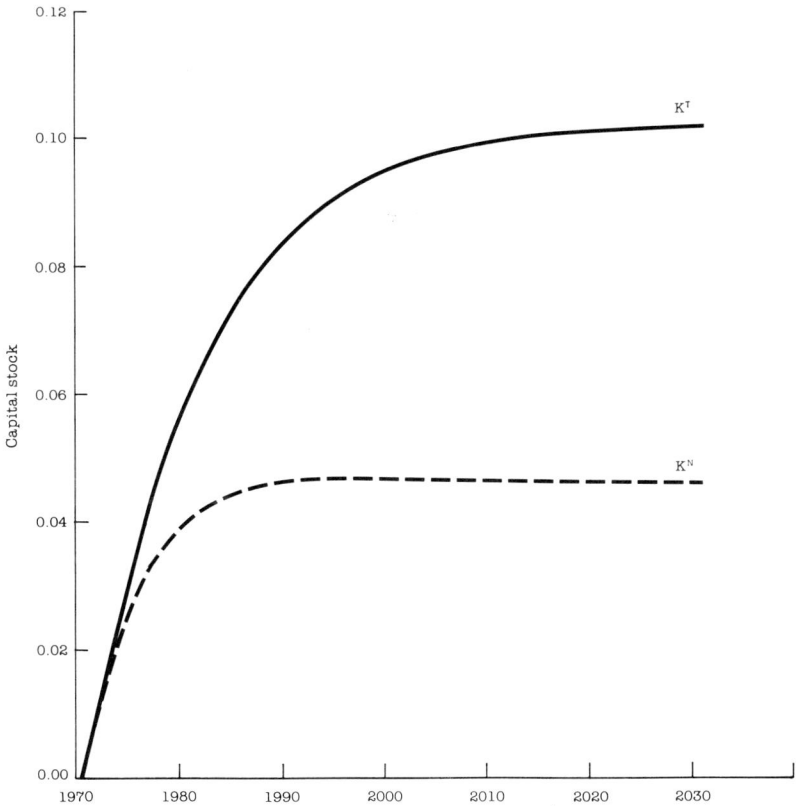

Figure A4
Paths of capital accumulation for K^T and K^N (percentage deviations from constant baseline).

Notes

1. Equation 2 implicitly assumes that Q_t is independent of C_t in each period, which is correct under the assumptions made. In more general models, with a variable labor supply or with work effort a function of C_t, we cannot simply maximize TB_t each period by setting $C_t = \bar{C}_t$.

2. Such a Ponzi scheme is called a rational speculative bubble in the finance literature, where it is shown that with $n > r$ the bubble can last forever. In a sense, the debt is an "unbacked asset" that maintains value because each creditor believes that future creditors will make the necessary loans to the debtor country.

3. By writing $C_1^L = Q_1 - (1 + r)D_1$, we are assuming that the borrower always repays D_1 and never opts to repudiate if credit rationing on D_2 in fact occurs.

4. By totally differentiating $U_1^N = -V_D^N/(1 + \delta)$, we have

$$\frac{D_2^N}{dD_1} = (1 + r)U_{11}^N/[U_{11}^N + V_{DD}/(1 + \delta)].$$

Since U_{11}^N and $V_{DD} < 0$,

$$0 < \frac{dD_2^N}{dD_1} < (1 + r).$$

5. Specifically,

$$\frac{dD_1}{d\pi} = \frac{1 + r}{1 + \delta} \frac{U_1^L - U_1^N}{U_{00} + \pi(1 + r)^2 U_{11}^L/(1 + \delta) + (1 - \pi)(1 + r)\gamma U_{11}^N/(1 + \delta)},$$

where $\gamma = (1 + r) - dD_2^N/dD_1 > 0$.

6. The proof is as follows. We start at an equilibrium with

$$U_1(C_1^N) = -(1 + r)V_D(D_2^N)/(1 + \delta)$$

and

$$U_1(C_1^L) > -(1 + r)V_D(0)/(1 + \delta).$$

Utility is given by

$$V_0 = U(C_0) + \pi[U(C_1^L)/(1 + \delta) + V(0)/(1 + \delta)^2]$$
$$+ (1 - \pi)[U(C_1^N)/(1 + \delta) + V(D_2^N)/(1 + \delta)^2].$$

The investment project has an income stream of $-dI_1, 0, (1 + \theta)^2 dI$ over the three periods, so that

$$dV = -U_0 dI_1 - [\pi V_D(0)/(1 + \delta)^2](1 + \theta)^2 \, dI_1$$
$$- [(1 - \pi)V_D(D_2^N)/(1 + \delta)^2](1 + \theta)^2 dI_1.$$

Now, by conditions of optimality,

$$U_0 = (1 + r)\pi U_1(C_1^L)/(1 + \delta) + (1 + r)(1 - \pi)U_1(C_1^N)/(1 + \delta).$$

Substituting in the dV equation, we find

$$\frac{dV}{dI_1} = -\pi[(1+r)U_1^L/(1+\delta) + (1+\theta)^2 V_D(0)/(1+\delta)^2]$$
$$-(1+\pi)[(1+r)U_1^N/(1+\delta) + (1+\theta)^2 V_D(D^N)/(1+\delta)^2].$$

Let
$$\gamma = U_1^L + (1+r)V_D(0)/(1+\delta).$$

Then, by substituting in dV the relationships between U_1 and V_D, we get

$$\frac{dV}{dI_1} = [\pi V_D(0)/(1+\delta)^2][(1+r)^2 - (1+\theta)^2]$$
$$+ [(1+\pi)V_D(D_2^N)/(1+\delta)^2][(1+r)^2 - (1+\theta)^2]$$
$$- \pi(1+r)\gamma/(1+\delta).$$

For $r = 0, dV/dI_1 = -\pi(1+r)\gamma/(1+\delta) < 0$. For $\theta \gg r, dV/dI_1 > 0$.

7. Table 3 is calculated from the following model, using the notation of the appendix:

$Q^T = Q_0^T + \rho K^T$,

$C^N = 0.5(P_N/P_T)^\varepsilon (Q - rD)$,

$Q^N = Q_0^N + \rho K^N$,

$Q^N = C^N$,

$Q = Q^T + Q^N$,

$K^N = \gamma D$,

$K^T = (1-\gamma)D$,

where $\rho = 0.15$, $r = 0.10$, $\varepsilon = -2.0$, and γ is shown parametrically as the first column of table 3. Q is calculated at initial prices, set at unity.

References

Arrow, K., and M. Kurz. 1970. *Public Investment, The Rate of Return, and Optimal Fiscal Policy*. Baltimore: Johns Hopkins University Press.

Bhagwati, J., and T. N. Srinivasan. 1976. "Optimal Trade Policy and Compensation Under Endogenous Uncertainty: The Phenomenon of Market Disruption." *Journal of International Economics* 6:317–336.

Blanchard, O. 1983. "Debt and the Current Account Deficit in Brazil." In P. Armella et al., eds., *Financial Policies and the World Capital Market: The Problem of Latin American Countries*. University of Chicago Press.

Blanchard, O., and J. Sachs. 1982. "Anticipations, Recessions, and Policy: An Intertemporal Disequilibrium Model." *Annales de L'Insee* 47–48, July–December.

Brecher, R. A., and C. F. Díaz-Alejandro. 1977. "Tariffs, Foreign Capital and Immiserizing Growth." *Journal of International Economics* 7 (November):317–322.

Bruno, M., and J. Sachs. 1982. "Input Price Shocks and the Slowdown in Economic Growth." *Review of Economic Studies* 49:679–705.

Bulow, J., and J. B. Shoven. 1978. "The Bankruptcy Decision." *Bell Journal of Economics* 9 (no. 2):437–456.

Díaz-Alejandro, C. 1984. Good-bye Financial Repression, Hello Financial Crash. Columbia University.

Dornbusch, R. 1985. "External Debt, Budget Deficits, and Disequilibrium Exchange Rates." In G. W. Smith and J. T. Cuddington, eds., *International Debt and the Developing Countries* (Baltimore: Johns Hopkins University Press).

Eaton, J., and M. Gersovitz. 1981. "Debt with Potential Repudiation: Theoretical and Empirical Analysis." *Review of Economic Studies* 48:289–309.

Hayashi, F. 1982. "Tobin's Marginal q and Average q: A Neoclassical Interpretation." *Econometrica* 50:213–224.

Jensen, M., and W. Meckling. 1976. "Theory of the Firm: Managerial Behavior, Agency Costs, and Capital Structure." *Journal of Financial Economics* 3:305–360.

Kharas, H. J. 1981. Constrained Optimal Foreign Borrowing by Less Developed Countries. Development Policy Staff, World Bank.

Lipton, D., and J. Sachs. 1983. "Accumulation and Growth in a Two-Country Model." *Journal of International Economics* 15:135–159.

McEachern, W. A. 1975. *Managerial Control and Performance*. Lexington, Mass.: Lexington Books.

Sachs, J. 1981. "The Current Account and Macroeconomic Adjustment in the 1970's." *Brookings Papers on Economic Activity*, no. 1, pp. 201–268.

Sachs, J. 1982a. "The Current Account in the Macroeconomic Adjustment Process." *Scandinavian Journal of Economics* 84 (no. 2):147–159.

Sachs, J. 1982b. "LDC Debt: Problems and Prospects." In P. Wachtel, ed., *Crises in the Economic and Financial Structure*. Lexington, Mass.: Lexington Books.

Sachs, J. 1983. "Energy and Growth under Flexible Exchange Rates." In J. Bhandari and B. Putnam, *The International Transmission of Economic Disturbances*. Cambridge, Mass.: MIT Press.

Sachs, J. 1984. "Theoretical Issues in International Borrowing." *Princeton Studies in International Finance*, no. 54.

Sachs, J., and D. Cohen. 1982. LDC Borrowing with Default Risk. NBER Working Paper no. 925.

Smith, C., and J. Warner. 1979. "On Financial Contracting: An Analysis of Bond Covenants." *Journal of Financial Economics* 7:117–161.

Stiglitz, J. E., and A. Weiss. 1981. "Credit Rationing in Markets with Imperfect Information: I." *American Economic Review* 71:393–410.

Wellons, P. A. 1977. *Borrowing by Developing Countries in the Euro-Currency Market*. Paris: OECD Development Centre.

11 Economic Interdependence and Coordination of Economic Policies

The term "economic interdependence" has come into widespread use during the past decade. This article will address the various meanings of this term, the possible reasons for increased economic interdependence, and the implications of that increased economic interdependence for the functioning of national economies, including national economic policy. Except in passing, it will not cover the rapid growth of empirical work on interdependence.

Definition of Terms

The O.E.D. defines interdependence as "the fact or condition of depending each upon the other; mutual dependence," and cites Coleridge as having used the term as early as 1822, followed by Huxley and Spencer, who used the term in connection with nature and social institutions, respectively. I have not done an exhaustive survey of use of the term by economists, but it was used in a meaning similar to that developed here by W. A. Brown, Jr. (1940, p. 77).[1]

The first serious examination of "interdependence" by economists arose, not in the literature on the international economy, but in discussion of the philosophical underpinnings of econometric analysis, during the 1950s. The question there was whether in reality economies were truly simultaneous, or "interdependent," in a *causal* sense, or whether causation did not run clearly and unambiguously from one variable to another, such that any properly specified model should be "recursive" in nature.[2] This distinction is important for econometric estimation, since "interdependence" among endogenous variables introduces biases into ordinary least-squares and other estimation techniques that were in almost universal use at that time. Whatever the merits of the underlying philosophical debate on the nature of causality, endogenous variables in many models of economic behavior may be assumed to influence one another within the time periods covered by our observations, and estimation techniques designed to correct for simultaneous equation bias have now come into almost routine use.

"Economic interdependence," in ordinary usage, typically refers to some measure of the value of economic transactions between two countries, or between a country and the rest of the world, perhaps scaled to total national output or to some measure of total financial assets. But these measures are not satisfactory from an analytical point of view. On close inspection, there are really two quite different phenomena that are commingled in the term "interdependence," each of which is multidimensional. The first concerns how costly it would be to do without the transactions in question, perhaps after a period of adjustment. Costly losses tend to be highly correlated with transactions levels, but it is possible to imagine instances in which a particular product is imported in small amounts but is such a crucial input into important productive processes, with no close substitutes, that its loss would entail large losses to the economy. This situation can be characterized as high dependence on another part of the world; if the dependence is reciprocal it may be called high interdependence, although for reasons given below I prefer to call it high mutual dependence, or reciprocal dependence. This kind of dependence is obviously multidimensional, since it concerns specific commodities. In the context of a total cessation of trade between two countries, e.g. due to a war or a trade embargo, the many dimensions can be collapsed into "loss of GNP" without the trade. The measurement should contain a time dimension to reflect the fact that optimal adjustments to the loss of critical materials typically take time. This concept is of special interest to political scientists, who are concerned with the use and the threatened use of power as sources of influence. It has been called "vulnerability interdependence" by Keohane and Nye (1977).[3] The second phenomenon concerns how much adjustment a country has to make to "foreign" events under conditions of normal economic activity, where frequency as well as cost is taken into account. When the requirements to adjust run both ways between two countries, Keohane and Nye call this "sensitivity interdependence." It involves marginal (as opposed to average) relationships, along with the magnitude and frequency of disturbances normally emanating from the foreign economies. The measures of sensitivity involve such factors congenial to economists as marginal propensities to spend on foreign products or assets, elasticities of substitution between foreign and domestic products or assets, elasticities of substitution in production, and relative size of the economies in question. This notion of interdependence is in harmony with the methodological discussion of interdependent systems of the 1950s, which also focused on marginal relationships between the variables under examination.

Some political scientists dislike this use of the term "interdependence" on the grounds that it creates terminological confusion with the other concept, which is relevant to them.[4] The difficulty is worse than that: sensitivity interdependence may be rising even when vulnerability interdependence is falling, and even for the same reasons. For example, as substitution possibilities increase as a result of technical changes that reduce cost differentials between home and foreign production of certain goods, the impact of normal foreign disturbances will rise while the cost (in a given time period) of a trade embargo will fall.

Each discipline must specify concepts and define terms in ways that are most suitable for its purposes. Economists do not focus on the threatened use of force so avidly as political scientists do, and are more concerned professionally with the relatively humdrum problems of analyzing and managing economies under conditions of normal economic intercourse. I would therefore suggest that we use the term "mutual dependence" when two countries are dependent on (i.e., vulnerable to) one another, and, O.E.D. notwithstanding, that we use the term "interdependence" to refer to the degree of two-way influence of one economy on another at the margin. The key point, whatever the labels, is that the concepts are different, and each is useful in its own context. The political scientist may be more interested in a flow chart of economic transactions between two countries and in statistics concerning the share of its total supply of a crucial product that a country imports from potential adversaries (although even those can merely represent staring points for his analysis.) The economist will be more interested in the matrix of partial derivatives linking a set of interesting variables, plus normal variation in the disturbances exogenous to his model, although when it comes to the impact of foreign disturbances on the domestic price level be too will be interested in import shares. Because of its implications for the framework of policymaking, however, political scientists should also take an interest in the economist's notion of interdependence.

Interdependence defined in this way must be distinguished from "openness," which refers simply to a country's exposure to the rest of the world.[5] It is only if the openness and size of an economy are such that the economy is itself affected by the impact of its own actions on the rest of the world that the openness becomes "interdependent." Nonetheless, because of its comparative simplicity, a small, open economy is frequently a useful point of departure for the analysis of interdependence.

Interdependence must also be distinguished from the integration of markets across national boundaries. We can take August Cournot's definition of a market, cited with approval by Alfred Marshall, as "the whole of any region in which buyers and sellers are in such free intercourse with one another that the prices of the same goods tend to equality easily and quickly"—after allowing for transfer costs. We can speak of international economic intergration to the extent that markets so defined cross national boundaries, the limiting case of course being the entire globe. However, markets here refer to single commodities and securities; a worldwide market implies that the law of one price obtains for those goods and securities. It is difficult to imagine a high degree of interdependence among nations in the presence of a low degree of market integration.[6] Nevertheless, a high degree of market integration can certainly exist without producing high interdependence, even when the countries involved are not so small that the impact of economic events on the rest of the world can be neglected. For instance, the elasticities of substitution between home and foreign goods or securities might be very low, despite highly integrated markets, or the marginal propensities to import goods or securities out of additional income or wealth might be very low.[7] Integration thus refers to a single product over space; interdependence typically refers to high substitutability between many products over space. In practice, high integration of markets is necessary for high interdependence but does not ensure it.

Finally, it will be useful in this discussion of concepts and definitions to distinguish several types of interdependence, the exact meaning of which will become clearer with the examples in later sections. There is first of all *structural* interdependence, whereby two or more economies are highly open (at the margin) with respect to one another, so that economic events in one strongly influence economic events in the other. It is this sort of interdependence that has been implicit in the discussion above. Its presence implies that each country will have a strong interest in information about both the structure of the other economy and likely events there. Detailed knowledge about developments in the German economy may be just as important for the framing of Dutch economic policies, for instance, as knowledge about the structure of the Dutch economy. Second, there may be interdependence among the *objectives* of economic policy; that is, one country may be concerned about the attainment of policy targets in the other country. This is trivial when the targets are the same, such as the exchange rate between the countries or, less obviously, when they are both subject to some overall constraint, such as that the current-account positions of the world must add up to zero. Less trivial cases involve direct concern for developments elsewhere. Such concern has been clearly manifested in noneconomic realms, as when country A's demand for defense expenditures depends directly on defense expenditures outside the country (positively when the foreigner is an adversary, negatively when he is an ally, unless institutional arrangements for burden-sharing are present), or when the residents of country A feel strongly about human-rights conditions in foreign countries. There are beginnings of this cross-targeting in the economic realm as well, especially with respect to the distribution of income and wealth between and within countries. Third, there may be low or high interdependence among the *exogenous disturbances* to two or more countries. As we will see, high structural interdependence implies that events in one country will cause disturbances in others (perhaps welcome ones) and vice versa. But here we are speaking of disturbances exogenous to both countries. If these disturbances are poorly (or inversely) correlated, high structural interdependence may actually, on balance, reduce their impact on economic variables of interest, such as national incomes or price levels (Cooper 1974). If they are highly correlated, however, they will reinforce one another and this diversifying effect will be diminished or lost. Unfortunately, the same tendencies that increase structural interdependence may also increase the correlations among the exogenous shocks to which economies are subjected. Fourth, there may be a high degree of *policy interdependence* between countries, in the sense that the optimal course of action for one country depends decisively on the action taken by another country and vice versa. Such policy interdependence arises directly from the structural interdependence or from the interdependence of objectives already mentioned. Here we stress the game-theoretic or strategic aspects of policy interdependence: Actions by country A will influence actions by country B, and vice versa, and each "player" should in general take these anticipated responses into account in framing his own actions. Moreover, the manner in which they are taken into account can influence strongly the extent to which countries may attain their national objectives. This type of interdependence will be discussed more fully below.

Most of the discussion that follows, under all the categories above, will concern macroeconomic interdependence. But similar issues and problems arise if one's principal concern is microeconomic issues of regulation or taxation. These will be discussed briefly in the final section.

Macroeconomic Interdependence: A Simple Illustration

To fix our ideas concerning the economist's approach to interdependence, let us consider first a small economy that exchanges goods and securities with the rest of the world. Here "small" is taken to mean that events in our country cannot appreciably influence the level of income, prices, or interest rates in the rest of the world; these are taken as given, exogenous, beyond our country's influence. We can then ask how much influence our country can have on its own level of income, prices, and interest rates through bond-financed government spending (fiscal policy) or through open-market operations by the central bank in domestic bonds (monetary policy). After examining the small, open economy, we can turn to an economy that is large enough to influence conditions in the rest of the world, to ascertain what difference that makes. For concreteness, the economy (and, when we introduce it, the rest of the world) will be assumed to have well-defined aggregate-demand schedules for composite goods, for money, for an interest-bearing one-period domestic security, and for an interest-bearing one-period foreign security. The prices of the composite goods will be assumed to be fixed, as is the exchange rate. The nominal interest rate and the real interest rate are thus identical. The analysis will be short-run in nature, with changes in stocks (e.g. of fixed capital or of outstanding government debt) assumed to be negligible during the period under consideration. These assumptions are strong and tenable only for short-period analysis, and in any case they are merely designed to introduce the key issues in a simplified but concrete manner, by way of illustration. They follow the early tradition of open-economy macroeconomic analysis pioneered by Meade (1951), Fleming (1962), and Mundell (1968).

For the single country we can write

$$Y = E(Y, r) + T(Y, Y') + G, \tag{2.1}$$

$$M = H + R = L(Y, r), \tag{2.2}$$

$$B = \Delta R = T(Y, Y') - \Delta F, \tag{2.3}$$

where

Y = national output,

E = national private expenditure,

G = government expenditure,

T = exports less imports,

M = high-powered money supply,

H = central-bank holdings of domestic bonds,

R = central-bank holdings of international reserves,

L = public demand for high-powered money,

B = balance of international payments,

F = private domestic holdings of foreign securities,

r = rate of interest on domestic bonds,

r' = rate of interest on foreign bonds.

A prime indicates that the variable is for the rest of the world.

We assume that the country is initially in short-run equilibrium in that the variables are unchanging and $B = 0$ by choice of an appropriate exchange rate. We then want to examine the impact of small changes in G and in H on the endogenous variables, Y and r, in the case of the small economy. Differentiate equations 2.1 and 2.2 totally with $dY' = dr' = 0$, let dx stand for the deviation of x from its initial value x_0, and rearrange terms:

$$(s + m)dY - E_r dr = dG, \tag{2.4}$$

$$L_y dY + L_r dr = dM, \tag{2.5}$$

or, in matrix terms,

$$\begin{pmatrix} s+m & -E_r \\ L_y & +L_r \end{pmatrix} \begin{pmatrix} dY \\ dr \end{pmatrix} = \begin{pmatrix} dG \\ dM \end{pmatrix}. \tag{2.6}$$

Here $m = -T_y$, $s = 1 - E_y$, both assumed to be positive, and subscripts indicate the variable of differentiation: $L_y > 0$, $L_r < 0$, $E_r < 0$. The balance of payments poses a problem in this model of fixed exchange rates: So long as $B \neq 0$, reserves will be changing, and so will the money supply in the absence of offsetting action. We will therefore assume that, during the period under examination, sterilization of balance-of-payments flows takes place. Thus, we assume $dM = dR + dS + dH$, so that for $dS = -dR$ we have $dM = dH$, where dS is the purchase or sale of domestic securities designed to offset the change in reserves (sterilization) and dH is the purchase or sale of domestic securities over and above that.

This formulation, while satisfactory in the short run, has the undesirable consequence of excluding transactions in international securities from having any influence on domestic variables. We will therefore make one further adjustment. Suppose that home demand for foreign securities depends on the interest-rate differential between our country and the rest of the world, $r' - r$. Suppose also that there is no foreign demand for home securities and that monies are not held by nonresidents. Then a change in this differential will lead to a once-for-all change $\Delta F = F_r(dr' - dr)$ in domestic holdings of foreign securities, where $F_r > 0$. Since the central bank fixes the exchange rate, this change in desired holdings by the public can be satisfied instantaneously. We will assume that this rapid adjustment occurs, and that the resulting change in reserves is not sterilized. That is, sterilization only applies to subsequent flow imbalances, arising through the trade account. So the central-bank account is revised to read

$$dM = dR_f + dR_t + dS + dH = dR_f + dH,$$

where f signifies reserve changes arising from (instantaneous) capital-account transactions, t signifies reserve changes arising from imbalances in trade, and $dS = -dR_t$. The reasons for this somewhat artificial distinction will become clear below. Alternatively, we can interpret our results as pertaining to very short-run equilibrium, before trade flows have influenced reserves enough to have discernible impact.

Since $dR_f = -F_r(dr' - dr)$, equation 2.5 can now be rewritten for $dr' = 0$ as

$$L_y dY + (L_r - F_r)dr = dH \tag{2.5'}$$

and equation 2.6 becomes

$$\begin{pmatrix} s + m & -E_r \\ L_y & L_r - F_r \end{pmatrix} \begin{pmatrix} dY \\ dr \end{pmatrix} = \begin{pmatrix} dG \\ dH \end{pmatrix}, \tag{2.6'}$$

or, for short, $Ay = x$, where A represents the "structure" of the economy around its equilibrium position. The economy's linkages with the rest of the world are captured in the coefficients m and F_r.

It is easy to show how the policy variables, G and H, affect the target variables:

$$\frac{dY}{dG} = \frac{L_r - F_r}{\Delta} > 0, \tag{2.7}$$

$$\frac{dY}{dH} = \frac{E_r}{\Delta} > 0, \tag{2.8}$$

$$\frac{dr}{dG} = \frac{-L_y}{\Delta} > 0, \tag{2.9}$$

$$\frac{dr}{dH} = \frac{s + m}{\Delta} < 0, \tag{2.10}$$

where

$$\Delta = (s + m)(L_r - F_r) + E_r L_y < 0.$$

That is, expansionary fiscal policy ($dG > 0$) or monetary policy ($dH > 0$) will raise output, and fiscal expansion will raise the interest rate but expansionary monetary policy will lower it, in each case by amounts that depend on all the structural coefficients of the economy.

How are the policy coefficients 2.7–2.10 influenced by the international linkages? This can be seen by differentiating them with respect to m and F_r, respectively. By doing so, we discover that increased linkages with the rest of the world (larger m and F_r) generally weaken the impact of a given increase in G or H on the target variables Y and r.[8] There are, however, two exceptions: (1) Higher F_r (a stronger response in holdings of foreign securities to a given interest differential) strengthens the impact of G on Y, by leading to a sale of foreign securities, augmenting reserves and hence the money supply, and thus weakening the drag on output of what otherwise would be higher domestic interest rates. This stimulative influence would of course be nullified if the capital movements were subject to sterilization. (2) Higher m increases the magnitude of the (negative) effect of higher H on r by reducing the stimulus to output and hence reducing the income-induced increase in demand for money. But in the six remaining combinations higher foreign linkages reduce the impact of domestic policy variables on target variables.

Is this general effect altered by allowing for interdependence—i.e., by dropping the assumption that our country is small? We can incorporate the rest of the world explicitly into the analysis by writing down equations analogous to 2.1 and 2.2 for the rest of the world, treating its policy actions as exogenous, but allowing its income Y' and its interest rate r' to respond to income and interest rates in the home country. Differentiating as before and putting the entire world system together yields

$$\begin{bmatrix} s+m & -E_r & 0 & -m' \\ L_y & L_r - F_r & F_r & 0 \\ 0 & F_r & L_r' - F_r & L_y' \\ -m & 0 & -E_r' & s'+m' \end{bmatrix} \begin{bmatrix} dY \\ dr \\ dr' \\ dY' \end{bmatrix} = \begin{bmatrix} dG \\ dH \\ dH' \\ dG' \end{bmatrix}, \quad (2.11)$$

or $Ay = x$ for short. Here the variables are defined as before, except that primes are neglected on the subscripts to L_r', L_y', and E_r' to avoid unduly complicated notation, and F_r must be interpreted as the change in holdings of foreign securities in response to a change in the interest differential, not in r alone. Now both countries are assumed to sterilize imbalances in payments (trade), except for the instantaneous adjustment in portfolios that occurs whenever the interest differential is altered.

The structural matrix A in equation 2.11 has been partitioned into two "domestic" blocks along the main diagonal, in the northwest and southeast corners—although they include some linkage coefficients—and two international blocks in the northeast and southwest corners. This will offer a convenient format for generalization to many countries.

As before, it is possible to calculate the policy multipliers on the target variables. We will focus on the influence of fiscal and monetary policy on national output; the interest rate is typically only an intermediate target or is not targeted at all.

It can readily be shown that in this larger system it is also true that $dY/dG > 0$ and $dY/dH > 0$, although the expressions are much more complex than 2.7 and 2.8.[9] What happens to these policy coefficients as international interdependence, as we may now call it, increases? In order to avoid unwanted compositional effects, we suppose that m and m' increase in the same proportion k; as before, F_r can also increase (independently).

It can be shown that dY/dG declines unambiguously as k increases. dY/dH also declines as k increases so long as the two economies are identical in their (marginal) structural coefficients, and in any case for sufficiently small values of F_r or (its equivalent) if capital flows are sterilized. For large F_r and economies that are sufficiently different, however, it is possible for an increase in openness as measured by m and m' to enhance the impact of open-market operations on national output. For instance, if E'_r/s' is greater than E_r/s, then monetary expansion at home will stimulate investment in the rest of the world sufficiently for that to increase the impact on home income through ever-higher values of m', despite the higher leakages through m.

dY/dH declines unambiguously as F_r increases if the two economies are similar in the sense that $E_r/L_r = E'_r/L'_r$, and will often decline even if this condition is not met.

dY/dG responds ambiguously to increases in F_r. For identical economies, increases in small values of F_r (any value below $-L_r$) lead to an increase in dY/dG, as the enhanced demand for money with higher output is satisfied by sales of foreign securities and conversion of the proceeds into domestic money at the central bank.[10] For values for F_r sufficiently above L_r, however, further increases in F_r will reduce dY/dG whether the economies are identical or not. This result stands in contrast to the small open economy, where the higher F_r becomes the greater is the impact of fiscal policy on home output.

Once the influence on income abroad is taken into account, higher capital mobility can reduce the effectiveness of fiscal policy via its depressing effects on foreign output (so long as $m, m' > 0$).

In summary, increased openness in terms of goods or securities generally weakens the effectiveness of the traditional instruments of macroeconomic policy on national output (substitution of tax reduction for increases in government expenditure would not fundamentally alter this analysis), although some exceptions can be found, arising mainly from consequential differences in the structures of the two economies.[11]

While the effectiveness of fiscal policy on output is reduced with increased trade linkages, by the same token its impact on income in the rest of the world is increased. Thus, with increased interdependence, policy actions in one country become larger "disturbances" in the other country. It does not follow, however, that the impact of a given dG on *world* output, $dY + dY'$, will remain unchanged. This will be so, in general, only if the two economies are identical in structure. If they are not, redistributing the policy impact between the two economies, as international linkages do, will alter the total impact on world output because of differences in response in the two economies. These compositional effects are also present within national economies, but we suppress them with the conventional assumptions of a single aggregate investment function, savings function, demand for money function, and the like.

This two-country model is presented here merely to introduce the notion of economic interdependence, in the form of trade flows and capital movements, and to indicate how changes in the international linkages will alter the effectiveness of some traditional instruments of macroeconomic policy. The simplification brings out the main elements, but it does so only by ignoring other elements and complexities that attend actual linkages among economies. It may be helpful to suggest directions in which the simplified model might be extended in the macroeconomic realm. Discussion of international linkages that affect other aspects of policy is reserved until the final section.

First, this model has assumed a constant price level—an assumption that may be plausible for an underemployed economy, but not for a fully employed one. It is relatively straightforward to allow demand stimulus to affect prices and output in different proportions in a closed economy (Tobin and Buiter 1980), but here we are dealing with two economies. If the two national price levels respond differently to a given disturbance or policy action, substitution between the (composite) goods of the two countries will presumably take place, so relative prices must be introduced as a factor affecting demand for each country's output. The magnitude of this elasticity represents another linkage between the two countries.[12] With many traded goods, there will of course be correspondingly many price relationships.

Second, the model could allow explicitly for response lags in the key variables, income, interest rates, trade, and capital movements, instead of assuming, as above, that the key variables move to their new (short-run) equilibrium values at once. In short, time could be introduced explicitly into the model.

Third, if time were to be introduced explicitly, allowance could and should be made for the cumulative influence of flow variables on stocks: of payments imbalances on reserves and (dropping the assumption of sterilization) money supply, of government deficits on outstanding bonds, of investment on capital stock, and of savings on wealth.

Fourth, the assumption of a fixed exchange rate can be relaxed. Going to the other extreme of a fully flexible exchange rate has the advantage of ensuring continuous balance in international payments and thus no influence of reserve changes on the money supply, but it has the disadvantage of altering radically the expectational environment concerning the future, for which credibly fixed exchange rates provide a firm point of reference. Allowance must be made for expectations regarding the durability or reversibility of any change in exchange rates, and therefore also for the influence of exchange rates on the rates of return on and the domestic-currency value of foreign-currency assets.[13]

Fifth, allowance could be made explicitly for the policy reactions in the rest of the world to "disturbances" that arise from policy actions in the home country, and then in turn for the new responses of the home country. The dynamics of policy interaction between interdependent economies and the possible gains from coordination of policy will be taken up below.

Reasons for Greater Economic Interdependence

Why might interdependence have risen in recent years? The roots lie in improvements in international transportation and communication, which have diffused both production and management techniques and reduced the dependence of exports on distinctive locational advantages. The result has probably been a sharp reduction in differences in comparative costs, which has given rise to greater substitution possibilities in production (Cooper 1968, chapter 3; Lindbeck 1973). In addition, knowledge about the possibilities of producing or buying abroad has greatly improved, giving rise to much greater integration of markets. Official barriers to trade have also been reduced, especially among industrialized countries, although they remain high in many developing countries. The "foreignness" in foreign transactions is diminishing. Greater familiarity with foreign financial markets, the emergence of the Eurocurrency market, and the lowering of barriers to capital movements have all increased the interdependence among national financial markets. The move to flexible exchange rates, in contrast, has probably reduced interdependence, *ceteris paribus*, by introducing a modest barrier of short-run uncertainty for both trade and international financial transactions.

Macroeconomic Interdependence: A General Dynamic Formulation

The formulation of structural interdependence introduced above can be generalized by considering the relationships between some set of target variables, y, determined within the economic system subject to analysis, and another set of variables, z, which are exogenous to that system but influence it. z can be considered as either disturbance variables, shocks from outside the system subject to analysis, or policy variables, which are assumed to be under control of the policymakers. We will consider y to be deviations of target variables from their desired target values y^*, and z as the outside influences that create nonzero values of y. It will sometimes be convenient to designate as x the subset of z that are policy instruments subject to control.

By linearizing in the neighborhood of y^*, we can describe the time path of the economic system for specified values of z as

$$\frac{\delta y}{\delta t} = Ay + Bz(t). \tag{4.1}$$

The matrices A and B describes the influences of the variables y and z, respectively, on the rate of change of y. (In a steady state, $\delta y/\delta t = 0$.) If both A and B are diagonal matrices, the variables y are independent of one another and each one depends on a single element of z. If A and B are triangular matrices, there is a "recursive" system involving hierarchical dependence, with the first element of y depending only on a single element of z, the second element of y depending on the first element of y and the first two elements of z, and so forth through the y and z vectors. If A and B are both full matrices, all the elements of y depend on one another and on all the elements of z. This system is called an interdependent economic system. A captures the structural interdependence defined in the first section, and B offers one way to capture the degree of interdependence among disturbances.

If now the elements of y and z are ordered so that the variables from different countries are grouped together, we can use equation 4.1 to characterize the world economy of different countries, as equation 2.11 did for two countries. If A and B are block diagonal the individual national economies will be independent of one another, but if A and B are full matrices all the national economies will be structurally interdependent. Obviously, many combinations of interdependence are possible. More interesting from our point of view, however, is the degree of interdependence, which in this formulation is measured by the magnitude of off-diagonal (or off-block diagonal) elements in the A and B matrices. Such an element in the B matrix indicates that a disturbance in country i, say, *directly* affects a variable in country j. Such an element in the A matrix indicates that a disturbance in country i indirectly affects a variable in county j, via the influence of a variable in country i. It is clear from this formulation that "interdependence" is multidimensional; in principle there are hundreds of off-diagonal elements, and while some are rising in absolute value over time (which implies higher interdependence) others may be falling. Thus, talk of "greater economic interdependence" among countries must refer to some unspecified average characterization of these off-diagonal elements.

The potential linkages among economies are numerous, but the most obvious channels involve direct shifts in demand for a country's products or securities, price linkages, interest-rate linkages, and direct links in the formation of expectations on the basis of universally available news. As interdependence rises, "disturbances" in one economy diffuse rapidly and widely to other economies. The meaning of "disturbance," of course, depends very much on the analytical framework within which one is operating. What is a disturbance in one framework is an endogenous response in another. In particular, political science has taken on the fundamentally difficult task of attempting to endogenize a number of actions—especially policy responses—that economists typically assume to be exogenous within their analytical framework.

If the original disturbances are not perfectly correlated, higher interdependence may actually reduce the disturbances that a national economy experiences in an interval of time by diffusing them widely and leading to some canceling out of effects (Kenen 1969; Cooper 1974). On the other hand, the same forces that have increased interdependence are also likely to increase the correlation among disturbances. Consumption fads in one country are more likely to be emulated in other countries, labor unions are more conscious of what their companion institutions are doing in neighboring countries, inflationary expectations are likely to be influenced by world events, and so on. In that case, the rapid diffusion of disturbances may not, on balance, diminish much the total impact of disturbances, since the scope for canceling out will be reduced. Moreover, greater interdependence may actually create disturbances on a global scale. For example, the smooth functioning of financial markets depends on the law of large numbers, on the mutual offsetting of numerous individual judgments and transactions. Where bandwagon effects become global in character, fostered by instant communication, this essential canceling out may be diminished or lost.

Just as disturbances spread more quickly and more widely under high interdependence, so do the policy actions of individual countries. (Recall that x, policy actions, is a subset of z.) This, in turn, has two consequences. First, policy actions in one country become "disturbances" in others—perhaps welcome, perhaps unwelcome. Second, as we saw above, policy actions may become less efficacious at home with respect to the objectives they have been seeking. That is, as the leakages abroad increase, the impact at home declines, so the instruments of policy generally have to be worked harder to achieve a given effect. Most policy instruments have multiple effects, and the costs associated with those side effects—e.g., the unwanted allocational effects of a general tax increase—typically rise with the extent to which the instrument is used. As a result, increased leakages will lead to greater side effects, domestic as well as foreign, in relation to the original intended effect.

The economic system characterized by equation 2.11 is a particular example of the more general formulation in equation 4.1 once we specify desired values y^* for the income and interest-rate variables and assume that the system has settled down so that $\delta y/\delta t = 0$. Extension of the system of equation 2.11 from two to many countries does not alter the general findings about the policy multipliers so long as all the countries are identical in their structure (which implies that bilateral relations between any pair of countries are the same for all possible pairs). However, once allowance is made for important differences in size and structure, compositional effects become much more important, and simple, strong generalizations break down.[14]

The dynamic economic system of equation 4.1 is stable around the desired values of y^* so long as the matrix A of structural coefficients is stable, that is, so long as its characteristic roots are negative. Under these circumstances, if we are concerned with macroeconomic variables, the role of stabilization policy is not literally to stabilize but to accelerate the return of target variables to their target values. This role will be the more important the longer are the lags with which the economic system "rights itself" after having been pitched away from its targets by outside disturbances. Stabilization policy becomes necessary if the economic system is not inherently stable around its targeted values, as is the case with some Keynesian systems with their underemployment equilibria. Policy variables then become crucial not merely for speeding up adjustment but for attaining the targets at all. As Tinbergen showed many years ago, attainment of n targets y^* in a linear system such as that of equation 4.1 will in general require an equal number of policy instruments.[15]

Sufficient instruments will ensure attainment of targets in this kind of system if there are no constraints on the use of instruments. Here, however, the instruments and the targets are assigned to different countries, and a natural question is whether the nationally autonomous pursuit of national targets will in fact converge to those targets in an interdependent system. Mundell (1968) proposed a "principle of effective market classification" to match targets with instruments in a decentralized system of policymaking. According to this principle, each instrument should be used in pursuit of that target for which it has comparative advantage. Mundell was mainly interested in the roles to be assigned to monetary and fiscal policy within a single economy, but the appropriate assignment of instruments to targets is a more general issue and is of greater interest when two or more countries are involved.[16] An assignment of instruments to targets on the basis of comparative impact will always ensure the stability of a decentralized system if there are only two targets and two instruments; however, the notion of "comparative advantage" becomes less clear in systems with a large number of instruments and targets, and no easy generalization is possible (Patrick 1973). Even with stability ensured, convergence to targets may be slow.

The problem can be stated more formally. Suppose that the instruments of policy are adjusted according to the rule

$$\frac{\delta x}{\delta t} = Cy, \qquad (4.2)$$

where y is the deviation of the targets variables from their target values y^* and where C can be considered a coordination matrix since it contains the information on which target variables are guiding which instruments. The following question then arises: If national governments target only their own national objectives in a system like that of equation 4.1, can they be assured of achieving their objectives? Or is it possible that actions by one country in pursuit of its targets would so dislodge the target variables of other countries that their policy responses in pursuit of their targets would have the consequence of driving the first country further away from its target, evoking further destabilizing action by the first country, and so on?

The policy-adjustment rule (equation 4.2) may be combined with the dynamic economic structure in equation 4.1 to produce

$Dx = C(D - A)^{-1}Bx,$

which with reorganization becomes

$$D(D - A)x - BCx = 0, \tag{4.3}$$

where D is a diagonal matrix of differential operators. This is a second-order system of differential equations, and it will converge to y^* only if the real parts of all roots are negative. The question concerning the workability of decentralized policymaking can then be posed as follows: Can a block-diagonal matrix C be found that will ensure the convergence of equation 4.3?

Aoki (1976) addresses this question for the special case in which the B matrix is structured so that policy actions in each country do not affect *directly* the target variables in the other countries, except where the targets are common to two or more of them (e.g. the exchange rate), that is, B is block diagonal except with respect to the common targets. Aoki supposes further that the coordination matrix C takes the special form

$$C = \begin{bmatrix} C_{11} & C_{12} & 0 \\ 0 & C_{22} & C_{23} \end{bmatrix} = \begin{bmatrix} g_1(w_1, w_2, 0) \\ g_2(0, w_3, w_4) \end{bmatrix}, \tag{4.4}$$

where the w's are the weights the national authorities attach to their respective objectives (the middle column reflecting the common objective) and g_i is the "gain" or strength they apply to their instrument variables in response to deviations from target. Under these circumstances, Aoki shows that for two countries, each with one instrument (but many possible targets, some held in common between two countries), values for g_1 and g_2 can be found that will ensure the stability of equation 4.3 provided A is stable. He suggests that this result can be generalized to many countries, but does not demonstrate it. Moreover, even in the two-country case, g_1 and g_2 must be chosen cooperatively if stability is to be ensured (that is, if policy is not to destabilize a basically stable system), or at a minimum one of them must be chosen with knowledge of the other taken into account.

The task of stabilization in a decentralized system can be eased if there is a direct feedback of policy actions on their own rates of change, that is, if instead of equation 4.2 the policy-adjustment rule takes the form

$$\frac{\delta x}{\delta t} = Cy + Ex. \tag{4.5}$$

This converts the total system, after substitution and rearrangement, to

$$D^2x - (A + C^{-1}EC)Dx - (BC - AC^{-1}EC)x = 0. \tag{4.6}$$

For E (block) diagonal, sufficiently large negative elements can be chosen to ensure that the decentralized system is stable if A is stable, i.e., if stabilization policy is necessary only to speed up the process of adjustment. If A is not stable, a suitable E can be found to stabilize the entire system in the 3×3 case; however, E must be chosen cooperatively, not with each country acting on its own.

Thus, it does not seem possible to ensure stability for decentralized policymaking in general terms,[17] although in most practical instances it is likely that an astute choice of policy-adjustment rule will permit decentralized policymaking to proceed successfully if there are sufficient instruments.[18]

Even if convergence to target were ensured, however, the path back to the targets after some disturbance might oscillate, involving much overshooting and delay in attainment of targets. The longer a country is away from its targets, the larger the loss in its welfare, *ceteris paribus*. In these circumstances, there is a strong case of international coordination of policy actions to ensure a minimum of working at cross-purposes and a speedy return of target variables to their target values. This issue has been explored through simulation of two-country systems by Cooper (1969) and Roper (1971).

The questions addressed in this section are of interest because nations in an interdependent world economy do in fact pursue their domestic targets of policy without explicit regard for what actions other countries are taking, except insofar as they impinge directly and visibly on each national economy. It is useful to know, therefore, whether decentralized policymaking of this type, with imperfect information about the prospective actions of others, is likely to achieve the desired results even in the absence of conflicting objectives, which pose a different set of problems.

Macroeconomic Interdependence: Conflict among Objectives

The preceding section was profoundly noneconomic in one respect: it assumed that all targets could be reached. With nations, as with individuals, aspiration generally exceeds attainment. We must allow for the likelihood that all targets cannot be achieved simultaneously, that choices must be made among them at the margin, and that national targets for jointly determined variables may even be in conflict.

To handle tradeoffs among targets requires an optimizing approach based on some national welfare (or loss) function, introduced to analysis of government policy by Theil (1964) and extended to the international context by Niehans (1968) and by Hamada in a series of pioneering articles.[19]

Hamada addresses the general question whether the behavior of nations, each pursuing its own national objectives in an interdependent world, will lead to a result that is optimal from the viewpoint of the community of nations. The general answer is that it will not. He therefore goes on to ask whether this general answer can be altered through institutional "rules of the game" within which nations pursue their objectives.

These exceedingly important questions have implicitly engaged the attention of statesmen over the years. However, they have not been addressed in their full generality by economists, in part because of their difficulty. Hamada explores some of the key elements in a simple two-country framework, briefly extended to three, in which each country is assumed to target its rate of inflation and its balance-of-payments position in a regime of fixed exchange rates. Each controls a single policy instrument: the level of domestic credit creation (in excess of what is normally required). In this framework, neither country can attain both its objectives by acting alone, except by coincidence; and of course the objectives between the two countries will typically conflict, again except by coincidence. Hamada then addresses how successful the countries might be if they were to cooperate in pursuit of their objectives, and compares this with two alternative approaches to policy: (1) each country pursuing its pair of objectives independently, taking actions by the other country as given and not anticipating how the other country will respond to its actions, and (2) each country pursuing its pair of objectives independently, but one country (the "leader") anticipating how the other country will react to its actions. This format gives rise to three different kinds of solution, well known from duopoly theory: a cooperative, joint solution (which will be Pareto optimal), a Cournot-Nash solution (which in general will not be Pareto optimal), and a Stackelberg-Nash solution (which in general will not be Pareto optimal, which will leave the leading country better off than the Cournot-Nash solution, and which may leave the follower either better or worse off).

The structure of this approach can be illustrated with a simple model in which two countries under flexible exchange rates are concerned with two targets (the rate of change in output and the rate of inflation) and each disposes of a single instrument of policy (the rate of monetary expansion).[20] (We will return to Hamada's fixed-exchange-rate example below). For simplicity, we will assume that the two countries are identical in economic structure and in preferences. Concretely, suppose that each country desires to minimize the loss function

$$U = -(q^2 + wp_c^2), \tag{5.1}$$

where q is the percentage rate of change in national output, p_c is the rate of inflation, and w is the weight that is accorded to inflation as opposed to output changes. Note that the function U is symmetric for increases and decreases, so changes in either direction cause disutility.

The structure of the economies is given by the following relationships:

$$q = \gamma(e + p^* - p) - \lambda i, \tag{5.2}$$

$$m - p = \alpha q - \beta i, \tag{5.3}$$

$$p_c = \mu(p^* + e) + (1 - \mu)p, \tag{5.4}$$

$$i = i^*. \tag{5.5}$$

Here e is the percentage change in the exchange rate (the domestic-currency price of a unit of foreign currency), m is the percentage change in the supply of money, i is the instantaneous change in the interest rate, and the asterisk designates the variables for the foreign country. Greek letters are structural coefficients, assumed constant and positive. Equation 5.2 represents the demand for output as a function of relative prices and the interest rate. Equation 5.3 is the demand for real-money balances as a function of output and the interest rate. Equation 5.4 gives the consumer price index as a weighted average of the price of domestic output and of imported goods. Equation 5.5 is an interest arbitrage condition, valid because of our assumption of symmetry between the two countries, implying no expected change in the exchange rate. We will assume that in the relatively short run under consideration the rate of inflation of domestic output prices is fixed and is identical in the two countries at $\bar{p} > 0$. This assumption implies that changes in nominal interest rates are the same as changes in real interest rates.

Equations 5.2–5.5 can be solved to yield reduced-form relationships in terms of the two policy variables, m and m^*, and the exogenous rate of inflation, $\bar{p}$:

$$q = am - bm^* + c\bar{p}, \tag{5.6}$$

$$e = (m - m^*)/2\alpha\gamma, \tag{5.7}$$

$$p_c = \bar{p} + \mu e = \bar{p} + \mu(m - m^*)/2\alpha\gamma, \tag{5.8}$$

where $a > b > 0$ and $c = b - a < 0$.[21] Comparable expressions hold for the starred country.

Because of the underlying symmetry, e must equal zero. But in that case $p_c = p_c^* = \bar{p}$, and the loss function 5.1 is minimized by setting $q = q^* = 0$. From equation 5.6 and its counterpart for the starred country, this result will be achieved when $m = m^* = \bar{p}$. This then represents the optimal, cooperative solution for these two economies, the best they can do under the postulated circumstances.

However, if the two countries act independently, each will believe that it can do better. The unstarred country, for example, can reduce its rate of inflation p_c by appreciating its currency, and will believe that it can do that by reducing the rate of growth of its money supply, m, because it assumes that m^* remains unchanged. Specifically, if $m^* = \bar{p}$, the unstarred country can minimize U by setting $dU/dm = 0$, which yields

$$m = gm^* - h\bar{p} < \bar{p}, \tag{5.9}$$

where $g < 1.$[22] Equation 5.9 specifies the m that the unstarred country desires as a function of m^*; it is the country's reaction function.

Of course, because of the underlying symmetry the starred country will reason in precisely the same way: for a given m, it can minimize its loss function U^* by choosing m^* such that

$$m^* = gm - h\bar{p}. \tag{5.10}$$

Equation 5.10 is the starred country's reaction function. Taken together with equation 5.9 it yields the noncooperative, Cournot-Nash solution to this policy game:

$$m = m^* = [-h/(1-g)]\bar{p}, \tag{5.11}$$

which is unambiguously less than $\bar{p}$. Thus, the noncooperative solution leads each country to contract monetary conditions in an effort to appreciate its currency in order to reduce inflation. In policy equilibrium, however, the exchange rate remains unchanged, as does the rate of inflation in each country; but by equation 5.6 output has fallen, so both countries are clearly worse off than they would be with the cooperative solution.

The contrast between the two solutions is illustrated graphically in figure 1. The two reaction functions 5.9 and 5.10 are plotted in the m-m^* plane; their intersection at N shows the noncooperative solution. The loss function 5.1 would be a family ellipses in the q-p_c plane, and since both of these variables are linear in m and m^* it is also a family of ellipses in the m-m^* plane. Its orientation depends upon the structural coefficients as well as upon $\bar{p}$. A similar, mirror-image utility map can be drawn for the starred country, with the 45° line providing the mirror. These are also sketched in figure 1. Pareto-efficient combinations of policies lie along the locus of tangencies between the two utility maps, and the cooperative solution C is the symmetric point along this locus, i.e. the one where $e = 0$ and therefore $m = m^*$. The reaction

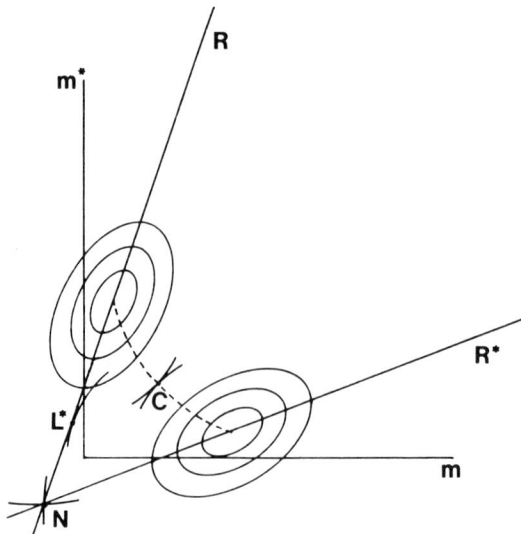

Figure 1

function R of the unstarred country is obtained by treating m^* as a parameter and is the locus of points on that country's utility map that have horizontal tangents. The reaction function R^* is the locus of vertical tangencies on the starred country's utility map.

It can be seen in figure 1 that if a country takes into account the other country's reaction to its own actions, it can do better than at N, the noncooperative solution. Thus, the starred country can maximize its utility noncooperatively by choosing an m^* at which its utility map is tangent to the other country's reaction function, shown as L^* in figure 1. The starred country, acting as a "leader" in the Stackelberg sense, overexpands in the knowledge that the follower will try to appreciate its currency and thereby induce global contraction. In this framework, the "leader" improves its position compared with N, but the gains of the follower are even greater, leading to the possibility that each country will wait for the other to take the first step (after you, Alphonse) while they both linger at N. L^* is clearly inferior to C for the starred country, although not, as drawn, for the unstarred one. In any case, at L^*, $e \neq 0$, so the interest-arbitrage condition 5.5 would have to be revised and the model solved under those new conditions.

Are there institutional arrangements that will lead both countries to the cooperative arrangement C? If the exchange rate is fixed by agreement, as under the Bretton Woods agreement, C will be ensured, since the temptation to appreciate to reduce home inflation will be removed. Under these circumstances, the starred country (say) will choose m^* to minimize U^* on the assumption that $e = 0$, i.e. that $dm = dm^*$. It can be shown that this will lead to the cooperative solution C, where the utility surfaces are tangent to one another.[23]

Even this simple formulation of policy interdependence is very complicated. The cooperative solution $m = m^* = \bar{p}$, which clearly maximizes mutual advantage in the short run, will also sustain the initial rate of inflation $\bar{p}$. The noncooperative solution, in contrast, has $m = m^* < \bar{p}$, which will not sustain the initial rate of inflation. It will subside gradually, over time, at rates depending on factors linking the decline in output to the price level that have not been specified. Thus, in this example the noncooperative solution may lead to higher utility in the long run whereas the one-period cooperative solution leads to higher utility in the short run. A total assessment thus also involves an intertemporal choice.[24] But in the short run, in this model, flexible exchange rates and decentralized decisionmaking will lead to excessive contraction in response to, say, an exogenous world supply shock that raise p and p^*. It can be argued that this kind of analysis captures the essentials of what actually happened to the world economy from 1980 to 1982.

The Bretton Woods system was designed specifically to avoid manipulation of exchange rates in the pursuit of national macroeconomic objectives. Historically, this manipulation involved competitive depreciation for the purpose of stimulating employment, but the rules would also have prohibited competitive appreciation in pursuit of anti-inflationary objectives. A system of fixed exchange rates has its own problems, however, even when the rates themselves are equilibrium exchange rates. Most of Hamada's discussion of policy interdependence takes place within a regime of fixed exchange rates, in which countries target the rate of inflation and the rate of increase in their international reserves. He shows that the noncooperative solution is suboptimal, as it is in the flexible-exchange-rate illustration given above. In particular, if both countries desire increases in reserves and manipulate their monetary policies to ensure balance-of-payments surpluses, the "world" will be subjected to economic contraction and inflation rates will be below the desired level (Hamada 1974).

If the sum of targets for payments balance exceeds the growth in world reserves in Hamada's models, monetary policy in a noncooperative regime will be more contractionary and inflation rates will be lower than desired, whereas some of these contractionary influences could be avoided in a cooperative regime. If, in contrast, the sum of desired payments balances falls short of world reserve growth, inflation in a noncooperative regime will be greater than desired.

Here is an instance in which the targets of the two countries are inconsistent and the attempt to achieve the inconsistent targets, while leading to a stable solution, as in the illustration with floating exchange rates, results in a general loss in welfare compared with what is possible. The natural "systemic" solution in this instance is for the international regime to create enough international reserves to satisfy the growing demand for them, so that both countries can run payments surpluses. Special Drawing Rights created by the International Monetary Fund can be viewed in this light as an outside source of international reserves for a world in which national demands for reserves are growing over time and nations are willing if necessary to conduct their policies so as to ensure some growth in their owned reserves.

This method for reconciling conflicting national goals would not work where the goals involved trade or current-account surpluses rather than increases in international reserves. In the former cases, there is a global consistency requirement summing the national balances to zero. Reconciliation in this case must involve changing the targets themselves (or, more generally, the way in which the targets enter national preferences), possibly by inducing a major country to adopt a position of indifference toward its trade or current-account balance and thus to act as a residual for the world as a whole.

Of course, if the countries participating in a policy "game" make up a substantial part of the world economy (as they do in a two-country model), it is unlikely that each government will ignore foreign response to its own actions. Taking these reactions into account, a Stackelberg leader can improve its position, in comparison with the Cournot-Nash noncooperative solution, by choosing a point on the foreigner's reaction curve that maximizes its welfare (such as the point L^* in figure 1). The welfare of the followers may range from deterioration to improvement much greater than that of the leader, when compared with the Nash noncooperative equilibrium, depending upon the exact assumptions of the "game" being played.

The analysis so far of policy interdependence has been somewhat artificial or contrived, as is duopoly theory in general. Outcomes depend critically on the details of structure, preferences, and information, and on the degree of anticipatory or strategic behavior by the actors. But these efforts capture an important point about the real world. National objectives may conflict, and countries—especially since there are many rather than only two—may fail to take adequately into account the behavior of other countries: national decisionmakers engage in partial rather than general equilibrium analysis with respect to the consequences of their actions. This phenomenon is especially likely in a world of roughly 160 nations, most of them small enough relative to the world as a whole that each can plausibly take events elsewhere as beyond its influence. The United States, the European Community, and Japan, in contrast, are all oligops in that they should recognize the consequences of their own actions for the system as a whole as well as for themselves. That realization has come only recently and incompletely to Japan, however, and the European Community is made up of ten nations that are still not fully harmonized, especially with regard to macroeconomic policy. The situation is further complicated by the fact that national policy actions in democratic societies are the results of diverse and usually conflicting domestic pressures, so that even when interdependence with the rest of the world is clearly present and intellectually recognized it will not be fully reflected in national policy actions.

Allusions have been made from time to time to competition among nations in the pursuit of their objectives, to the matching of instruments to targets along the lines of comparative advantages, and so on. These allusions are drawn from economic analysis of private markets and agents. Yet we know that under certain general conditions "competition" among private agents, while thwarting their individual objectives to some extent, conduces to the social good; and we know that, even though all objectives cannot be attained, the operation of a price system under competition will reconcile competing claims to output in a way that is efficient and often even harmonious. Might not the same line of reasoning apply to nations? Might not noncooperative behavior among them nonetheless lead to an overall optimum outcome?

This is a profound question, yet it has received little analysis.[25] No analysis will be attempted here, but two general remarks about the analogy can be made. First, private competitive markets are known to "fail"—that is, produce suboptimal results—in the presence of externalities of all kinds. In particular, they produce too few public goods—goods with pervasive externalities in the sense that, once produced, they can be enjoyed by many at little or no extra cost. Are there international public goods (or bads)? The clearest example, periodically preoccupying to many people around the world, is national expenditures on strategic nuclear weapons. Their existence raises the possibility of global devastation, clearly a public bad. Control of contagious disease (e.g., the elimination of smallpox) falls clearly into the category of international public goods. Economic stabilization in the major industrial countries of the world, most notably the United States, can also be said to fall into this category. Although what exactly is meant by stabilization is subject to disagreement, there is little doubt that economic management in the United States (and Europe and Japan) has strong externalities for the rest of the world—externalities which the major countries have not typically taken into account in framing their economic policies. Second, the structure of the world of nations lies far from what would be required to meet the conditions of perfect competition. There are only about 160 members to the community of nations, many of which are large enough to influence some of the markets in which they operate and a few of which are large enough to influence all the markets in which they operate. In short, the community of nations exists in the presence of extensive monopoly power—although, as with private monopoly power, it is limited by the alternative opportunities that other nations have. The attempt to exercise this limited monopoly in the pursuit of national objectives—to improve the terms of trade or to draw resources from the rest of the world—violates the conditions of "competition" and gives rise to the pervasive possibility of pushing economic policies toward global suboptimality. That, in turn, gives rise to possible gains from collusion, or, as it is more politely called in the context of economic policy, cooperation and coordination in order to enhance attainment of national economic objectives.

Possible Responses to Economic Interdependence

The responses to increased economic interdependence have varied in character and direction. One response involves steps toward disintegration, to reduce the degree of interdependence and restore some freedom of action to national policymakers. A second response involves attempts to coordinate national policy actions in one fashion or another, sometimes through conscious collaboration among nations and sometimes by one nation attempting to impose its preferred course of action on others. A third response involves the search for new instruments of policy not subject to the same degree of erosion as the traditional instruments, or even choosing instruments that capitalize on the increased economic openness and mobility.

New barriers to foreign trade and international movement of capital would be examples of disintegration, of efforts to reduce interdependence by providing for increased separation between national markets. We have experienced some of that during the past decade or two. Many countries have maintained some control over inward or outward movements of capital. Even the United States, with its relative commitment to free markets, attempted to limit outward movements of capital from 1963 to 1973 with its interest-equalization tax and its directives to banks. There have also been periodic revivals of protectionism. On the whole, however, disintegrative responses to increased interdependence have been limited, partly in recognition of the great gains from interdependence and from (not quite the same thing) the great costs associated with trying to restore effective national insulation from the world economy.

The most significant step toward less interdependence has been the movement to flexible exchange rates that took place among the major currencies in 1973. That move was complicated in its effects. It may have sustained interdependence by helping to preserve relative freedom of trade and capital movements, which would have been restricted much more severely under the pressures of the 1970s if countries had tried to maintain fixed exchange rates. However, one interpretation of the movement to flexible exchange rates is that it reflected the unwillingness of countries to accept the restraints on national monetary policies entailed by a commitment to maintain fixed exchange rates in a world of high capital mobility. It therefore represented an effort to restore some monetary autonomy in a world of high interdependence. It also increases the impact of monetary actions, via the exchange rate, on real economic activity. Yet flexible exchange rates do not insulate national economies from the rest of the world completely.[26]

I will touch on the search for new instruments of policy below; however, the main response to greater interdependence has been to call for greater coordination of national economic policies. Since "coordination" is always difficult, especially among independent nations, we must try to distinguish among various kinds of coordination and indicate why and under what circumstances each might be necessary.

What Is to Be Coordinated?

Several aspects of economic policy can be coordinated. First, the goals might be coordinated. These goals may be common goals, competitive goals, or goals that relate to one another only through general economic interactions. Second, information may be "coordinated," or exchanged, on goals, forecasts, economic structure, and intended actions. Third, the choice, magnitude, and timing of policy actions might be coordinated.

Sometimes countries will share an objective that requires costly actions for its attainment. Under these circumstances, attainment of the goal will require the interested countries to coordinate (that is, assign) their respective contributions toward that common goal. Without such coordination, or "burden sharing," countries will be tempted to try to enjoy the benefits without paying the costs, by letting other countries take the necessary actions. And if all countries thus try to become free riders, the goal will not be achieved. There is a natural analogy with domestic public goods, where compulsory taxation may be necessary to finance them. With countries of unequal size, the larger ones may purchase some of the international public good even without contributions by the smaller countries, but the purchase will be suboptimal except under special conditions.[27] Examples of these international public goods would be military alliances, the encouragement of economic development through foreign aid (e.g., contributions to the International Development Association), and attempts to limit the world demand or supply of oil. The International Energy Agency attempted in 1979 to assign targets for reductions in oil imports among industrialized consumer countries during a period of world oil shortage; OPEC's members attempted in 1982 to restrict output during a period of world oil surplus. In each of these instances, the setting of the overall target and the assignment of shares were, in practice, inseparable.

Another example of a common goal with the necessity for assigning roles is recovery from a world recession, where each country would prefer to experience export-led recovery engineered by other countries. Under these circumstances the recovery is likely to be delayed, to the disadvantage of all.[28]

Because of the problem of distributing costs, a common goal is often converted into a competitive game, with each country maneuvering to incur as low a cost as possible without jeopardizing the goal. One tactic used in such maneuvers is suggesting that the goal may not be all that important, i.e. concealing the country's true preferences. In this competitive negotiating environment, the common goal is often lost to view.

Sometimes goals are directly competitive, in the sense that they are arithmetically related; the currencies of two countries have a common exchange rate, the payments or trade positions of all countries must sum to zero, and so on. If countries set target values for these variables, they may be inconsistent and thus nonrealizable no matter how policy measures are manipulated. For concreteness, consider overall balance-of-payments targets. *Ex post*, and apart from recording errors, payments positions must add to zero for the world as a whole unless there is some outside source of international reserves, i.e. some reserve asset that is not the liability of any country. Consistency must be achieved, however, even if targeted reserve changes do not add to zero; if they do not, the costs of attaining their targets will eventually reach the point at which countries choose to adjust them and the *ex post* condition is met. In the end, the targets will be reconciled. But the outcome of this process, as we saw above, may be socially suboptimal. This result can be avoided in several ways. One is to coordinate the targets at the outset so that they are consistent; a second is to adjust the total quantity of outside reserves (such as through the issuance of Special Drawing Rights by the International Monetary Fund) so that it accomodates the *ex ante* targets; a third (really a special variant of the first) is to persuade one country to abandon its target and act as a residual for the rest of the world.

As was noted earlier, the second solution could be made to work for reserve increases but not for current account or trade balances. There was some attempt to "allocate" current-account deficits among OECD countries after the sharp increase in oil prices and the emergence of a huge surplus in the oil-exporting nations in 1974. The attempt did not succeed formally, but it probably served the purpose of helping to avoid a self-defeating race among countries to reduce deficits that were irreducible so long as oil-exporting countries had large surpluses.

The third solution—designating a residual country to solve the so-called nth-country problem, whether one is dealing with exchange rates or payments balances—is technically workable but may be unacceptable both to the nth country and to other countries.[29] The perception that the United States could run large payments deficits in the 1960s and its "benign neglect" of the exchange rate in the 1970s and early 1980s were both sources of great resentment abroad. In the early 1970s, the United States resented the fact that it could not effectively control its exchange rate. And for the United States to have run the "residual" current account deficit that corresponded to the OPEC surpluses of 1974–75 and 1980–81 surely would have evoked strong protectionist reactions from Americans.

Suppose that consistency of targets is ensured through one solution or another. Can coordination stop here? Unfortunately, no. The resulting outcome of independent national pursuit of targets may still lead to less-than-optimal results if countries are proceeding on different assumptions regarding the magnitude of their (noncompetitive) targets, their forecasts of exogenous variables, their views of the structure of the interdependent world economy (including in particular the policy multipliers), or their forecasts of the actions of other countries. The question of information is complex, since in reality no one has perfect information and the result of action based on diverse, independent views of what will happen might conceivably be superior to the result of action taken on the basis of agreed but erroneous views concerning forecasts and economic structure. Nonetheless, pooling information is likely to improve the performance of the world economy as a whole. One may presume that, with respect to its own targets and prospective actions, each country has superior information that can be usefully shared with others. Exchanging views on forecasts and on economic structure is also likely to improve comprehension of where the greatest uncertainties lie, even if no consensus is reached on the information pool.

With consistent goals and with full information on forecasts, structure, and prospective action by others, there is a basis for successful, independent pursuit of objectives. Even then, however, the results may be inferior to those that could be achieved through close coordination of actions. The prospective actions reported to others will in general be contingent on the actions to be taken by others. A single iteration may be insufficient for the contingent prospective actions to converge to actions that are actually desired all around. If countries take the actions they have reported to others, they will generally discover that they have not reached their objectives because of actions taken simultaneously by others. A series of iterations through time may be necessary for convergence on the policy targets, but this process of iteration will lead to avoidable divergences from targets while it occurs, i.e., to welfare losses as compared with full coordination of actions (Cooper 1969; Roper 1971). In other words, even with consistent targets and exchange of information, the magnitude, mix, and timing of policy actions may lead to overshooting or undershooting of targets. This may have been the principal characteristic of the world boom in 1972 and of the severity of the world recession in 1975, as countries in each case undertook macroeconomic actions without making full allowance for the actions being taken by other countries.

Of course, in principle countries could act independently if they knew fully not only the structure of foreign economies but also their policy responses under all likely contingencies. Each country could then "solve the entire system" for its own optimal policy responses and move directly to the appropriate result. Since the same (correct) information base would be shared by all countries, convergence to the desired results would be rapid. However, the information requirements for this kind of solution would be enormous. Information about structure is not typically correct. Moreover, most governments do not know their likely reactions until they are confronted with actual choices. In practice, the exchange of information on policy responses under all likely contingencies would hardly be distinguishable from coordination of policy actions as the contingencies arose.

The European Community—whose very creation can be interpreted as a response to growing economic interdependence—has on occasion attempted to coordinate not only the macroeconomic targets of its members but also the use of instruments. McKinnon (1982) has suggested that monetary actions in the United States, Japan, and West Germany, at a minimum, must be closely coordinated to achieve smooth global macroeconomic performance, including avoidance of inflation, because of the high substitutability among the financial assets of these countries.

Decentralized Action within Agreed Regimes

Coordination of policy targets and actions on a continuous basis is difficult under the best of circumstances, and among democratic nations it could never be more than a very imperfect process. These difficulties raise the important question whether it is possible to establish rule-bound regimes—constitutions, as it were—which would permit decentralized national pursuit of national objectives within the rules of the regime to lead to socially optimal outcomes, or at least to avoid the worst of the unregulated, decentralized solutions. Such a framework has been successfully achieved in such areas as containment of contagious diseases, the nuclear test ban treaty (for those who signed), and the nuclear nonproliferation treaty. In the economic arena, it has been attempted with some success in the General Agreement on Tariffs and Trade (GATT) and in the Bretton Woods agreement concerning international monetary relations.

A simple, damage-limiting view of the GATT is that it was designed to avoid the mutually disadvantageous Nash solution of countries seeking to maximize their national welfare through trade restrictions without allowing for retaliation by others, described by Scitovsky (1942). Actually it was more ambitious than that. Not only did it prohibit new restrictions on trade except under carefully controlled circumstances (and it allowed for controlled retaliation when this prohibition was violated), but it also called for nondiscrimination in trade restrictions[30] (thereby reducing greatly opportunities for tariff-induced improvements in terms of trade) and for trade liberalization under conditions of reciprocity. Over the entire period for which the GATT has been in operation, it must be reckoned a great success in accomplishing its objectives.

The Bretton Woods arrangements, with their call for fixed exchange rates that would be adjustable with international agreement, were established in part to avoid the suboptimal practices of competitive depreciation and exchange controls for purposes of generating employment and ensuring payments equilibrium or even surplus. But implicit in fixed exchange rates with high capital mobility (the implications of which were not fully comprehended in the 1940s) is coordination of national monetary policies. Exchange-market intervention (to maintain the agreed exchange rate) is monetary policy, and monetary policy governed by the need to fix the exchange rate ensures coordination among national monetary policies, although it leaves open the question of how world monetary policy is determined.[31]

In 1970 the International Monetary Fund began to issue special drawing rights (SDRs), on the assumption that countries' targets for increases in owned reserves exceeded the amount of additional gold that was available for increments to monetary reserves, and that an increase in outside reserves was preferable to a scramble for payments surpluses or to continued deficits by the United States as other countries added to their dollar holdings. Implicit in this novel arrangement was the assumption that the demand was for *owned* reserves and not for *earned* reserves, i.e., that countries really wanted to add to their reserves and were not merely or mainly interested in the employment and growth effects of payments surpluses.

Rule-based regimes have considerable merit if the rules are widely accepted, and this constitutional approach to international economic coordination has demonstrated some success during the past three decades. If appropriate rules can be found, rule-based regimes have the advantage over noncooperative regimes of leading to superior outcomes while at the same time preserving the reality of national autonomy and decentralization in economic decisionmaking. The nation-state and the forms of decisionmaking that have been developed within it are predicated on the assumption of the efficacy of decisions taken at the national level. Through infrequent international negotiations of treaties or less formal agreements, a framework can perhaps be found that will preserve these forms while reducing their costs in an interdependent world.

Decisionmaking at the supranational level, or its analytical near-equivalent, continuous international coordination of national policy actions, can always in principle lead to results that are superior to those produced by rule-based regimes (since when appropriate they encompass those regimes); but they do so only by threatening existing decisionmaking arrangements at the national level. Constitutional change at the national level entails costs as well. The search for rule-based international regimes is designed to compromise between these conflicting considerations.

Of course, in practice rule-based regimes go beyond simply laying down rules once and for all. They establish procedures for enforcing the rules, for adjudicating disputes, and for modifying the rules as necessary. They thus encourage continual consultations, if not formal decisionmaking, among their member states. Indeed, while it is difficult to separate the two, the consultative process may sometimes be even more important than the rules themselves. But the rules form a useful psychological and legal bulwark against domestic pressures for short-run, national optimizing behavior predicated (often unrealistically) on the assumption that other nations will not respond in similar manner and the regime will survive.[32]

Rule-based regimes do not usually solve the problem of conflicts in timing of economic actions, however. Moreover, a constitutional regime is typically not highly adaptable in the face of evolutionary change in economic conditions. Constitutional rules tend to be rigid (they derive much of their usefulness, while they are useful, from their inflexibility) and are not easily changed except under strong provocation. Hence, there is a danger that rule-based regimes will sooner or later collapse or will erode into irrelevance as they are increasingly ignored.

Obstacles to Economic Coordination

The coordination of policy actions among countries is rare. There is, perhaps paradoxically, a somewhat better record at the creation and maintenance of rule-based regimes, but it has proved extremely difficult to alter them in an orderly way. The reasons for the lack of coordination lie in different perspectives and different interests among nations, even in settings in which all recognize the potential gains from coordination.

First, countries may not agree on the objectives. Among like-minded countries (e.g., excluding those committed to a completely different system of economic or political organization, such as Communist countries), there are not likely to be radical differences of view; they operate within the same general conceptual framework. But they still may differ on such matters as the balance to be struck in macroeconomic management between combating inflation and protecting employment. To claim that there is no tradeoff between inflation and employment is a pious wish, clearly at variance with experience in the short to medium run and untested in the long run, which is a series of short runs.) Such differences inhibit coordinated macroeconomic action. Also, even with commonly agreed ultimate objectives, the distribution among nations of benefits and costs will differ depending on the exact measures undertaken, and these divergent distributional objectives may inhibit collective action.

Second, even if countries have compatible objectives and similar circumstances, they may differ on their forecasts of future events, either with respect to the course of events without changes in policy or with respect to the influence of policy actions on the targeted variables. In short, they may disagree on the structure of the economy, and hence on the relationship of means to ends. This factor seemed to be part of the problem (although disagreement on objectives may also have lain beneath the surface) between the United States and West Germany in 1977, when the German government thought that a given fiscal stimulus would have a greater influence on the price level, relative to employment and output, than American officials did.[33]

Third, there may be lack of trust between nations. This factor can be important even for a single episode of coordination, since heads of government typically do not take final action; they merely set in motion a political process which with luck and skill will lead to the desired action. If some leaders are thought to be unable to deliver on their commitments, that will inhibit cooperation by others. Trust is even more important in a rule-based regime with durability over time. The rules of a regime cannot cover all contingencies, and few are so airtight that they are self-enforcing in the sense that deviation leads automatically to penalties sufficiently severe to deter those deviations. Thus, rule-based regimes depend for their effectiveness on adherence to the spirit as well as the letter of the agreed rules. If other participants are suspected of being unwilling or unable to adhere to the spirit as well as the letter, countries will be reluctant to undertake commitments that they fear will prove to be one-sided. Decisionmakers may have an incentive to deviate from previously agreed-upon paths in new circumstances or—most important in this context—if they believe that other governments will follow the rules. Where such deviations would work to the disadvantage of the other countries, their lack of trust will inhibit the conclusion of otherwise mutually beneficial schemes of cooperation.[34]

Fourth, public sentiment for preserving national freedom of action still runs sufficiently strong in many countries to make coordination of economic policy—especially agreement on restraints on future action—politically difficult. The illusion of national autonomy is still widespread, and it is widely confused with national sovereignty. The latter concerns the formal ability of a nation to act on its own rather than under the instruction of another nation. That remains undiminished. National autonomy, in contrast, is the ability of a nation to attain its objectives through unilateral action. That is heavily constrained, as we have seen, in an environment of high interdependence. Economic cooperation may restore some effectiveness in the pursuit of objectives. Far from undermining national sovereignty, such cooperation often represents a wise exercise of that sovereignty.

Finally, cooperation may be inhibited by the fact that no nation is willing to take the lead to achieve it. In view of the difficulties and inhibitions enumerated above, building a coalition within and among nations for effective international cooperation requires a clear view of the objective and constant effort and persuasion to achieve it. The importance of this kind of leadership, as opposed simply to taking the first move in the static games of the preceding section (although willingness to take the first move may be important) has been emphasized by Kindleberger (1973), who sees faltering world leadership a major cause of the Great Depression of the 1930s, by Cooper (1972), and by Whitman (1979).

The Search for New Instruments of Policy

Two directions for economic policy created by higher interdependence have been addressed: disintegrative steps to reduce interdependence and attempts to coordinate policies. A third involves the search for new instruments of policy that have not been subject to erosion or that have actually been enhanced in their effectiveness by higher interdependence. The introduction of new instruments of policy is often neglected by economists because it falls outside their usual framework for analysis, with its relatively fixed structure; however, it has undeniably occurred. In particular, as the general instruments of macroeconomic policy (overall government spending and taxation, and monetary policy) diminished in efficacy as tools for economic stabilization and growth, governments turned elsewhere to restore some control. "Fiscal" policy has for some countries increasingly become "industrial" policy, that is, the provision of industry-specific tax breaks and government expenditures designed to stimulate both domestic and foreign investment in the desired activity. To the extent that mobile foreign capital and firms can be attracted into the country, employment and growth will be stimulated. In effect, residents are willing (via the tax/expenditure system) to reduce their real after-tax rewards per unit of effort for the sake of greater employment or growth. This process has proceeded farthest in small, highly open countries, where the leakages from overall monetary or fiscal actions are most obvious and where the possible gains (relative to the size of the economy) from attracting internationally mobile firms are also obvious. The process can also be seen among states and provinces within the United States and Canada.[35]

Other Areas of Interdependence

National economic policy in the modern economy goes well beyond macroeconomic stabilization and growth; it tries to inform and protect consumers and investors, to encourage specific forms of investment, to provide public goods and services, and to redistribute income. In each case, successful policy action requires that the jurisdiction of government have a span of control that covers the domain of geographical mobility of those economic agents that are the objects of regulation or redistribution. Otherwise, those agents can escape the regulation or taxation by moving beyond the government's jurisdictional reach.

As the domain of mobility increases with improved information and communication—as international interdependence increases—the capacity of national governments to regulate and to tax economic activity is eroded.[36] Of course, the increased mobility of firms, capital, or individuals makes it attractive for some countries to provide tax or regulatory incentives to relocate, as noted in the previous section. Thus, tax havens, flags of convenience, and havens from bank regulation have sprung up around the world. Countries compete with one another in the reduction of onerous conditions imposed on desired, mobile economic agents, of which the 1981 passage of the International Banking Act permitting "offshore" banking in the United States is only one recent example.

In some cases this mobility beyond the regulating jurisdiction may improve the world's allocation of resources. Consider as an example air pollution, which is relatively localized in it effects. If country A finds its air polluted to an unacceptable degree, it may impose antipollution regulations on its firms. Some of these firms may then find it economical to shift their activities to country B, which has no antipollution regulations. If the residents of country B are prepared in full knowledge to accept the additional pollution (perhaps because they have much less to start with), and if the air pollution has only local effects, both countries will be made better off in the long run by the move. For pollution that is pervasive or global in its effects, in contrast, competition in regulatory laxity will leave the world worse off than would a coordinated approach to regulation. As in some cases of macroeconomic management, international coordination of policy actions could avoid mutually damaging competition to reduce regulations. Coordination will be necessary to ensure Pareto-optimal results.

This article is already too long to undertake a detailed analysis of these other dimensions of interdependence and their implications for economic policy and for cooperation among nations. Further discussion can be found in Vernon 1971, Cooper 1968, and Cooper 1974.

Notes

1. The term "interdependence" was used once by Albert Hirschman in his *National Power and the Structure of Foreign Trade* (1945, p. 10). Baldwin (1980) adopts the

dubious procedure of imputing to Hirschman's casual use of the term a meaning based on the content of his entire book to argue that economists used this term to apply to power relationships among countries. Brown's use, which parallels that adopted below, antedates Hirschman's. There is more on this issue below, because there has been some divergence between economists and political scientists on the meaning and importance of economic interdependence.

2. See, e.g., Bentzel and Hansen 1954–55.

3. An example of vulnerability interpendence would be the dependence of Iran on the United States for spare parts for its military and telecommunications equipment (which became evident after the invasion of Iran by Iraq in 1980 while Iran was under a U.S. embargo) combined with the dependence of the United States on Iran for oil and for intelligence stations crucial to the monitoring of Soviet missile tests and other strategic military activity.

4. See Waltz 1970 and Baldwin 1980.

5. Bryant (1980, pp. 156–159) uses the terms "openness" and "interdependence" more or less interchangably. Certainly in reality there will be a close correspondence between them, but it is worth maintaining the distinction for two reasons: (1) "Openness' refers to average relationships, such as the ratio of imports to GNP, whereas "interdependence" as used here refers mainly to marginal relationships, such as the marginal propensity to import. (2) A single country can be open (in marginal as well as average terms), yet not interdependent because it is too small to influence conditions in the rest of the world appreciably.

6. But it is not completely impossible; for instance, because of natural endowments, each of two countries might produce goods that were demanded only in the other country.

7. Allen and Kenen (1980, p. 377 and passim) identify integrated markets with high elasticities of substitution between home and foreign goods and securities. This usage is somewhat confusing, since markets that are "perfect" in the sense that the law of one price prevails could, on this definition, be poorly integrated. It seems preferable to use high substitution elasticities as one measure of openness and, when the magnitudes are appropriate, of interdependence.

8. We assume that the remaining structural coefficients are unchanged. This assumption needs to be questioned for large changes in m and F_r.

9. Here

$$\frac{dY}{dG} = \frac{1}{\Delta}\{(s' + m')[L_r L'_r - F_r(L_r + L'_r)] + (L_r - F_r)E'_r L'_y\} > 0,$$

where

$$\Delta = (ss' + m's + ms')[L_r L'_r - F_r(L_r + L'_r)] + (s + m)(L_r - F_r)E_r L'_y$$
$$+ (s' + m')(L'_r - F_r)E_r L_y + E_r L_y E'_r L'_y - F_r(mE_r L'_y + m'E'_r L_y) > 0.$$

10. $F_r < -L_r$ implies that domestic bonds and domestic money are closer substitutes than are foreign and domestic bonds.

11. Chapter 12 of Bryant 1980 contains a lucid discussion of the influence of openness on policy multipliers, emphasizing the difficulties in making strong generalizations about them.

12. It has lately become fashionable to study international trade on the assumption of a single internationally traded good competing for national expenditure with nontraded goods in each country. On this more complex formulation (since two relative prices are involved), the elasticities of substitution between traded and nontraded goods within each country measure the degree of linkage.

13. Tobin and Braga de Macedo (1980) formulate a two-country instantaneous model under flexible exchange rates approached from the perspective of portfolio holdings of foreign and domestic assets and money; the goods market is suppressed but implicit. They do not discuss the influence of greater interdependence on policy coefficients, but they do demonstrate that a consistent balance-sheet approach casts doubt on some of the strong generalizations about policy coefficients that were made in the Meade-Fleming-Mundell tradition concerning policy coefficients, basically because of the possible effects (even in the short run) of changes in stocks.

14. See chapters 13 and 15 of Aoki 1981 for a discussion of these compositional effects and a method for analyzing them.

15. For a variety of reasons, including uncertain knowledge of the structural coefficients and constraints on wide use of some instruments, it is desirable to have more instruments than objectives. In the optimizing approach taken up below, the equation between instruments and targets is also avoided by expressing a national objective function explicitly. On the influence of uncertainty on the use of policy instruments, see Brainard 1967.

16. Mundell (1971) later addressed the appropriate assignments of national monetary policies in a closed, interdependent world economy with fixed exchange rates. He suggested that all countries except for the United States should target their international payments positions, and that the United States should target the world price level.

17. Aoki, an engineer by training, takes for granted that instability is possible. See Aoki 1981, p. 273.

18. Generalization of Mundell's principle of market classification to many targets and instruments has been attempted by Patrick (1973) and Aoki (1976). Aoki states the conditions required for the presence of comparative advantage of instrument with respect to target in a system given by equations 4.1 and 4.5, on the assumption that this system is stable. Successful decentralization on this principle is not ensured when these conditions are not satisfied, or, even if they are, if the appropriate pairing of instrument to target crosses a national boundary, such that country A controls the instrument appropriate for pursuit of one of country B's targets.

19. See especially Hamada 1979 and the references there cited; also Bryant 1980, pp. 464–470. A direct conflict among objectives arises when one party desires $\hat{y}$ and another party desires (not $\hat{y}$). A generalized conflict among objectives, calling for choice, arises when a party wants both $\hat{x}$ and $\hat{y}$, but circumstances (the opportunity set) do not permit him to get arbitrarily close to both objectives at the same time; he

must choose one or the other, or some compromise between them. The use of a national welfare function allows both kinds of conflict to be handled when more than one objective is involved by introducing the possibility of an opportunity cost to the attainment of objectives.

20. This illustration is a variant, suggested by Jeffrey Sachs, of an analysis found in Canzoneri and Gray 1983.

21. $a = (\beta + 2\alpha\lambda)/2\alpha(\beta + \alpha\lambda)$; $b = \beta/2\alpha(\beta + \alpha\lambda)$; $c = -\lambda/(\beta + \alpha\lambda)$.

22. Here

$$g = \frac{ab + wk^2}{a^2 + wk^2}$$

and

$$h = \frac{ac + k}{a^2 + wk^2},$$

where $k = \mu/2\alpha\gamma$. It can be shown that $m > 0$ for $\bar{p} > 0$ unless α, the elasticity of demand for real money balances with respect to output, is well under $\frac{1}{4}$—an unlikely possibility. In this example, e becomes an intermediate target for both countries, which have conflicting objectives.

23. $dU^*/dm^* = \partial U^*/\partial m^* + (\partial U^*/\partial m)(dm/dm^*) = 0$ implies, for $dm = dm^*$, that $\partial U^*/\partial m^* = -\partial U^*/\partial m$. By symmetry in the model, therefore, $(\partial U^*/\partial m^*)/(\partial U^*/\partial m) = (\partial U/\partial m^*)/(\partial U/\partial m)$, i.e. a tangency between the utility surfaces. This condition plus $e = 0$ establishes the cooperative solution.

24. Sachs (1983) has shown that noncooperative solutions are inferior to multiperiod cooperative ones in an extended model involving many periods.

25. For partial attempts along these lines, see Cooper 1974 and Corden 1981.

26. See chapter 23 of Bryant 1980 for a discussion of the extent to which flexible exchange rates may be expected to permit autonomy in the national use of monetary policy and to insulate a national economy from disturbances originating in the rest of the world. (For the improved effectiveness of monetary policy under flexible as compared with fixed exchange rates, and some qualifications, see pp. 423 ff.)

27. The particular case of financing a military alliance has been examined by Olson and Zeckhauser (1966) and by van Ypersele (1967). For a general discussion of the problem of public goods, not focusing on the international aspects, see Olson 1971.

28. For a discussion of the "locomotive" proposal for coordinated expansionist actions by the United States, Japan, and West Germany in 1977, see Cooper 1982.

29. For a rigorous examination of optimal exchange-rate arrangements to ensure output stability, and the necessity for a residual country or for the imposition of a consistency rule on all countries, see Jones 1982.

30. Except for customs unions and free-trade areas, an exception that preserved the purpose of limiting opportunities for tariff-induced improvements in the terms of trade.

31. Mundell's (1971) suggestion that this was the proper role for monetary policy in the United States was another manifestation of the nth-country solution.

32. For a skeptical discussion of the merits of rule-based regimes as compared with continual coordination, see Bryant 1980, pp. 470–475.

33. It is possible that both were right with respect to their own economies. That is, they found themselves in different circumstances. Sachs (1979) has argued that a high fraction of the unemployment in Germany, in contrast to the United States, was due to excessive real wages in the wake of the 1974 oil-price increase rather than to deficient aggregate demand. The German government at this time encouraged increased export sales, however, which suggests that German officials did not consistently hold Sachs's view.

34. The verification issue in arms-control agreements reflects deep lack of trust among the participants. In some formal economic literature this question of trust (or lack of it) has been labeled "time inconsistency"—a misleading and inappropriate term, since the "inconsistency" refers only to a particular analytical framework for solving for optimal policy over a finite period of time, and in any case the problem of forward-looking expectations has been exaggerated within that framework. On the last points, see Kydland and Prescott 1977 and Chow 1980.

35. Some evidence for this shift in emphasis to attracting mobile firms is found in Cooper 1968 and 1974 and in Lindbeck 1973.

36. Two qualifying distinctions must be made here. First, to the extent that taxation finances desired public goods, and these are available only within the tax jurisdiction, taxation does not induce the departure of mobile firms, capital, or individuals. Taxation for redistribution or to finance public goods that are available outside the tax jurisdiction, e.g. general foreign or defense policies, will encourage movement. Second, to the extent that regulation applies to products rather than production processes, governmental jurisdictions can apply the regulations to imports and thus can preserve their efficacy.

Acknowledgments

I am grateful to Ralph Bryant and Peter Kenen for detailed comments on an earlier version of this chapter.

References

Allen, P. R., and P. B. Kenen. 1980. *Asset Markets, Exchange Rates, and Economic Integration: A Synthesis.* New York: Cambridge University Press.

Aoki, 1976. "On Decentralized Stabilization Policies and Dynamic Assignment Problems." *Journal of International Economics* 6 (May): 143–171.

Aoki, M. 1981. *Dynamic Analysis of Open Economies.* New York: Academic.

Baldwin, D. A. 1980. "Interdependence and Power: A Conceptual Analysis." *International Organization* 34 (autumn): 471–506.

Bentzel, R., and B. Hansen. 1954–55. "On Recursiveness and Interdependency in Economic Models." *Review of Economic Studies* 22: 153–168.

Brainard, W. C. 1967. "Uncertainty and the Effectiveness of Policy." *American Economic Review* 57 (May): 411–425.

Brown, W. A., Jr. 1940. *The International Gold Standard Reinterpreted, 1914–1934.* New York: National Bureau of Economic Research.

Bryant, R. C. 1980. *Money and Monetary Policy in Interdependent Nations.* Washington, D.C.: Brookings Institution.

Canzoneri, M. B., and J. Gray. 1983. Two Essays on Monetary Policy in an Interdependent World. Federal Reserve Board International Finance Discussion Paper no. 219.

Chow, G. C. 1980. "Econometric Policy Evaluation and Optimization under Rational Expectations." *Journal of Economic Dynamics and Control* 2 (February): 47–60.

Cooper, R. N. 1968. *The Economics of Interdependence.* New York: McGraw-Hill.

Cooper, R. N. 1969. "Macroeconomic Policy Adjustments in Interdependent Economies." *Quarterly Journal of Economics* 83 (February): 1–24.

Cooper, R. N. 1972. "Trade Policy Is Foreign Policy." *Foreign Policy* 9: 18–36.

Cooper, R. N. 1974. *Economic Mobility and National Economic Policy.* Stockholm: Almquist and Wiksell.

Cooper, R. N. 1975. "Prolegomena to the Choice of an International Monetary System." *International Organization* 29 (winter): 63–97.

Cooper, R. N. 1982. "Global Economic Policy in a World of Energy Shortage." In J. Pechman and J. Simler, eds., *Economics in the Public Service.* New York: Norton.

Corden, W. M. 1981. "The Logic of the International Monetary Non-system." In F. Machlup, ed., *Reflections on a Troubled World Economy: Essays in Honor of Herbert Giersch.* New York: Macmillan 1983.

Fleming, J. M. 1962. "Domestic Financial Policies Under Fixed and Flexible Exchange Rates." *International Monetary Fund Staff Papers* 9(3): 369–379.

Hamada, K. 1974. "Alternative Exchange Rate Systems and the Interdependence of Monetary Policies." In R. Z. Aliber, ed., *National Monetary Policies and the International Financial System.* University of Chicago Press.

Hamada, K. 1979. "Macroeconomic Strategy and Coordination under Alternative Exchange Rates." in R. Dornbusch and J. A. Frenkel, eds., *International Economic Policy.* Baltimore: Johns Hopkins University Press.

Hirschman, A. O. 1945. *National Power and the Structure of Foreign Trade.* Berkeley: University of California Press.

Jones, M. 1982. "Automatic Output Stability and the Exchange Arrangement: A Multi-Country Analysis." *Review of Economic Studies* 49: 91–107.

Kenen, P. B. 1969. "The Theory of Optimum Currency Areas: An Eclectic View." in R. A. Mundell and A. K. Swoboda, eds., *Monetary Problems of the International Economy*. University of Chicago Press.

Keohane, R. O. and J. S. Nye. 1977. *Power and Interdependence: World Politics in Transition*. Boston: Little, Brown.

Kindleberger, C. P. 1973. *The World in Depression, 1929–1939*. Berkeley: University of California Press.

Kydland, F. E., and E. C. Prescott. 1977. "Rules Rather Than Discretion: The Inconsistency of Optimal Plans." *Journal of Political Economy* 85 (June): 473–491.

Lindbeck, A. 1973. *The National State in an Internationalized World Economy*. Rio de Janeiro: Conjunto Universitario Candido Mendes.

McKinnon, R. I. 1982. "Currency Substitution and Instability in the World Dollar Market." *American Economic Review* 72 (June): 320–333.

Meade, J. E. 1951. *The Theory of International Economic Policy*, vol. 1, *The Balance of Payments*. London: Royal Institute for International Affairs.

Mundell, R. A. 1968. *International Economics*. New York: Macmillan.

Mundell, R. A. 1971. *Monetary Theory: Inflation, Interest, and Growth in the World Economy*. Pacific Palisades, Calif.: Goodyear.

Niehans, J. 1968. "Monetary and Fiscal Policies in Open Economies under Fixed Exchange Rates: An Optimizing Approach." *Journal of Political Economy* 76 (July/August): 893–920.

Olsen, M. Jr. 1971. *The Logic of Collective Action*, second edition. Cambridge, Mass.: Harvard University Press.

Olsen, M. Jr., and R. Zeckhauser. 1966. "An Economic Theory of Alliances." *Review of Economics and Statistics* 48 (August): 266–279.

Patrick, J. D. 1973. "Establishing Convergent Decentralized Policy Assignment." *Journal of International Economics* 3 (February): 37–51.

Roper, D. E. 1971. "Macroeconomic Policies and the Distribution of the World Money Supply." *Quarterly Journal of Economics* 85 (February): 119–146.

Sachs, J. 1979. "Wages, Profits, and Macroeconomic Adjustment: A Comparative Study." *Brookings Papers on Economic Activity*.

Sachs, J. 1983. International Policy Coordination in a Dynamic Macroeconomic Model. NBER Working Paper 1166.

Scitovsky, T. 1942. "A Reconsideration of the Theory of Tariffs." *Review of Economic Studies* 9 (summer): 89–110. Reprinted in *Readings in the Theory of International Trade* (Philadelphia: Blakiston, 1949).

Theil, H. 1964. *Optimal Decision Rules for Government and Industry.* Amsterdam: North-Holland.

Tinbergen, J. 1952. *On the Theory of Economic Policy.* Amsterdam: North-Holland.

Tobin, J., and W. Buiter. 1980. "Fiscal and Monetary Policies, Capital Formation, and Economic Activity." In G. von Furstenberg, ed., *The Government and Capital Formation.* Cambridge, Mass.: Ballinger.

Tobin, J., and J. Braga de Macedo. 1980. "The Short-run Macroeconomics of Floating Exchange Rates: An Exposition." In J. S. Chipman and C. P. Kindleberger, eds., *Flexible Exchange Rates and the Balance of Payments.* Amsterdam: North-Holland.

van Ypersele, J. 1967. "Sharing the Defense Burden among Western Allies." *Review of Economics and Statistics* 49 (November): 527–536.

Vernon, R. 1971. *Sovereignty at Bay.* New York: Basic Books.

Waltz, K. 1970. "The Myth of Interdependence." in C. P. Kindleberger, ed., *The International Corporation.* Cambridge, Mass.: MIT Press.

Whitman, M. v. N. 1979. *Reflections of Interdependence.* University of Pittsburgh Press.

Acknowledgments of Sources

Article 1: Copyright 1972 by Princeton University Press. Reprinted by permission. An earlier version was presented in December 1970 at the Council on Foreign Relations Conference on Trends Affecting International Relations.

Article 2: Copyright 1983 by Cambridge University Press. Reprinted by permission.

Article 3: Copyright 1982 by J. A. Pechman and N. J. Simler. Reprinted by permission.

Article 4: Reprinted by permission of the Wicksell Lecture Society.

Article 5: Copyright by International Economic Association. Reprinted by permission.

Article 6: Copyright by Macmillan Company. Reprinted by permission.

Article 7: Copyright by President and Fellows of Harvard College. Reprinted by permission.

Article 8: Reprinted by permission from *Scandinavian Journal of Economics.*

Article 9: Copyright by George Allen and Unwin. Reprinted by permission. Parts of this article draw extensively on R. N. Cooper, Currency Devaluation in Developing Countries, Princeton Essays in International Finance, no. 86 (1971). I wish to thank the Princeton International Finance Section for permission to reproduce certain sections of this article. Copyright by The World Bank.

Article 10: Reprinted by permission.

Article 11: Copyright by Elsevier Science Publishers. Reprinted by permission.

Index

Ability-to-pay principle, 88
Adverse development, degrees of, 24
Allocational efficiency, 111
Allocational incentives, 75–78
Aoki, M., 305, 326n18
Assignment problem, 175n5
Autonomy, 6, 9–12, 15

Bagehot, Walter, 75, 99–100
Balance of payments
  continuous equilibrium in, 184
  crisis in, 31
  domestic expenditures and, 161
  financing of, 58
  monetary approach to analysis of, 184
  policies for, 12–13
Banking crisis, 26–28, 33, 35–41
Banking, international problems of, 40
Benefit principle, 88
Bhagwati, Jagdish, 121n46, 251
Bond covenants, 257
Bonds, international, 138–140, 142
Bonn economic summit, 63–64
Borrowing
  external, 234–235, 247–253, 258–259, 262–265, 267 (see also Debt, external)
  optimal strategy for, 230, 240–241, 248–249, 258, 272–274
Braga de Macedo, J., 326n13
Breakdown, as degree of adverse development, 24, 48
Breton, A., 131
Bretton Woods Agreement, 7–8, 13, 29–30, 311
Bretton Woods system, breakdown of, 31–33
Bryant, R. C., 325n5, 326n11
Burke, Edmund, 98–99

Cairncross, A. K., 134
Callaghan, James, 224
Capital markets
  distinguished from money markets, 137
  domestic, 148
  indirect linkages between, 141–142
  integration of, 140, 144, 147, 151–154
  interdependence of, 148–151
Capital mobility, 155, 159, 168, 179. *See also* Capital movements
  domestic implications of, 147–148
  and exchange-rate policy, 151
  in Fleming's open-economy model, 182–184
  interest sensitivity of, 181–182, 184, 189
  and interest taxation, 150
  restrictions on, 8, 196
  short-term, 141
Capital movements, 138–142. *See also* Capital mobility
  and foreign-trade multipliers, 160–162
  equilibrium models of, 183–190
  interest sensitivity of, 173–174, 182
  portfolio balance and, 174
  short-term, 105
Carter, Jimmy (President), 62
Catastrophe, as degree of adverse development, 24
Caves, R., 183
Central American Common Market, 134
Centralization, 15–18, 134–135
Choudry, N., 183
CIEC, 59
Closed economies, 80
  and expenditure location, 79–81
  monetary policy in, 180
  repudiation risk in, 236
Cohen, D., 253, 256

Index 336

Colbert, J. B., 97, 98
Collapse. *See* Breakdown
Commodity markets, internationalization of, 78
Concessional aid, 270
Conference on International Economic Cooperation, 59
Consumption smoothing rule, 240
Cooper, C. A., 126
Cooperation, international
 advantages of, 309–310
 developing countries and, 48–49
 erosion of, 47–49
 oil crisis and, 59–60
Coordination of economic policy, 64–66, 155–178, 314–319
 lack of, 173
 and national objectives, 173
 obstacles to, 321–323
Corporate havens, 107
Country factor, in international lending, 261
Cournot, August, 71, 292, 307, 312
Cournot-Nash noncooperative solution, 307, 312
Credit rationing, 235
Credit squeeze, with devaluation, 212
Crisis, as degree of adverse development, 24, 48
Currency speculation, 188

Debt, external, 138
 of government, 261
 and macroeconomic policy, 259–261
 taxation of, 251
Debt/GDP ratio, 265, 267–269
Debt maturity, 251–253, 272
Debtor utility, 237
 instantaneous, 238
 intertemporal, 238–239, 244
Debt policy, goal of, 237
Debt relief, 236, 247
Debt repudiation, 253–259
Debt rescheduling, 37–38
Debt-servicing ratio, 265
Debt servicing, taxation and, 244, 247, 270
Decentralization. *See* Centralization
Decentralized system, stabilization in, 305–306
Default, 36–38
Demand
 aggregate, 73, 94, 206–213, 224

deficient, 94–95
Devaluation
 accompanied by expansionary policies, 213
 concerns about, 200, 214–215, 223
 in developing countries, 200, 202
 effects of, 200–226, 260
 management of, 222, 224–226
 in multiple-exchange-rate system, 200–202
 standard analysis of, 200, 203, 213–224
 and wage-price spiral, 218, 222
Developing countries
 devaluation in (*see* Devaluation, effects of)
 and foreign-exchange system, 200
 inflationary policies pursued by, 203
 integration of, 134
 laissez faire as borrowing strategy in, 261
 as markets, 62
Díaz-Alejandro, C. F., 211, 250
Distance, economic, 78–80, 113–114
Distributional aims, 109, 111
Distributive effect, 210
Disturbance, as degree of adverse development, 24
Disturbances, 126, 128–130
 exogenous, 293
 of expenditure, 161, 167–172
 monetary, 161, 167–179
 pooling of, 83
Dornbusch, R., 186, 191, 230
Dual-exchange-rate system, 213
Dynamic adjustment model, 156–174
Dynamic budget constraint, 230–231
Dynamic economic structure, equation for, 301

Economies of scale, 75, 90, 96, 126–127, 132–133
Educational subsidies, and national market, 76
Enclaves, 117n6
Endogenous disturbances, interdependence among, 289
Energy policy, in macroeconomic policy, 66–67
Equilibrium change, 79–81, 160
Equity markets, integration in, 144, 149
Eurocurrency market, 35, 105, 107, 141–142
European Economic Community, 20, 44, 106, 124, 133, 313, 318–319

Index   337

Exchange rates. *See also* Fixed exchange
  rate; Floating exchange rate
  alteration of, by monetary action, 87
  and capital markets, 143
  manipulation of, 28, 201–203
  and national policies, 9
  regime for, 12, 85, 197
Export-credit concessions, 12
Export goods, 203–204
Externalities, 75, 83, 89–90, 96, 126–127,
  132

Factor markets, 78
Factor mobility, 128–129, 132
Factor-price level, changes in, 194–196
Federal Reserve System, 39–41, 50n4,
  67n5, 100
Fiscal policy
  coordination of, 63, 66
  effectiveness of, 73–74, 78, 81–85
  and interest rates, 169
  in mathematical models, 159, 294–297,
    299
Fixed exchange rate, 7, 8, 16, 32, 105, 186,
  189, 311
  in Bretton Woods system, 32
  in cooperative model, 311–312
  in dynamic adjustment model, 157, 173
  and external borrowing, 260
  and monetary control, 260
  in small-country models, 181–183, 185,
    294–297
Flags of convenience, 9–10, 20
Fleming, M., 179–180, 184
Fleming open-economy model, 180–183,
  185
  fiscal policy in, 182
  fixed vs. floating exchange rates in,
    181–182
  monetary policy in, 181–182
  results of, 182–183, 186, 190
  small-country assumptions of, 181
  weaknesses of, 183–198
Floating exchange rate, 12, 17, 32–35,
  65–66, 106, 189–190, 192, 195
  in cooperative models, 307–311
  and financial markets, 86–87
  in Genberg-Kierzkowski model, 186–188
  insulation provided by, 192–194
  and interdependence, 301, 315
  in open economy, 181–183
  policy dilemmas resulting from, 34

  as shock absorber, 35
Flow equilibrium model, 186
Foreign borrowing. *See* Borrowing,
  external; Debt, external
Foreign exchange
  crisis in, 33–34
  rationing of, 204–205
Franklin National Bank, 38–40, 50n15, 61
Free markets, historical development
  toward, 73, 96–108
Friedman, Milton, 50n4
Functional federalism, 112, 132–133

Galbraith, J. K., 23, 222
GATT. *See* General Agreement on Tariffs
  and Trade
Genberg, H., 186, 188
Genberg-Kierzkowski open-economy
  devaluation model, 186–189
General Agreement on Tariffs and Trade,
  29–30, 111, 124, 319
Geographic effects, in expansionary fiscal
  policy, 73–74
Gold standard, 27–28
Government expenditure, in mathematical
  models, 157, 161, 294, 296
Government responsibility, in external
  borrowing, 250, 258, 262–265

Hamada, K., 306–307, 311
Hanson, J., 186
Heckscher, Eli, 98
Heckscher-Ohlin-Samuelson theorem, 128
Heller, Walter, 59–60
Hirschman, Albert, 324n1
Hoover, Herbert (President), 26, 28–29
Human capital, 76
Hume, David, 184

IEA. *See* International Energy Agency
IMF. *See* International Monetary Fund
Import liberalization, with devaluation,
  212, 215–218, 225
Import-substituting investment, 200–201,
  203
Income redistribution, 87–89, 91, 95, 104
Industrial locations, competition for, 106
Industrial policy, 323
Infinite-horizon problem, 239, 275–276
Information, exchange of, 315, 317–318
Integrated area, optimal size of, 124–125,
  127–133

Integration, 129–130, 291–292
 distinctions within concept of, 124–126
 institutional, 124
 regional vs. global, 134
Interdependence
 causal, 289
 economic, vs. psychological, 5
 institutional, 5
 vs. integration, 292–292
 multidimensionality of, 290, 302
 and national policies, 5–9, 13–21, 85, 294–299
 national responses to, 9–13, 148–151, 314–319
 parameters of, 156, 173–174
 sensitivity, 19, 290–291
 structural, 292–300
 types of, 292–293
 vulnerability, 325n3
Interest-equalization tax, 148, 258, 315
Interest rates
 change in, 185
 convergence of, 143–144
 differentials in, 159
 as marginal cost measure, 238
 as policy target, 160
 and solvency constraint, 133–134
International Bank for Reconstruction and Development. See World Bank
International economic system, 33, 51n21
International Energy Agency, 44–45, 57
International Monetary Fund, 30, 34, 46, 58, 199, 202
Investment
 direct, 141–142, 271
 foreign equity, 270–271

Japan, as oligop, 313
Jensen, M., 256
Johnson, H. G., 126

Kaiser, Karl, 21n3
Kemp, Murray, 227n5
Kenen, P. B., 129–130, 185–186
 open-economy model of, 185
Keohane, R. O., 290
Keynes, J. M., 54–55, 73, 84–85, 109, 173
Kharas, H. J., 246
Kierzkowski, H., 186, 188
Kindleberger, C. P., 26, 121n44, 323
Kissinger, Henry, 57

Laissez faire, 97–99, 110
 and foreign borrowing, 241, 249–251, 261–265
Laursen-Metzler effect, 227n5
Lender of last resort, 40–41, 61
Lending cutoff, and optimal borrowing strategy, 248–249
Lindahl, Erik, 88
Linkages, international, 297–299
Liquidity risks, short-run, 248–249
Locomotive theory, 61–64, 68n9, 68n10

Machlup, F., 201
McKinnon, R. I., 114, 130, 184, 190
Marginal propensity to import, 78, 113–114, 117n3, 156, 165, 168–169, 173–174, 189–190
Markets
 classification of. See Assignment problem
 failure of, 75–76
 fragmentation of, 5, 10
 growth of, 96–108
 internalization of, 71–72, 85–87
 national, 72–73
 reliance on, 72–78
 secondary, 139–140
Marshall, Alfred, 71–72, 209, 292
Marshall-Lerner condition, 209
Massel, B. V. E., 126
Meckling, W., 256
Metzler, L. A., 155, 227n5
Mobility
 and allocation of resources, 89
 and domestic policies, 78, 94, 101–105, 107
 and jurisdiction size, 128
 policy responses to, 94–96, 108
 and regulation, 89, 93, 128, 324
 and world economy, 105–108
Monetary policy
 and balance-of-payments position, 147
 capital-market integration and, 147
 demand and, 169
 and national markets, 74–75, 87
 in noncooperative regime, 311–312
Money illusion, 130, 194–196
Money markets, 99, 137, 141. See also Capital markets
Monnet, Jean, 125
Monopoly, 93
Multilateral Trade Negotiations, 47
Mundell, R. A., 129–130, 155–156, 163,

Solvency constraint, 231–234, 239–247, 267
  defined, 232
  and interest rates, 233–234
Sovereignty, economic, 21n4. *See also* Autonomy
Special Drawing Rights, 5, 32, 201, 312, 317, 320
Speculative effect, in devaluation, 210
Srinivasan, T. N., 251
Stabilization, 126, 128–130, 132, 185–186, 191
  under decentralized system, 111
  and exchange-rate regimes, 185, 191
  expenditure locus in, 78–79
  fiscal policy used for, 73, 78–85, 186
  monetary policy used for, 141, 147–148, 186
Stackleberg, H. von, 307, 312
Stackleberg–Nash solution, 307, 312
Stock-equilibrium model, 183–188
Subsidies, and national markets, 75–78
Supranational state, as ideal type, 15–16, 150
System capacity, 131

Tariff war, 26
Taxation
  beyond national boundaries, 150
  history of, in U.S., 101–105
  redistributive, 92
  by states, 102–103
Tax ceiling, and solvency constraint, 245
Tax/expenditure system, 88–91, 323
Tax jurisdiction, mobility and, 92
Temin, Peter, 26
Tiebout, Charles, 89, 95–96, 118n12
Tinbergen, J., 156, 304
Tobin, J., 187, 326n13
Tradeables, in optimal borrowing model, 241–243, 267–268
Trade credits, 271–272
Trade wars, 33, 46–47
Trading blocs, 123, 126
Triffin, Robert, 125

Unemployment, exportation of, 4
United States
  hegemony of, 16
  expansionary monetary policy of, 62–63, 105
  as oligop, 313
  regulation of corporations by states in, 102

Viner, J., 126

Wage-settlement process, 55
Waltz, Kenneth, 21n1, 22n9
Warner, J., 257
Westphalian system, 19–20
Wicksell, Knut, 71–72, 88, 112
Wilson, Harold, 9
World Bank, 30, 38, 138

Index

179, 183, 185, 304, 326n18
Mutual dependence, 290–291
Myrdal, Gunnar, 22n11

Nash, G. D., 236, 307, 312
Nash bargaining solution, with repudiation, 236
Nation-states, as ideal type, 15–16
New Economic Policy of 1971 (U.S.), 22n12
Noncooperative solution, outcome of, 313–314
Nontradeables, in optimal borrowing model, 241–243, 267–268
Nordhaus, William, 69n14
nth-country problem, 317
Nye, J. S., 290

Oates, Wallace, 114, 120n41
OECD. *See* Organization for Economic Cooperation and Development
Ohlin, B., 117n3
Oil crisis
 current threat of, 31, 33, 41–46
 IEA sharing plan for, 45, 57
 inadequacy of preparation for, 43, 48
 military action in, 45–46
 of 1974, 41–42, 44, 53–55
 of 1979, 41–42, 45
 secondary impact on economies of, 42–43
Oil import dependency, reduction of, 44
Oil price increase, effects of, 42, 53–56, 66–67
Oligops, 313–314
OPEC. *See* Organization of Petroleum Exporting Countries
Openness, 291, 325n5, 325n7
Optimal borrowing models, 230–259, 274–285
Optimal-tariff theory, 219
Organization for Economic Cooperation and Development, 46, 49, 57–60, 62, 66, 140
Organization of Petroleum Exporting Countries, 36, 39–49, 53–54, 57, 59, 66
Overborrowing, 246, 250, 257
Overshooting, 65
Oxenstierna, Axel, 97–98

Patinkin, D., 187
Payments, fundamental disequilibrium of, 199, 206

Phelps, E. S., 67n2
Policy-adjustment model, 162–174.
Policy-adjustment rule, 304
Policy coefficients, 326n13
Policy instruments, 156, 200, 212, 313–314
 and mobility, 94–95, 314
 and openness, 299, 314
 and higher interdependence, 323
 in mathematical models, 159–160, 162–163, 294–297
 search for, 314–315, 323
Policy interdependence, 293
Policy making, decentralized, 156, 319–324
Policy-objective interdependence, 292–293
Portfolio-equilibrium model. *See* Stock-equilibrium model
Protectionism, 46–47, 315, 317
Public expenditure, financing of, 88
Public goods, 125–127
 financing of, 88
 international, 313
 optimal provision for, 89–90, 126, 130–132, 134

Reciprocal dependence. *See* Mutual dependence
Recycling problem, 58
Regional economic jurisdictions, 123–126, 133–135
Regulation
 history of, in U.S., 101–105
 of incorporated businesses, 102
 in late Middle Ages, 97–99
 and mobility, 93
 and national markets, 77–78
 as a public good, 92–93
 redistribution as motive for, 93
Repudiation risk, in external borrowing, 235–237, 253–259, 267
Resource efficiency effect, 212–213
Reuber, G., 183
Revaluation, 199, 211–212
Rhomberg, R., 183
Rule-bound international regimes, 319–321

Sachs, J., 230, 240, 253, 256, 328n33
Samuelson, P. A., 132
Schwartz, Anna, 50n4
Small-country assumptions, 181
Smith, Adam, 98, 110–111, 257
Social-welfare function, 230, 237, 241